Full Moon
O Sagashite

3

Story & Art by Arina Tanemura

Table of Contents

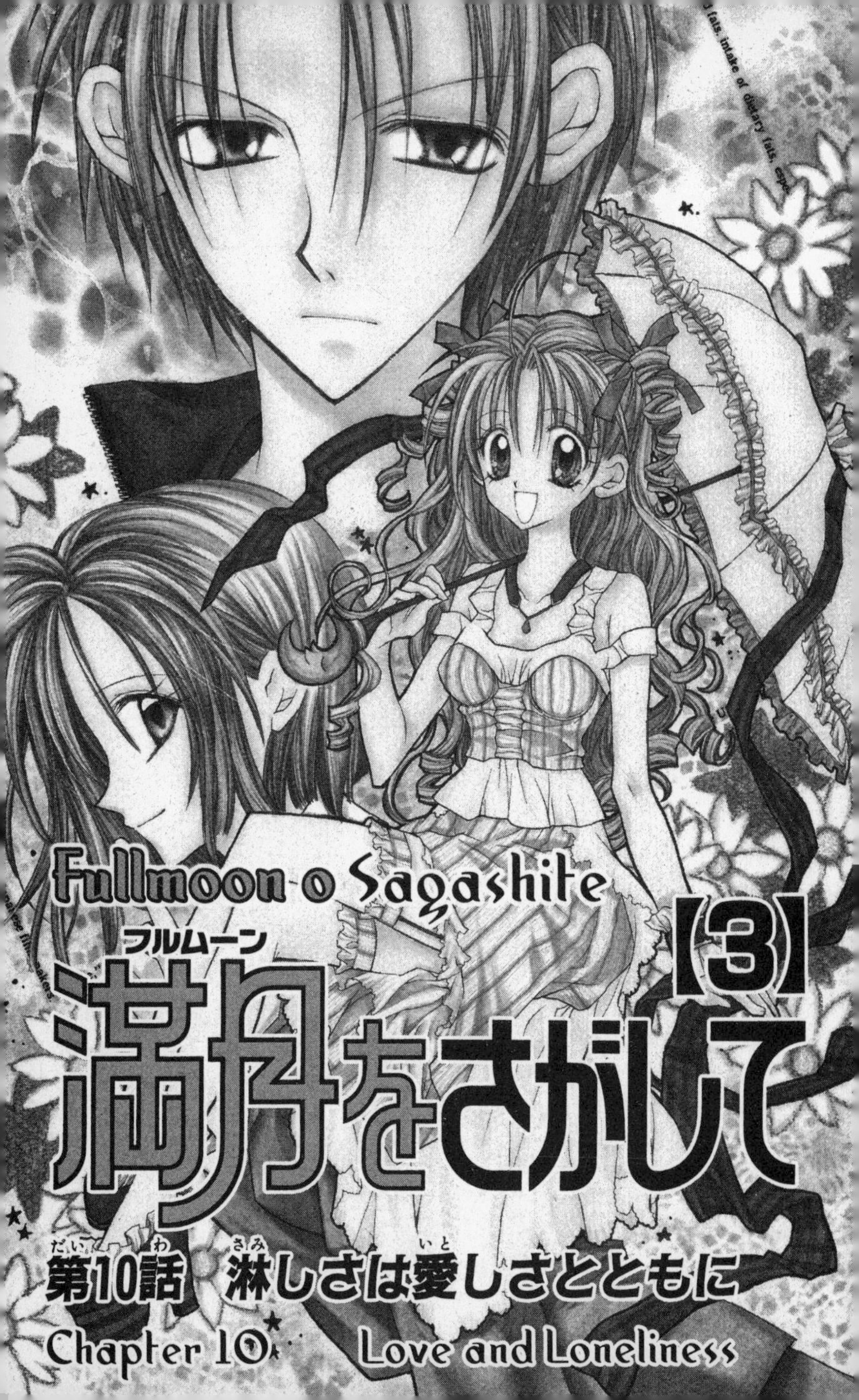
Fullmoon o Sagashite
フルムーン
満月をさがして
(3)
第10話　淋しさは愛しさとともに
Chapter 10　Love and Loneliness

CHARACTER INTRODUCTIONS

MEROKO
A Shinigami who turns into a rabbit. She likes her partner, Takuto.

TAKUTO
A Shinigami who turns into a cat.

EICHI
He's studying in the U.S. Mitsuki has loved him since she was little.

MITSUKI KOYAMA (AGE 12)
She has throat cancer, and can't talk or sing loud. She's not good at competing or quarreling.

MITSUKI KOYAMA (AGE 16)
Mitsuki's alter ego, who debuts as the singer "Fullmoon."

Full Moon o Sagashite

Mitsuki is twelve. She loves Eichi, who's studying in the U.S., and she dreams of fulfilling her promise to him by becoming a singer. Mitsuki has a form of cancer in her throat called sarcoma, and Dr. Wakaoji has recommended that she have an operation. But she refuses to go through with it, since the operation would destroy her singing voice. One day, a pair of Shinigami named Takuto and Meroko appears, and tries to stop Mitsuki from going to an audition. However, Takuto is moved by Mitsuki's ardent wish to become a singer, and helps her audition by transforming her into a healthy 16-year-old. Mitsuki is able to sing in her new body, and wins the competition. She makes her musical debut as "Fullmoon." Mitsuki's debut single "Ange" is a smash hit, and Takuto begins to fall in love with her as he watches her confidence grow with her success. Meroko realizes what is going on, and she calls up her former partner Izumi to stop the two from getting any closer. Mitsuki's rival, Madoka Wakamatsu, plagiarizes Mitsuki's lyrics for a TV commercial competition, and Izumi is behind the incident. Izumi's objective is to retrieve Mitsuki's soul on her fated day of death. He believes that by doing this, he will be able to make Takuto a successful Shinigami, and free up Meroko so that Izumi can be her partner. But Izumi's attitude begins to change when he comes in contact with Mitsuki's pure heart. The deadline for recording Mitsuki's second single is approaching, and the record company has hired a new producer..Dr. Wakaoji!

STORY THUS FAR

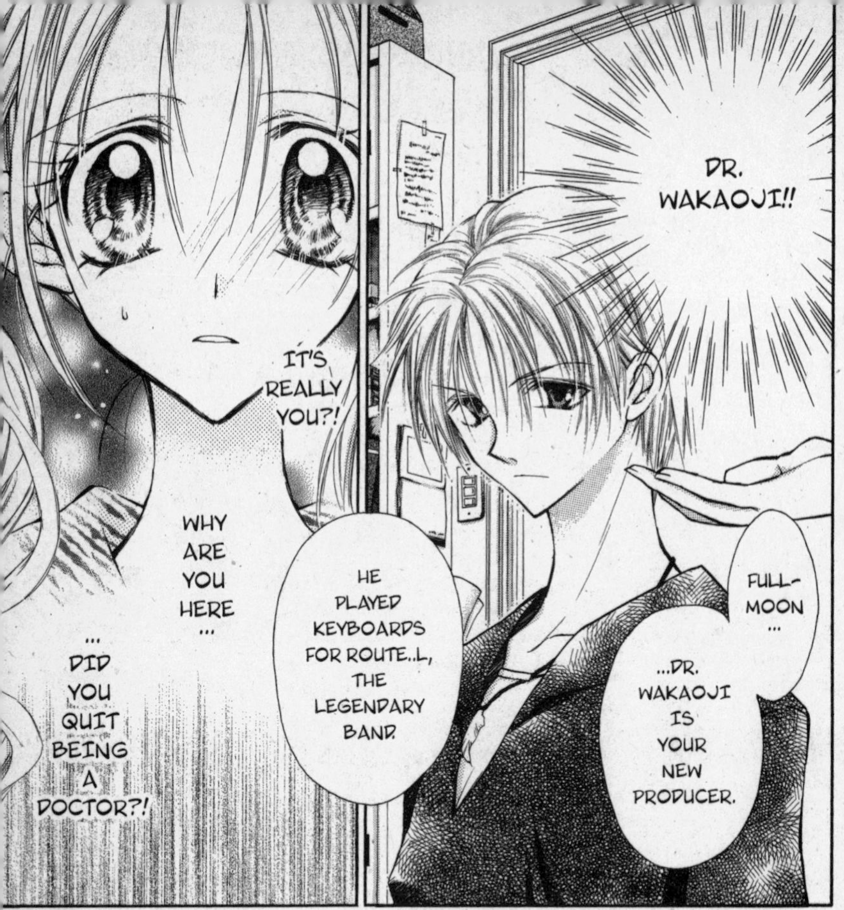
DR. WAKAOJI!!
FULL-MOON ...
...DR. WAKAOJI IS YOUR NEW PRODUCER.
HE PLAYED KEYBOARDS FOR ROUTE..L, THE LEGENDARY BAND.
IT'S REALLY YOU?!
WHY ARE YOU HERE ...
... DID YOU QUIT BEING A DOCTOR?!

Chapter 10 Loneliness Comes Together with Love (spoilers follow)

Cover Copy **Expectations make her shine even more!**

The cover illustration is the third in the series of "Mitsuki and XX," Ms. Oshige and Dr. Wakaoji. I like this illustration quite a bit. I like the three-shot of Mitsuki (Fullmoon) and Negi-Ramen, panel 1 of page 5. It's...good. I also love Jonathan! I just love him!! I'm really happy and proud I created him! ♪

Dr. Wakaoji jumps to conclusions. Once he thinks of things one way, he tends to stick to that point of view. I like that part about him, I find it cute. But it's difficult drawing him. I'm always frazzled when drawing him. Why am I talking like a gay guy? The Meroko on page 18 next to the words "It can't be..." apparently looks funny (My assistant Niki-chan says that). ...It is really weird. I must have been really sleepy then.

...I don't have much to talk about this chapter...

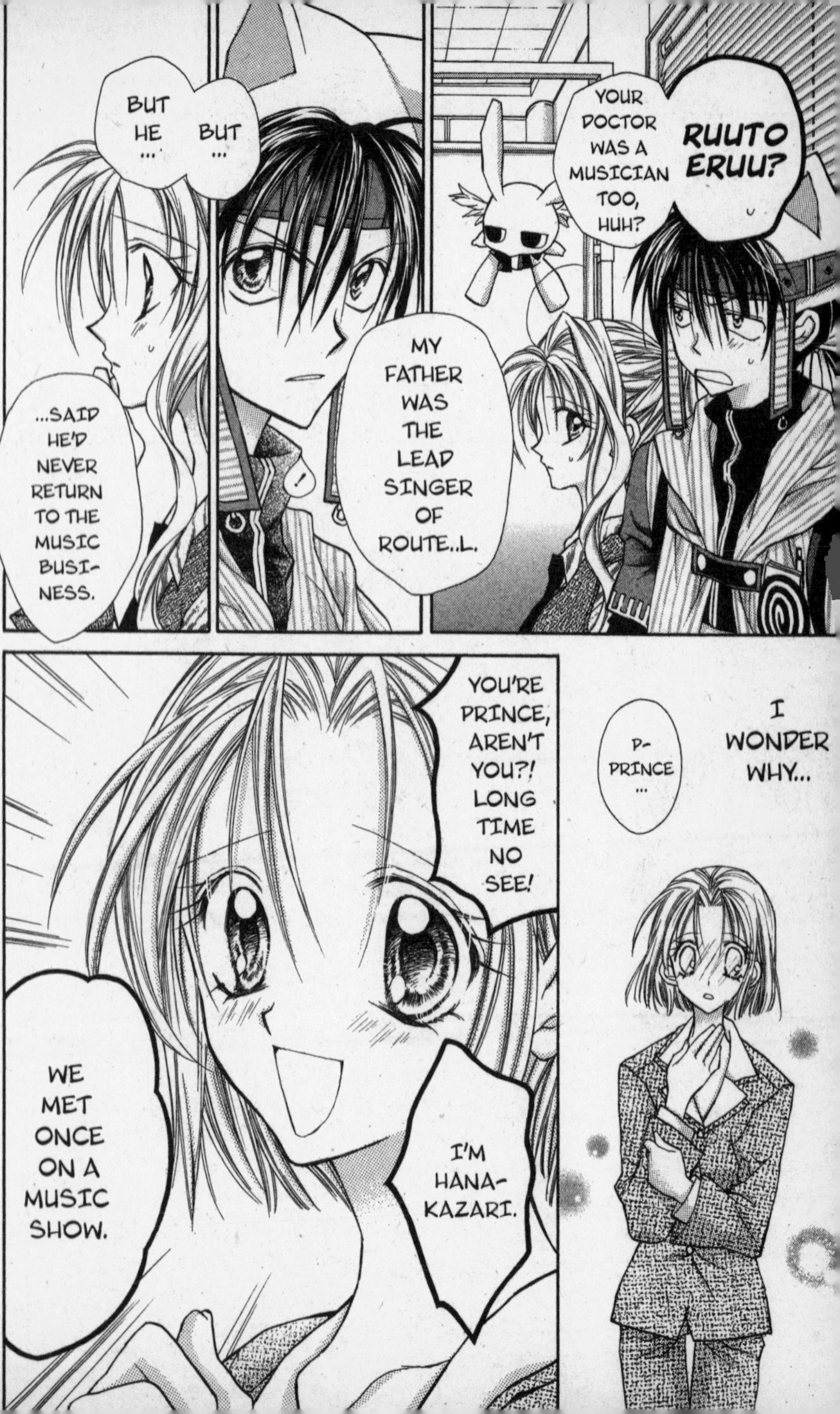
RUUTO ERUU?
YOUR DOCTOR WAS A MUSICIAN TOO, HUH?
MY FATHER WAS THE LEAD SINGER OF ROUTE..L.
BUT ...
BUT HE ...
...SAID HE'D NEVER RETURN TO THE MUSIC BUSI-NESS.
I WONDER WHY...
P-PRINCE ...
YOU'RE PRINCE, AREN'T YOU?! LONG TIME NO SEE!
I'M HANA-KAZARI.
WE MET ONCE ON A MUSIC SHOW.

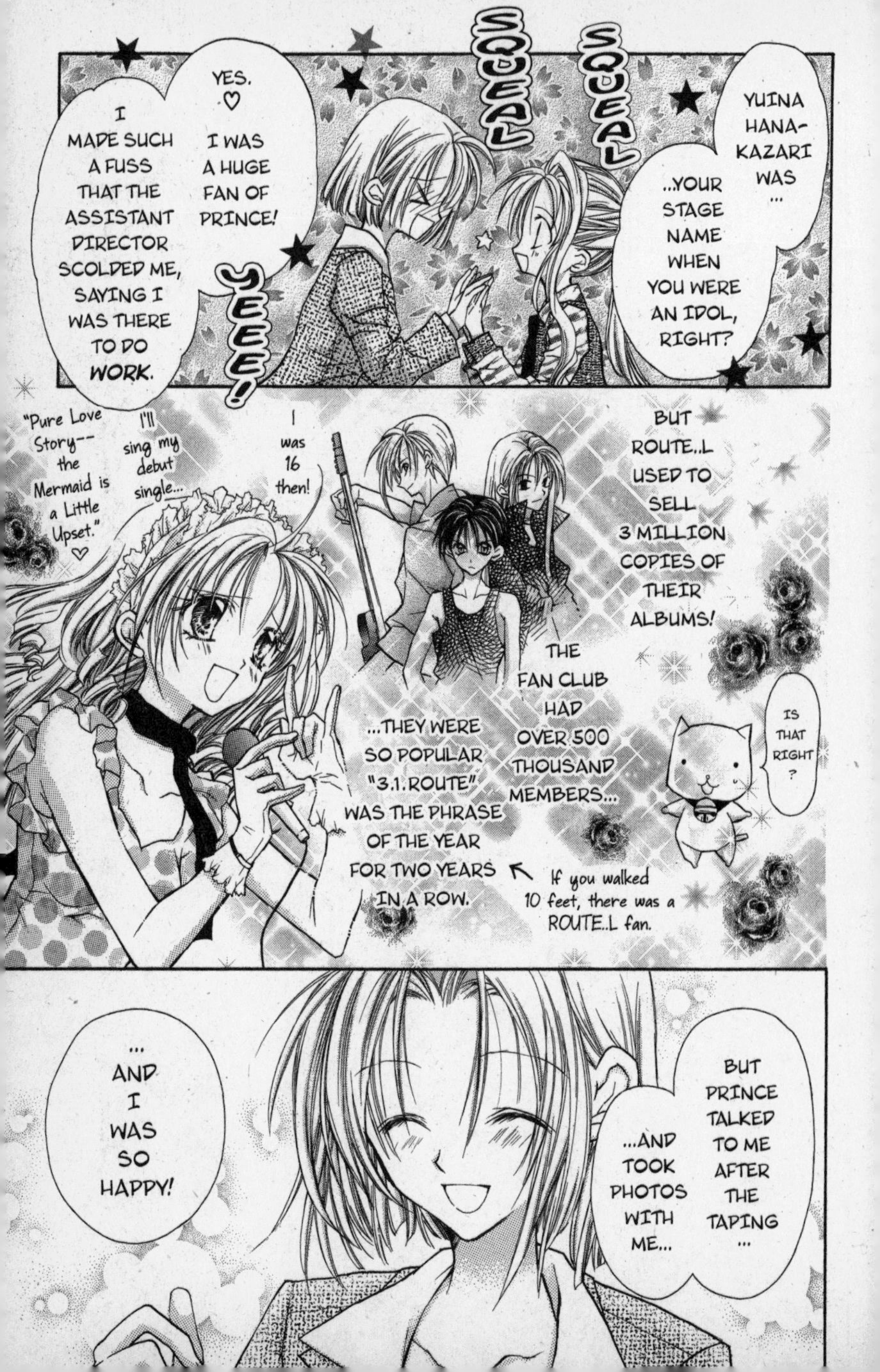

YUINA HANA-KAZARI WAS ...
...YOUR STAGE NAME WHEN YOU WERE AN IDOL, RIGHT?
SQUEAL
SQUEAL
YES. ♡ I WAS A HUGE FAN OF PRINCE!
YEEEE!
I MADE SUCH A FUSS THAT THE ASSISTANT DIRECTOR SCOLDED ME, SAYING I WAS THERE TO DO **WORK**.
BUT ROUTE..L USED TO SELL 3 MILLION COPIES OF THEIR ALBUMS!
IS THAT RIGHT?
THE FAN CLUB HAD OVER 500 THOUSAND MEMBERS...
...THEY WERE SO POPULAR "3.1. ROUTE" WAS THE PHRASE OF THE YEAR FOR TWO YEARS IN A ROW.
If you walked 10 feet, there was a ROUTE..L fan.
I was 16 then!
I'll sing my debut single...
"Pure Love Story--the Mermaid is a Little Upset." ♡
BUT PRINCE TALKED TO ME AFTER THE TAPING ...
...AND TOOK PHOTOS WITH ME...
... AND I WAS SO HAPPY!

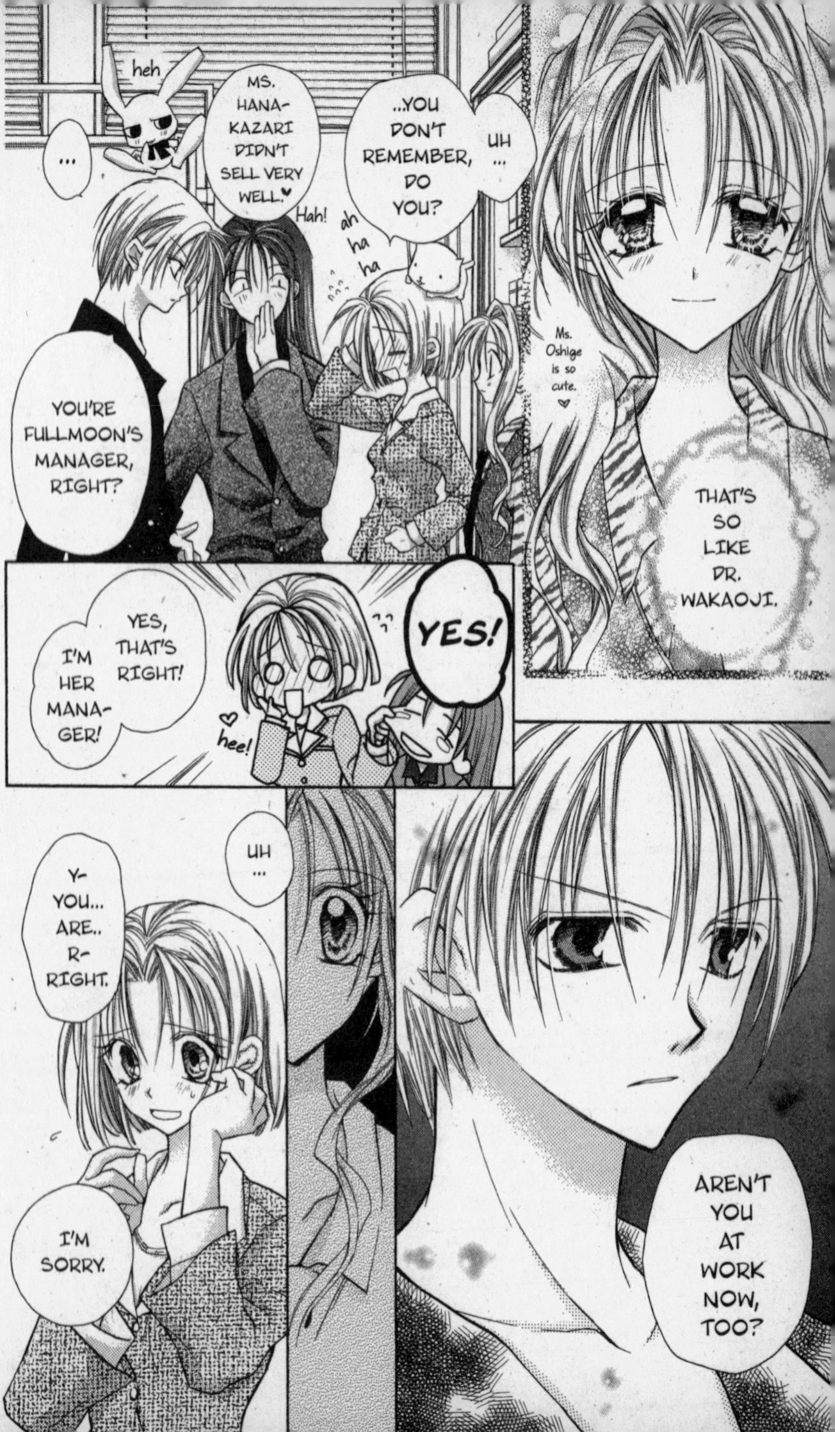
Ms. Oshige is so cute. ♥
THAT'S SO LIKE DR. WAKAOJI.
UH ...
...YOU DON'T REMEMBER, DO YOU?
ah ha ha
Hah!
MS. HANA-KAZARI DIDN'T SELL VERY WELL.♥
heh
...
YOU'RE FULLMOON'S MANAGER, RIGHT?
YES!
hee! ♥
YES, THAT'S RIGHT!
I'M HER MANA-GER!
AREN'T YOU AT WORK NOW, TOO?
UH ...
Y-YOU... ARE.. R-RIGHT.
I'M SORRY.

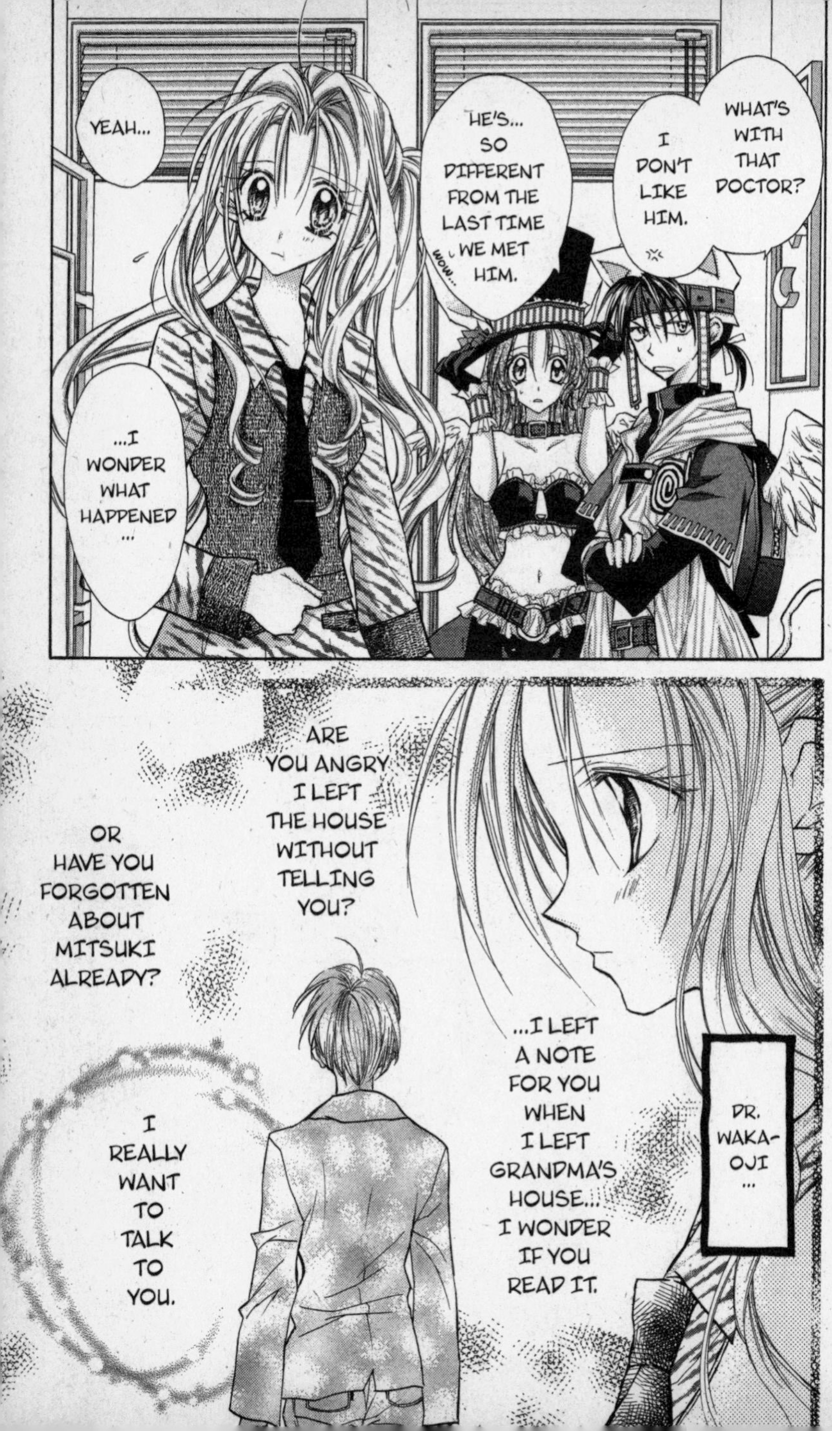
WHAT'S WITH THAT DOCTOR?
I DON'T LIKE HIM.
HE'S... SO DIFFERENT FROM THE LAST TIME WE MET HIM.
WOW...
YEAH...
...I WONDER WHAT HAPPENED...
DR. WAKA-OJI...
...I LEFT A NOTE FOR YOU WHEN I LEFT GRANDMA'S HOUSE... I WONDER IF YOU READ IT.
ARE YOU ANGRY I LEFT THE HOUSE WITHOUT TELLING YOU?
OR HAVE YOU FORGOTTEN ABOUT MITSUKI ALREADY?
I REALLY WANT TO TALK TO YOU.

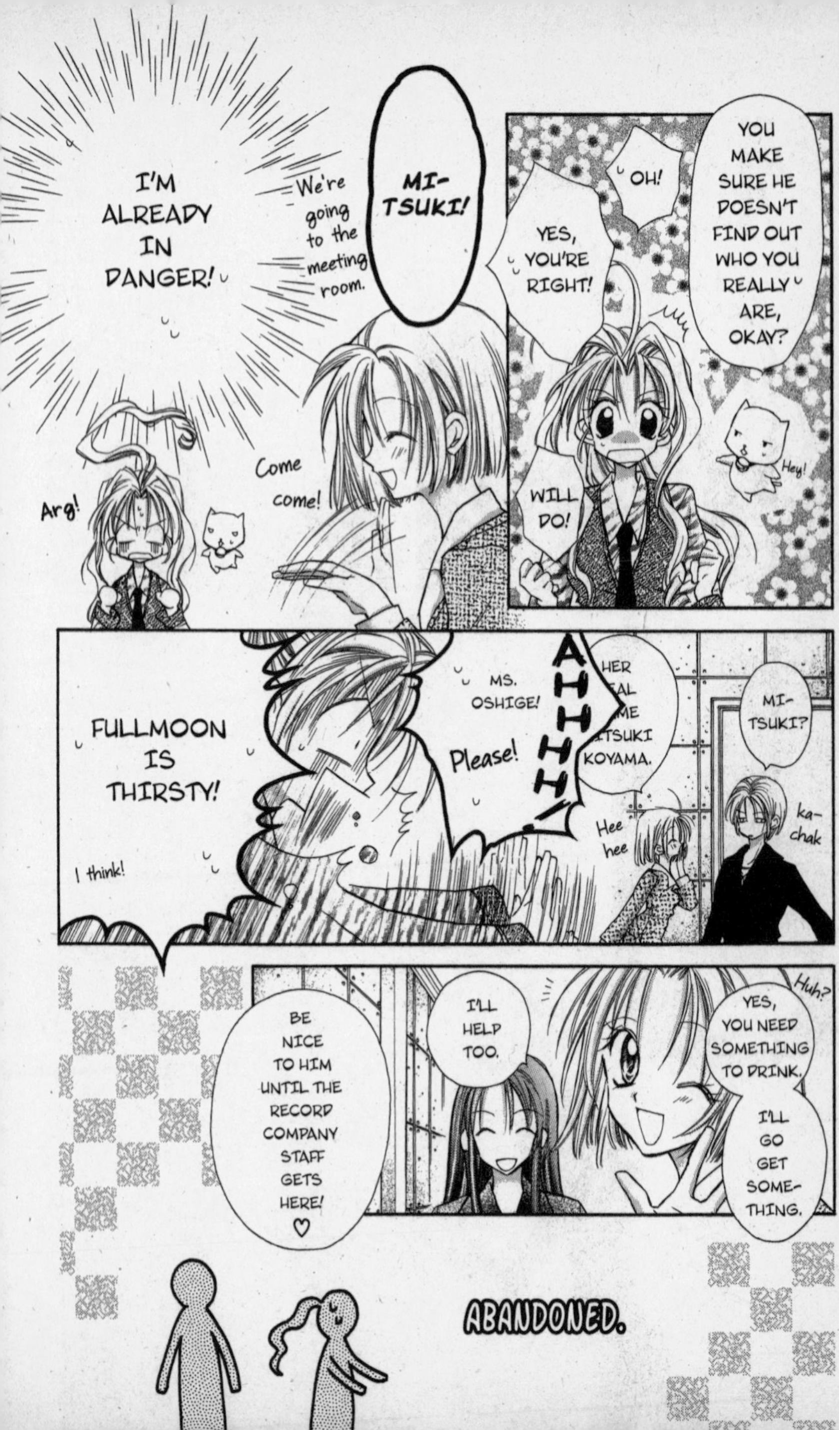
YOU MAKE SURE HE DOESN'T FIND OUT WHO YOU REALLY ARE, OKAY?
OH!
YES, YOU'RE RIGHT!
Hey!
WILL DO!
MI-TSUKI!
We're going to the meeting room.
Come come!
I'M ALREADY IN DANGER!
Arg!
MI-TSUKI?
ka-chak
HER EAL ME ITSUKI KOYAMA.
Hee hee
AHHHHH!
MS. OSHIGE!
Please!
FULLMOON IS THIRSTY!
I think!
Huh?
YES, YOU NEED SOMETHING TO DRINK.
I'LL GO GET SOME-THING.
I'LL HELP TOO.
BE NICE TO HIM UNTIL THE RECORD COMPANY STAFF GETS HERE! ♡
ABANDONED.

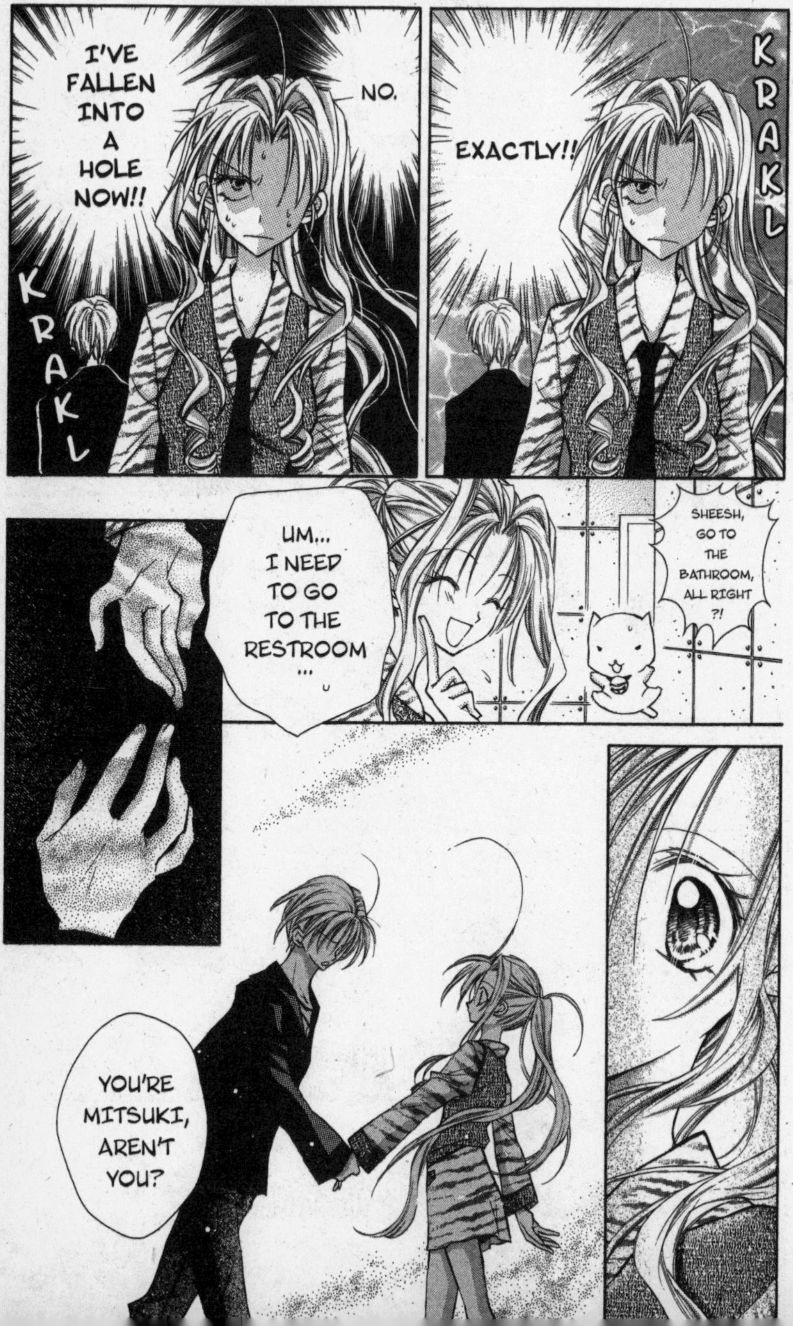
KRAKL
EXACTLY!!
NO.
I'VE FALLEN INTO A HOLE NOW!!
KRAKL
SHEESH, GO TO THE BATHROOM, ALL RIGHT ?!
UM... I NEED TO GO TO THE RESTROOM ...
YOU'RE MITSUKI, AREN'T YOU?

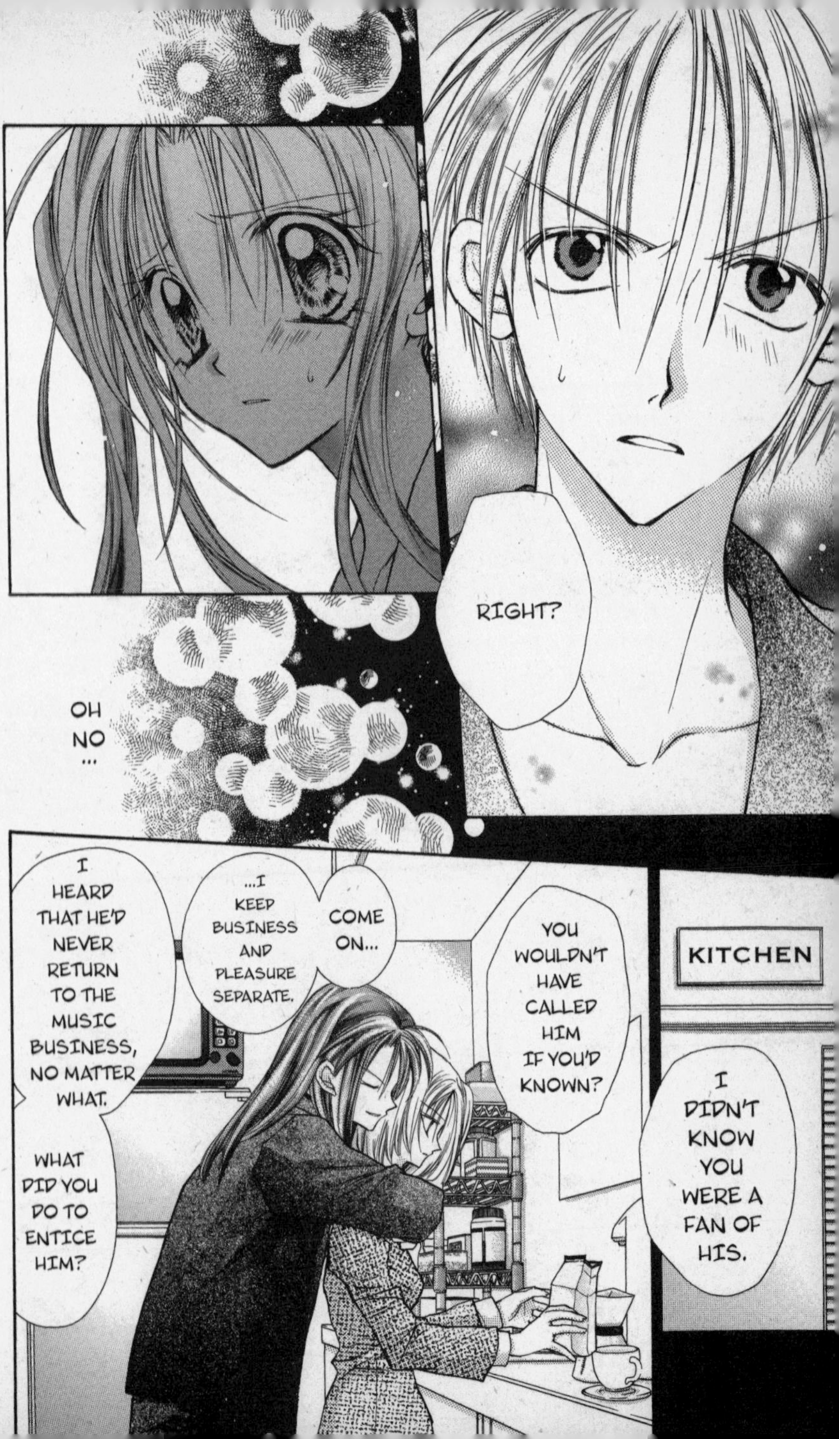
RIGHT?
OH NO ...
KITCHEN
I DIDN'T KNOW YOU WERE A FAN OF HIS.
YOU WOULDN'T HAVE CALLED HIM IF YOU'D KNOWN?
COME ON...
...I KEEP BUSINESS AND PLEASURE SEPARATE.
I HEARD THAT HE'D NEVER RETURN TO THE MUSIC BUSINESS, NO MATTER WHAT.
WHAT DID YOU DO TO ENTICE HIM?

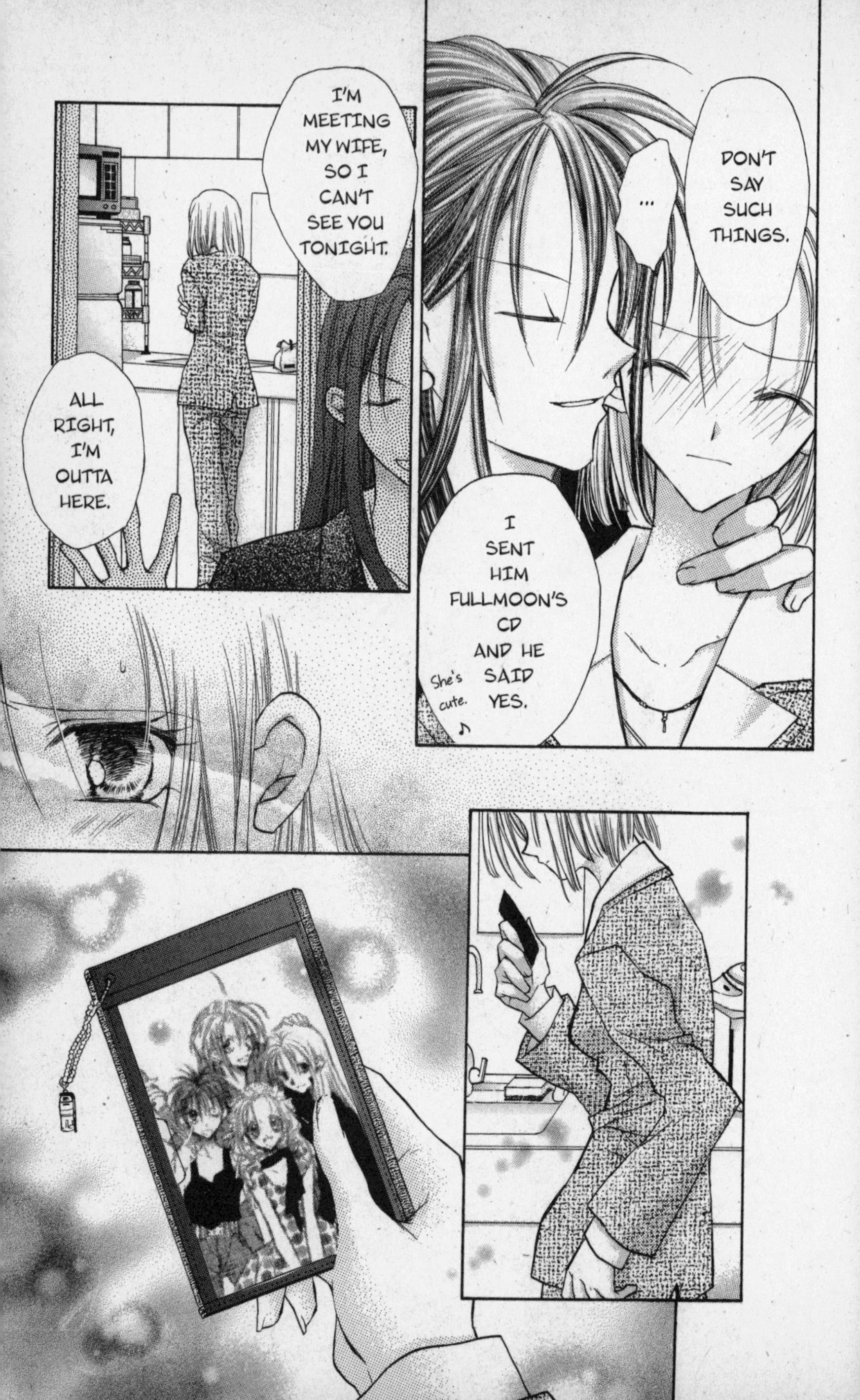
DON'T SAY SUCH THINGS.
...
I SENT HIM FULLMOON'S CD AND HE SAID YES.
She's cute. ♪
I'M MEETING MY WIFE, SO I CAN'T SEE YOU TONIGHT.
ALL RIGHT, I'M OUTTA HERE.

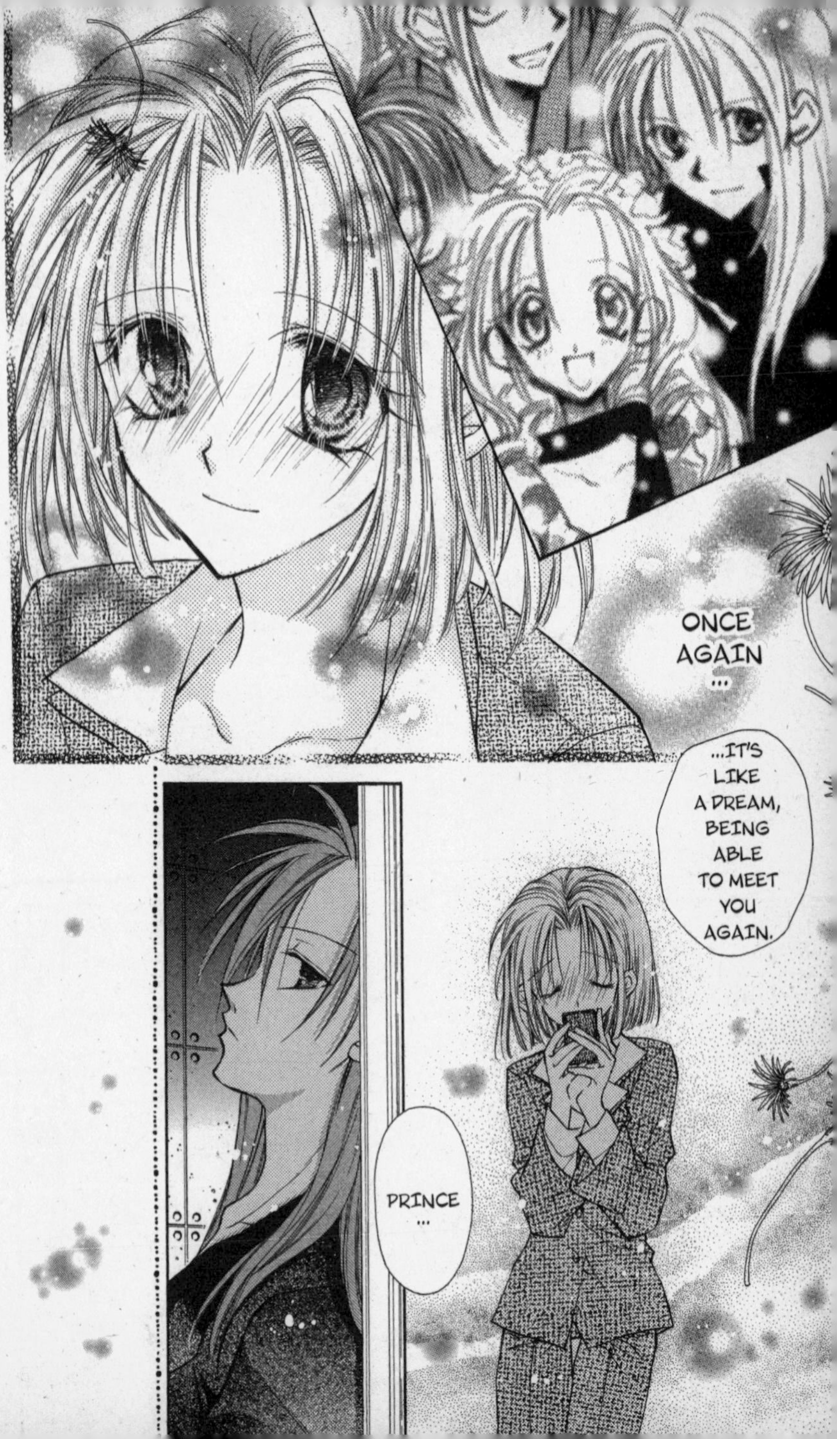
ONCE AGAIN ...
...IT'S LIKE A DREAM, BEING ABLE TO MEET YOU AGAIN.
PRINCE ...

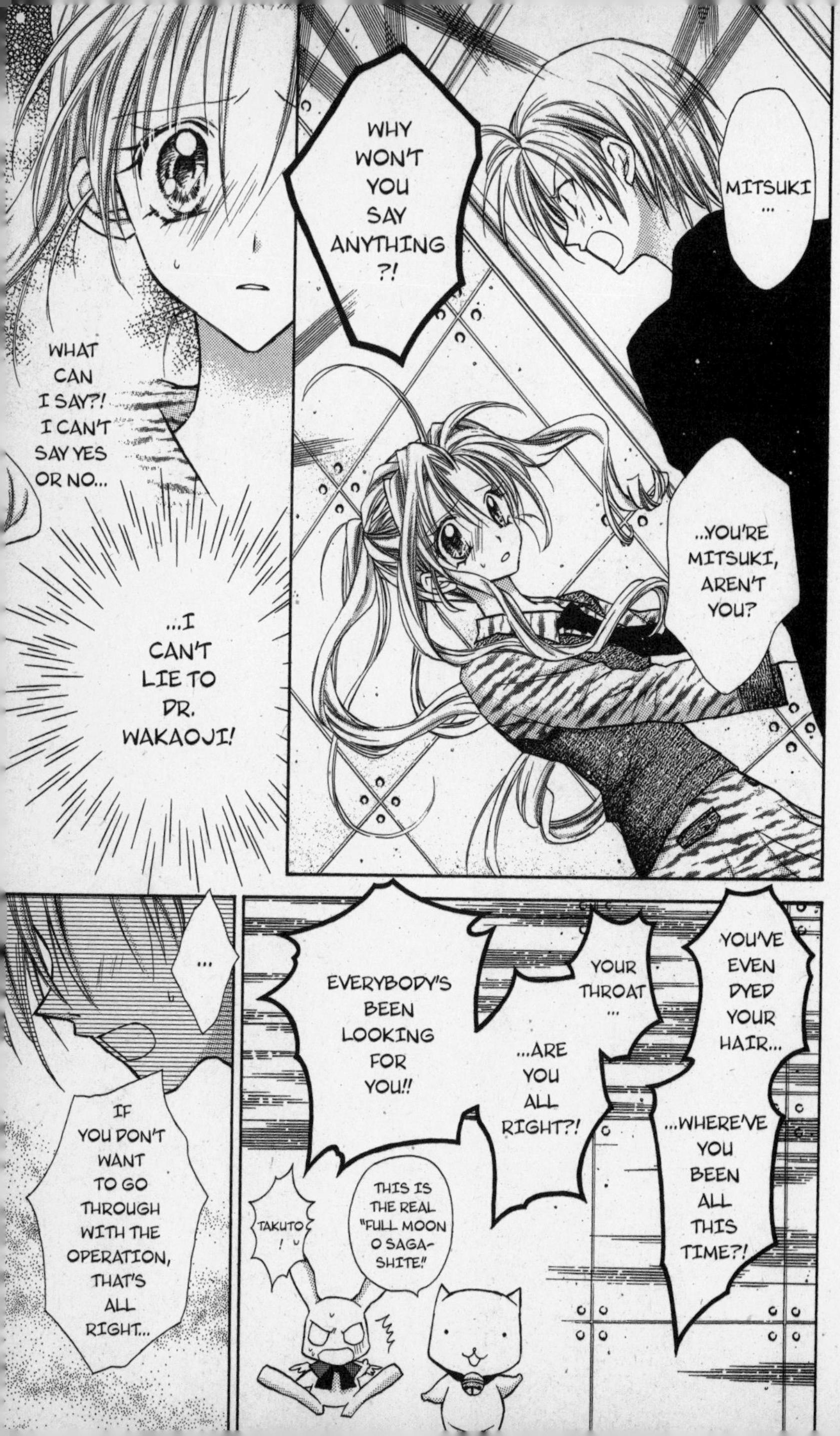
MITSUKI...
WHY WON'T YOU SAY ANYTHING?!
...YOU'RE MITSUKI, AREN'T YOU?
WHAT CAN I SAY?! I CAN'T SAY YES OR NO...
...I CAN'T LIE TO DR. WAKAOJI!
YOU'VE EVEN DYED YOUR HAIR...
...WHERE'VE YOU BEEN ALL THIS TIME?!
YOUR THROAT...
...ARE YOU ALL RIGHT?!
EVERYBODY'S BEEN LOOKING FOR YOU!!
THIS IS THE REAL "FULL MOON O SAGA-SHITE!"
TAKUTO!
...
IF YOU DON'T WANT TO GO THROUGH WITH THE OPERATION, THAT'S ALL RIGHT...

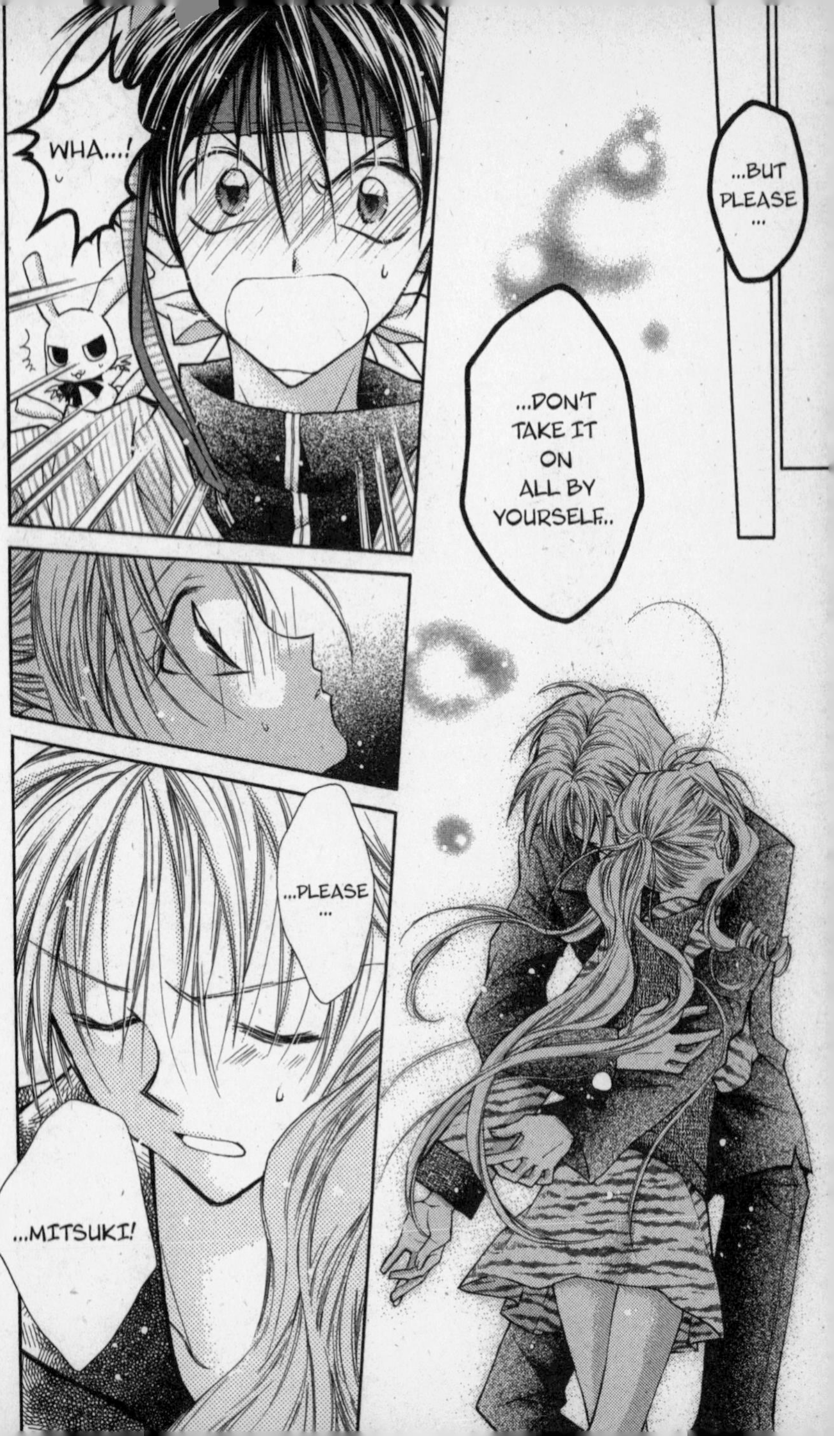
...BUT PLEASE ...
...DON'T TAKE IT ON ALL BY YOURSELF..
WHA...!
...PLEASE ...
...MITSUKI!

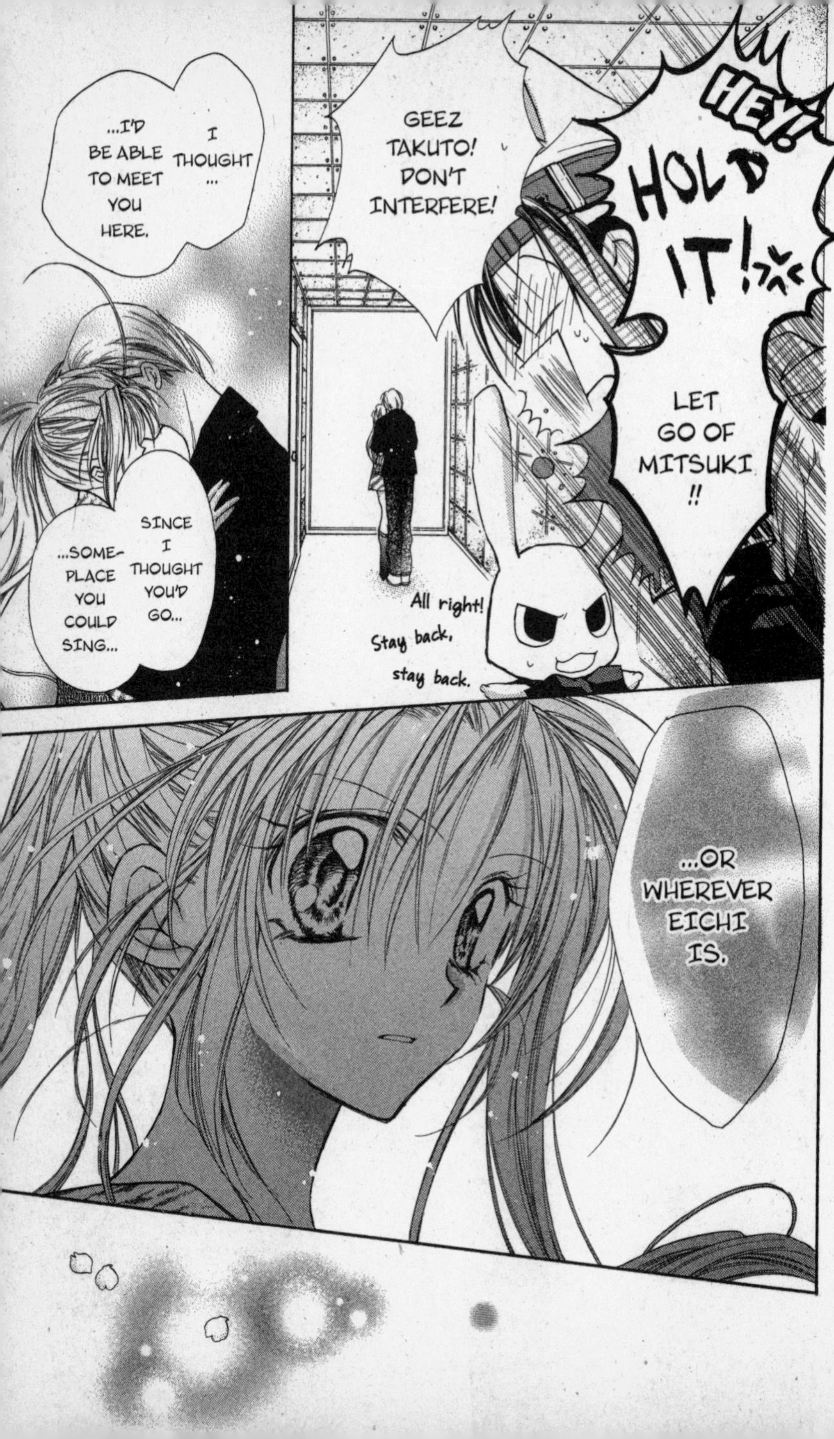
HEY! HOLD IT!
LET GO OF MITSUKI!!
GEEZ TAKUTO! DON'T INTERFERE!
All right! Stay back, stay back.
I THOUGHT...
...I'D BE ABLE TO MEET YOU HERE.
SINCE I THOUGHT YOU'D GO...
...SOMEPLACE YOU COULD SING...
...OR WHEREVER EICHI IS.

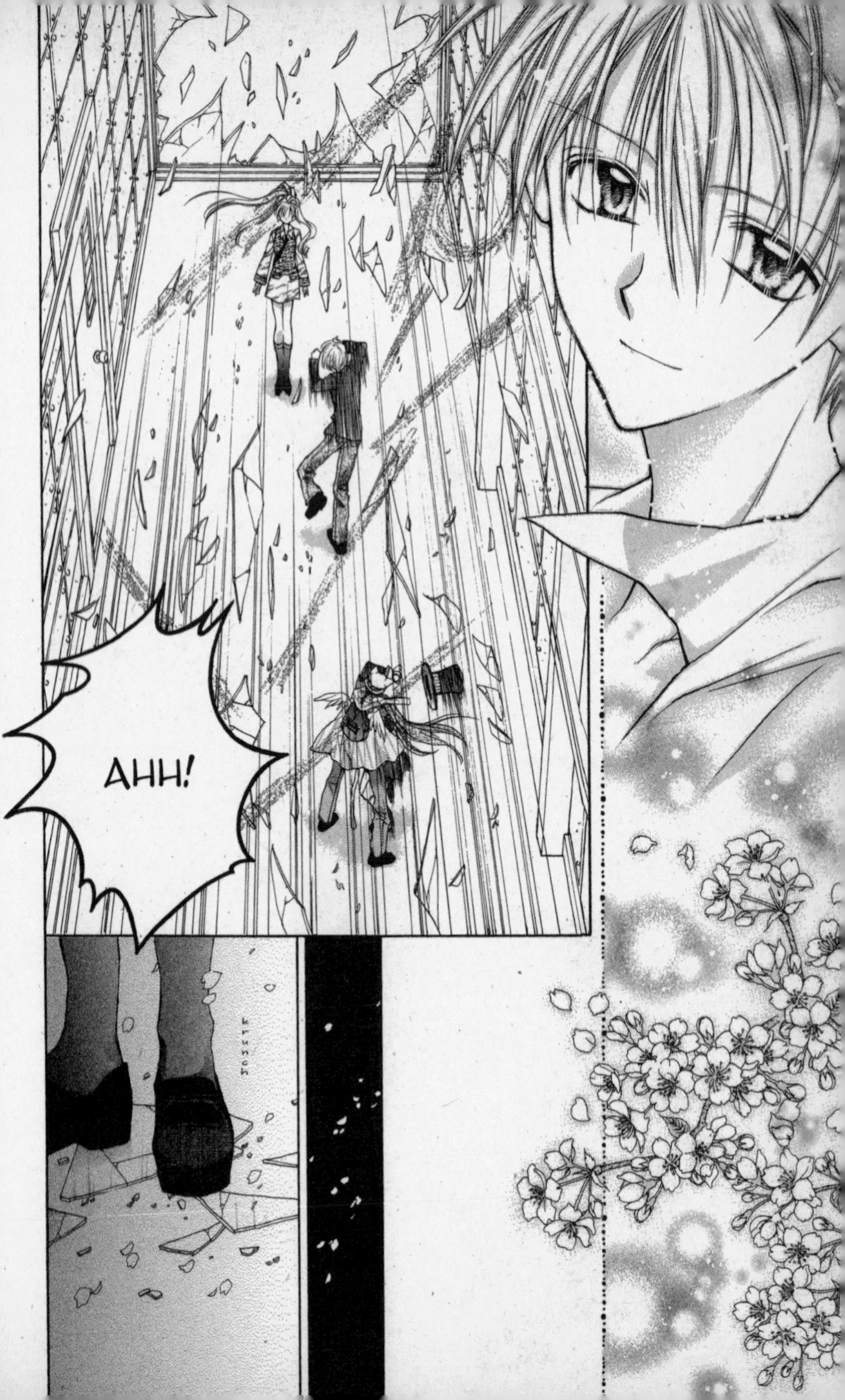
AHH!

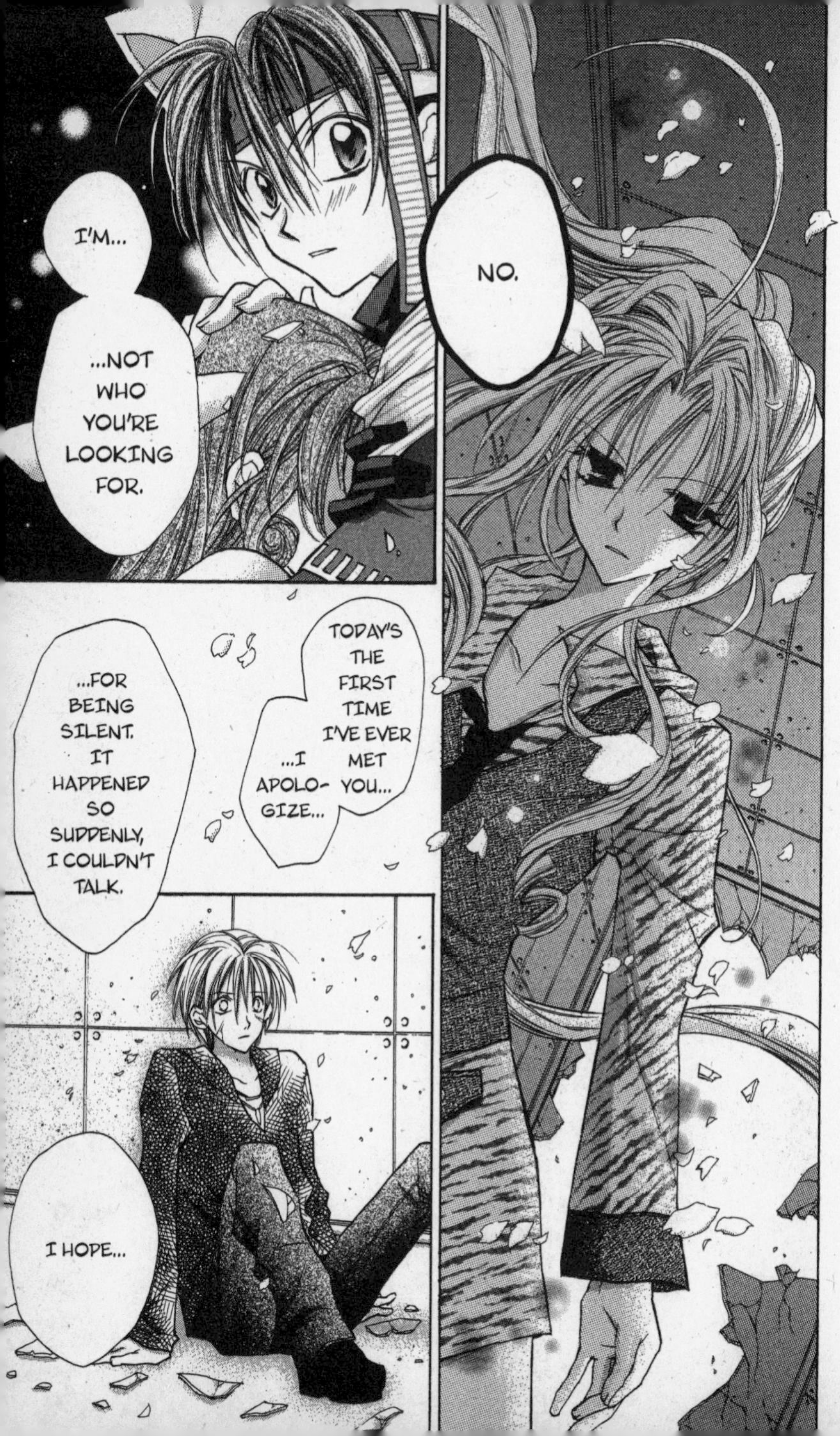
NO.
I'M...
...NOT WHO YOU'RE LOOKING FOR.
TODAY'S THE FIRST TIME I'VE EVER MET YOU...
...I APOLO-GIZE...
...FOR BEING SILENT. IT HAPPENED SO SUDDENLY, I COULDN'T TALK.
I HOPE...

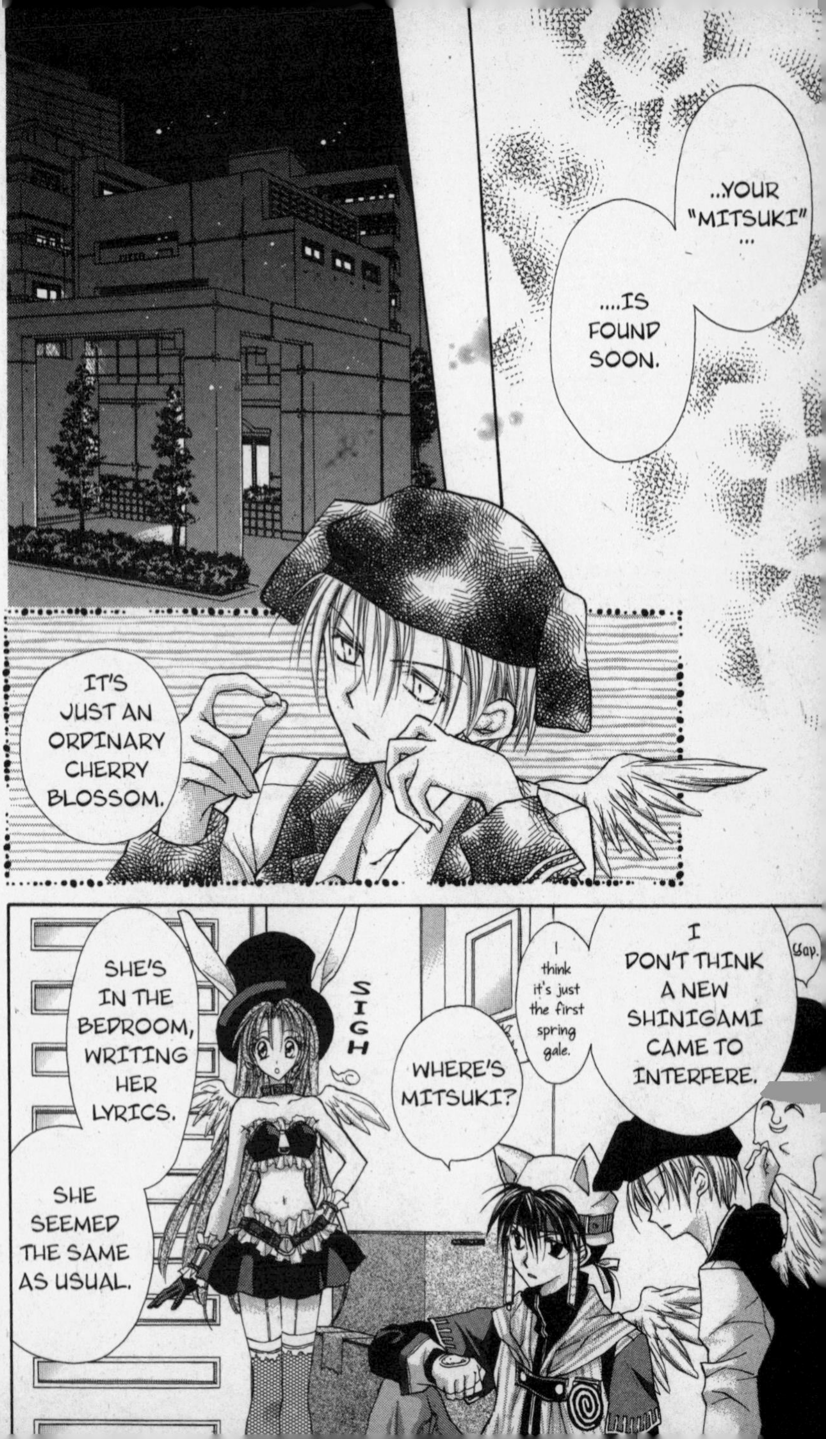
...YOUR "MITSUKI" ...
....IS FOUND SOON.
IT'S JUST AN ORDINARY CHERRY BLOSSOM.
Yay.
I DON'T THINK A NEW SHINIGAMI CAME TO INTERFERE.
I think it's just the first spring gale.
WHERE'S MITSUKI?
SIGH
SHE'S IN THE BEDROOM, WRITING HER LYRICS.
SHE SEEMED THE SAME AS USUAL.

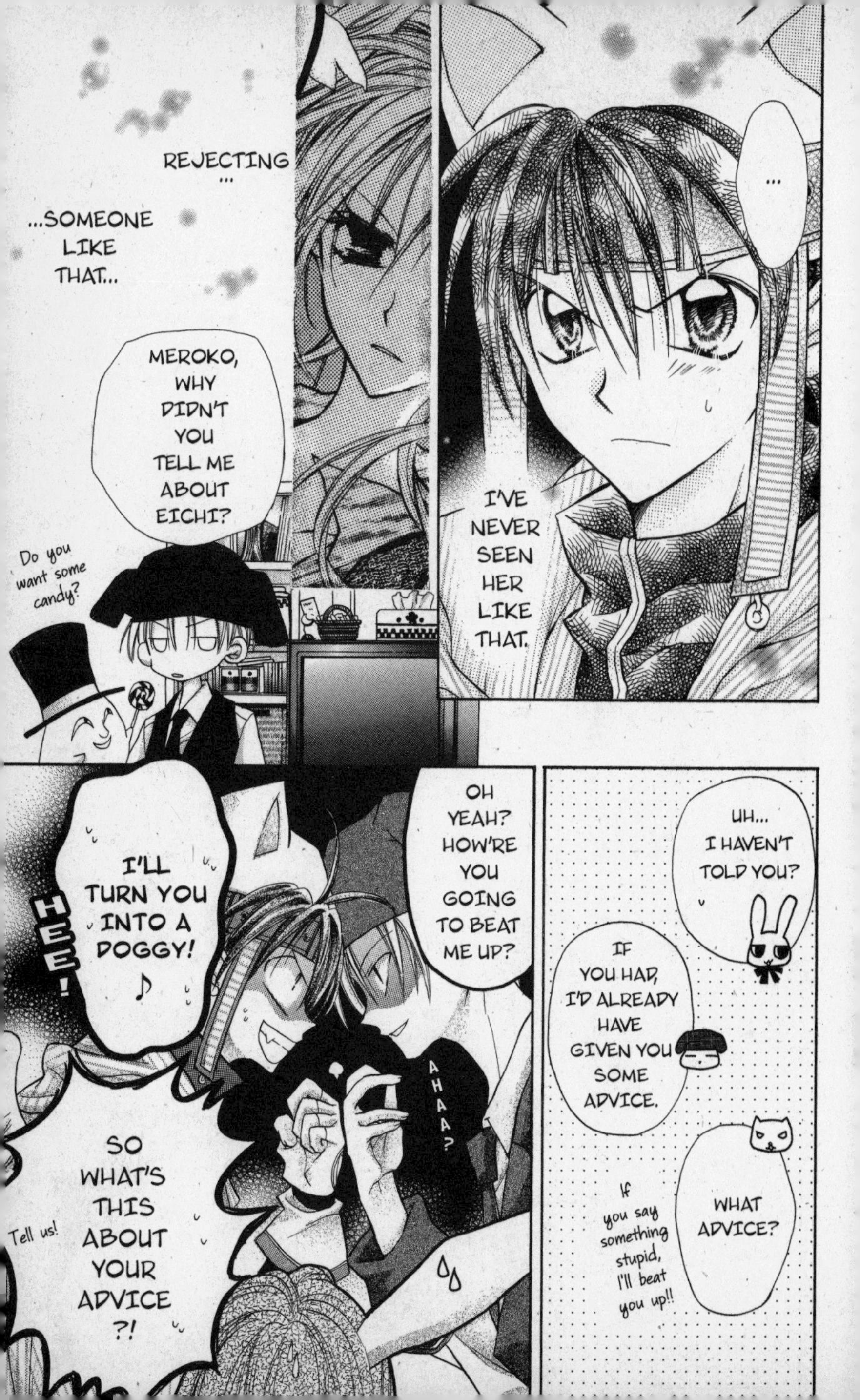
...
I'VE NEVER SEEN HER LIKE THAT.
REJECTING...
...SOMEONE LIKE THAT...
MEROKO, WHY DIDN'T YOU TELL ME ABOUT EICHI?
Do you want some candy?
UH... I HAVEN'T TOLD YOU?
IF YOU HAD, I'D ALREADY HAVE GIVEN YOU SOME ADVICE.
WHAT ADVICE?
If you say something stupid, I'll beat you up!!
OH YEAH? HOW'RE YOU GOING TO BEAT ME UP?
I'LL TURN YOU INTO A DOGGY! ♪
HEE!
AHAA?
SO WHAT'S THIS ABOUT YOUR ADVICE?!
Tell us!

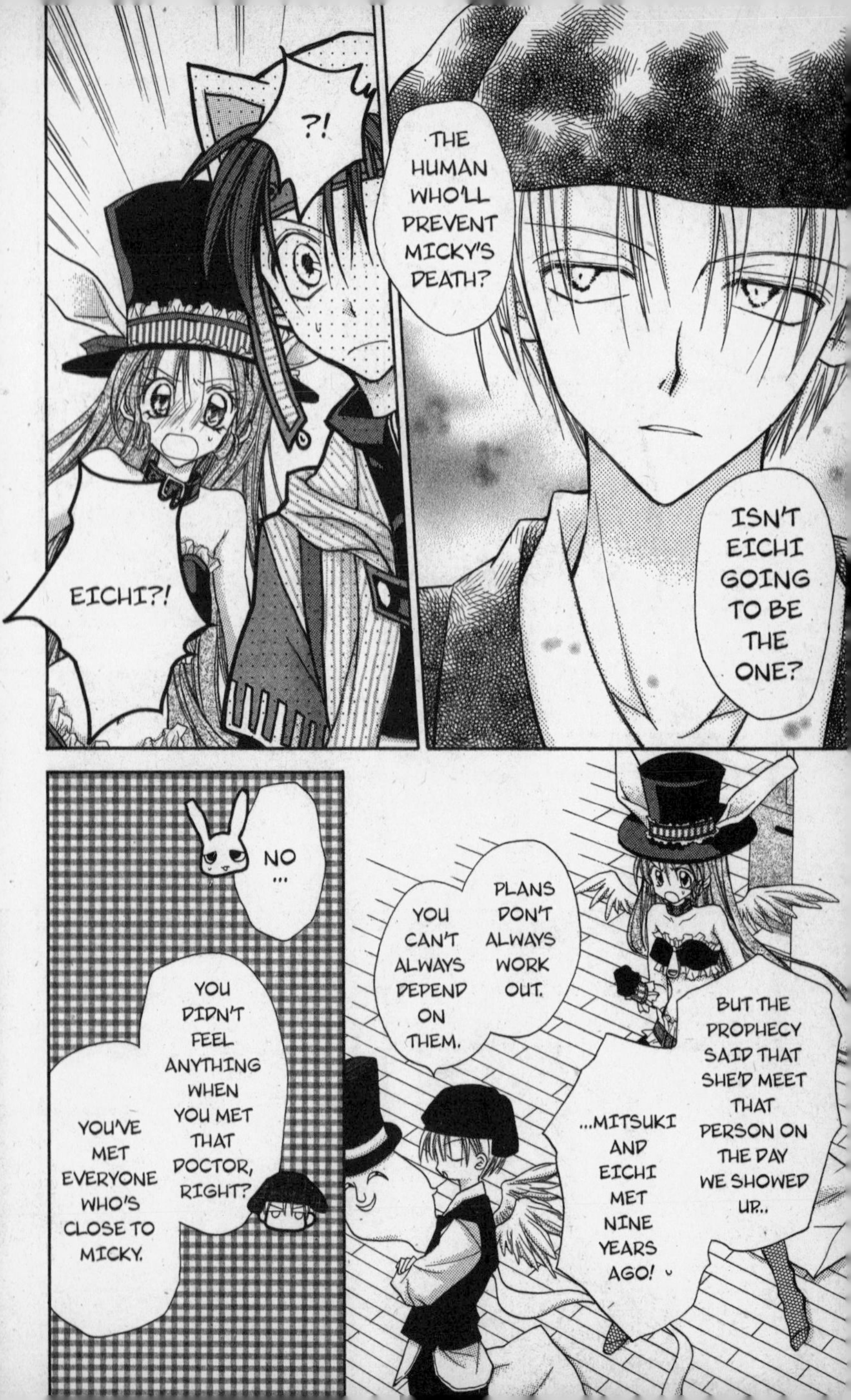
THE HUMAN WHO'LL PREVENT MICKY'S DEATH?
ISN'T EICHI GOING TO BE THE ONE?
?!
EICHI?!
BUT THE PROPHECY SAID THAT SHE'D MEET THAT PERSON ON THE DAY WE SHOWED UP..
...MITSUKI AND EICHI MET NINE YEARS AGO!
PLANS DON'T ALWAYS WORK OUT.
YOU CAN'T ALWAYS DEPEND ON THEM.
NO ...
YOU DIDN'T FEEL ANYTHING WHEN YOU MET THAT DOCTOR, RIGHT?
YOU'VE MET EVERYONE WHO'S CLOSE TO MICKY.

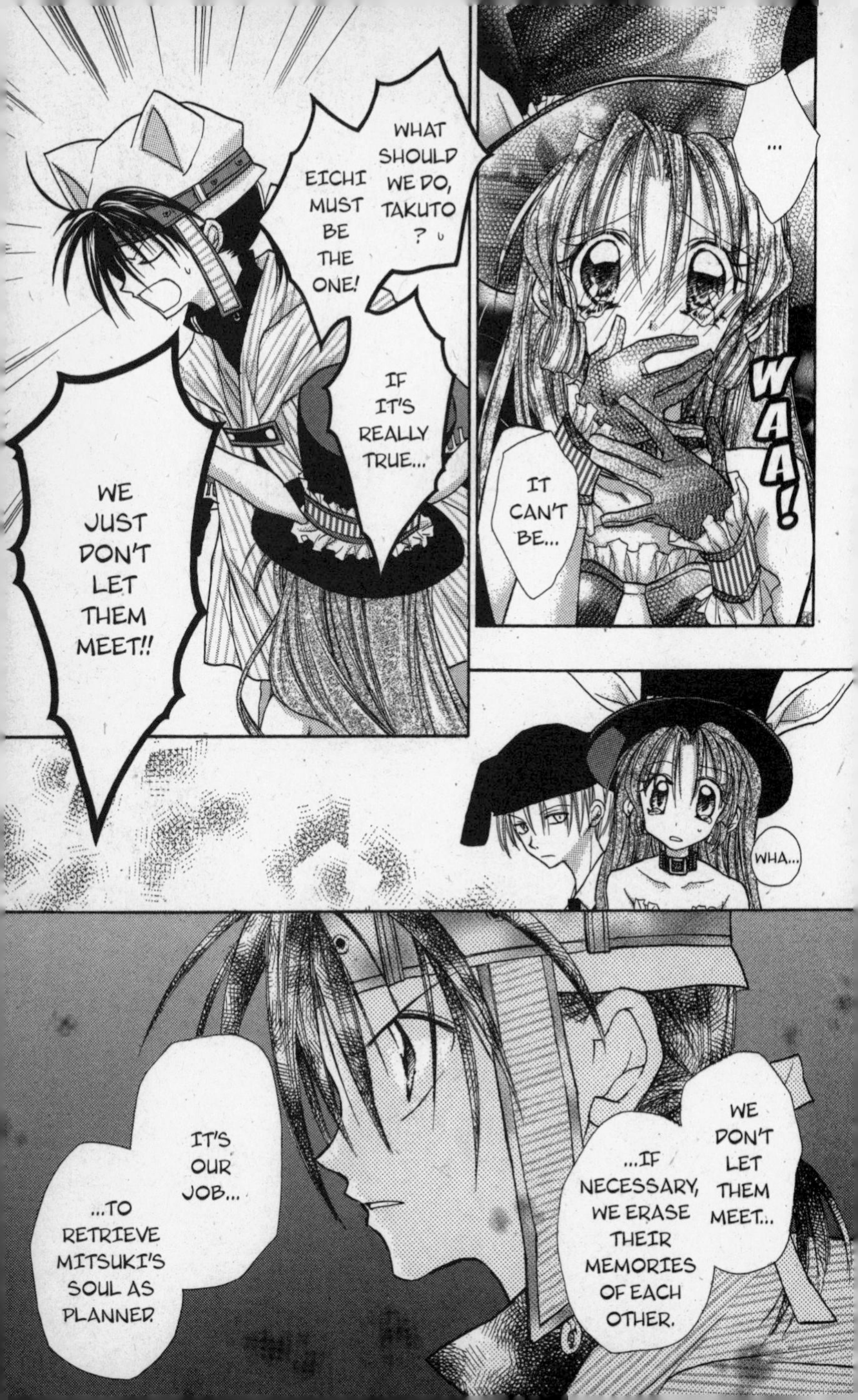
...
WAA!
IT CAN'T BE...
WHAT SHOULD WE DO, TAKUTO?
EICHI MUST BE THE ONE!
IF IT'S REALLY TRUE...
WE JUST DON'T LET THEM MEET!!
WHA...
WE DON'T LET THEM MEET...
...IF NECESSARY, WE ERASE THEIR MEMORIES OF EACH OTHER.
IT'S OUR JOB...
...TO RETRIEVE MITSUKI'S SOUL AS PLANNED.

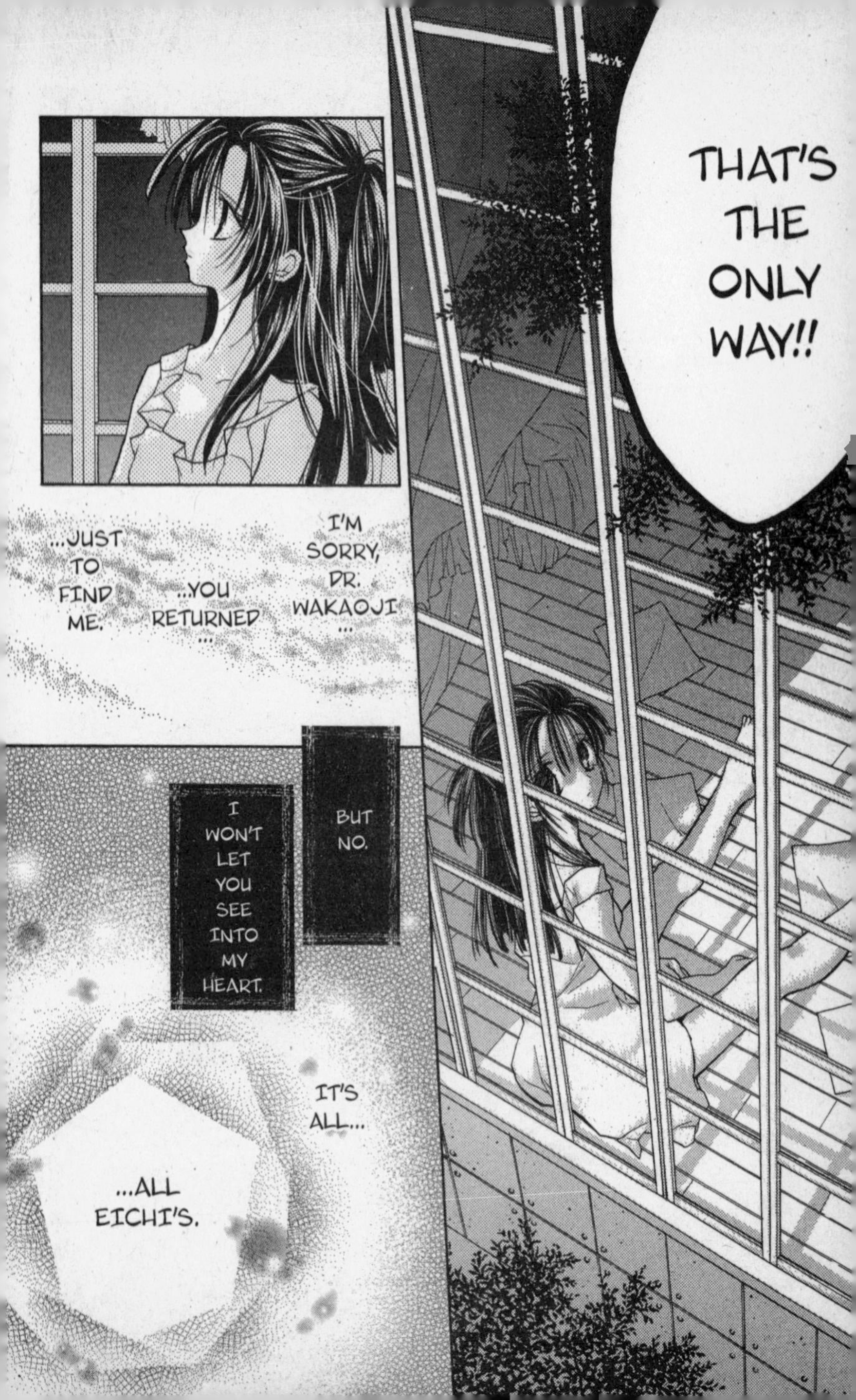
THAT'S THE ONLY WAY!!
I'M SORRY, DR. WAKAOJI...
...YOU RETURNED...
...JUST TO FIND ME.
BUT NO.
I WON'T LET YOU SEE INTO MY HEART.
IT'S ALL...
...ALL EICHI'S.

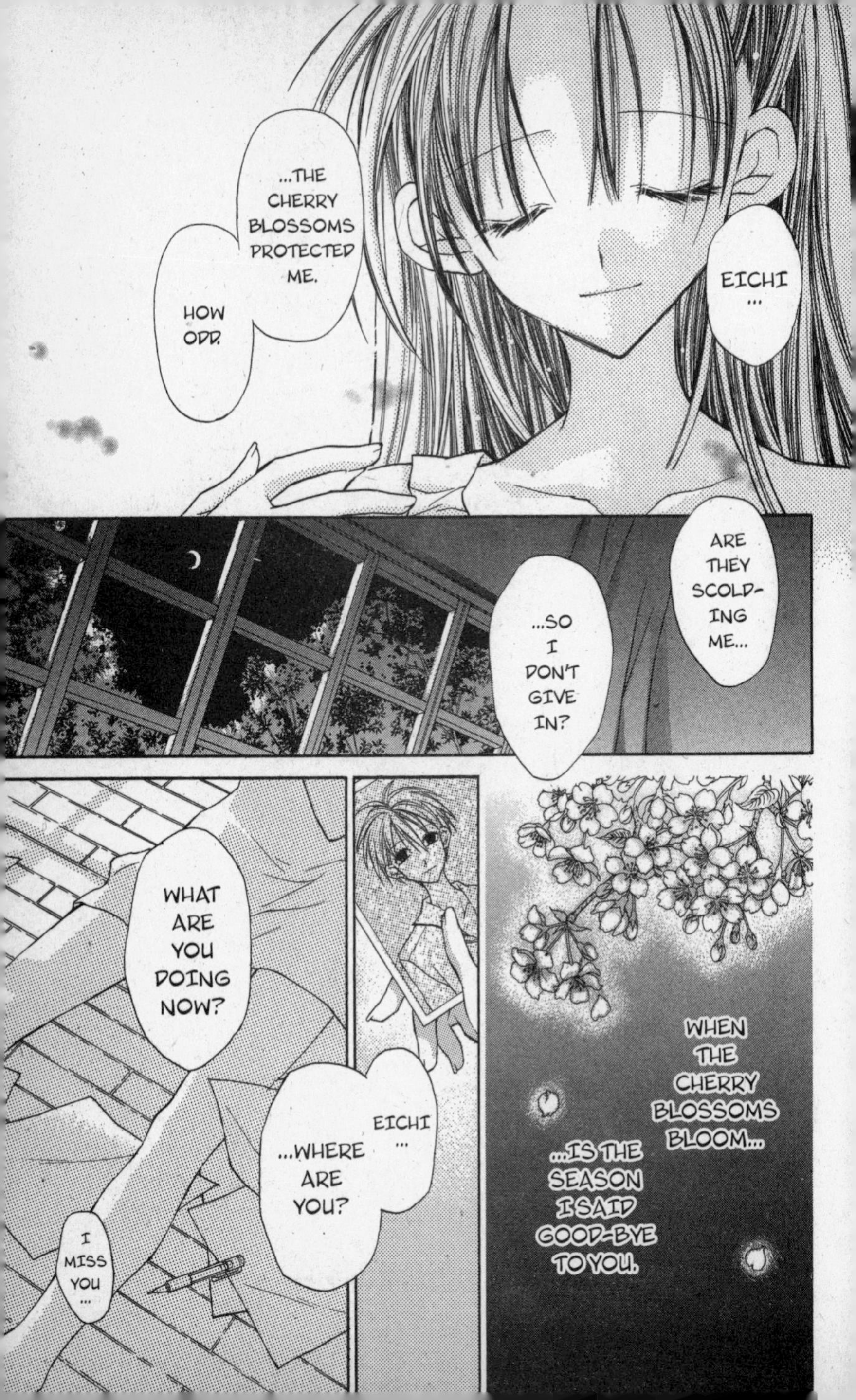
EICHI...
...THE CHERRY BLOSSOMS PROTECTED ME.
HOW ODD.
ARE THEY SCOLD-ING ME...
...SO I DON'T GIVE IN?
WHEN THE CHERRY BLOSSOMS BLOOM...
...IS THE SEASON I SAID GOOD-BYE TO YOU.
EICHI...
...WHERE ARE YOU?
WHAT ARE YOU DOING NOW?
I MISS YOU...

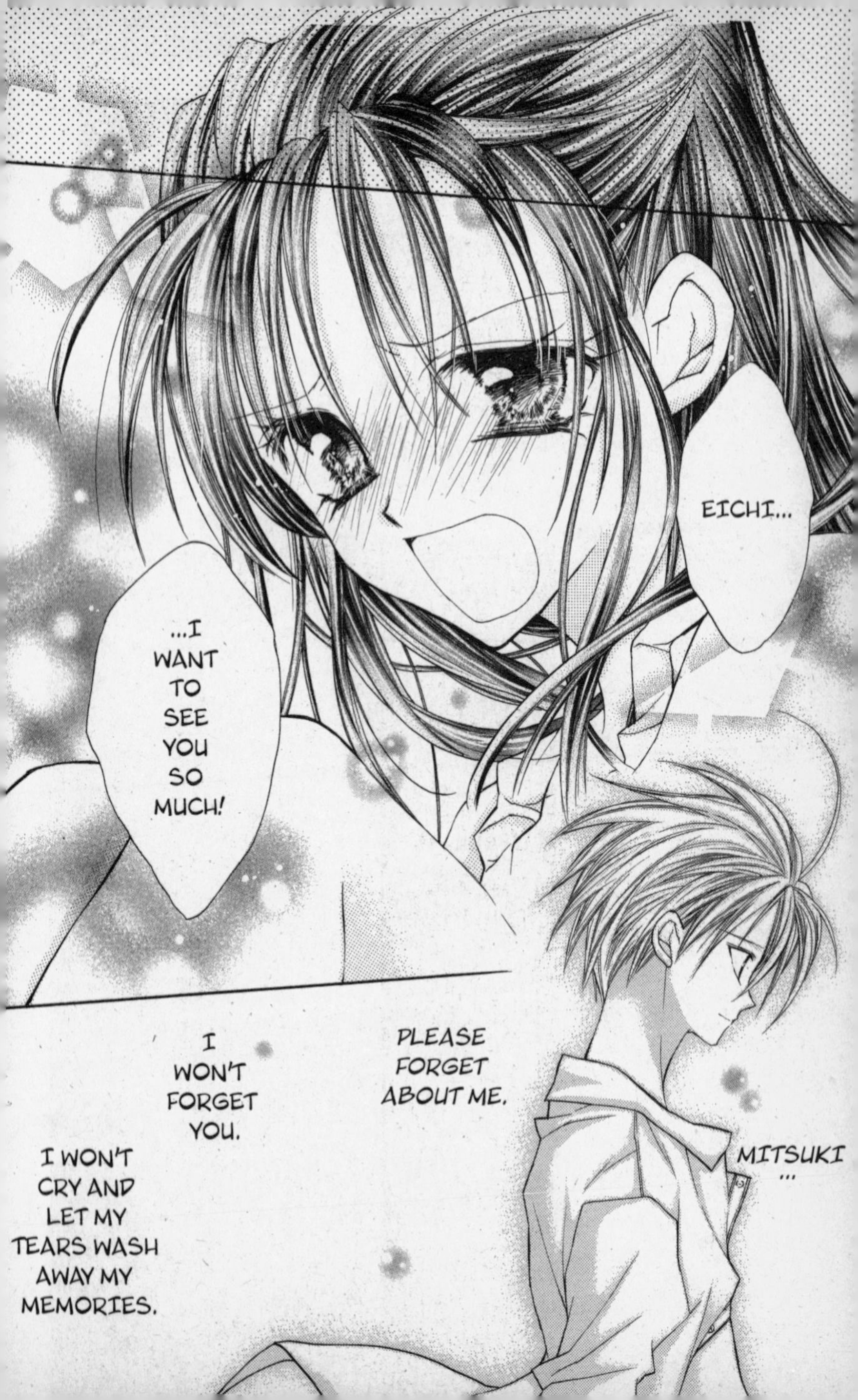
EICHI...
...I WANT TO SEE YOU SO MUCH!
MITSUKI ...
PLEASE FORGET ABOUT ME.
I WON'T FORGET YOU.
I WON'T CRY AND LET MY TEARS WASH AWAY MY MEMORIES.

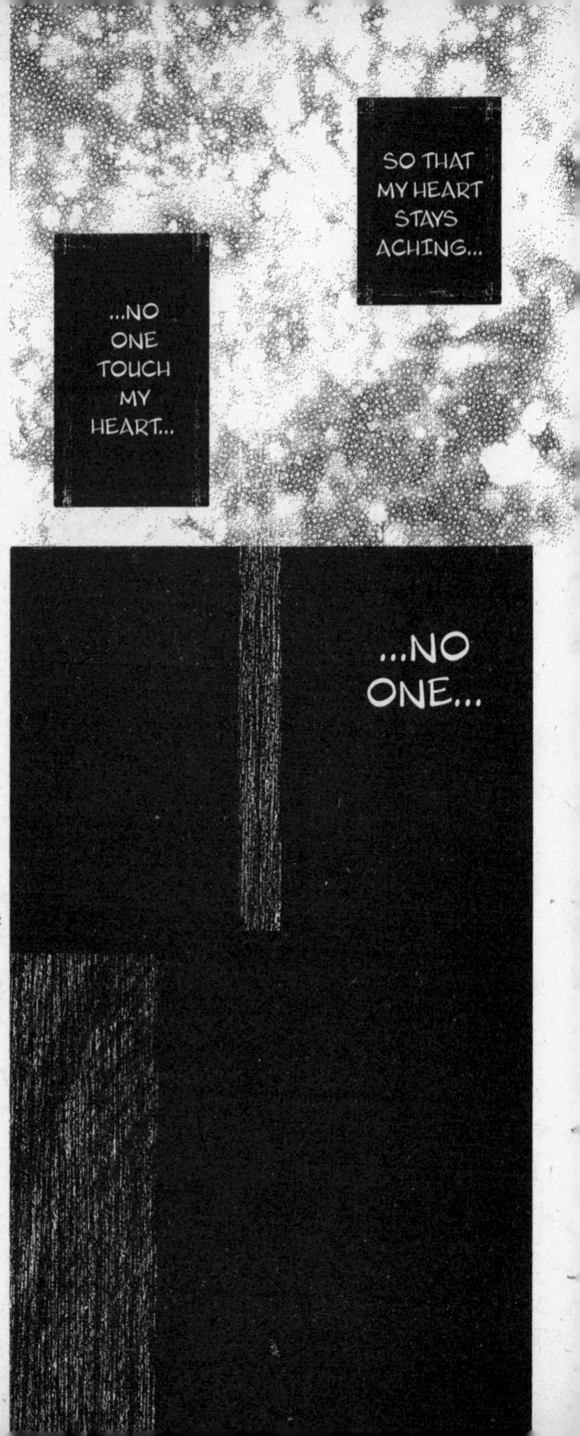
SO THAT MY HEART STAYS ACHING...
...NO ONE TOUCH MY HEART...
...NO ONE...

Greetings

Hello! It's Arinacchi. I came to deliver you "Full Moon o Sagashite" Vol.③! I'm sorry the cover looks like the cover for Volume ①. It wasn't supposed to be this way...

In February 2003 "Full Moon Anime Edition" was on sale. Did everyone **GET** it?
Actually, there was supposed to be an anime edition for "Jeanne," but in the end it didn't come out, so I was happy there was one out for "Full Moon." ♪ la la la!
Talking about real-time stuff, the anime will be over soon. It was reaaaaaaally good, so I'm sad. Awww...
To every staff member, thank you very very much!! I loved the "Full Moon" anime!! How to say...I first had trouble deciding how to portray the incident that happens in this volume, and then in the anime the alternative version was used, so I'm really happy. It's a surprise every episode.
And my favorites, Ms. Oshige and Dr. Wakaoji being so in **LOVE** is good. Yes...really good.

If you live in a place where the anime wasn't broadcast, please watch it on DVD if possible.

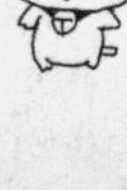

Watch it.

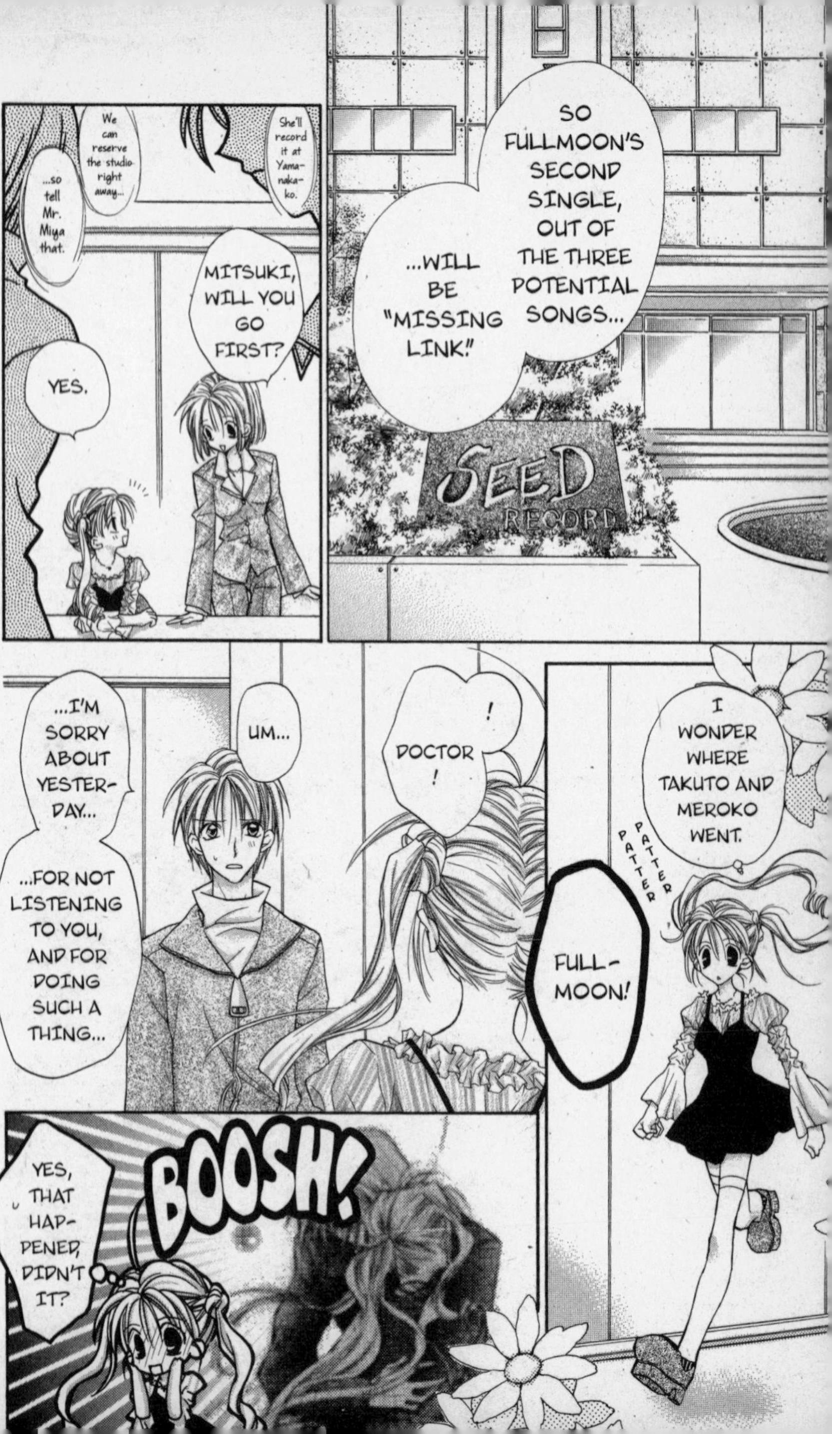
SO FULLMOON'S SECOND SINGLE, OUT OF THE THREE POTENTIAL SONGS...
...WILL BE "MISSING LINK."
She'll record it at Yamanakako.
We can reserve the studio right away...
...so tell Mr. Miya that.
MITSUKI, WILL YOU GO FIRST?
YES.
I WONDER WHERE TAKUTO AND MEROKO WENT.
PATTER PATTER
FULL-MOON!
!
DOCTOR!
UM...
...I'M SORRY ABOUT YESTERDAY...
...FOR NOT LISTENING TO YOU, AND FOR DOING SUCH A THING...
BOOSH!
YES, THAT HAPPENED, DIDN'T IT?

In the Ribon Website, Mitsuki's Room...

This Month's Highlight!

A little while ago in the "Mitsuki's Room" section of Ribon's website, I was writing the highlight of each month's "Full Moon o Sagashite." (To be exact, I email or FAX a summary to Ribon, and they write the highlight for me). But what I write about isn't the most important part.

It's not!

I most want people to read the manga (since people buy Ribon on different dates) and look at the drawings. So I usually write the third most important part, or I write gags. *Runs away*

If you have a computer, and you can access the net but have never seen "Mitsuki's Room," please access it. ♪

It's usually updated on the first of the month, but I write it right after I've finished drawing the chapter, so my messages tend to be pretty real. ☺

And thank you to all the people who send support emails to the website. When I get emails from people who've read the manga on the day Ribon goes on sale, I'm really happy. It makes me want to do my work!!

I don't cry when I do my storyboards (sometimes I'm close to tears, but I hold it back), but sometimes I cry when I read all your opinions. Awww! Especially this volume...yes.

Ribon Website↓

http://ribon.shueisha.co.jp

The Takuto-cat and the Meroko-rabbit on the front page are cute!!

Yay!

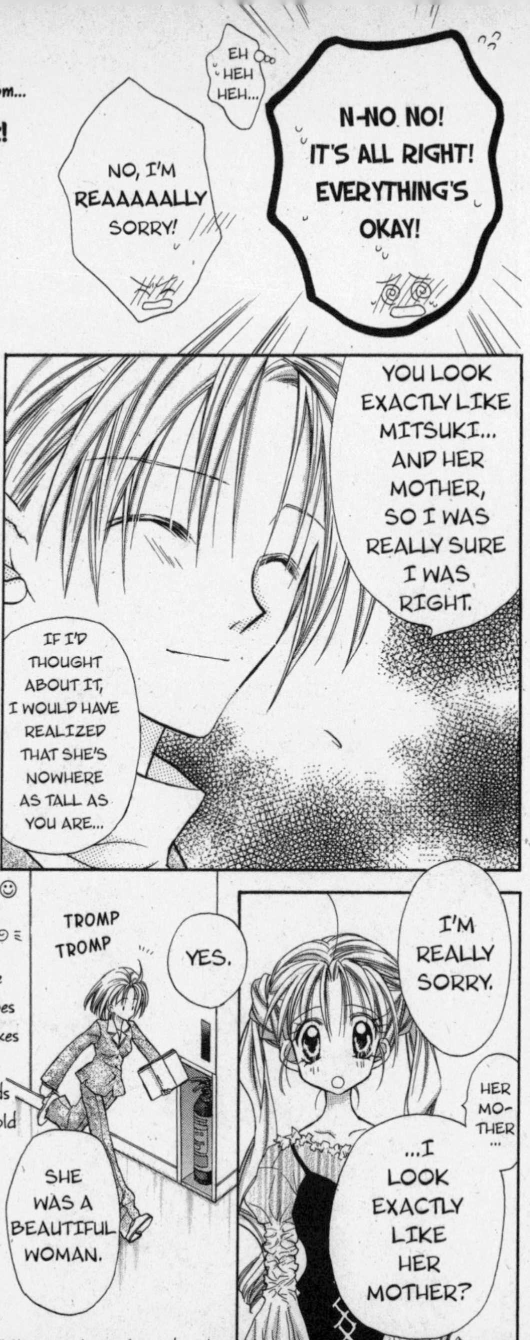
N-NO NO! IT'S ALL RIGHT! EVERYTHING'S OKAY!
EH HEH HEH...
NO, I'M REAAAAALLY SORRY!
YOU LOOK EXACTLY LIKE MITSUKI... AND HER MOTHER, SO I WAS REALLY SURE I WAS RIGHT.
IF I'D THOUGHT ABOUT IT, I WOULD HAVE REALIZED THAT SHE'S NOWHERE AS TALL AS YOU ARE...
I'M REALLY SORRY.
HER MO-THER...
...I LOOK EXACTLY LIKE HER MOTHER?
YES.
TROMP TROMP
SHE WAS A BEAUTIFUL WOMAN.

Full Moon is no longer featured on the Ribbon site, but there are lots of other fun things to look at. -Ed.

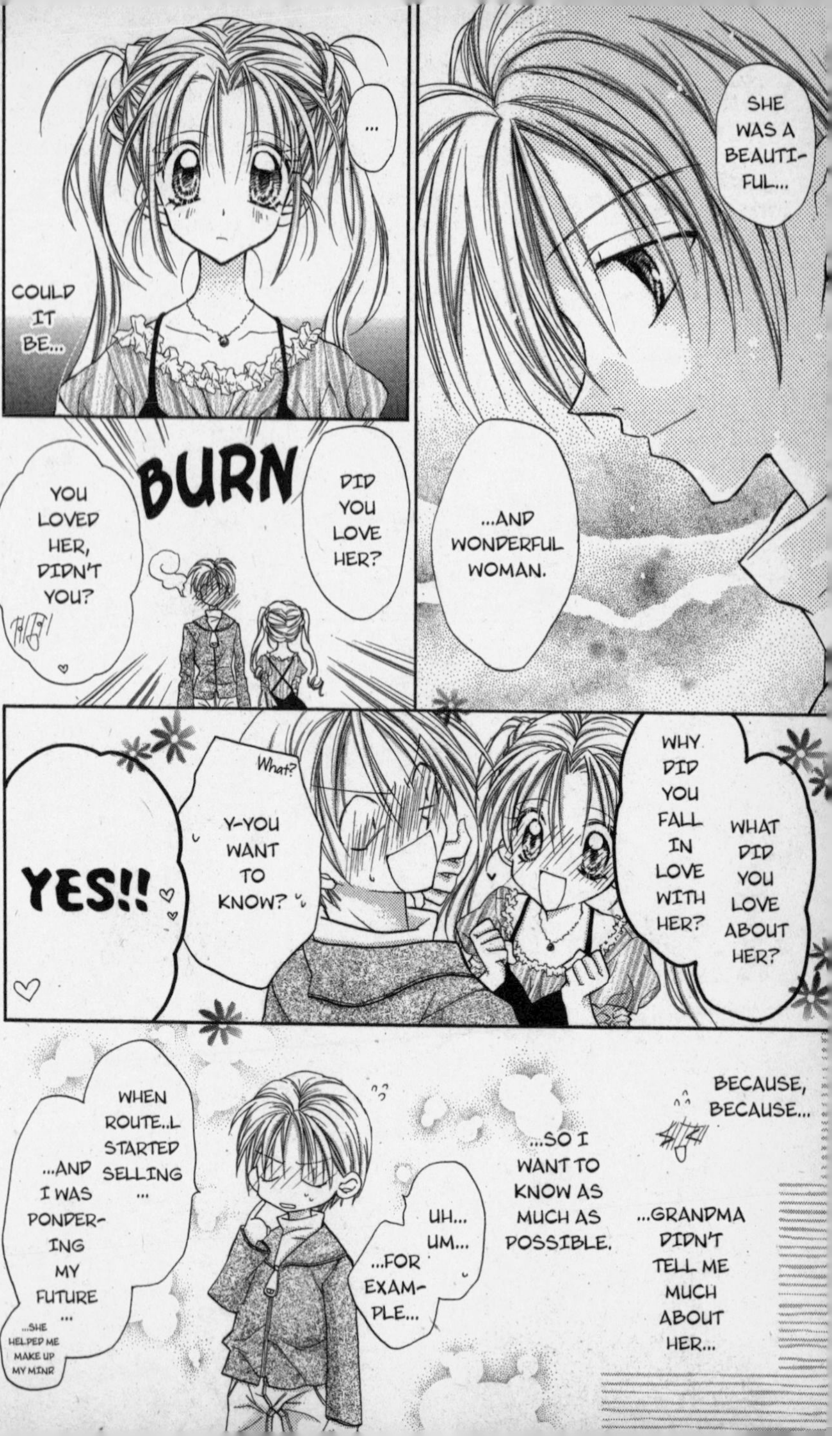
SHE WAS A BEAUTIFUL...
...AND WONDERFUL WOMAN.
...
COULD IT BE...
DID YOU LOVE HER?
BURN
YOU LOVED HER, DIDN'T YOU?
WHY DID YOU FALL IN LOVE WITH HER?
WHAT DID YOU LOVE ABOUT HER?
What?
Y-YOU WANT TO KNOW?
YES!!
BECAUSE, BECAUSE...
...GRANDMA DIDN'T TELL ME MUCH ABOUT HER...
...SO I WANT TO KNOW AS MUCH AS POSSIBLE.
UH... UM...
...FOR EXAMPLE...
WHEN ROUTE..L STARTED SELLING...
...AND I WAS PONDERING MY FUTURE...
...SHE HELPED ME MAKE UP MY MINR

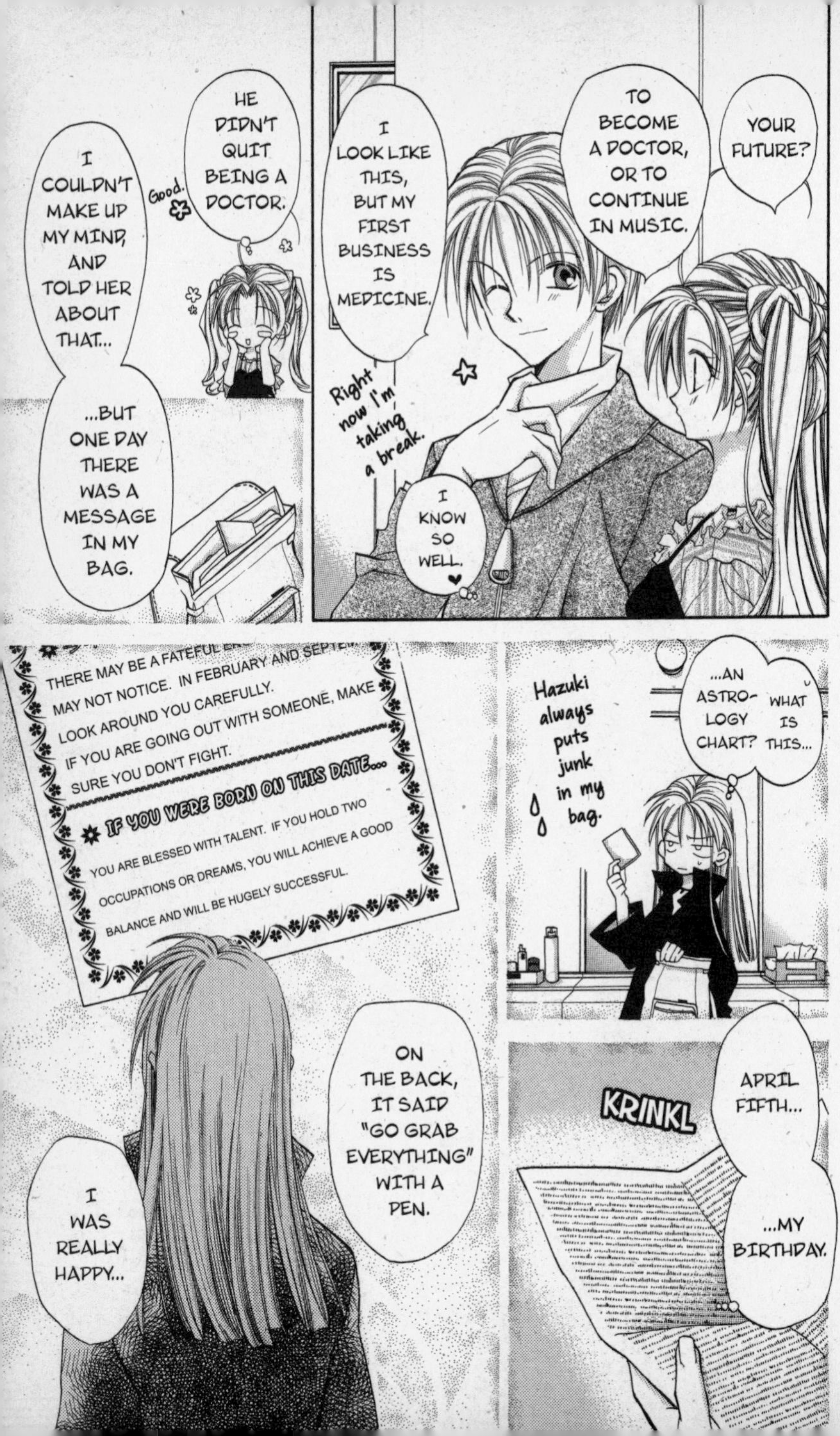
YOUR FUTURE?
TO BECOME A DOCTOR, OR TO CONTINUE IN MUSIC.
I LOOK LIKE THIS, BUT MY FIRST BUSINESS IS MEDICINE.
Right now I'm taking a break.
I KNOW SO WELL.
HE DIDN'T QUIT BEING A DOCTOR.
Good.
I COULDN'T MAKE UP MY MIND, AND TOLD HER ABOUT THAT...
...BUT ONE DAY THERE WAS A MESSAGE IN MY BAG.
WHAT IS THIS...
...AN ASTROLOGY CHART?
Hazuki always puts junk in my bag.
KRINKL
APRIL FIFTH...
...MY BIRTHDAY.
THERE MAY BE A FATEFUL
MAY NOT NOTICE. IN FEBRUARY AND
LOOK AROUND YOU CAREFULLY.
IF YOU ARE GOING OUT WITH SOMEONE, MAKE SURE YOU DON'T FIGHT.
IF YOU WERE BORN ON THIS DATE...
YOU ARE BLESSED WITH TALENT. IF YOU HOLD TWO OCCUPATIONS OR DREAMS, YOU WILL ACHIEVE A GOOD BALANCE AND WILL BE HUGELY SUCCESSFUL.
ON THE BACK, IT SAID "GO GRAB EVERYTHING" WITH A PEN.
I WAS REALLY HAPPY...

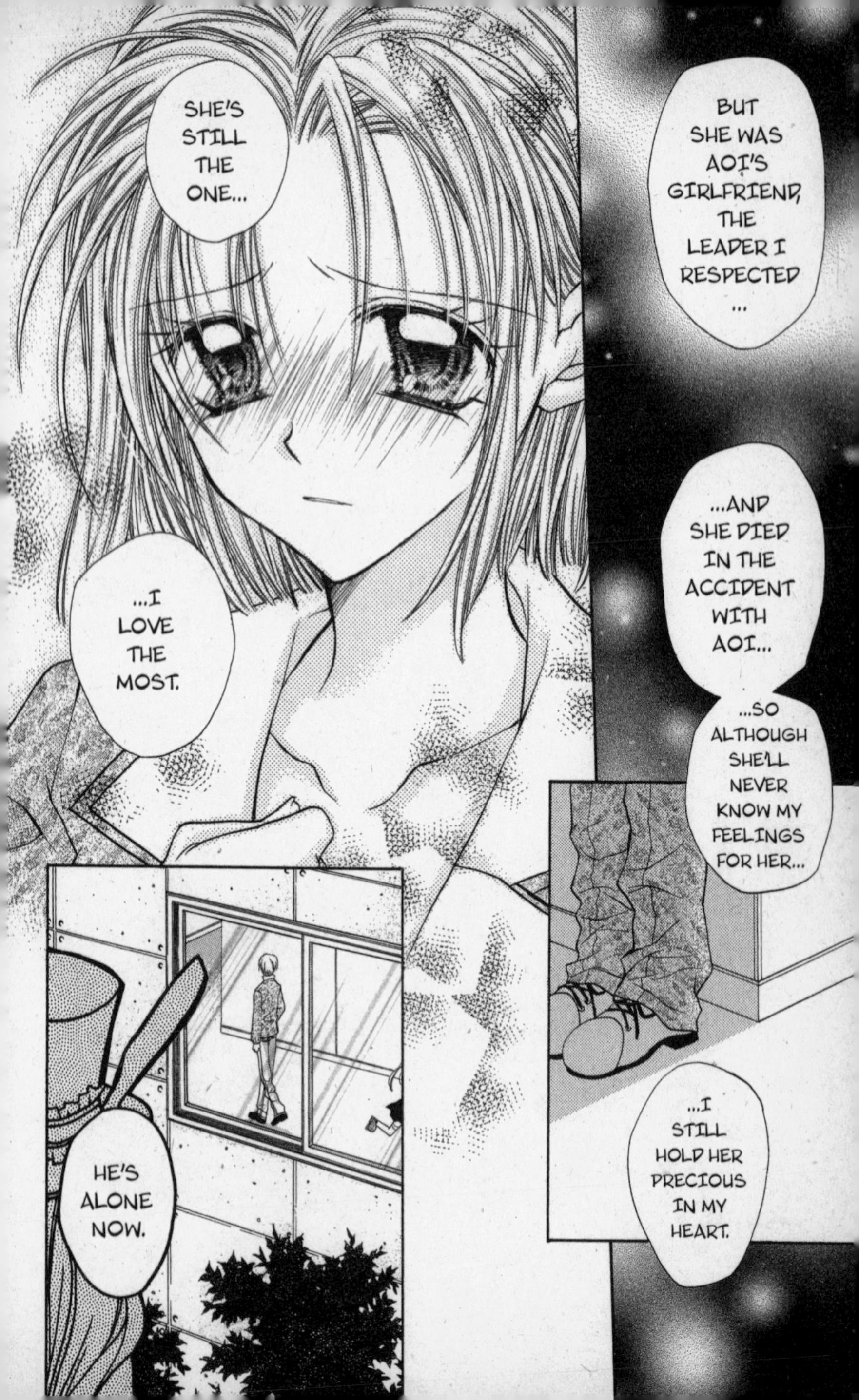
BUT SHE WAS AOI'S GIRLFRIEND, THE LEADER I RESPECTED ...
...AND SHE DIED IN THE ACCIDENT WITH AOI...
...SO ALTHOUGH SHE'LL NEVER KNOW MY FEELINGS FOR HER...
...I STILL HOLD HER PRECIOUS IN MY HEART.
SHE'S STILL THE ONE...
...I LOVE THE MOST.
HE'S ALONE NOW.

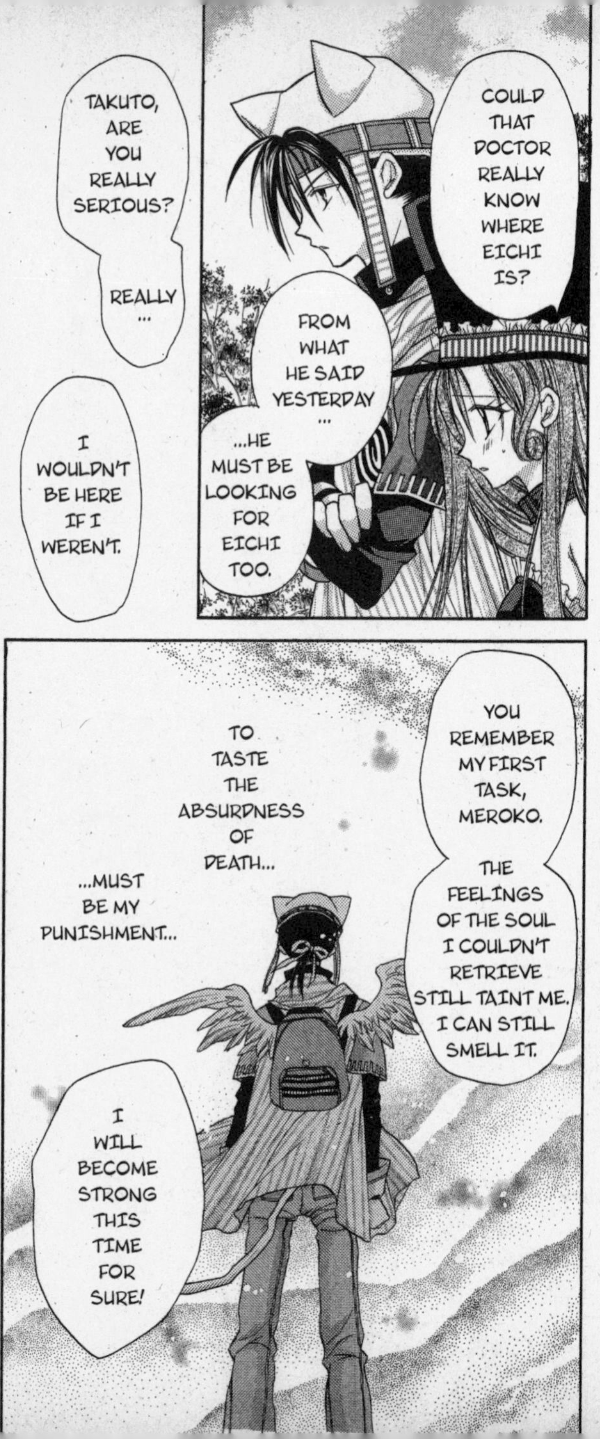
COULD THAT DOCTOR REALLY KNOW WHERE EICHI IS?
FROM WHAT HE SAID YESTERDAY...
...HE MUST BE LOOKING FOR EICHI TOO.
TAKUTO, ARE YOU REALLY SERIOUS?
REALLY...
I WOULDN'T BE HERE IF I WEREN'T.
YOU REMEMBER MY FIRST TASK, MEROKO.
THE FEELINGS OF THE SOUL I COULDN'T RETRIEVE STILL TAINT ME. I CAN STILL SMELL IT.
TO TASTE THE ABSURDNESS OF DEATH...
...MUST BE MY PUNISHMENT...
I WILL BECOME STRONG THIS TIME FOR SURE!

Arina Tanemura's

"Penchi de Shakin?"

episode 55

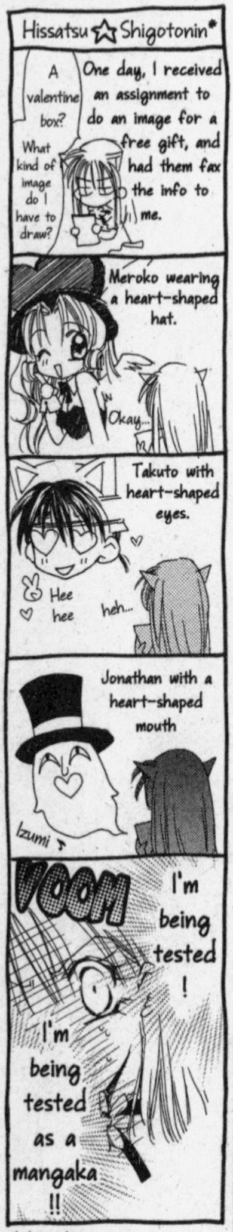
Hissatsu☆Shigotonin*
One day, I received an assignment to do an image for a free gift, and had them fax the info to me.
A valentine box?
What kind of image do I have to draw?
Meroko wearing a heart-shaped hat.
Okay...
Takuto with heart-shaped eyes.
Hee hee
heh...
Jonathan with a heart-shaped mouth
Izumi ♪
VOOM
I'm being tested!
I'm being tested as a mangaka!!

I didn't draw it...
By the way...
If you have the BOX, look at my clumsy drawing and laugh...

*The name of an old TV show. Shigotonin were assassins who went after the bad guys. —Ed.

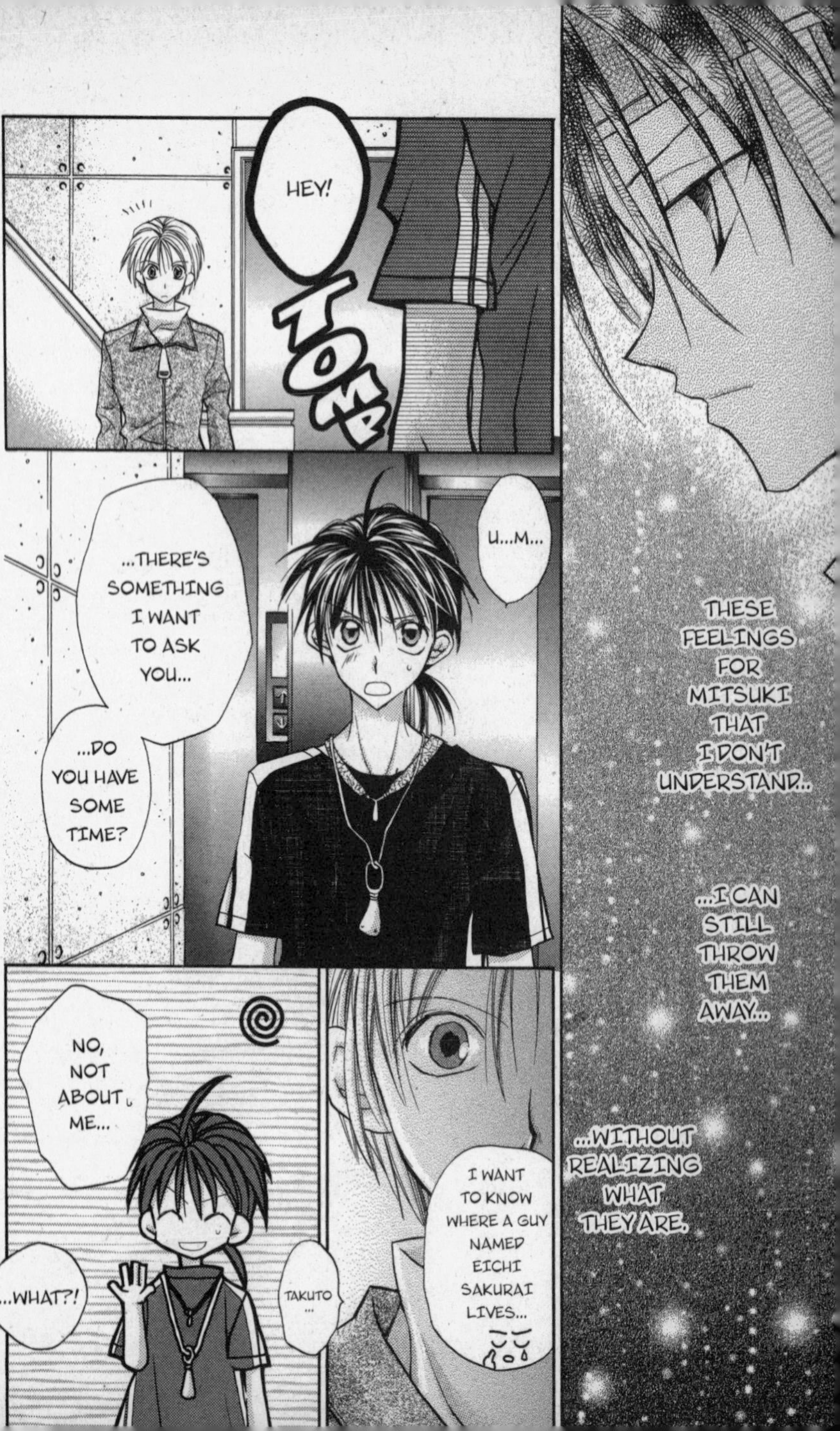
THESE FEELINGS FOR MITSUKI THAT I DON'T UNDERSTAND..
...I CAN STILL THROW THEM AWAY...
...WITHOUT REALIZING WHAT THEY ARE.
HEY!
TOMP
U...M...
...THERE'S SOMETHING I WANT TO ASK YOU...
...DO YOU HAVE SOME TIME?
I WANT TO KNOW WHERE A GUY NAMED EICHI SAKURAI LIVES...
TAKUTO ...
NO, NOT ABOUT ME...
...WHAT?!

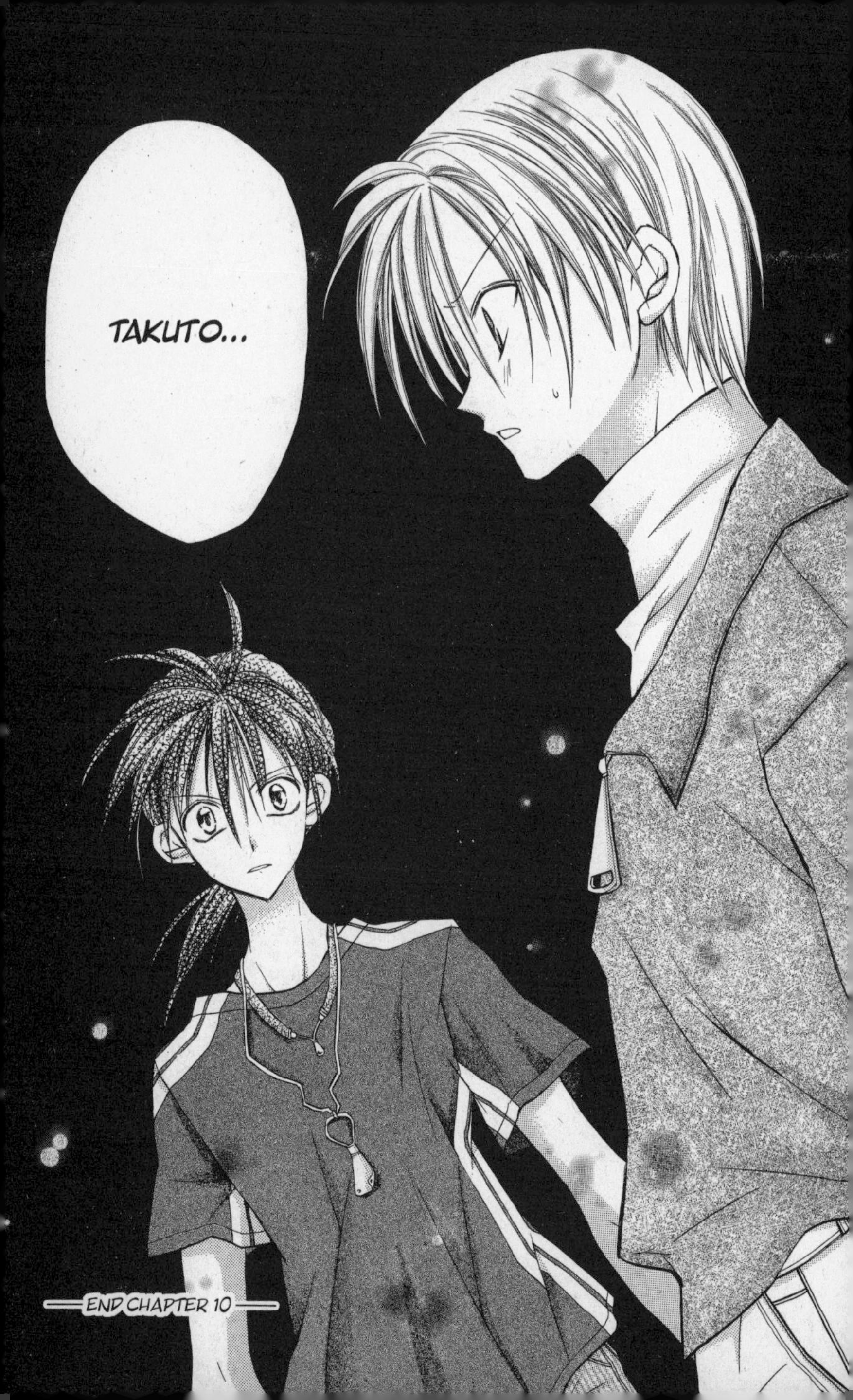
TAKUTO...
END CHAPTER 10

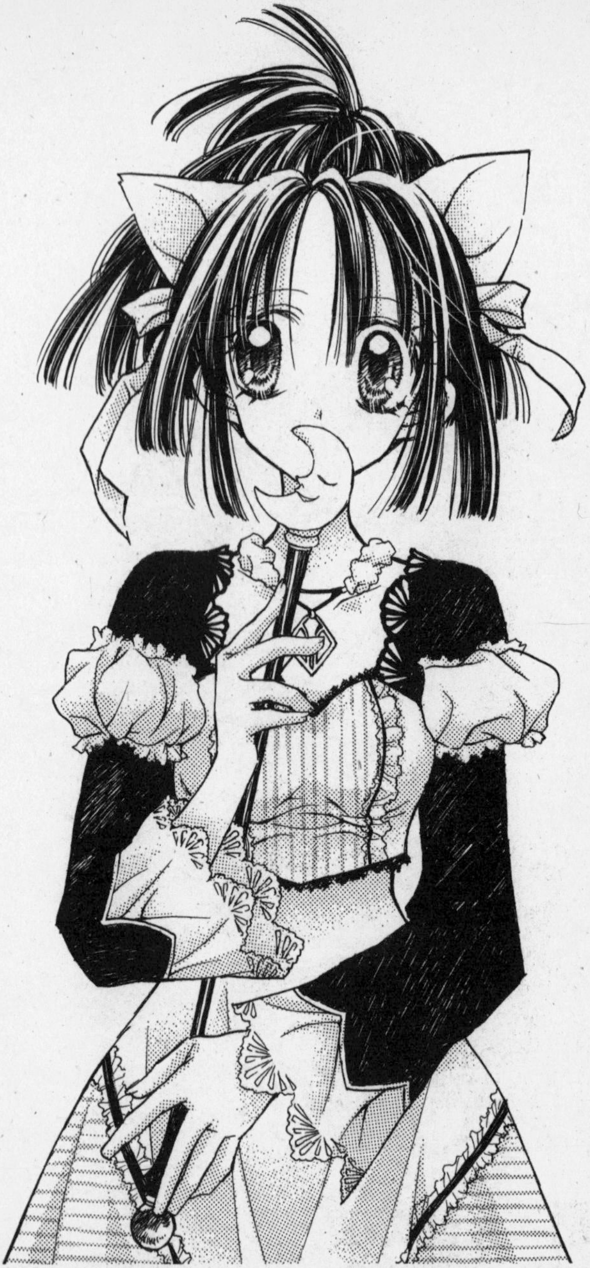

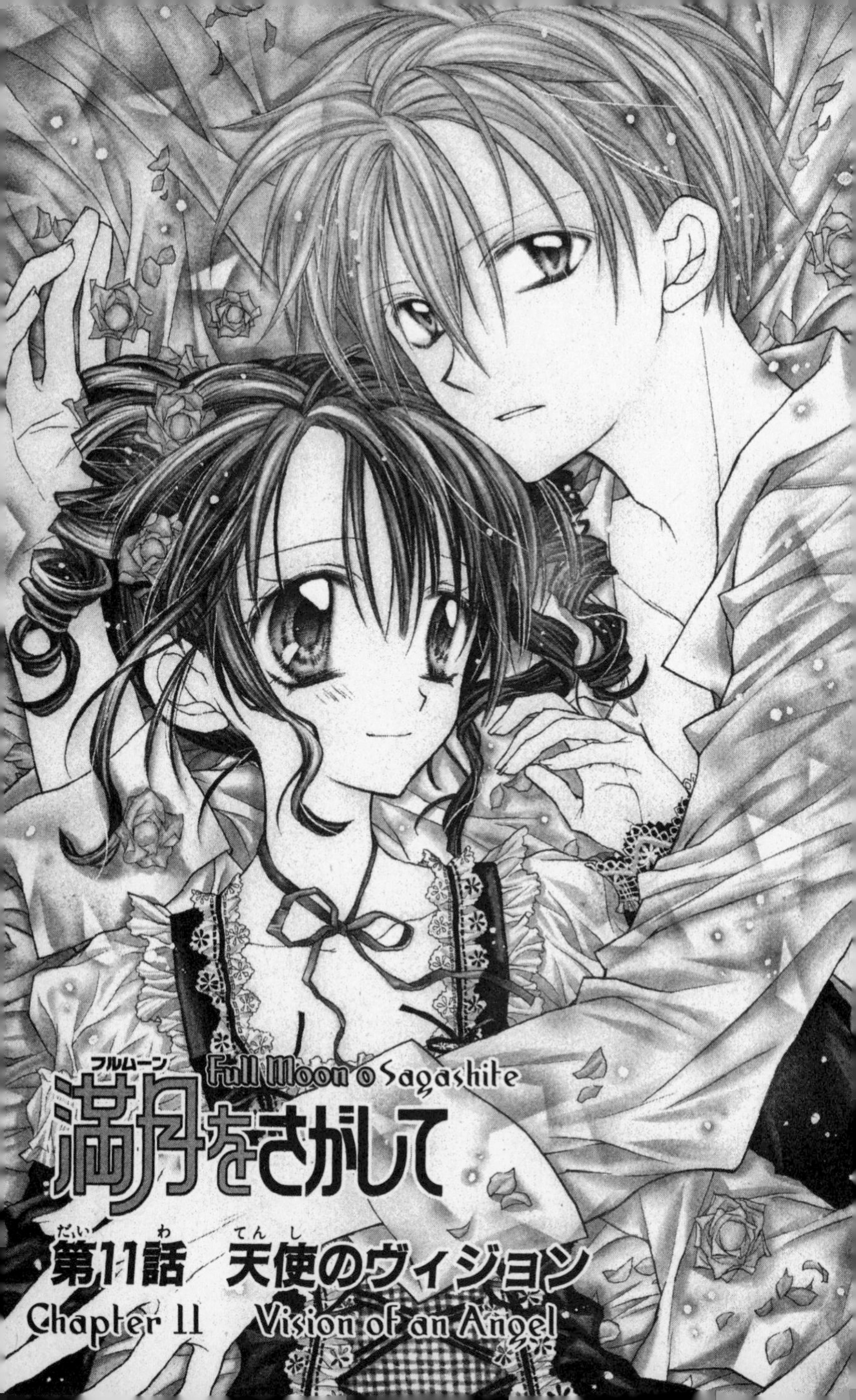
フルムーン
Full Moon o Sagashite
満月をさがして
第11話 天使のヴィジョン
Chapter 11 Vision of an Angel

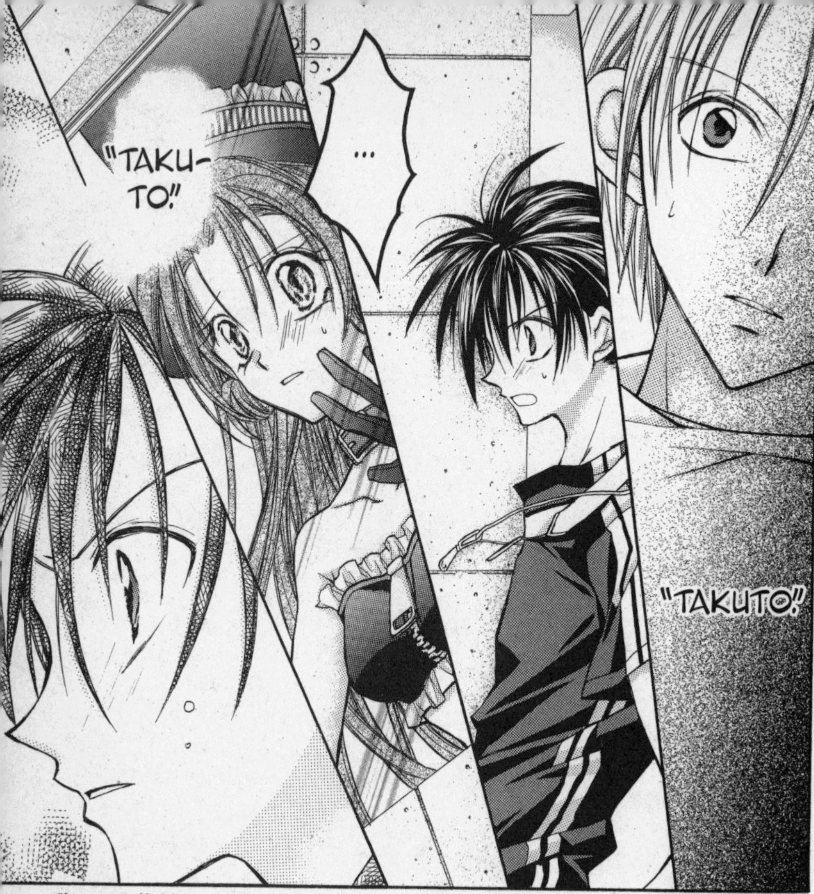
"TAKUTO!"
...
"TAKU-TO!"

Chapter 11 Vision of an Angel (spoilers follow)

Cover Copy I will always be with you.

The cover illustration is the last of the "Mitsuki and XX" series, Mitsuki and Eichi. The two make a good picture, and their illustrations all have the same atmosphere, but I think that's okay.
When I started this series, I received letters saying "You are taking life lightly," and other similar comments, but I don't intend to respond to them (probably...even after the series is done). But if I were to say anything, it would be "What is important or what is trivial, it's all vague and I don't understand it well myself. But I have only one life given to me too." Everyone is groping around.

...please understand the rest (of what I want to say) by reading the manga.

To tell the truth, I started drawing this story for a friend. But actually, I may be drawing it to ease my regrets about not being able to say anything to them at that time. I can't be honest except in this way.

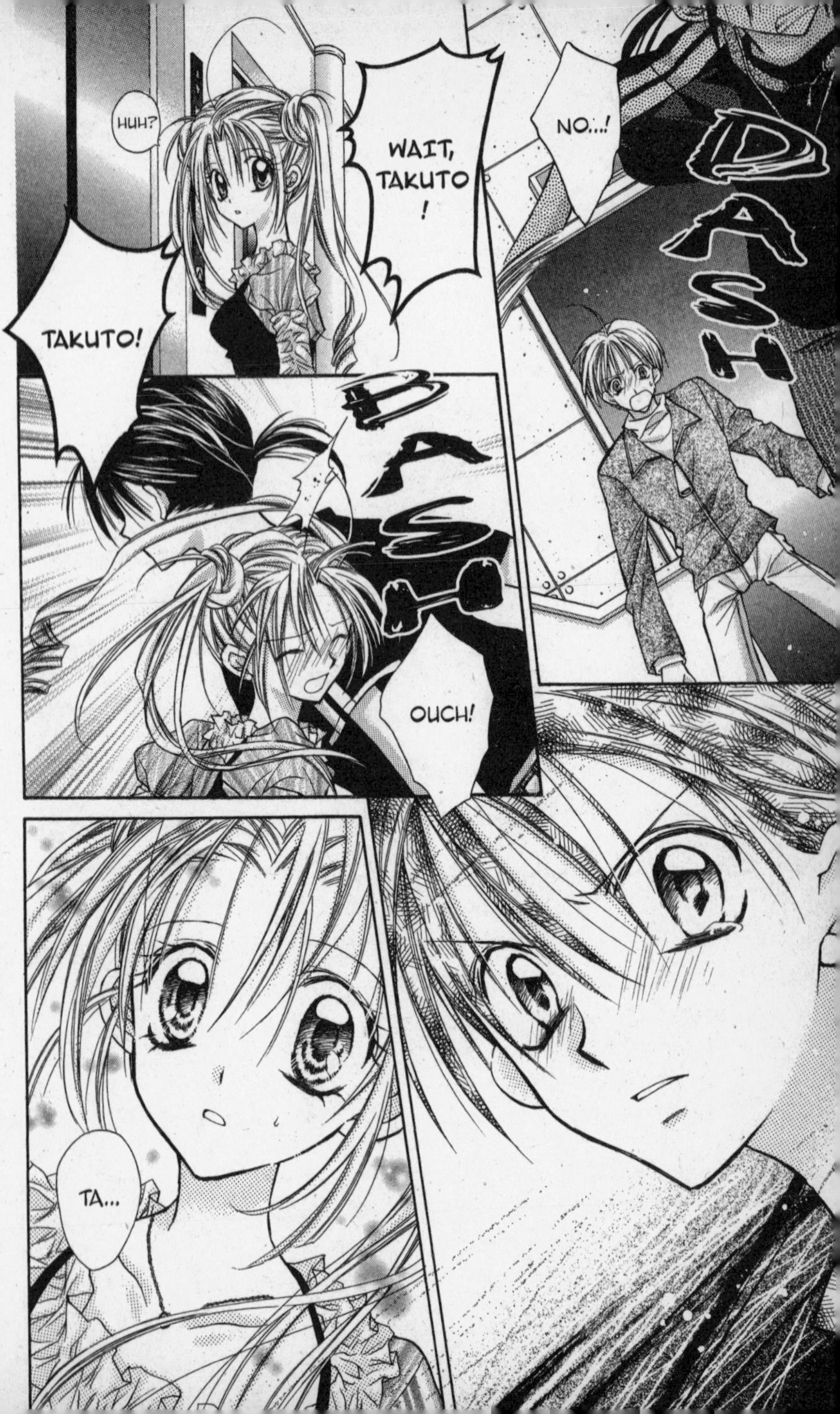
NO...!
DASH
WAIT, TAKUTO!
HUH?
TAKUTO!
DASH
OUCH!
TA...

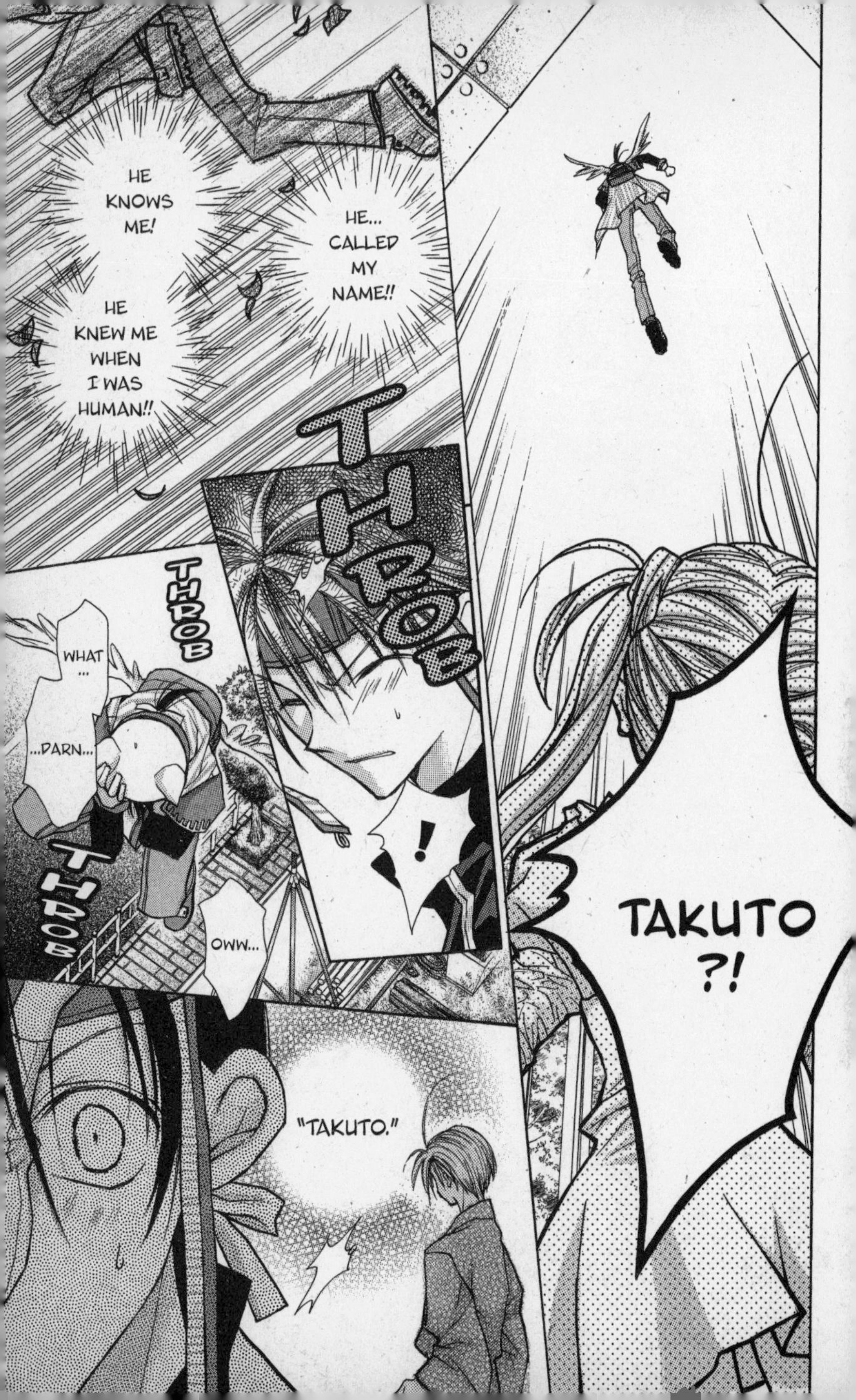
TAKUTO ?!
HE... CALLED MY NAME!!
HE KNOWS ME!
HE KNEW ME WHEN I WAS HUMAN!!
THROB
THROB
WHAT ...
...DARN...
THROB
OWW...
"TAKUTO."

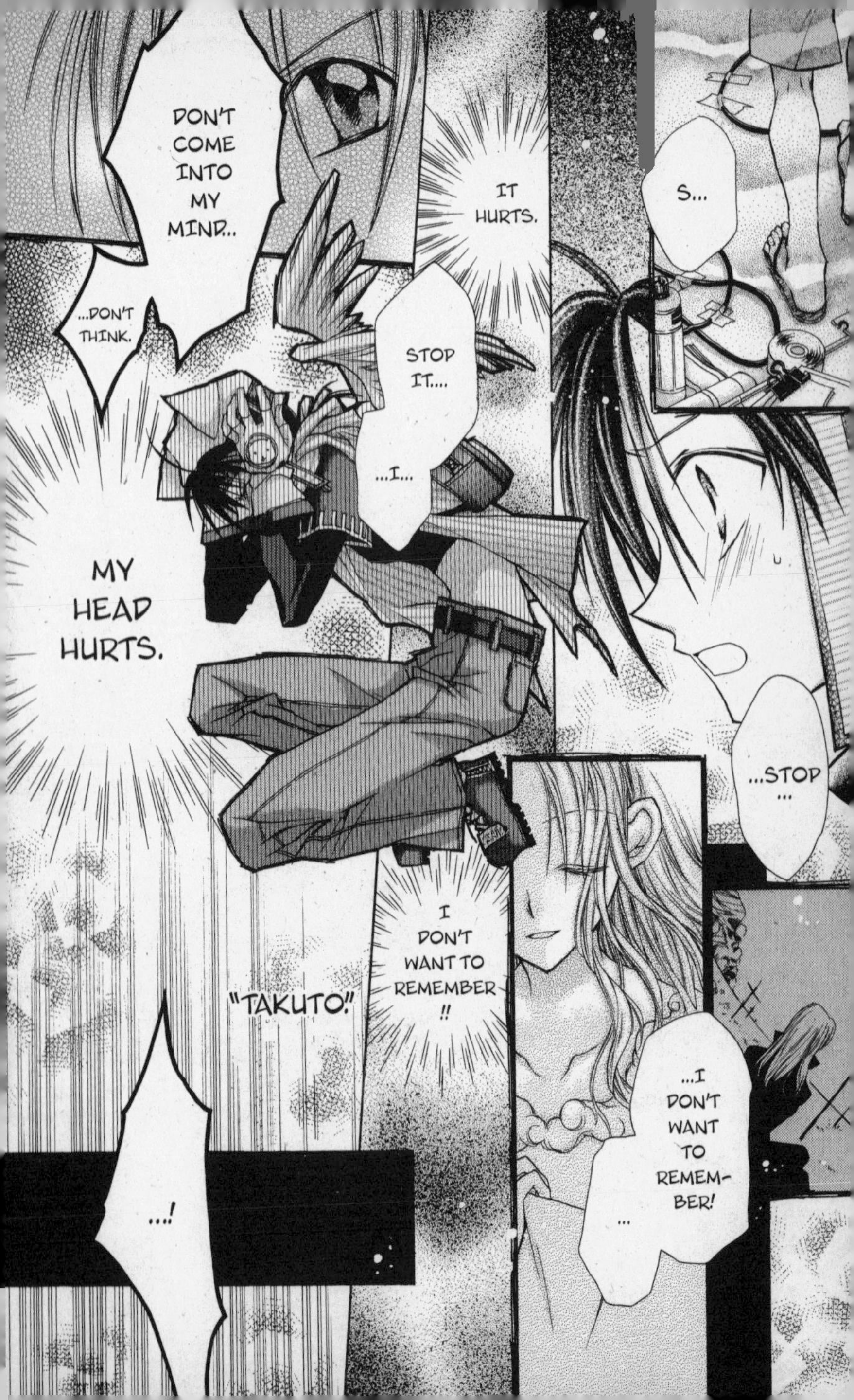
S...
...STOP ...
IT HURTS.
DON'T COME INTO MY MIND...
...DON'T THINK.
STOP IT....
...I...
MY HEAD HURTS.
...I DON'T WANT TO REMEMBER!
...
I DON'T WANT TO REMEMBER !!
"TAKUTO!"
...!

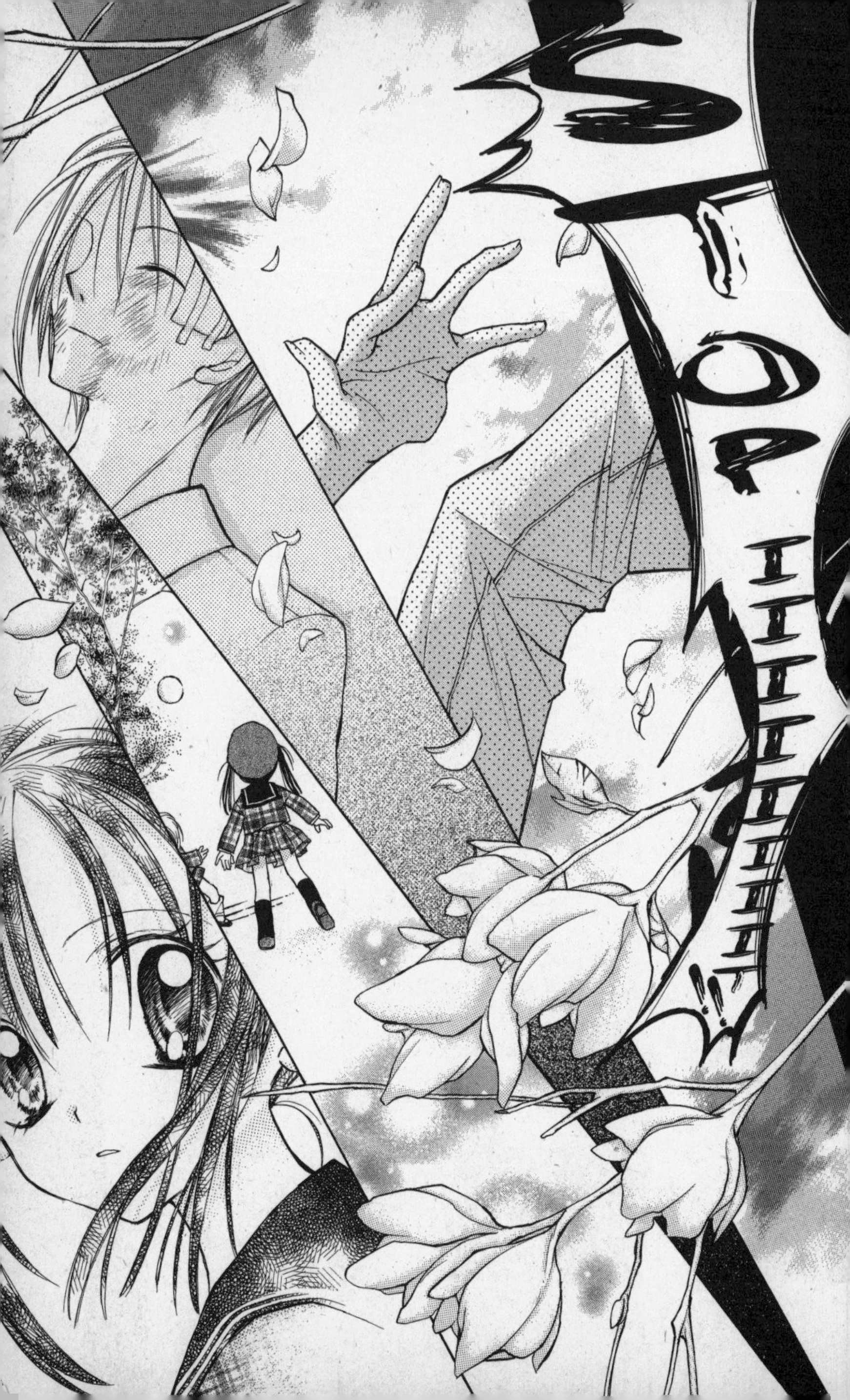
STOP IIIIIIIIT!!

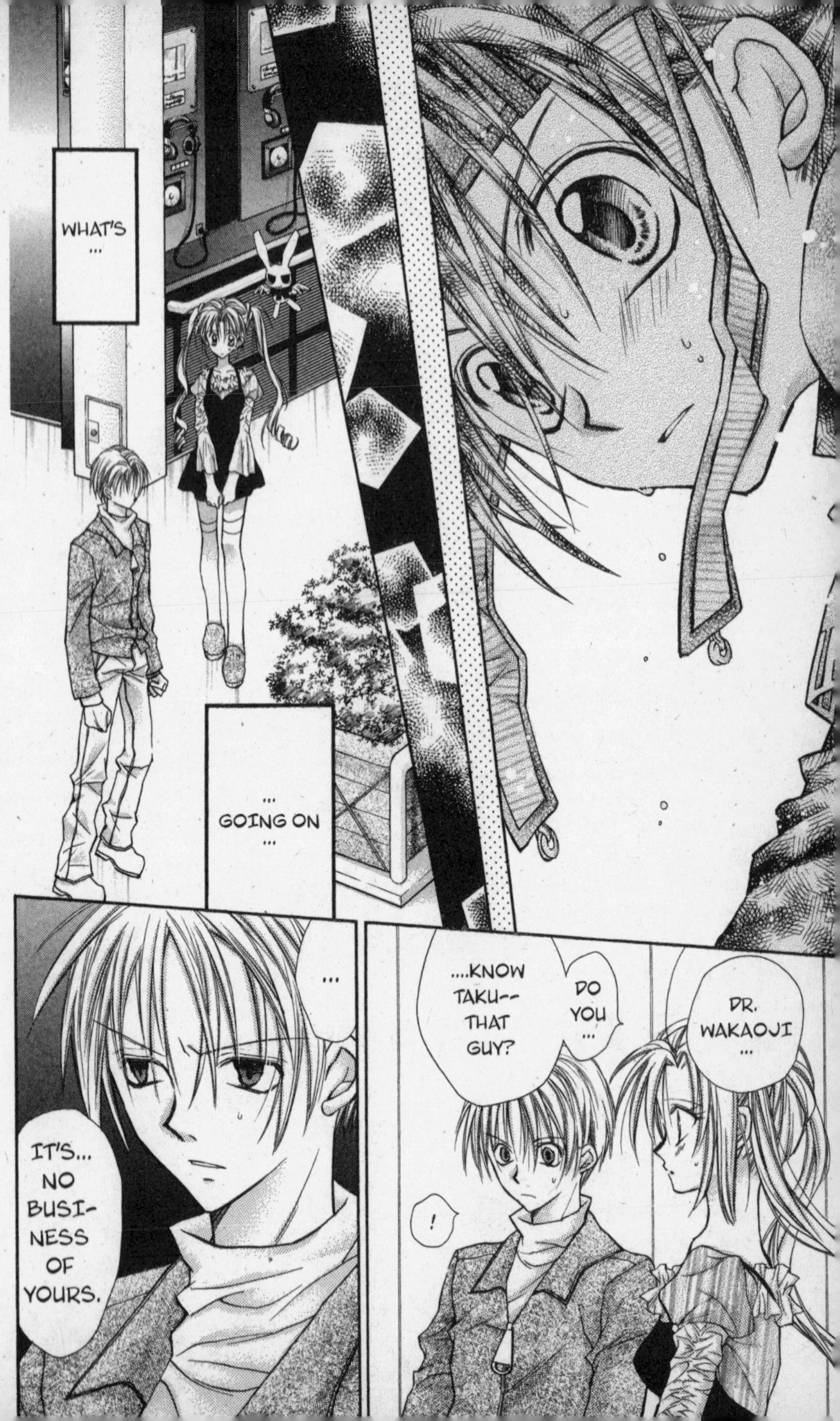
WHAT'S ...
... GOING ON ...
DR. WAKAOJI ...
DO YOU ...
....KNOW TAKU--THAT GUY?
!
...
IT'S... NO BUSI-NESS OF YOURS.

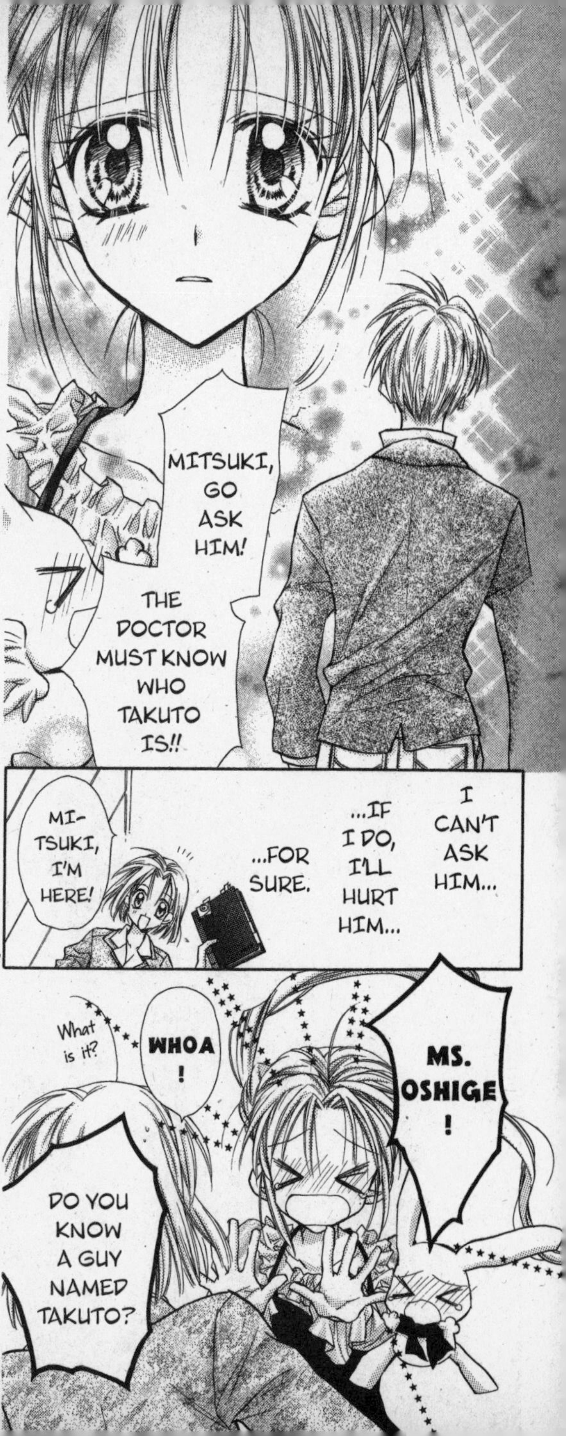
MITSUKI, GO ASK HIM!
THE DOCTOR MUST KNOW WHO TAKUTO IS!!
I CAN'T ASK HIM...
...IF I DO, I'LL HURT HIM...
...FOR SURE.
MI-TSUKI, I'M HERE!
MS. OSHIGE!
WHOA!
What is it?
DO YOU KNOW A GUY NAMED TAKUTO?

King Squid

Now I think I'll talk about the King Squid (suddenly).

I just love love love love love love love creatures of the sea. And crabs and squids, which are really hard, or really soft, or ones that look like "why did you turn out that way?!" are simply great!!

Like, horseshoe crabs are great!!

Among them all, the one I dearly love is, let's say it, King Squid! Sometimes you see "Huge Squid Washed Up on Shore" in the news, and that squid is my dear Mr. King Squid!

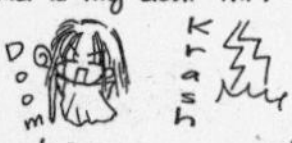
Doom
krash

According to divers, some squid get to be 60 feet long, including tentacles, but they live deep in the sea, so they haven't been seen much.

In a museum in Washington in the U.S., there is supposedly a 10-foot stuffed specimen, but since I'm busy, there's no way I can travel overseas...

But I want to see it~!!!

To explain how much I love Mr. King Squid, if I could see a 60-foot Mr. King Squid live, I wouldn't mind being killed by that Mr. Squid. (I don't want to be killed, but if I can see it, I wouldn't mind giving my life up!!) But it has to be a 60-footer.

Oooh...I love you...

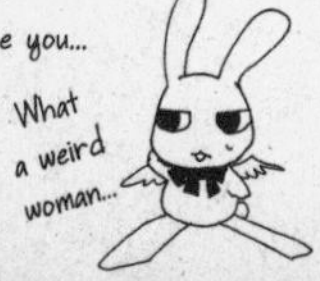
What a weird woman...

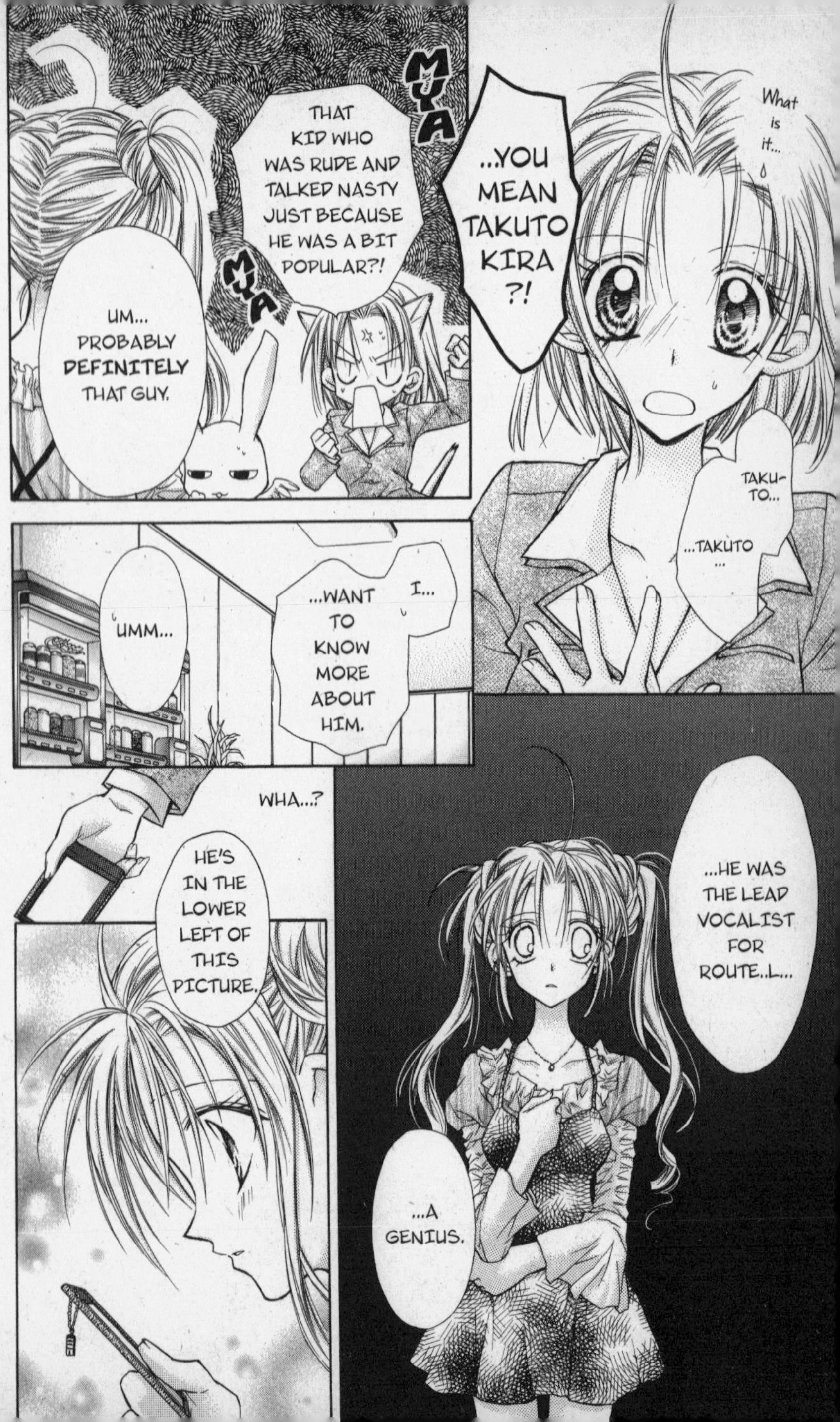
What is it...
...YOU MEAN TAKUTO KIRA ?!
TAKU-TO...
...TAKUTO ...
MYA
MYA
THAT KID WHO WAS RUDE AND TALKED NASTY JUST BECAUSE HE WAS A BIT POPULAR?!
UM... PROBABLY DEFINITELY THAT GUY.
I...
...WANT TO KNOW MORE ABOUT HIM.
UMM...
...HE WAS THE LEAD VOCALIST FOR ROUTE..L...
...A GENIUS.
WHA...?
HE'S IN THE LOWER LEFT OF THIS PICTURE.

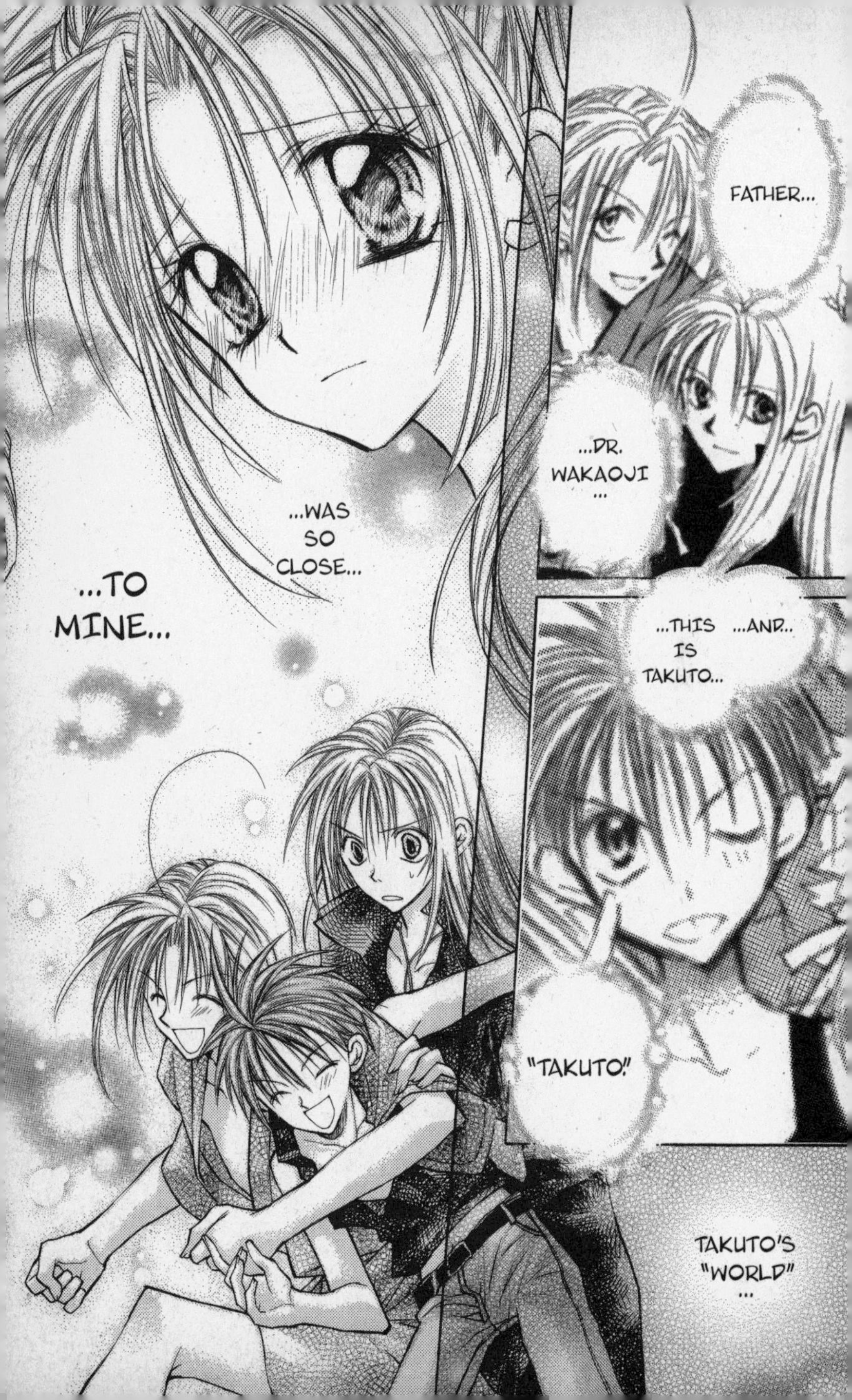
FATHER...
...DR. WAKAOJI...
...AND...
...THIS IS TAKUTO...
"TAKUTO!"
TAKUTO'S "WORLD"...
...WAS SO CLOSE...
...TO MINE...

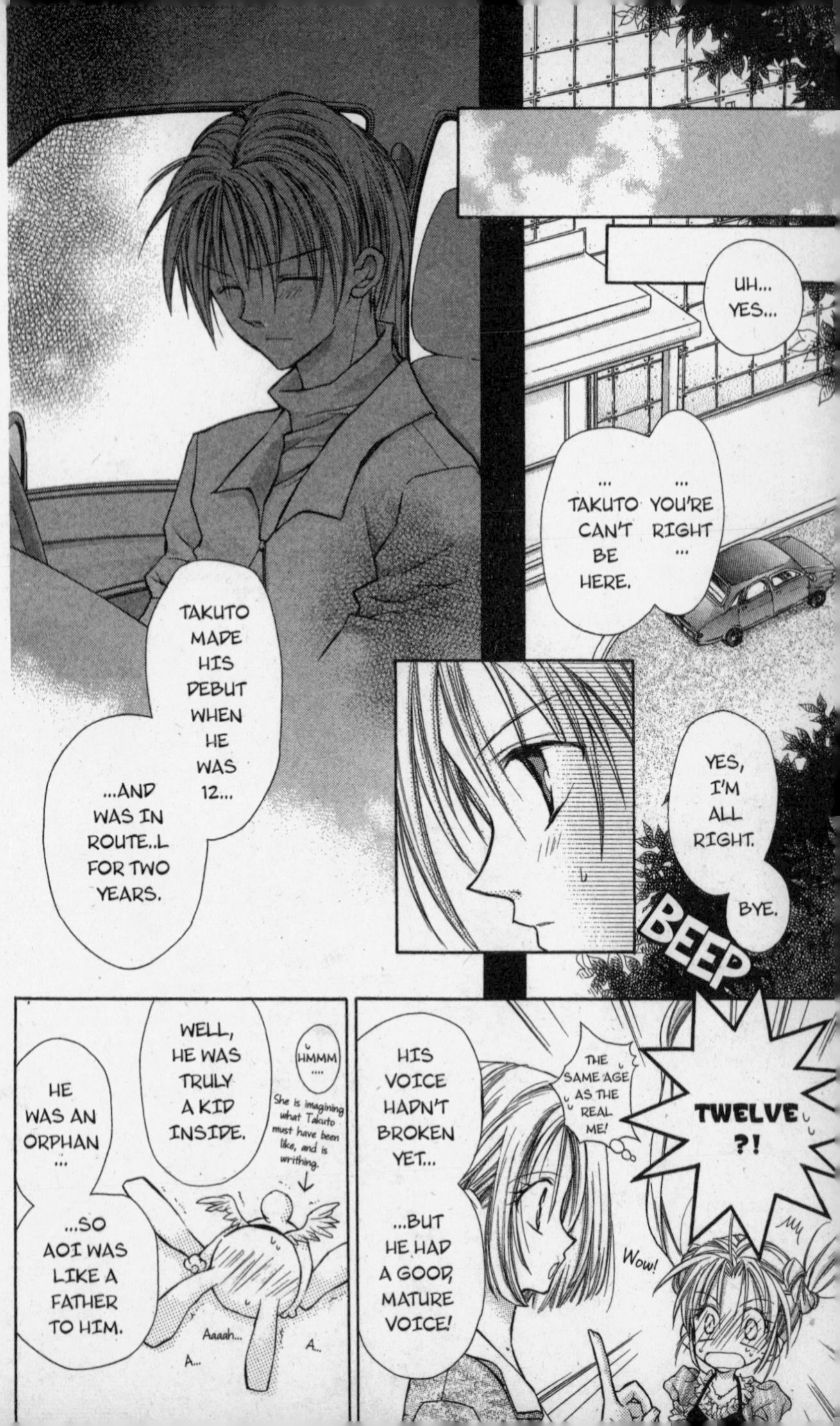
UH... YES...
... YOU'RE RIGHT ...
... TAKUTO CAN'T BE HERE.
YES, I'M ALL RIGHT.
BYE.
BEEP
TAKUTO MADE HIS DEBUT WHEN HE WAS 12...
...AND WAS IN ROUTE..L FOR TWO YEARS.
TWELVE ?!
THE SAME AGE AS THE REAL ME!
HIS VOICE HADN'T BROKEN YET...
...BUT HE HAD A GOOD, MATURE VOICE!
Wow!
HMMM....
She is imagining what Takuto must have been like, and is writhing.
WELL, HE WAS TRULY A KID INSIDE.
HE WAS AN ORPHAN ...
...SO AOI WAS LIKE A FATHER TO HIM.
Aaaah...
A...
A...

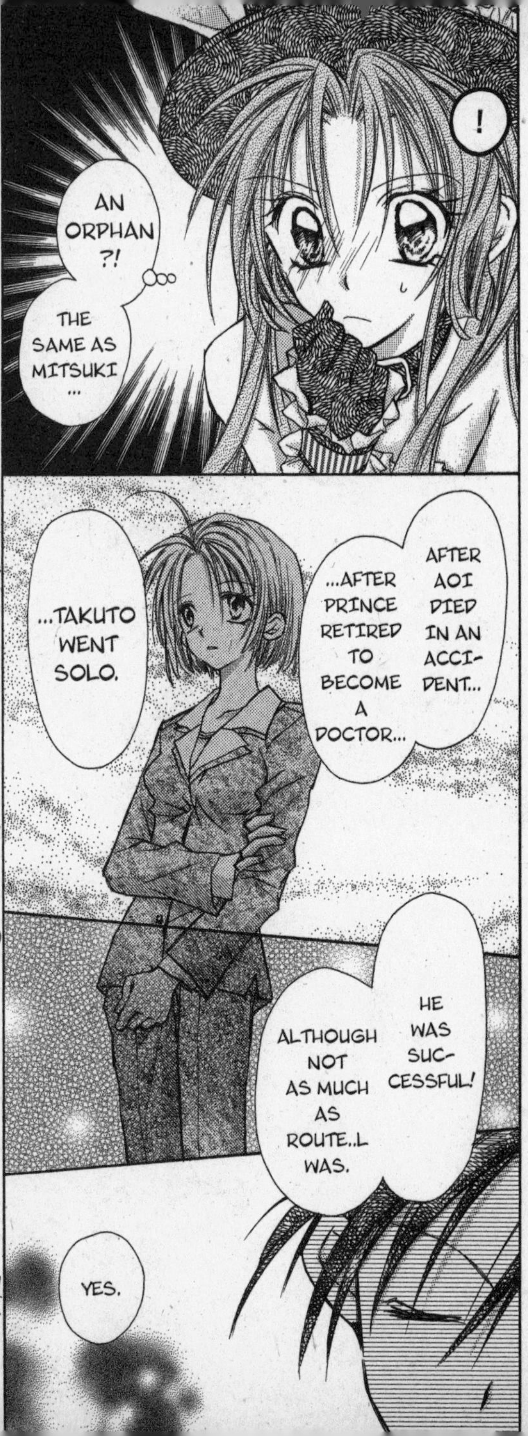
!
AN ORPHAN ?!
THE SAME AS MITSUKI ...
AFTER AOI DIED IN AN ACCI-DENT...
...AFTER PRINCE RETIRED TO BECOME A DOCTOR...
...TAKUTO WENT SOLO.
HE WAS SUC-CESSFUL!
ALTHOUGH NOT AS MUCH AS ROUTE..L WAS.
YES.

Penchi de Shakin ☆ Special version

The Gingi is Getting Cold!!

The "shuraba" (pandemonium) that a mangaka often experiences. Let's look at Arinaccho Tanemura's workplace to see what it's like.

Sorry...the room is cold and my fingers are frozen. My writing is messy but please forgive me.

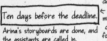

Ten days before the deadline. ← It varies depending on the month. (It could be four days before)

Arina's storyboards are done, and the assistants are called in.

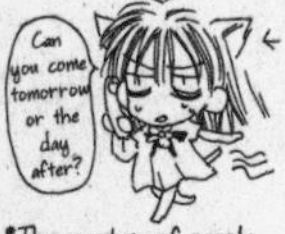
Can you come tomorrow or the day after?

← At this point, I'm pretty tired. The background team — three people (or four) come first.

*The number of people is the ideal number. Sometimes people can't come.

Nine Days Before

Arina does the first half (16 pages) of the penciling at a fast pace. Depending on the month, due to the printing schedule, I have to do the first half fast, so it's difficult.

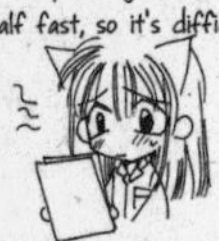

← In the beginning, the penciling takes time. I take about two hours (more?) per page.

The background assistant team does their penciling based on my rough sketch. Since I'm particular about details, it takes a lot of time.

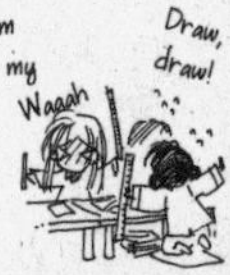
Draw, draw!
Waaah

This takes about two days. Everyone gets about six hours of sleep per night. (When there's time, seven or eight hours)

Assistants come to wake me up, but I take time waking up.

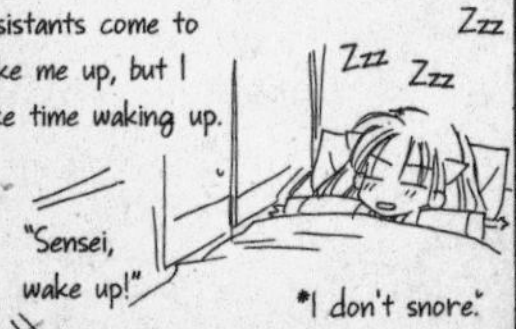
Zzz
Zzz Zzz
"Sensei, wake up!"
*I don't snore.

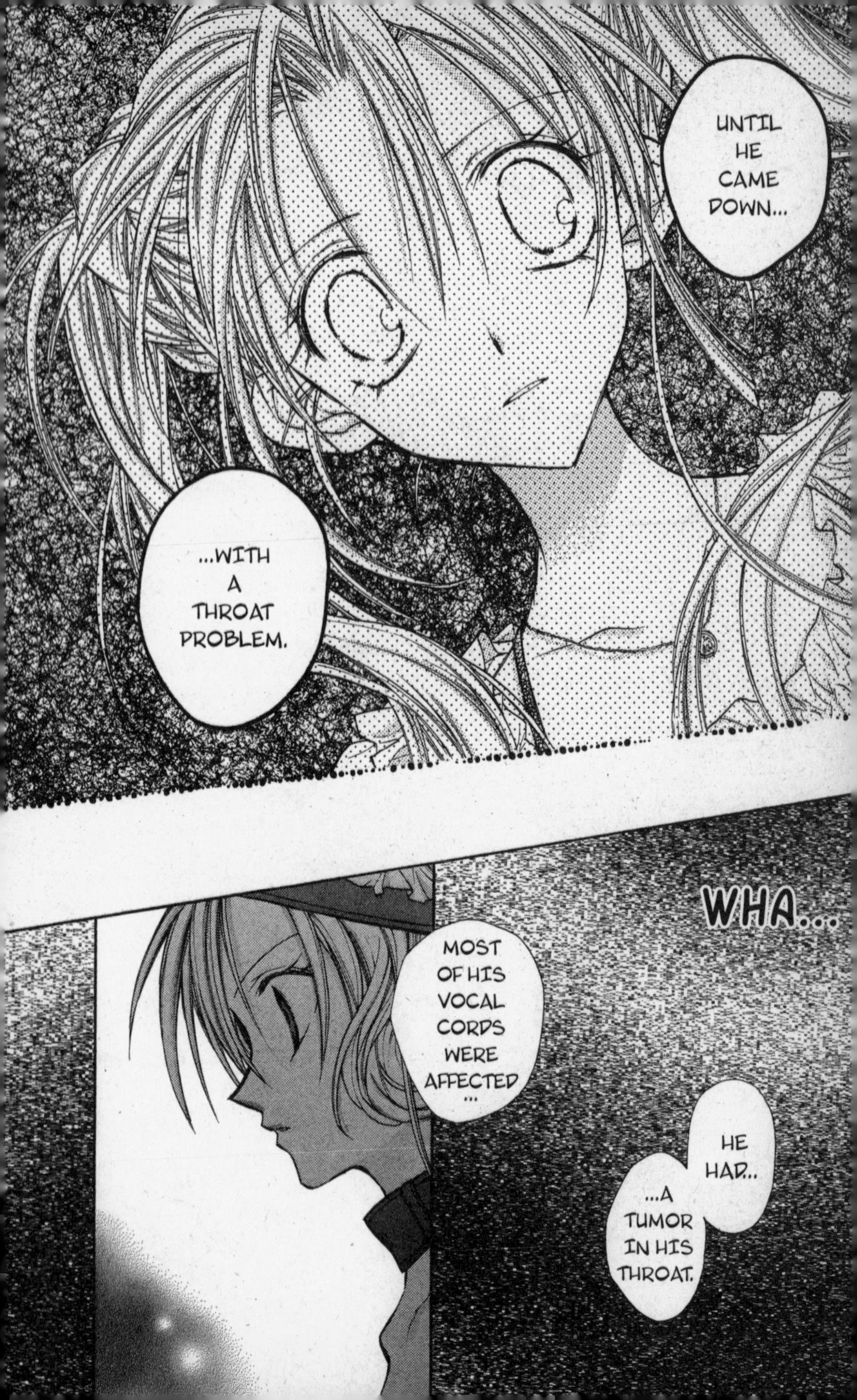
UNTIL HE CAME DOWN...
...WITH A THROAT PROBLEM.
WHA...
HE HAD..
...A TUMOR IN HIS THROAT.
MOST OF HIS VOCAL CORDS WERE AFFECTED...

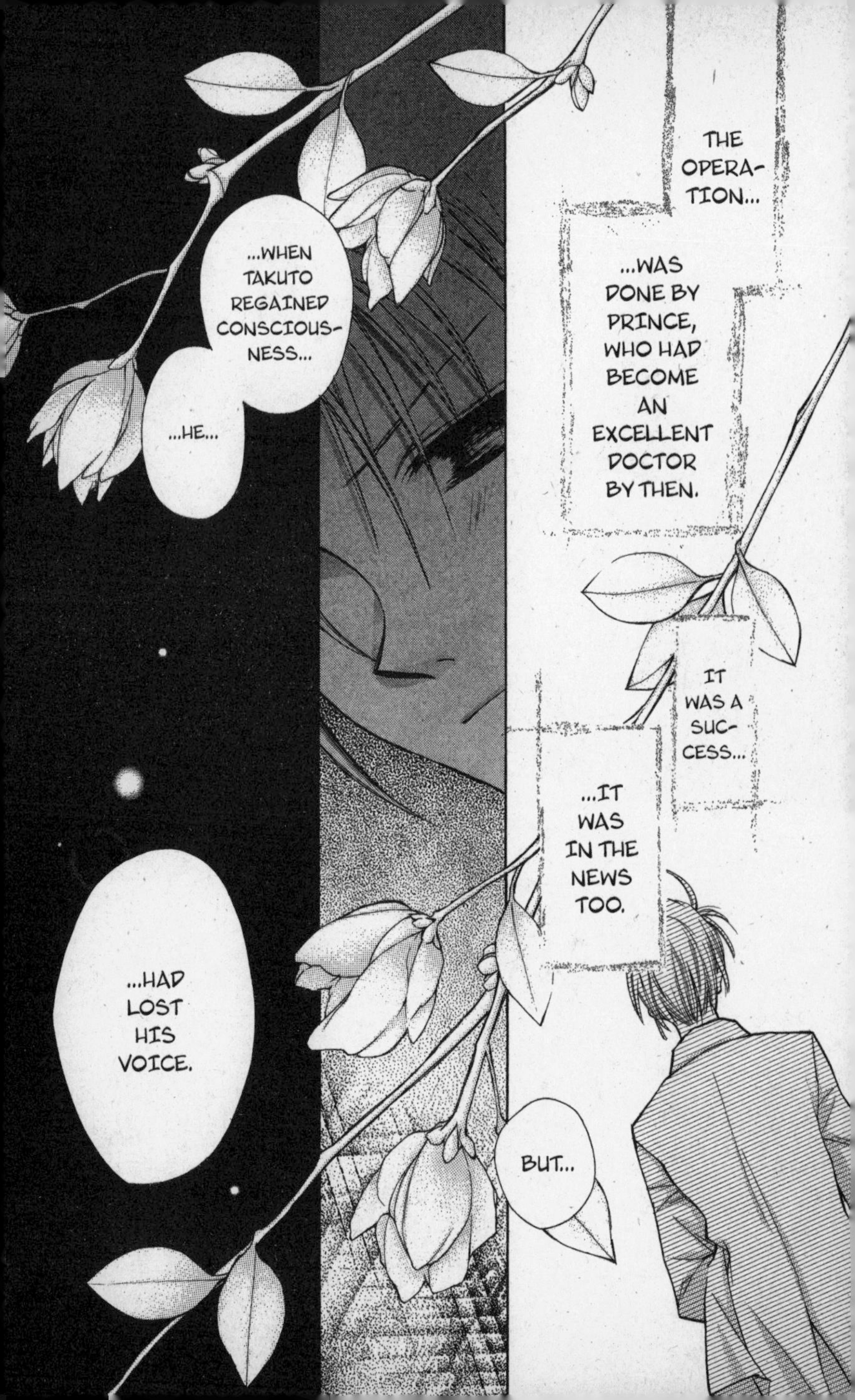
THE OPERATION...
...WAS DONE BY PRINCE, WHO HAD BECOME AN EXCELLENT DOCTOR BY THEN.
IT WAS A SUCCESS...
...IT WAS IN THE NEWS TOO.
BUT...
...WHEN TAKUTO REGAINED CONSCIOUSNESS...
...HE...
...HAD LOST HIS VOICE.

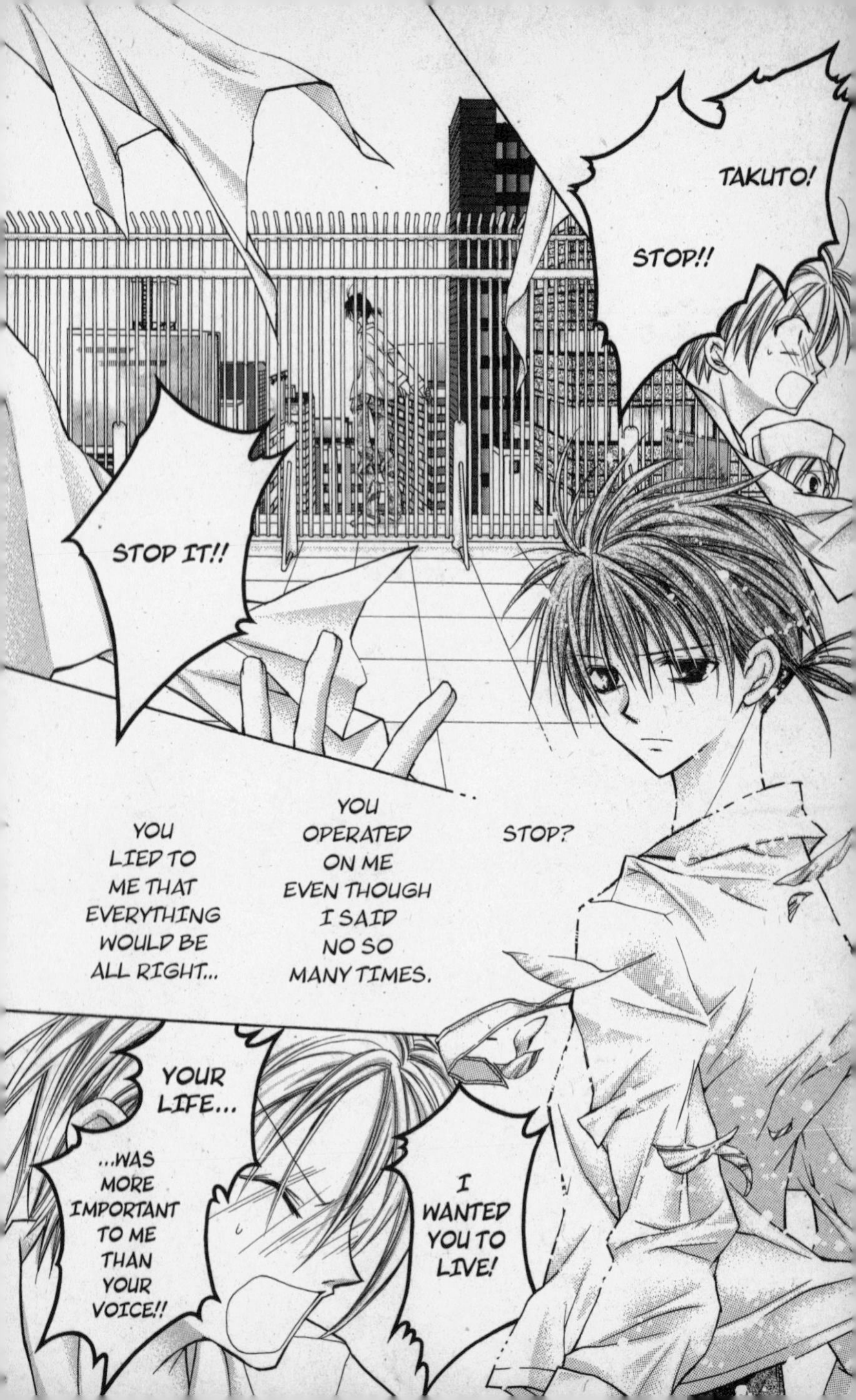
TAKUTO!
STOP!!
STOP IT!!
STOP?
YOU OPERATED ON ME EVEN THOUGH I SAID NO SO MANY TIMES.
YOU LIED TO ME THAT EVERYTHING WOULD BE ALL RIGHT...
I WANTED YOU TO LIVE!
YOUR LIFE...
...WAS MORE IMPORTANT TO ME THAN YOUR VOICE!!

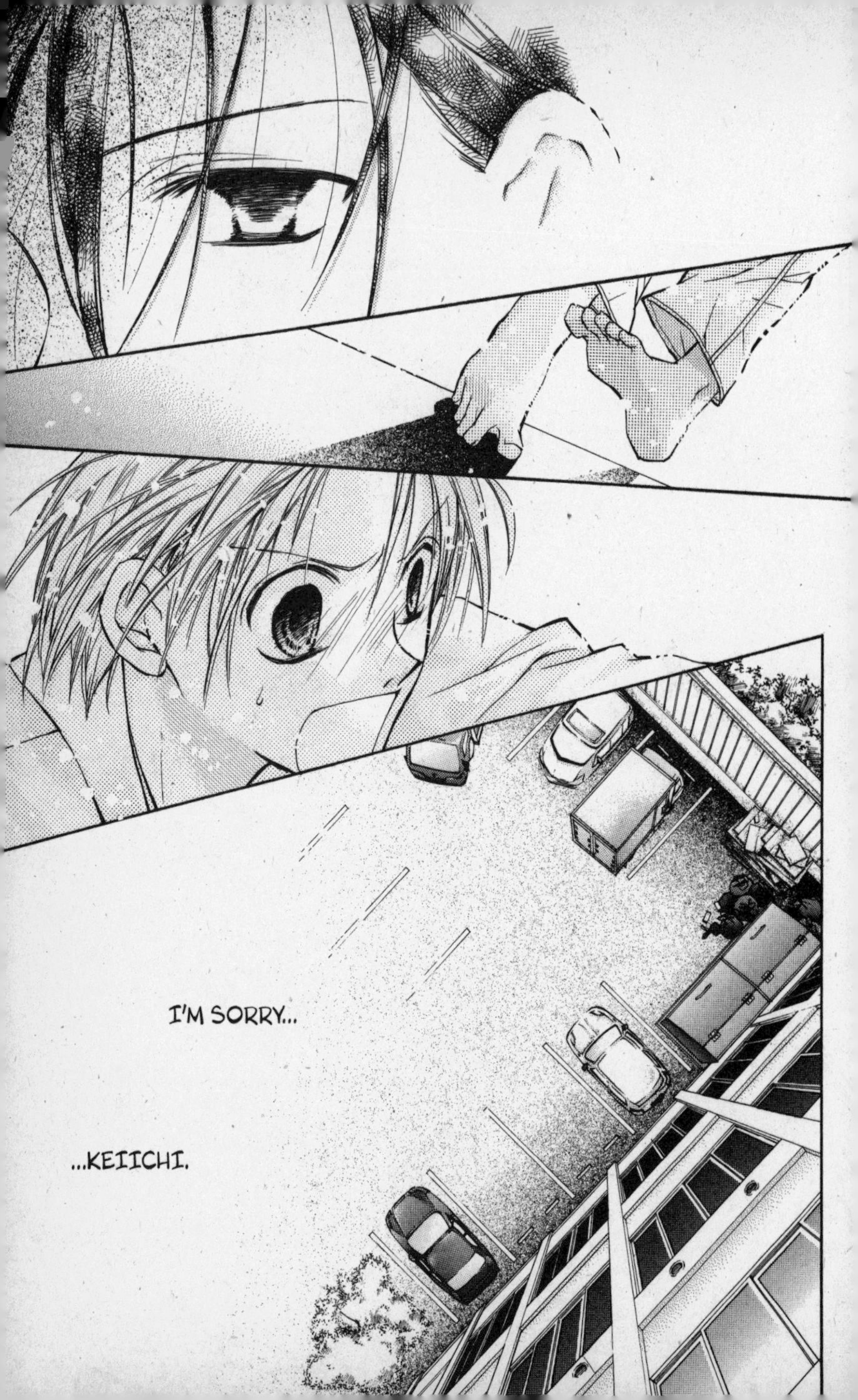
I'M SORRY...
...KEIICHI.

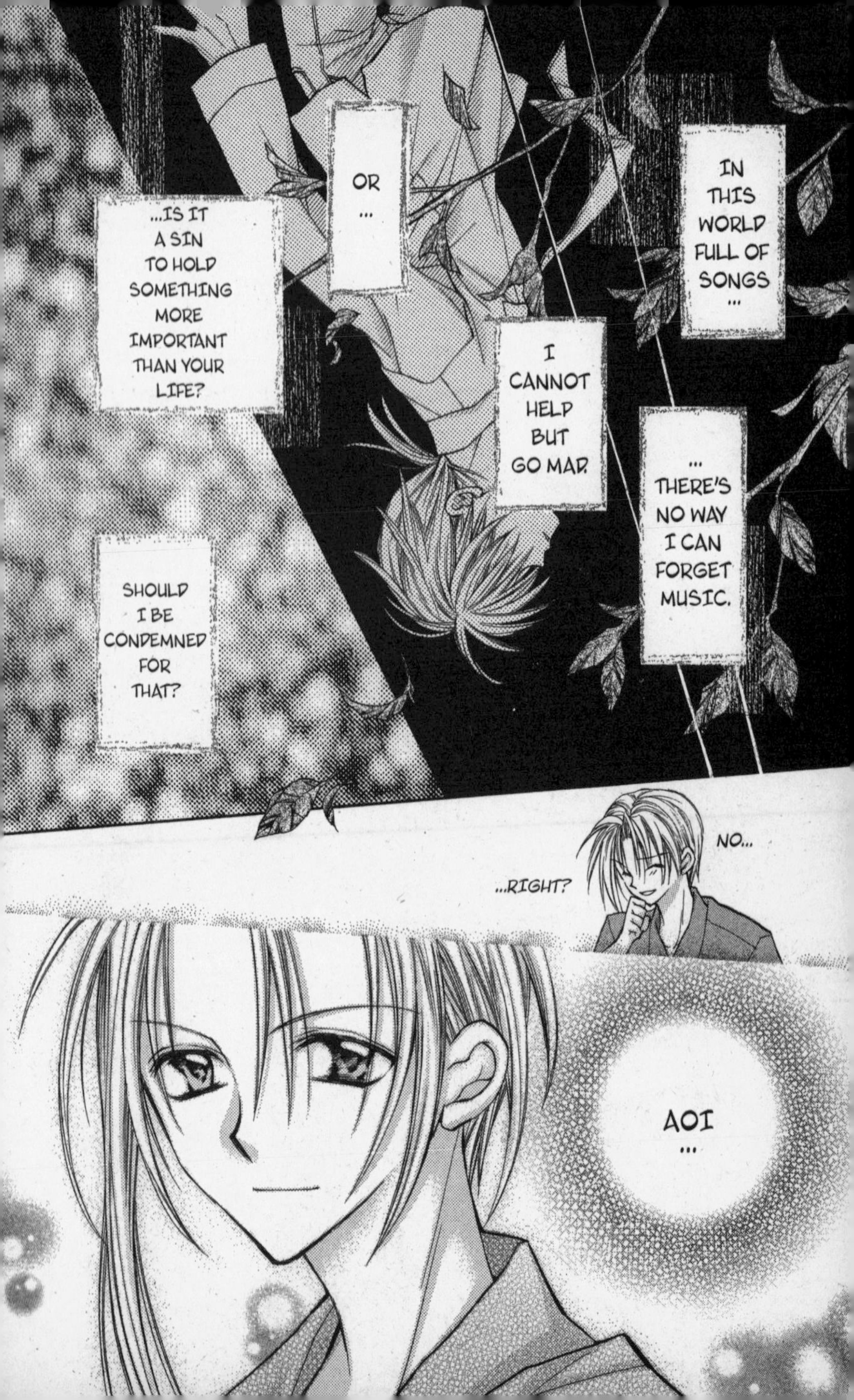
IN THIS WORLD FULL OF SONGS...
...THERE'S NO WAY I CAN FORGET MUSIC.
I CANNOT HELP BUT GO MAD.
OR...
...IS IT A SIN TO HOLD SOMETHING MORE IMPORTANT THAN YOUR LIFE?
SHOULD I BE CONDEMNED FOR THAT?
NO...
...RIGHT?
AOI...

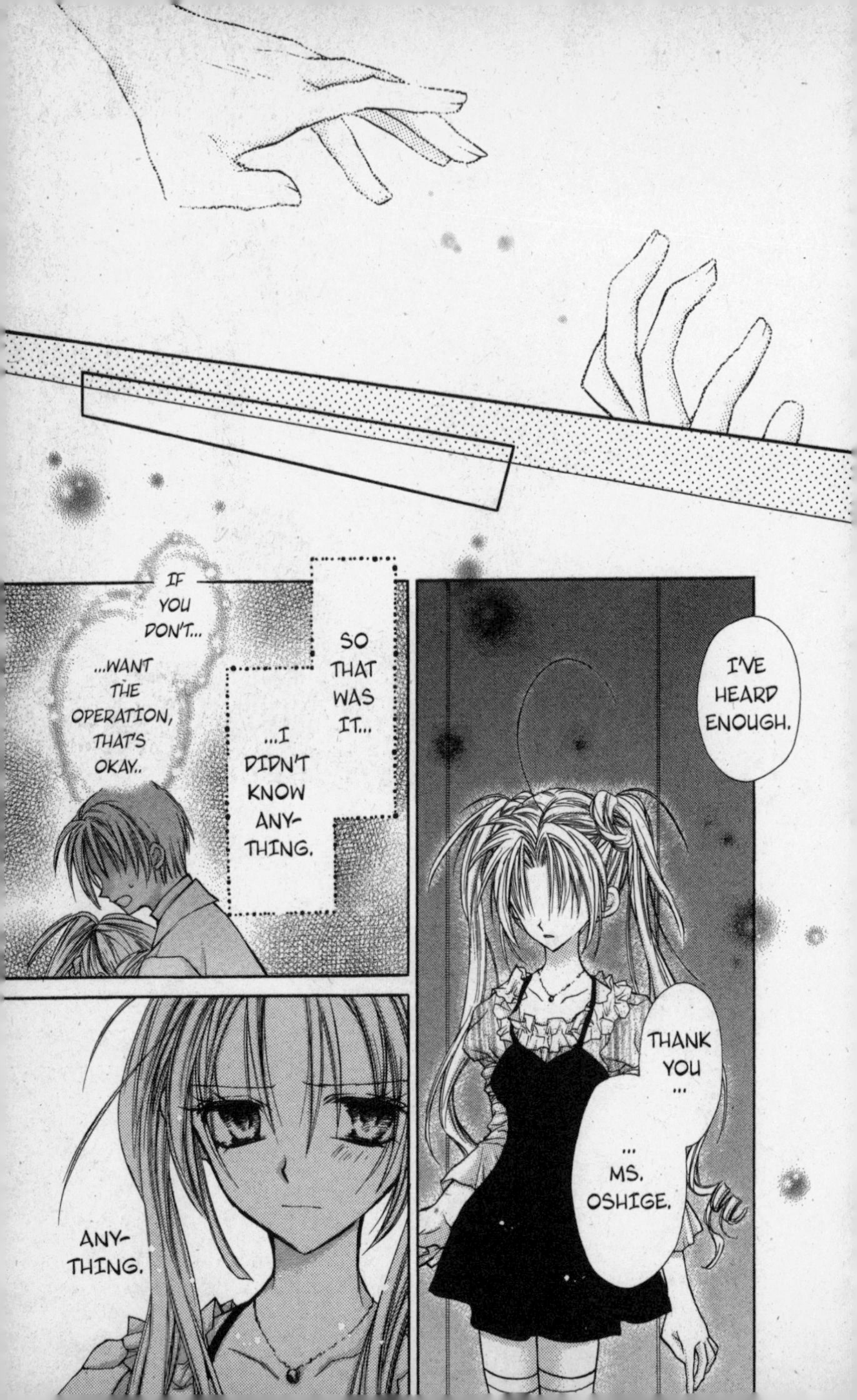
I'VE HEARD ENOUGH.
THANK YOU ...
... MS. OSHIGE.
SO THAT WAS IT...
...I DIDN'T KNOW ANY-THING.
IF YOU DON'T...
...WANT THE OPERATION, THAT'S OKAY..
ANY-THING.

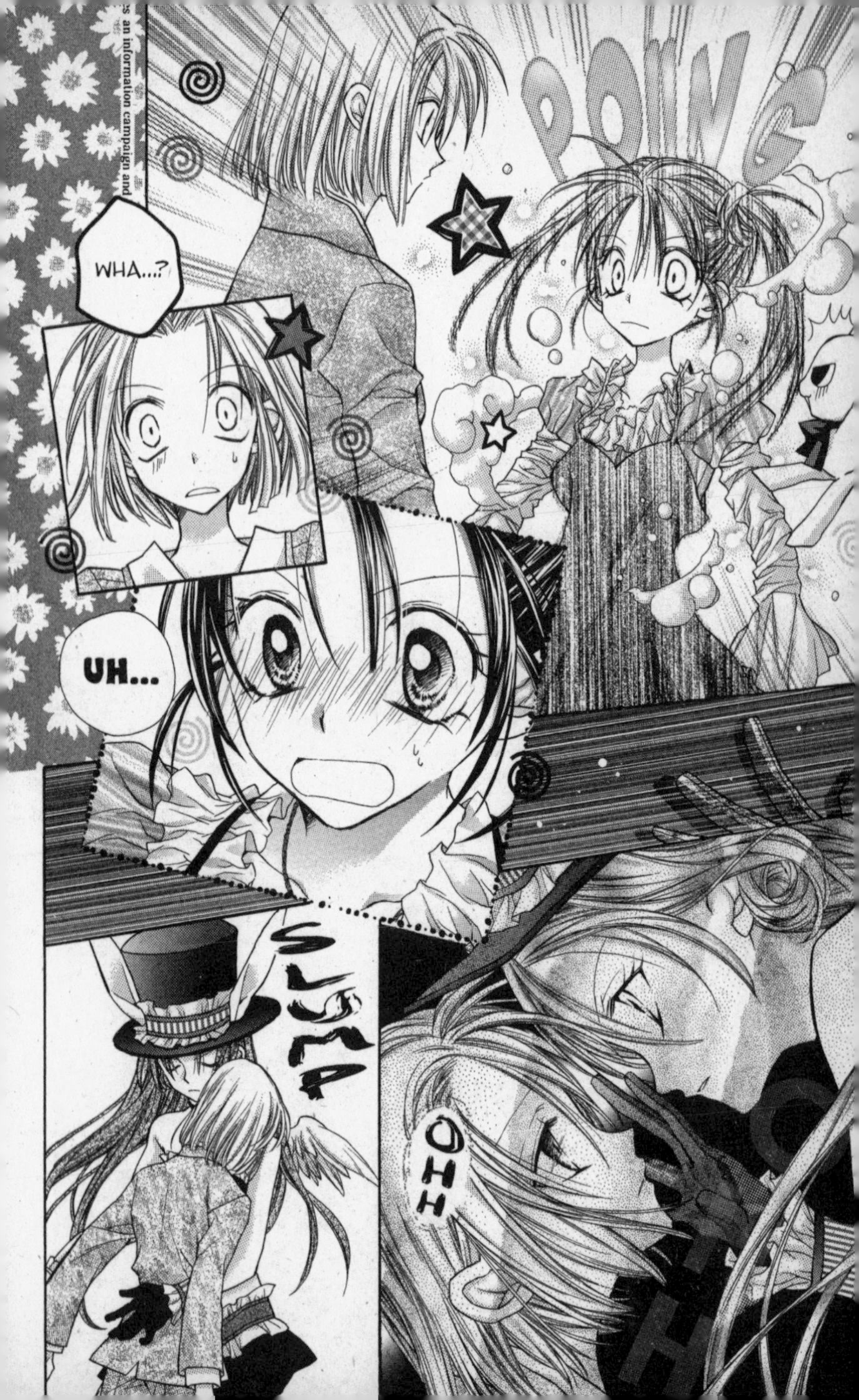
...s an information campaign and
POING
WHA...?
UH...
OHHH
SLUMP

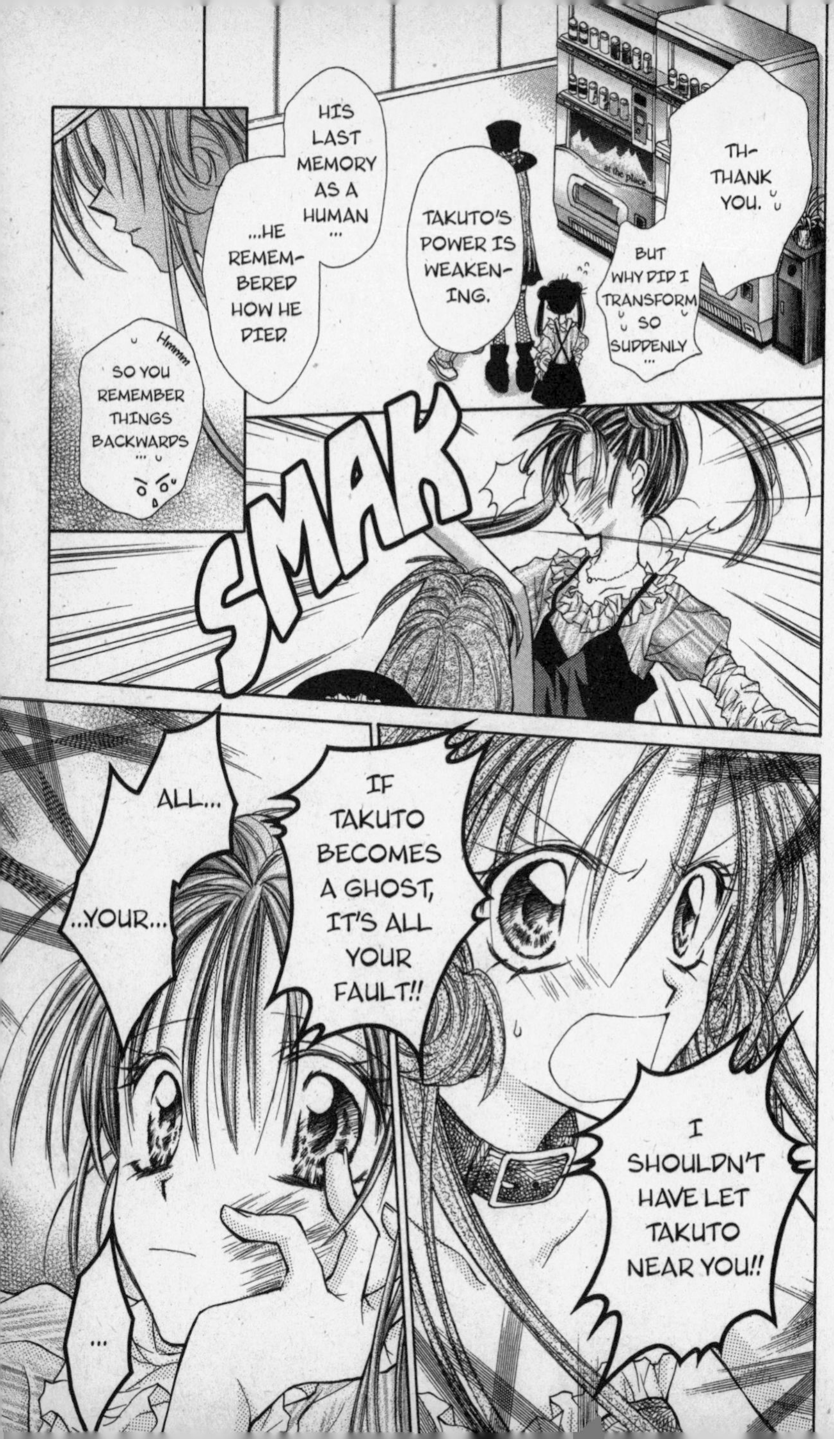
TH-THANK YOU.
BUT WHY DID I TRANSFORM SO SUDDENLY...
TAKUTO'S POWER IS WEAKENING.
HIS LAST MEMORY AS A HUMAN...
...HE REMEMBERED HOW HE DIED.
Hmmm
SO YOU REMEMBER THINGS BACKWARDS...
SMAK
IF TAKUTO BECOMES A GHOST, IT'S ALL YOUR FAULT!!
I SHOULDN'T HAVE LET TAKUTO NEAR YOU!!
ALL...
...YOUR...
...

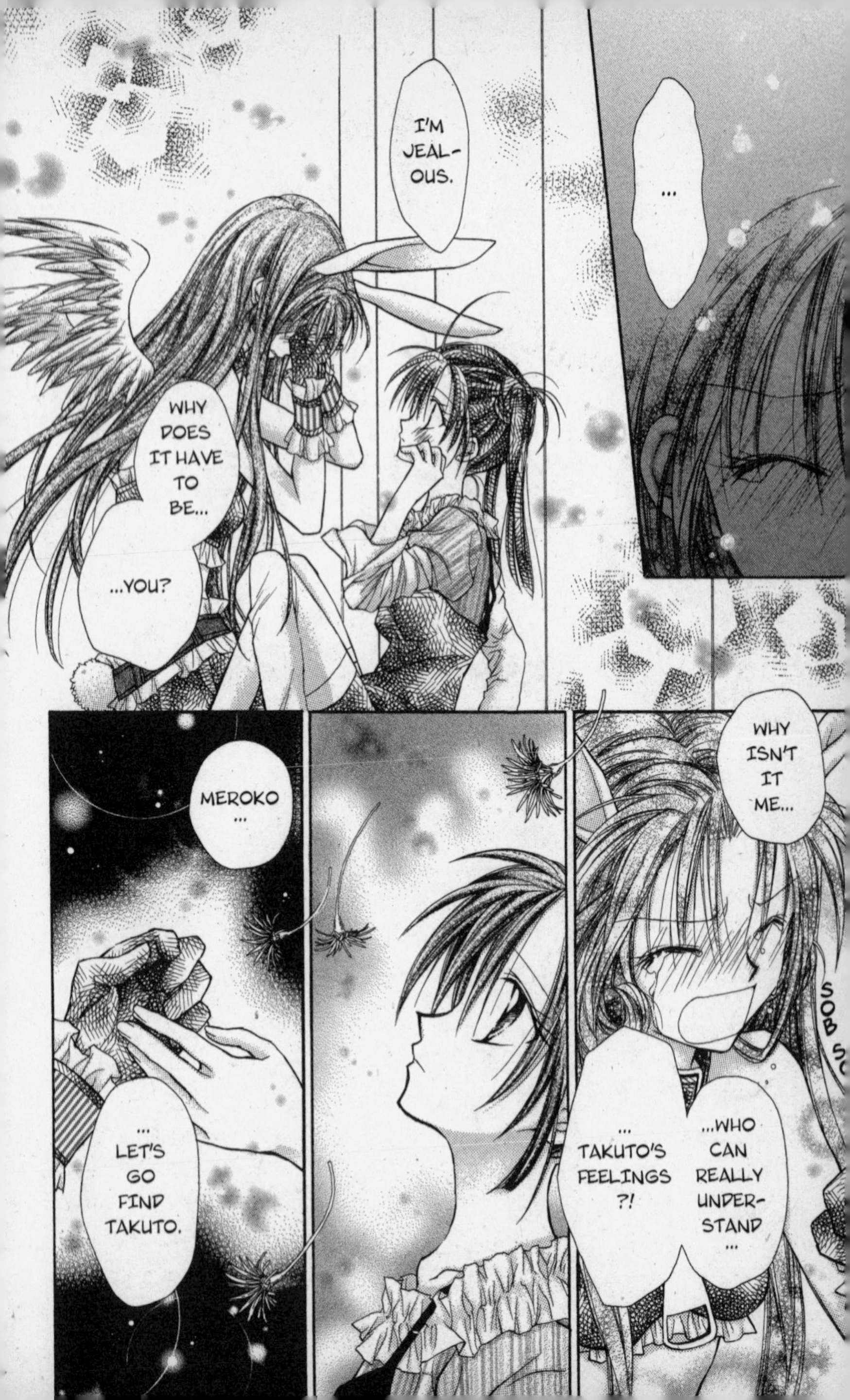
...
I'M JEAL-OUS.
WHY DOES IT HAVE TO BE...
...YOU?
WHY ISN'T IT ME...
...WHO CAN REALLY UNDER-STAND ...
... TAKUTO'S FEELINGS ?!
SOB
MEROKO ...
... LET'S GO FIND TAKUTO.

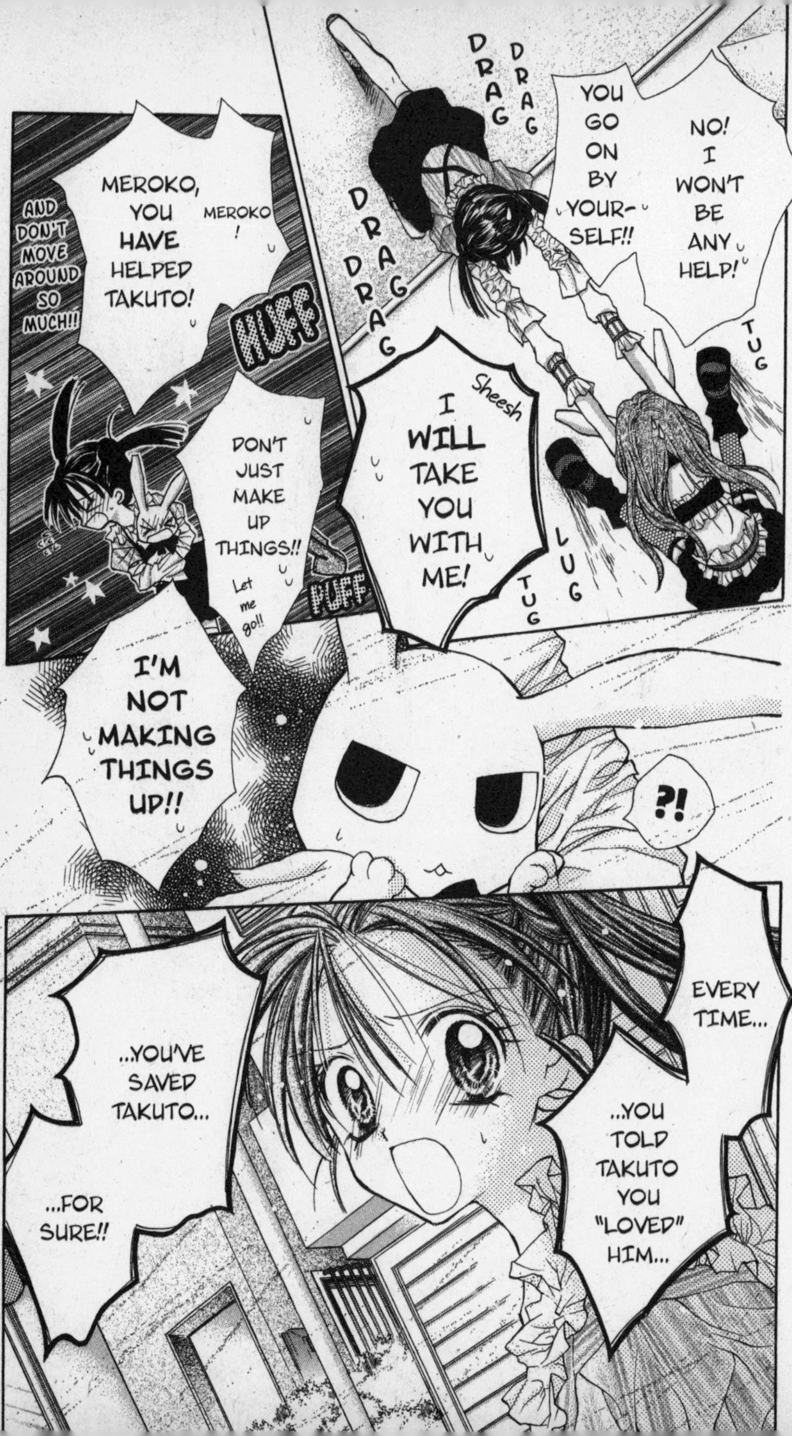
DRAG DRAG
NO! I WON'T BE ANY HELP!
YOU GO ON BY YOURSELF!!
DRAG DRAG
TUG
Sheesh
I WILL TAKE YOU WITH ME!
TUG LUG TUG
MEROKO!
MEROKO, YOU HAVE HELPED TAKUTO!
AND DON'T MOVE AROUND SO MUCH!!
HUFF
DON'T JUST MAKE UP THINGS!!
Let me go!!
PUFF
?!
I'M NOT MAKING THINGS UP!!
EVERY TIME...
...YOU TOLD TAKUTO YOU "LOVED" HIM...
...YOU'VE SAVED TAKUTO...
...FOR SURE!!

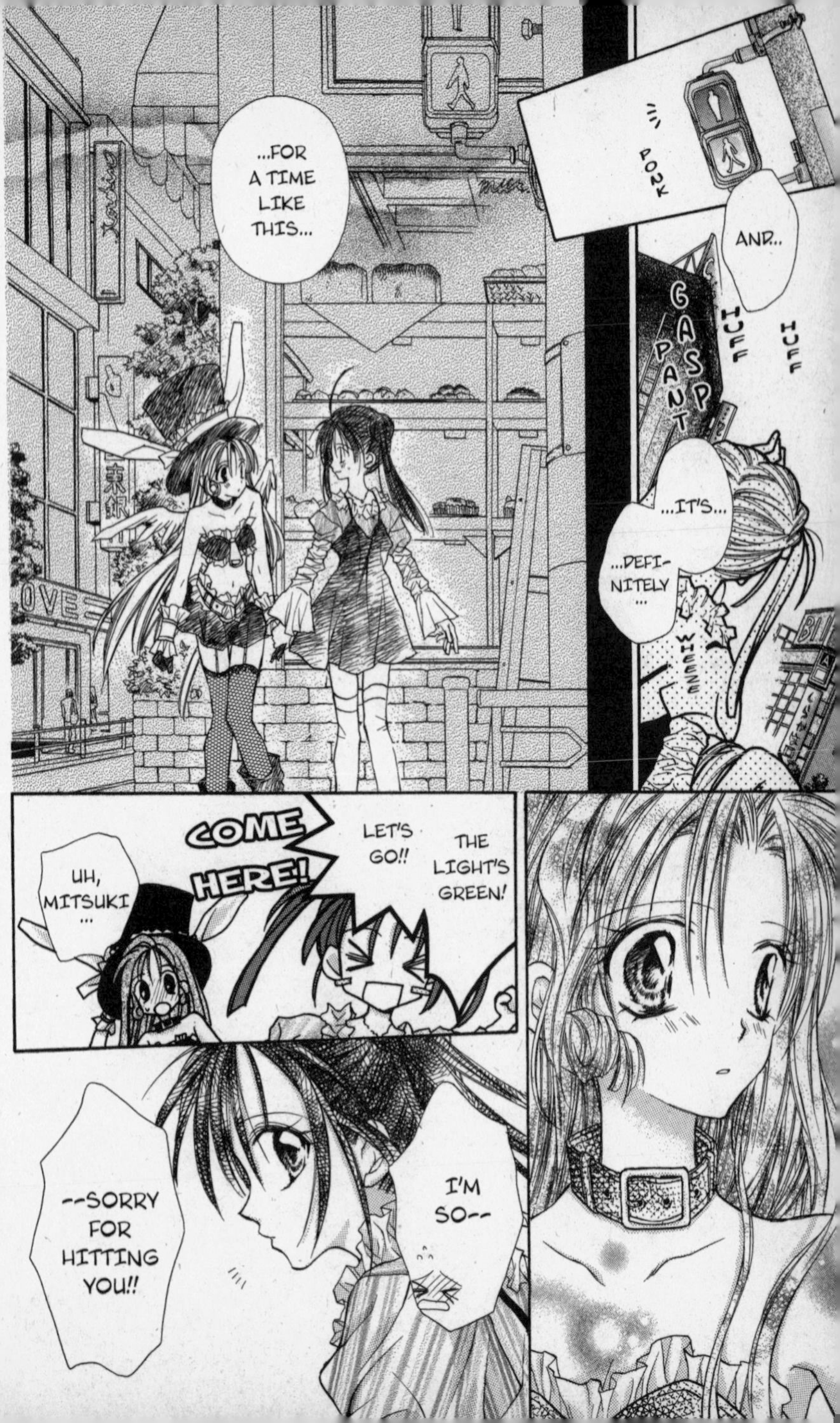
PONK
AND..
HUFF HUFF
GASP PANT
...IT'S...
...DEFI-NITELY...
WHEEZE
...FOR A TIME LIKE THIS...
THE LIGHT'S GREEN!
LET'S GO!!
COME HERE!
UH, MITSUKI...
I'M SO--
--SORRY FOR HITTING YOU!!

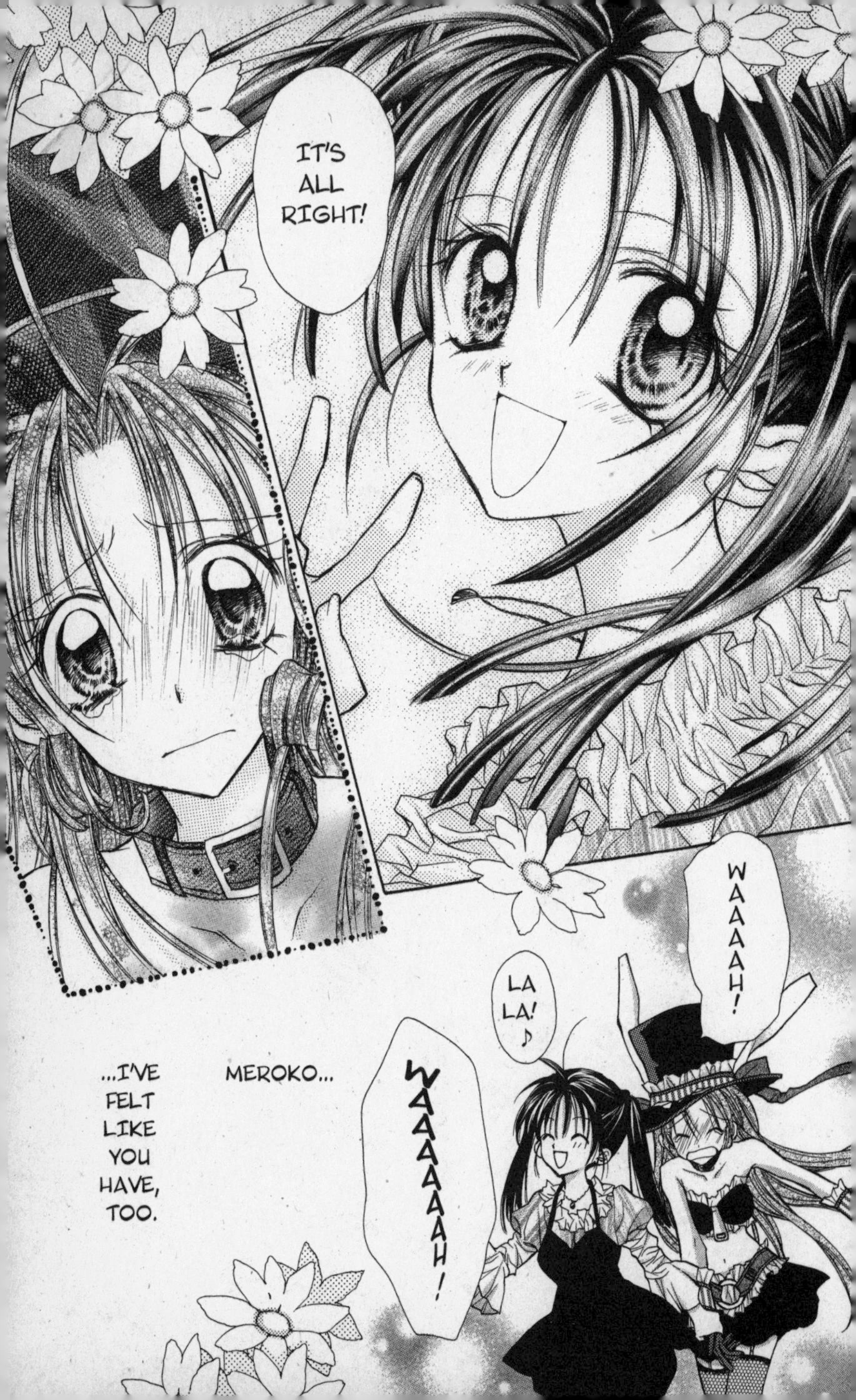
IT'S ALL RIGHT!
WAAAAAH!
LA LA! ♪
WAAAAAAAH!
MEROKO...
...I'VE FELT LIKE YOU HAVE, TOO.

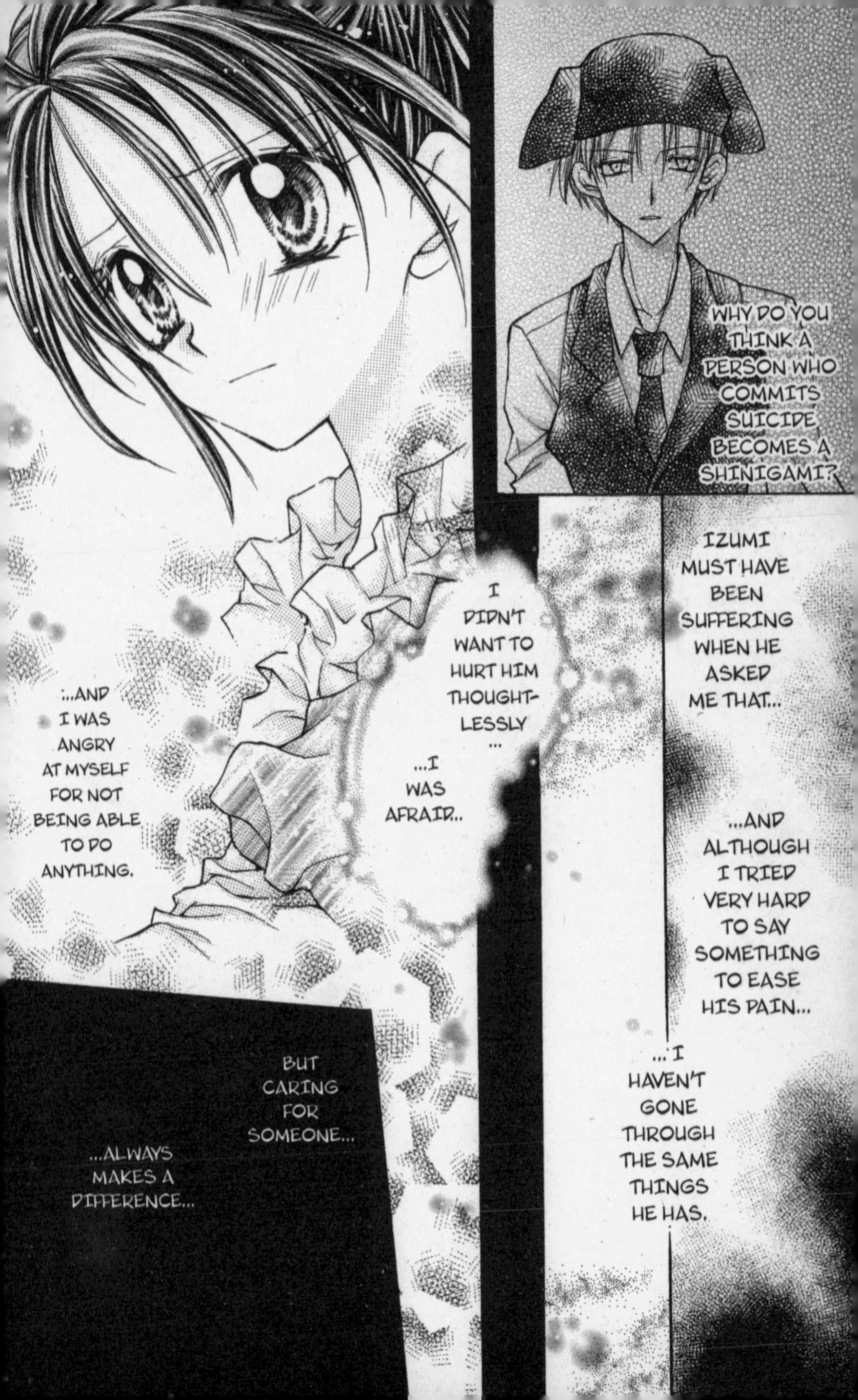
WHY DO YOU THINK A PERSON WHO COMMITS SUICIDE BECOMES A SHINIGAMI?
IZUMI MUST HAVE BEEN SUFFERING WHEN HE ASKED ME THAT...
...AND ALTHOUGH I TRIED VERY HARD TO SAY SOMETHING TO EASE HIS PAIN...
...I HAVEN'T GONE THROUGH THE SAME THINGS HE HAS.
I DIDN'T WANT TO HURT HIM THOUGHTLESSLY...
...I WAS AFRAID...
...AND I WAS ANGRY AT MYSELF FOR NOT BEING ABLE TO DO ANYTHING.
BUT CARING FOR SOMEONE...
...ALWAYS MAKES A DIFFERENCE...

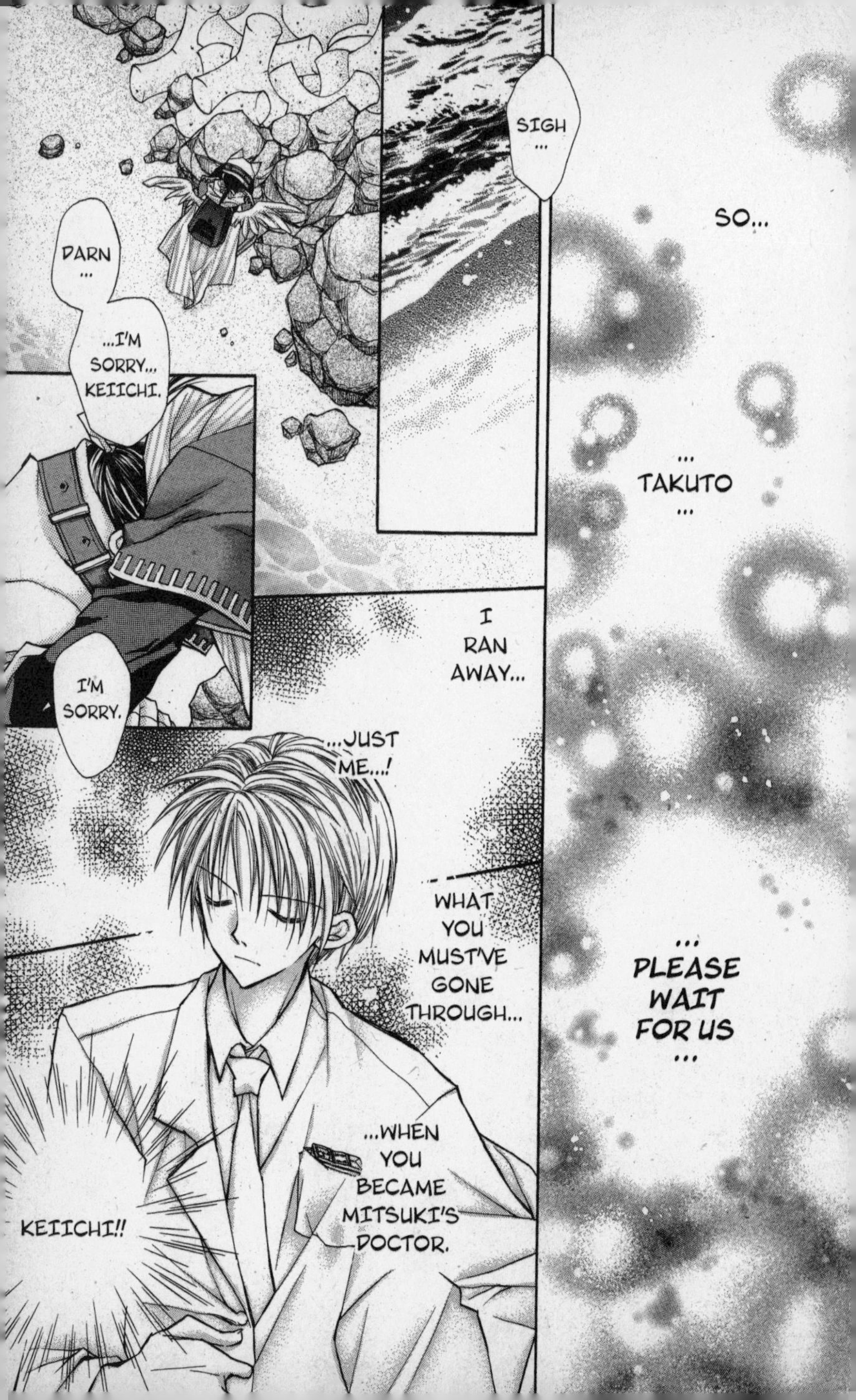
SO...
... TAKUTO ...
... PLEASE WAIT FOR US ...
SIGH ...
DARN ...
...I'M SORRY... KEIICHI.
I'M SORRY.
I RAN AWAY...
...JUST ME...!
WHAT YOU MUST'VE GONE THROUGH...
...WHEN YOU BECAME MITSUKI'S DOCTOR.
KEIICHI!!

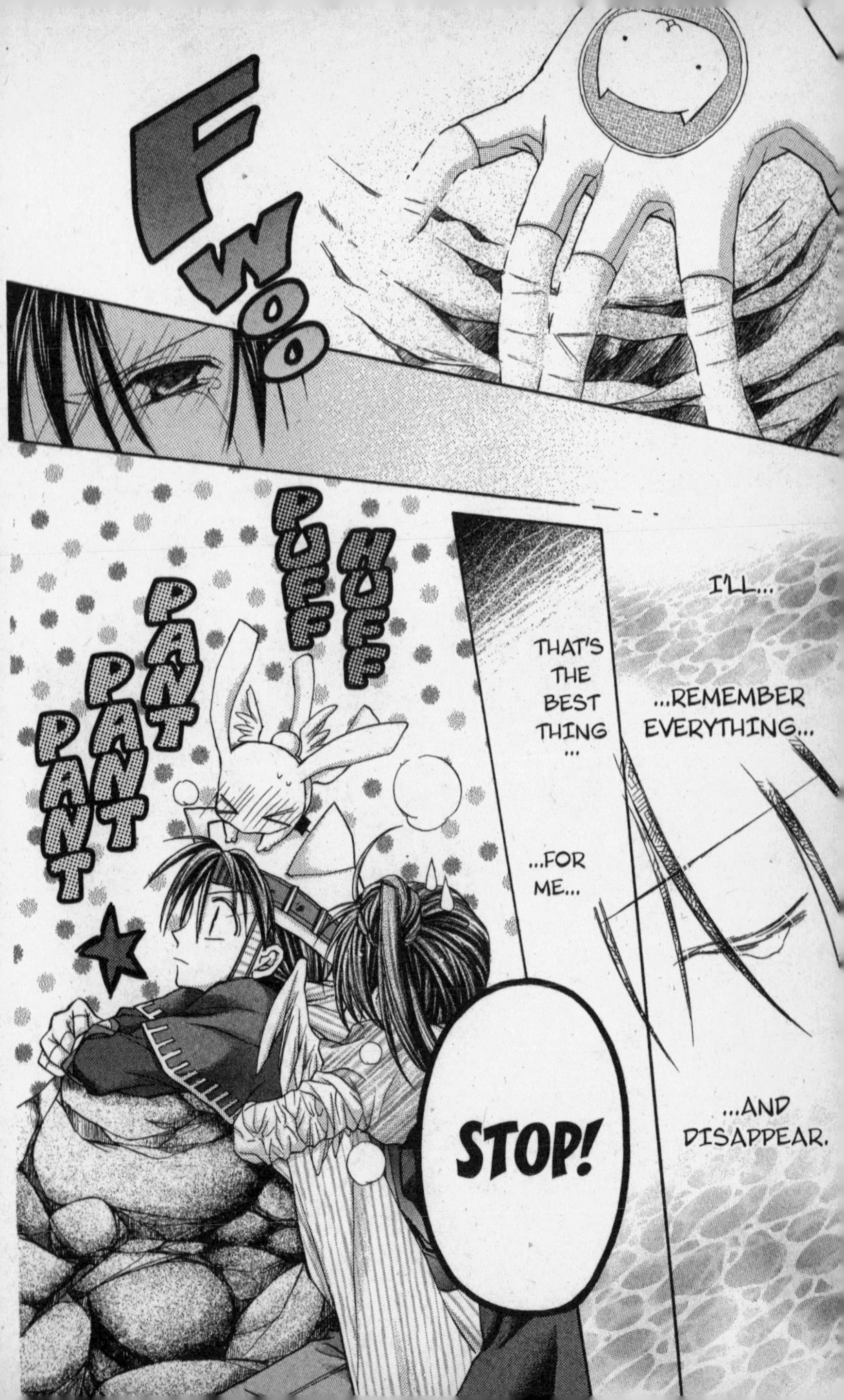
FWOO
I'LL...
...REMEMBER EVERYTHING...
...AND DISAPPEAR.
THAT'S THE BEST THING...
...FOR ME...
STOP!
HUFF
PUFF
PANT
PANT
PANT

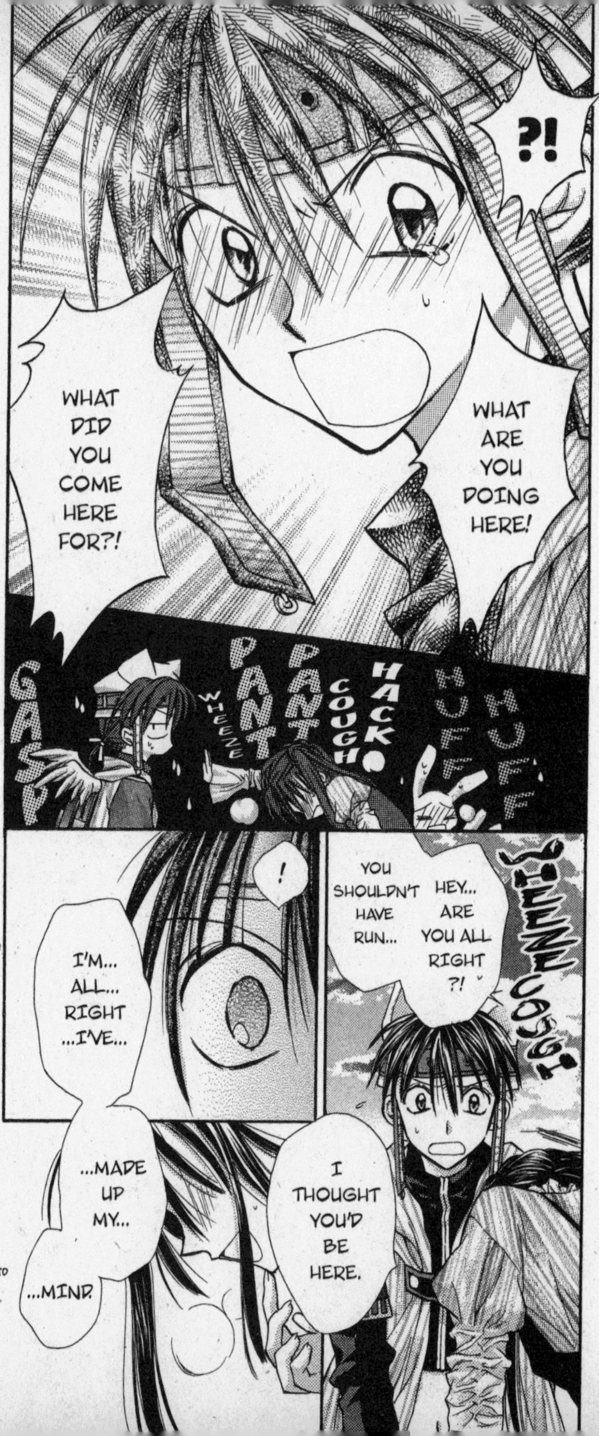
?!
WHAT ARE YOU DOING HERE!
WHAT DID YOU COME HERE FOR?!
HUFF
HUFF
HACK
COUGH
PANT
PANT
WHEEZE
GASP
WHEEZE COUGH!
HEY... ARE YOU ALL RIGHT?!
YOU SHOULDN'T HAVE RUN...
!
I'M... ALL... RIGHT ...I'VE...
...MADE UP MY...
...MIND.
I THOUGHT YOU'D BE HERE.

I've reached my limit.
I'm dead tired. I can't do any more sidebars.

Please forgive me with the friends of the forest.

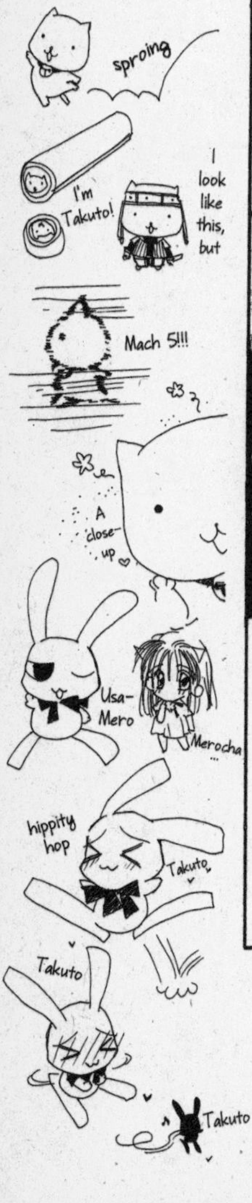
sproing
I'm Takuto!
I look like this, but
Mach 5!!!
A close-up
Usa-Mero
Merocha...
hippity hop
Takuto
Takuto
Takuto

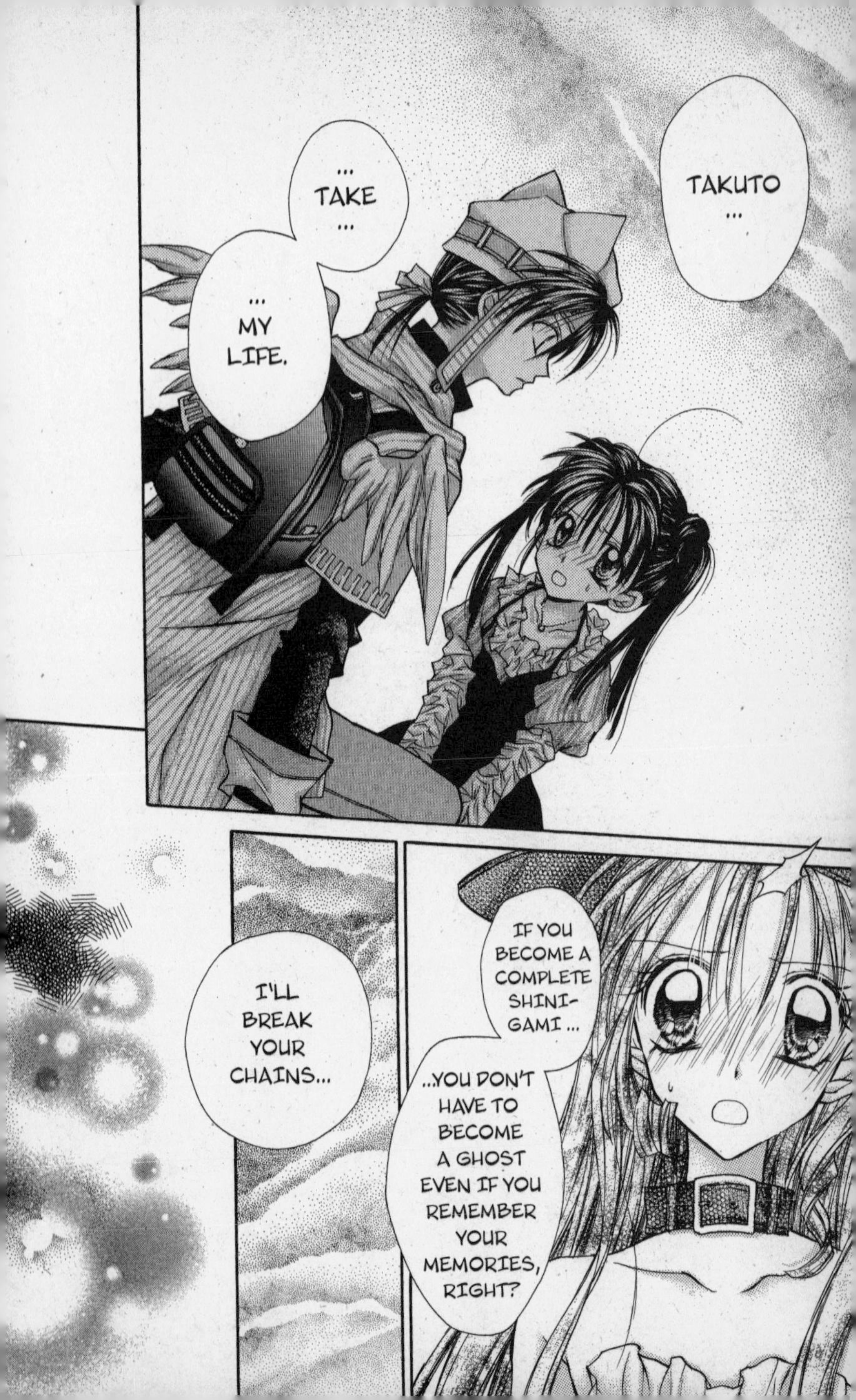
TAKUTO ...
... TAKE ...
... MY LIFE.
IF YOU BECOME A COMPLETE SHINI-GAMI ...
...YOU DON'T HAVE TO BECOME A GHOST EVEN IF YOU REMEMBER YOUR MEMORIES, RIGHT?
I'LL BREAK YOUR CHAINS...

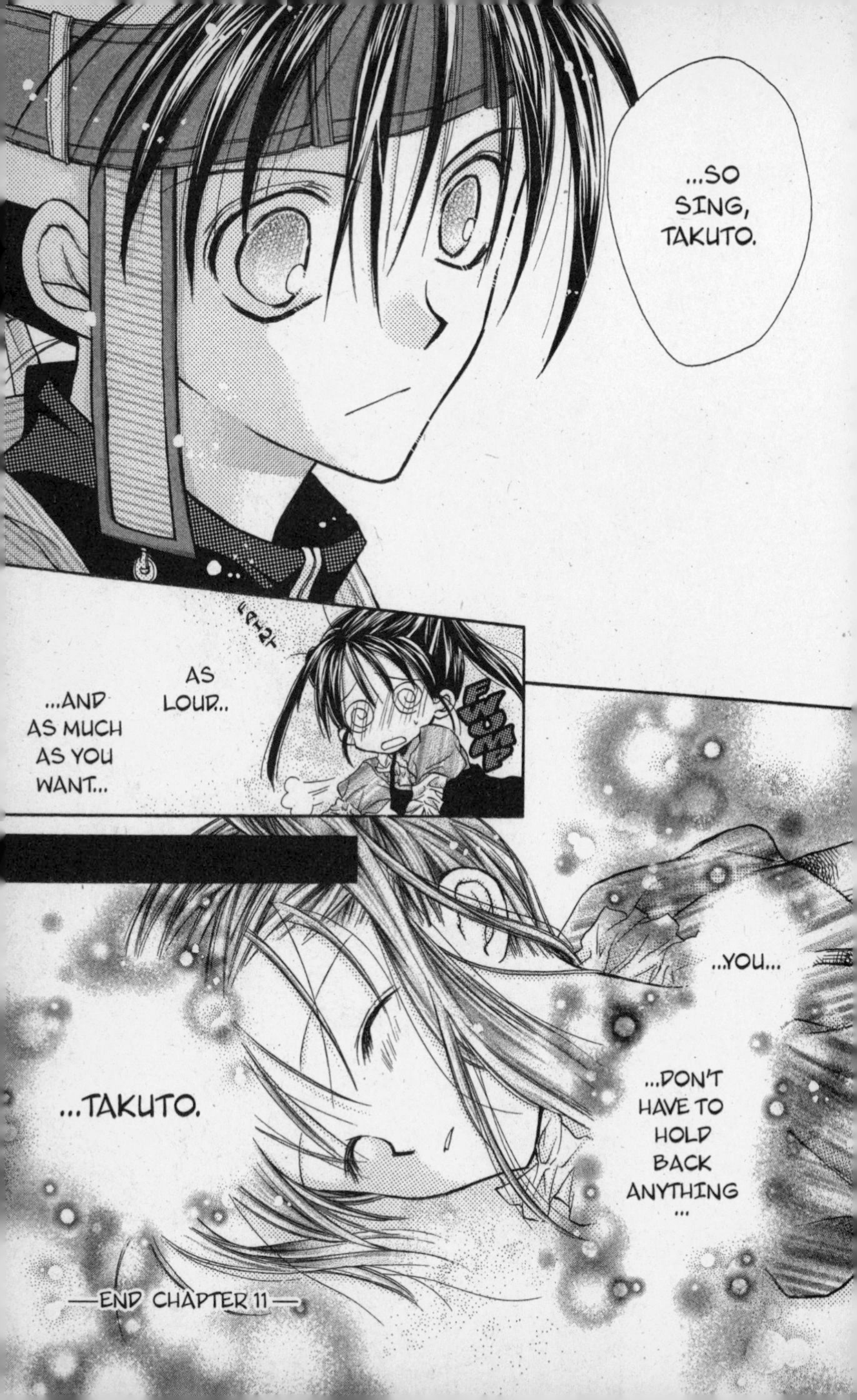
...SO SING, TAKUTO.
AS LOUD...
...AND AS MUCH AS YOU WANT...
...YOU...
...DON'T HAVE TO HOLD BACK ANYTHING ...
...TAKUTO.
—END CHAPTER 11—

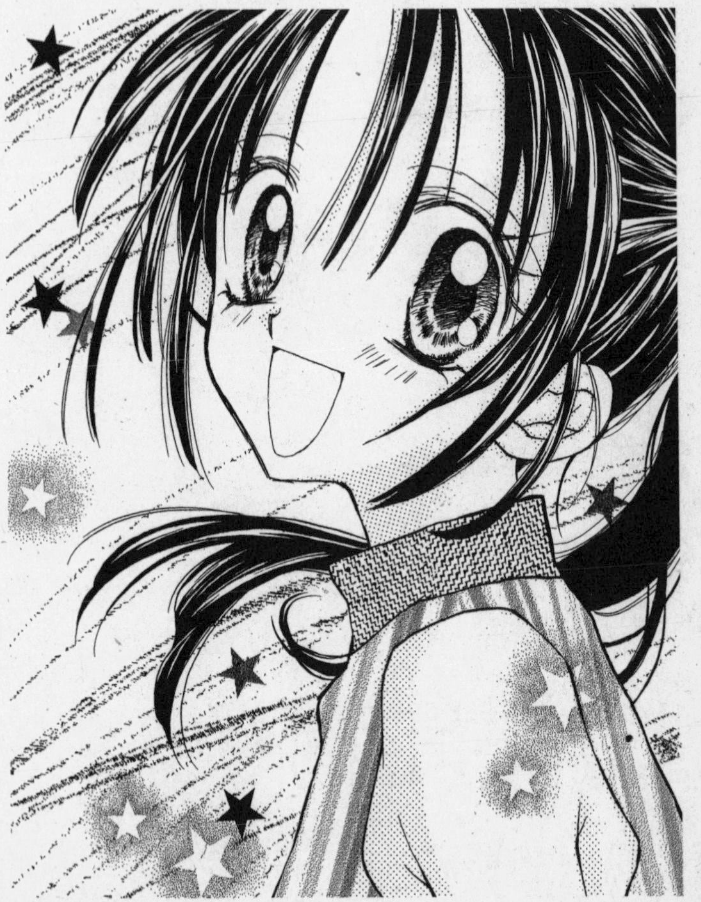

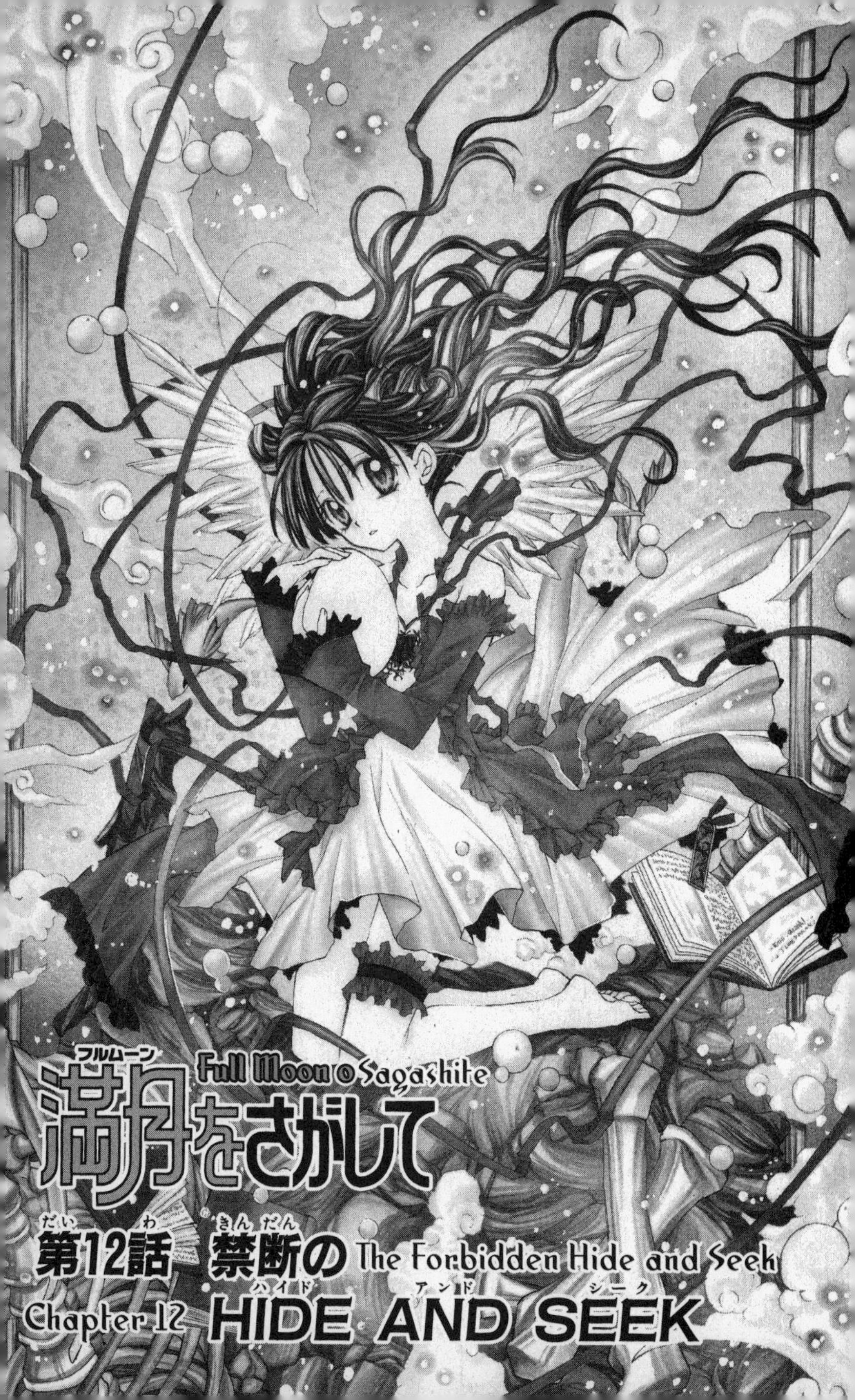
フルムーン
満月をさがして
Full Moon o Sagashite
第12話 禁断の HIDE AND SEEK
The Forbidden Hide and Seek
Chapter 12 HIDE AND SEEK

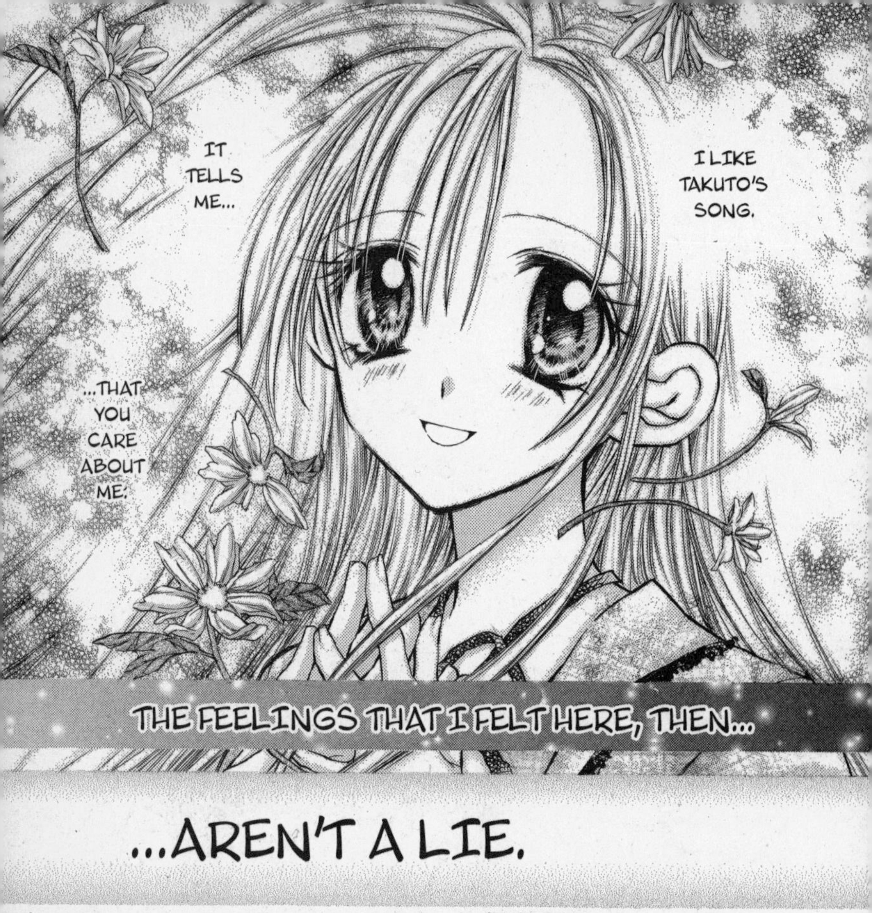
I LIKE TAKUTO'S SONG.
IT TELLS ME...
...THAT YOU CARE ABOUT ME.
THE FEELINGS THAT I FELT HERE, THEN...
...AREN'T A LIE.

Chapter 12 The Forbidden Hide and Seek (spoilers follow)

Cover Copy **Feelings drift in a mysterious world**

About the cover illustration...before I drew it, I went to Tokyo Disneyland. And at the end of Big Thunder Mountain (I rode it seven times!), you go through an arch of bones (oops, my Japanese is funny). I saw those bones and I wanted to draw bones and the illustration turned out this way.

About the story...among the recent ones, I like this one quite a bit. My editor looked at the penciling (was it? Or the final version?) and said "You've become good at drawing facial expressions," and I was very happy ♪ Yay! ♡ No matter how long I've been drawing, I don't gain confidence, but I do my best. So I'm very very happy when people compliment my drawing. I'm a little relieved then. Like, I've managed to get a passing mark.

Fans really liked the human Takuto wearing the cap.
The ending...had major repercussions. Oh dear.

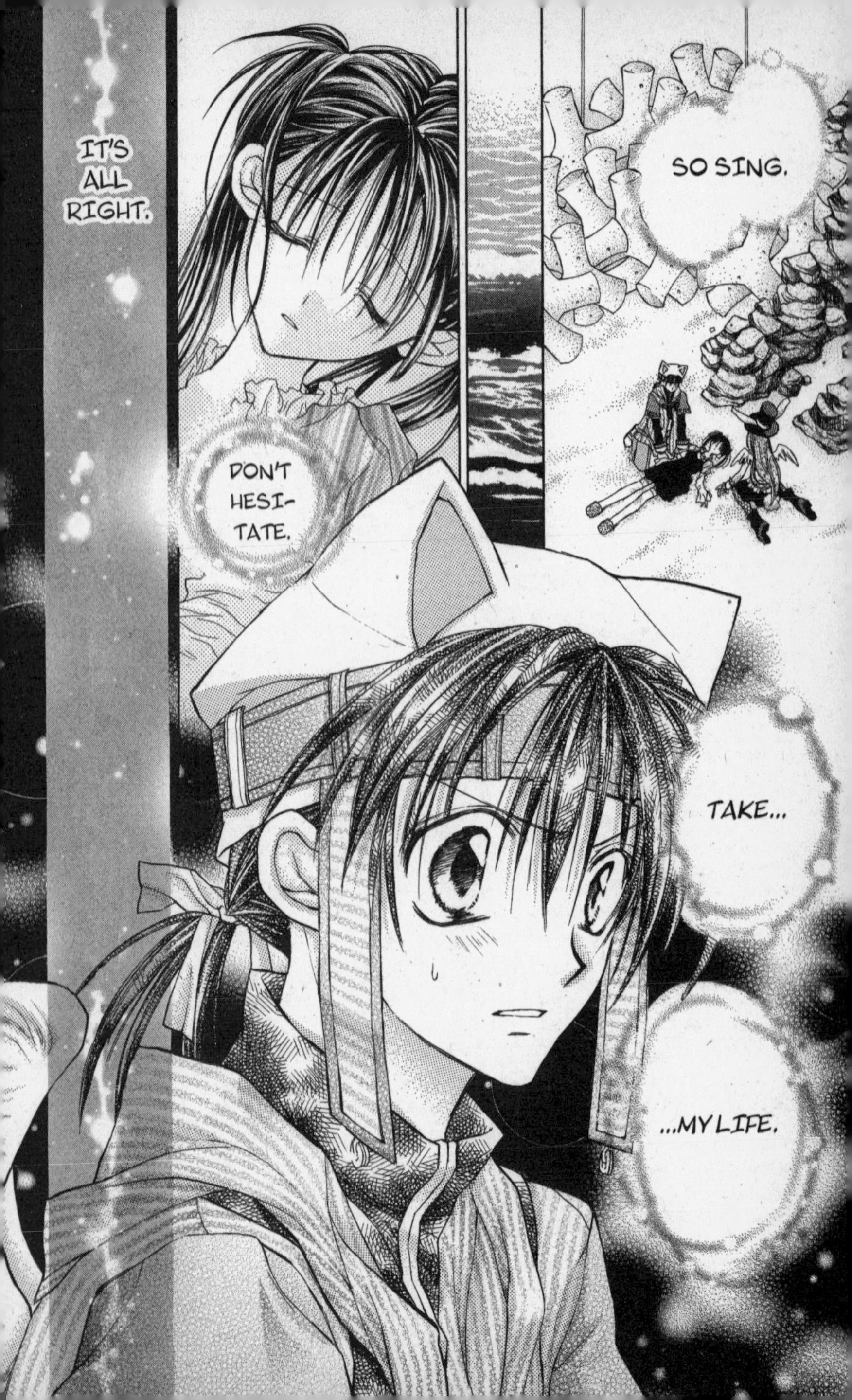
SO SING.
DON'T HESI-TATE.
TAKE...
...MY LIFE.
IT'S ALL RIGHT.

7 Days Before

Arina is about to finish the first half of the penciling tonight. The screentone team comes in (about four people). Until then...

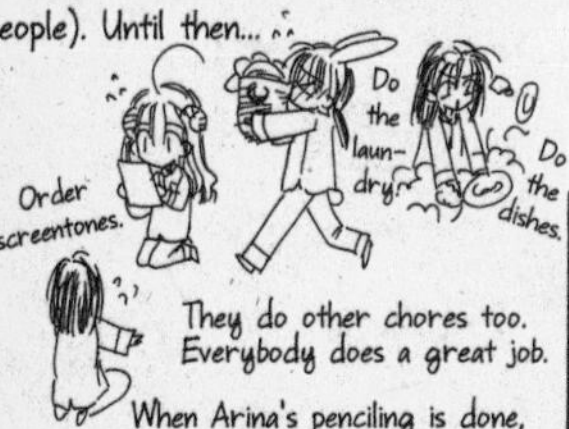
Do the laundry.
Do the dishes.
Order screentones.

They do other chores too. Everybody does a great job.

When Arina's penciling is done, two of the screentone team go to the convenience store to make copies.

Buy a copier.

I start inking. ♡

6 Days Before

Around this time, something becomes popular at work. (Example: Gundam SEED, the most amazing classmate, Tenzaru-Udon.) We usually order takeout for meals. My workplace is in an apartment, so we get lots of fliers, and that's good.

Nagatanien Love!
Kentucky Fried Love!

I pay my assistants meal allowances. (Because I want them to eat well and do good work.) Of course, I pay for their commute too.

↑ This depends on the mangaka. Sometimes the family of the mangaka cooks meals for assistants, so it really depends.

Arina starts inking. Around this time (it varies, depending on the month) people get about four hours of sleep (those who don't have work right now). I'm sorry everybody.

Depending on the month, I can hardly sleep from this point on...(two or three hours every two days?) ← But when my eyes stop functioning, I take a break.

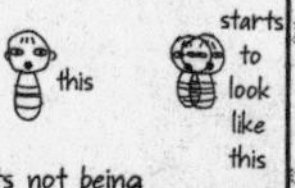
this
starts to look like this

The background team starts not being able to sleep too...(Niki-sama sleeps as she wishes. She just can't keep awake no matter what...) Even if you have to sleep, as long as you do your work, it's okay. ♡

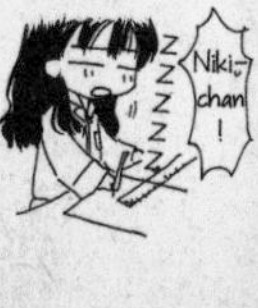
Niki-chan!
ZZZZZ

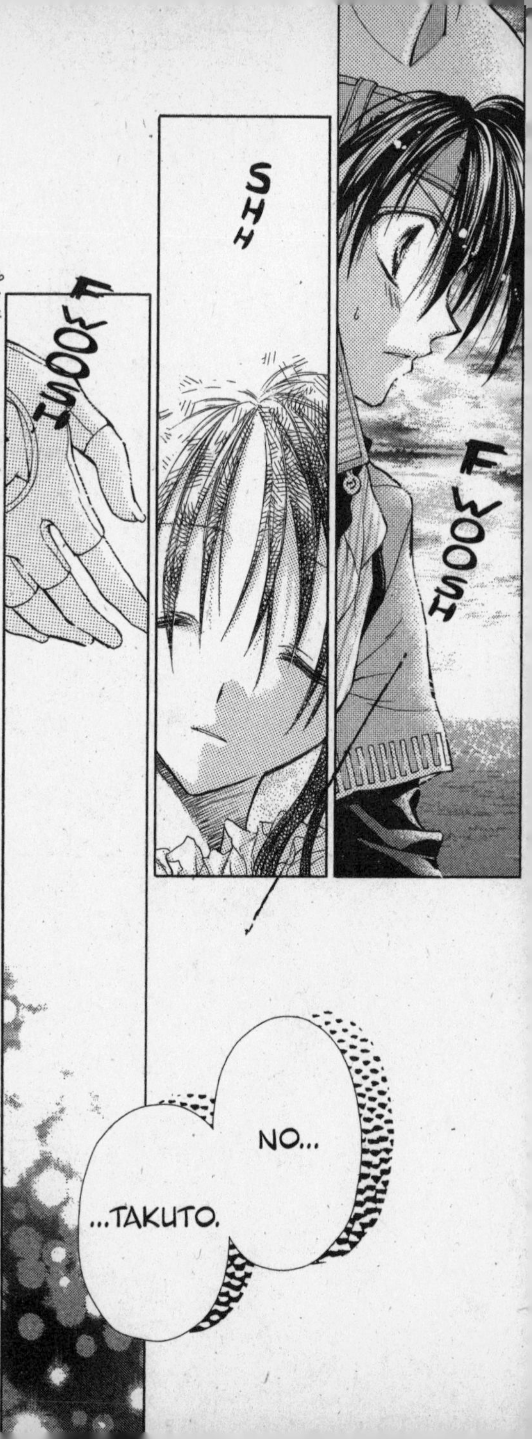
FWOOSH
SHH
FWOOSH
NO...
...TAKUTO.

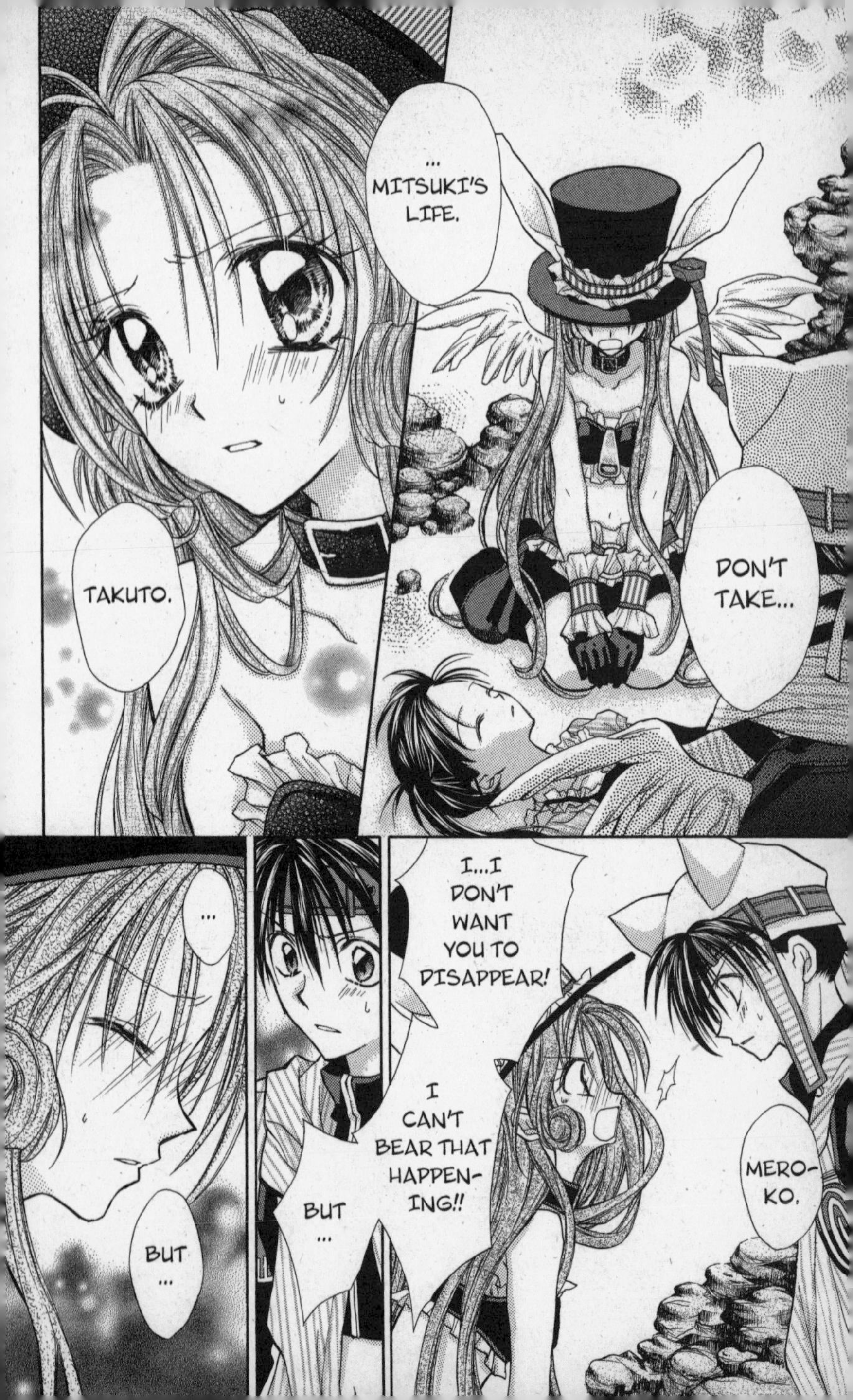
DON'T TAKE...
... MITSUKI'S LIFE.
TAKUTO.
I...I DON'T WANT YOU TO DISAPPEAR!
MERO-KO.
I CAN'T BEAR THAT HAPPEN-ING!!
BUT ...
...
BUT ...

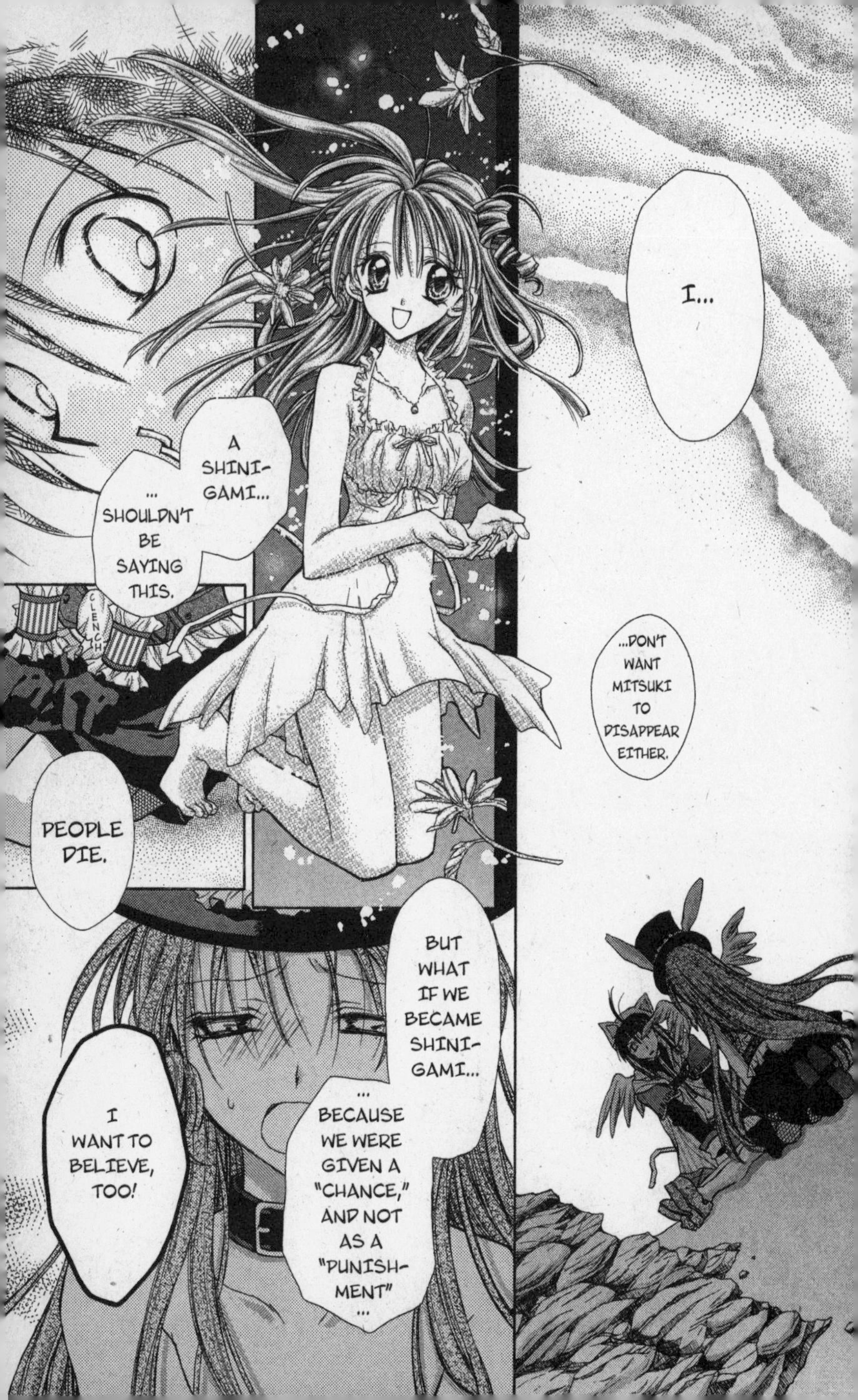
I...
...DON'T WANT MITSUKI TO DISAPPEAR EITHER.
A SHINIGAMI...
...SHOULDN'T BE SAYING THIS.
CLENCH
PEOPLE DIE.
BUT WHAT IF WE BECAME SHINIGAMI... ...BECAUSE WE WERE GIVEN A "CHANCE," AND NOT AS A "PUNISHMENT"...
I WANT TO BELIEVE, TOO!

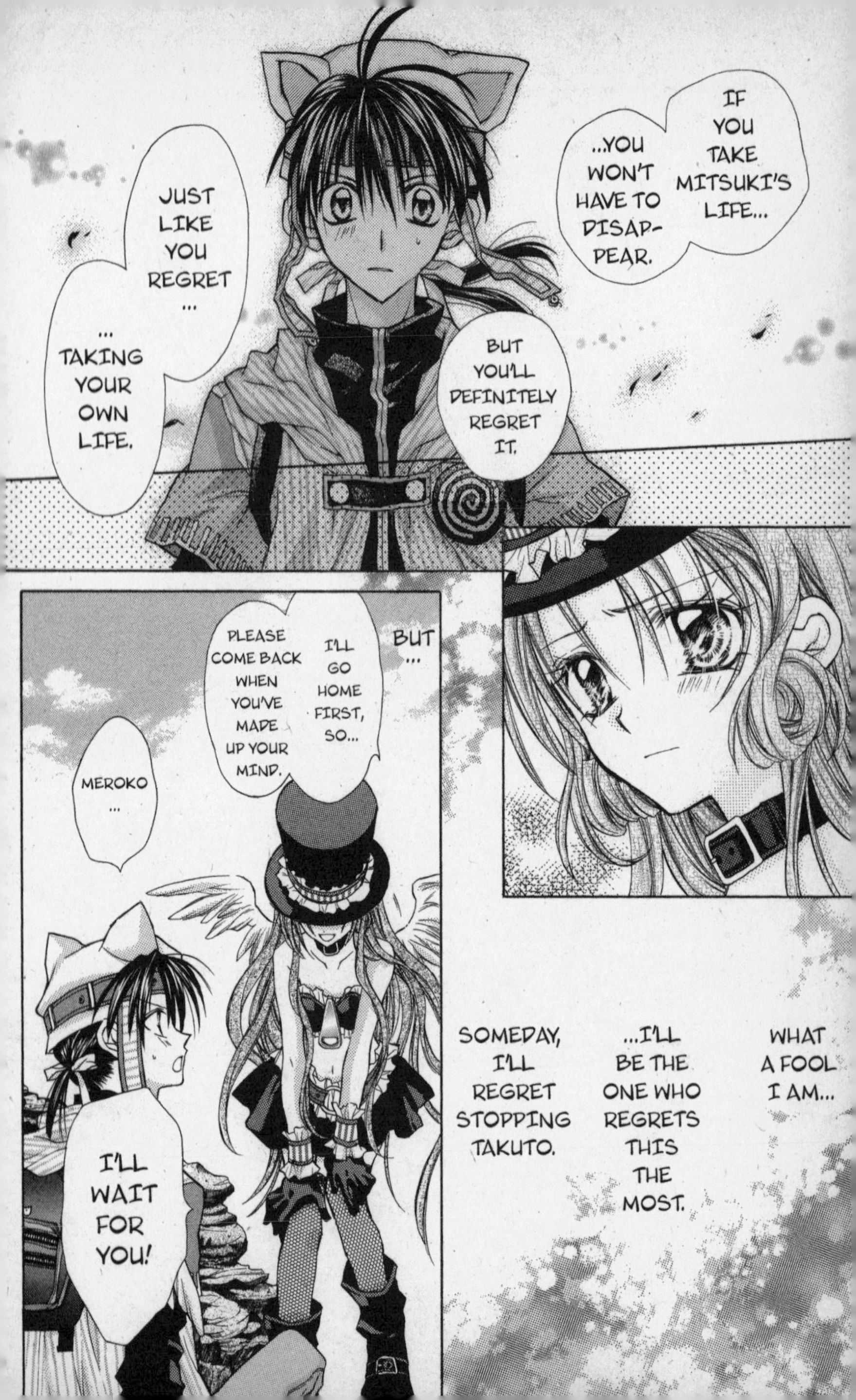
IF YOU TAKE MITSUKI'S LIFE...
...YOU WON'T HAVE TO DISAP-PEAR.
BUT YOU'LL DEFINITELY REGRET IT.
JUST LIKE YOU REGRET ...
... TAKING YOUR OWN LIFE.
WHAT A FOOL I AM...
...I'LL BE THE ONE WHO REGRETS THIS THE MOST.
SOMEDAY, I'LL REGRET STOPPING TAKUTO.
BUT ...
I'LL GO HOME FIRST, SO...
PLEASE COME BACK WHEN YOU'VE MADE UP YOUR MIND.
MEROKO ...
I'LL WAIT FOR YOU!

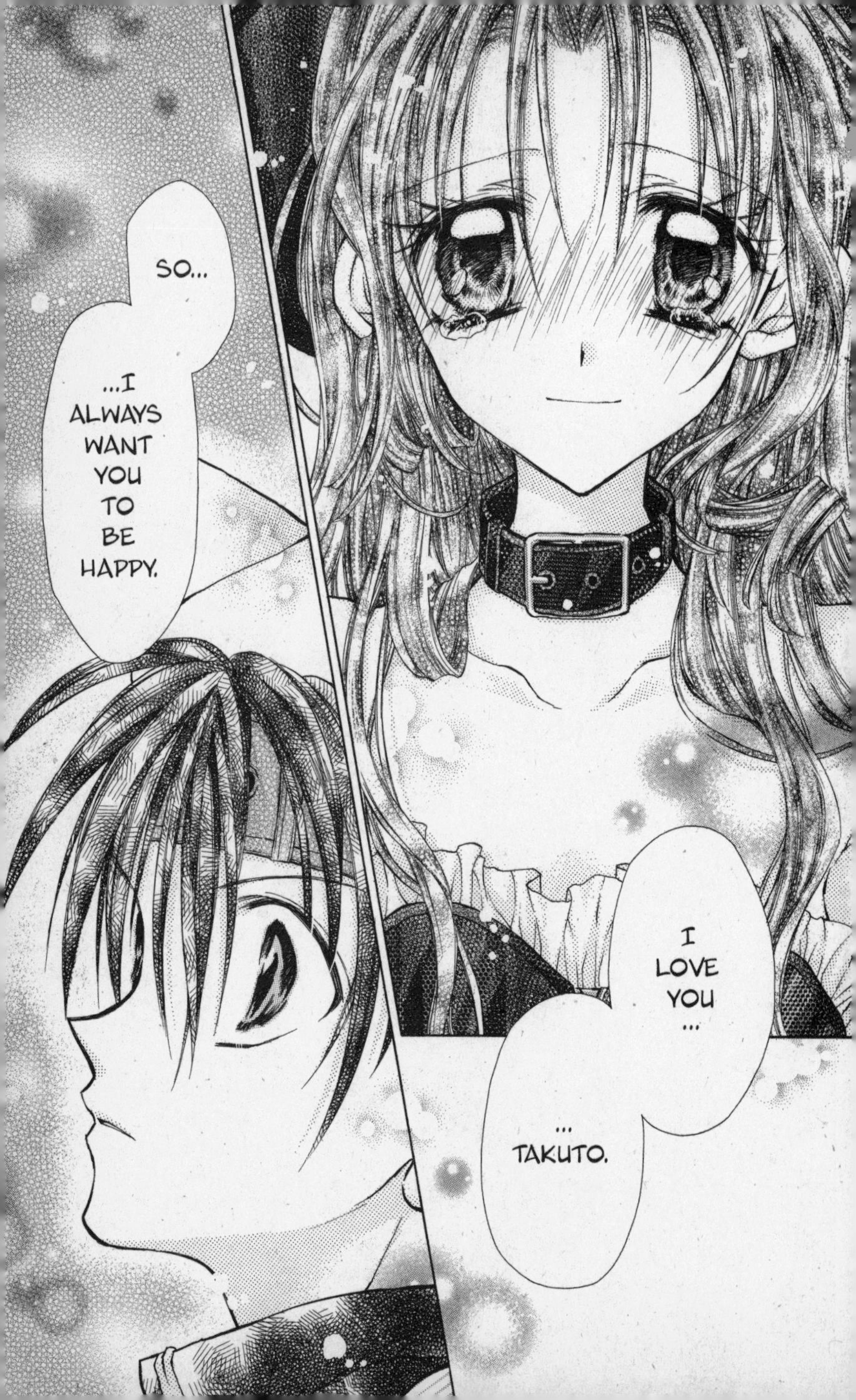
SO...
...I ALWAYS WANT YOU TO BE HAPPY.
I LOVE YOU ...
... TAKUTO.

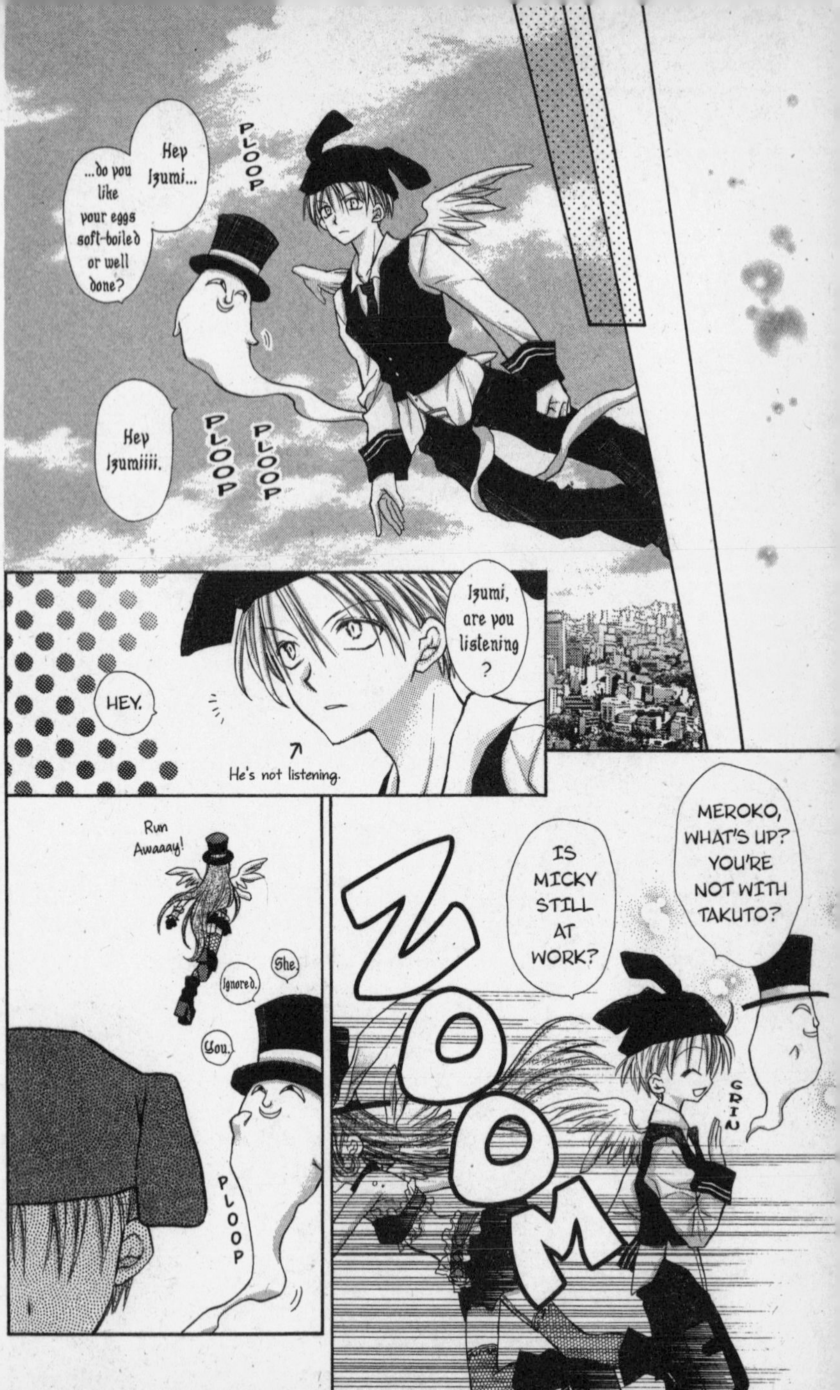
Hey Izumi...
...do you like your eggs soft-boiled or well done?
PLOOP
Hey Izumiiii.
PLOOP
PLOOP
Izumi, are you listening?
HEY.
He's not listening.
MEROKO, WHAT'S UP? YOU'RE NOT WITH TAKUTO?
IS MICKY STILL AT WORK?
ZOOM
GRIN
Run Awaaay!
She.
Ignored.
You.
PLOOP

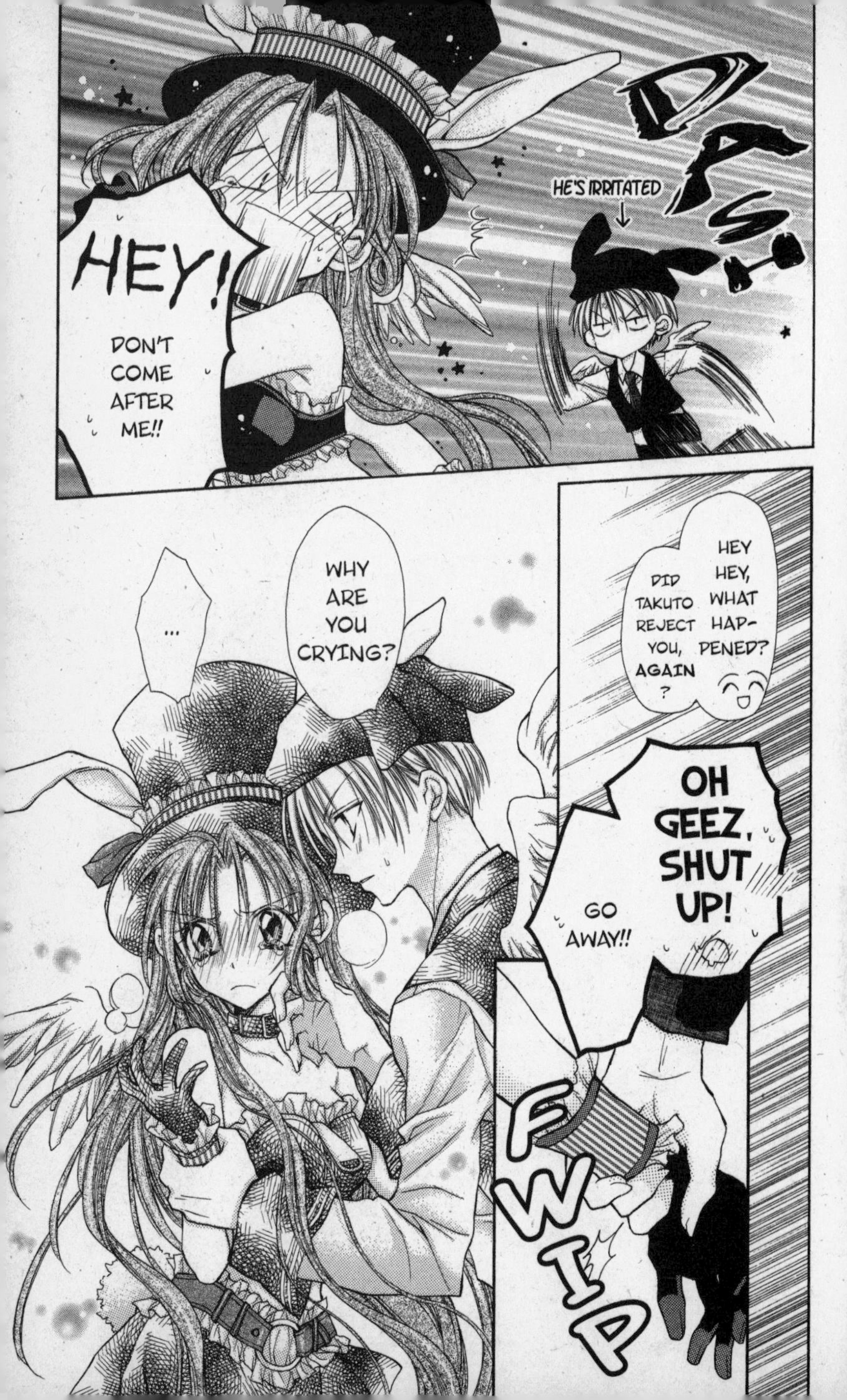
DASH!
HE'S IRRITATED
HEY!
DON'T COME AFTER ME!!
HEY HEY, WHAT HAPPENED?
DID TAKUTO REJECT YOU, AGAIN?
OH GEEZ, SHUT UP!
GO AWAY!!
FWIP
WHY ARE YOU CRYING?
...

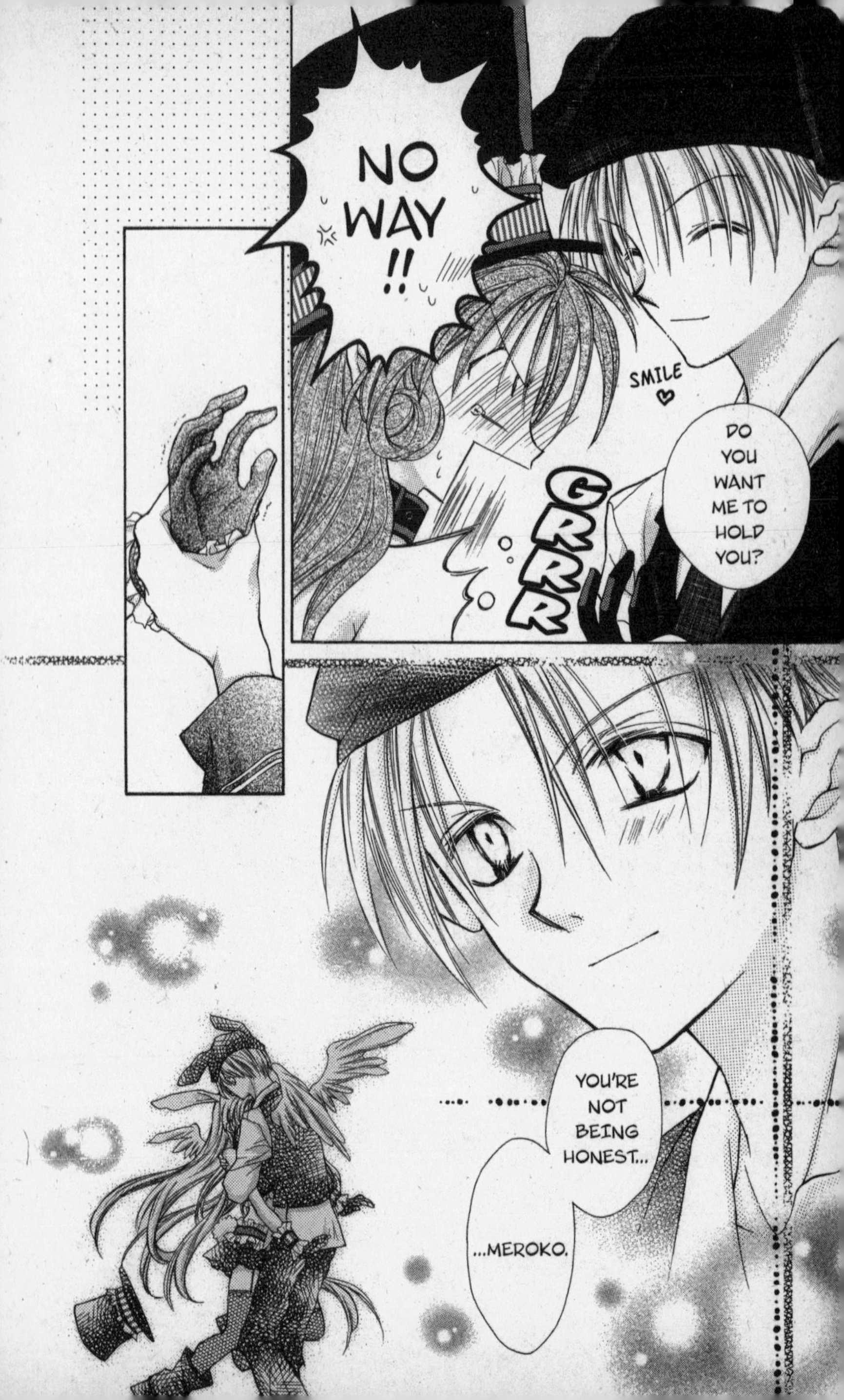
NO WAY!!
SMILE
DO YOU WANT ME TO HOLD YOU?
GRRR
YOU'RE NOT BEING HONEST...
...MEROKO.

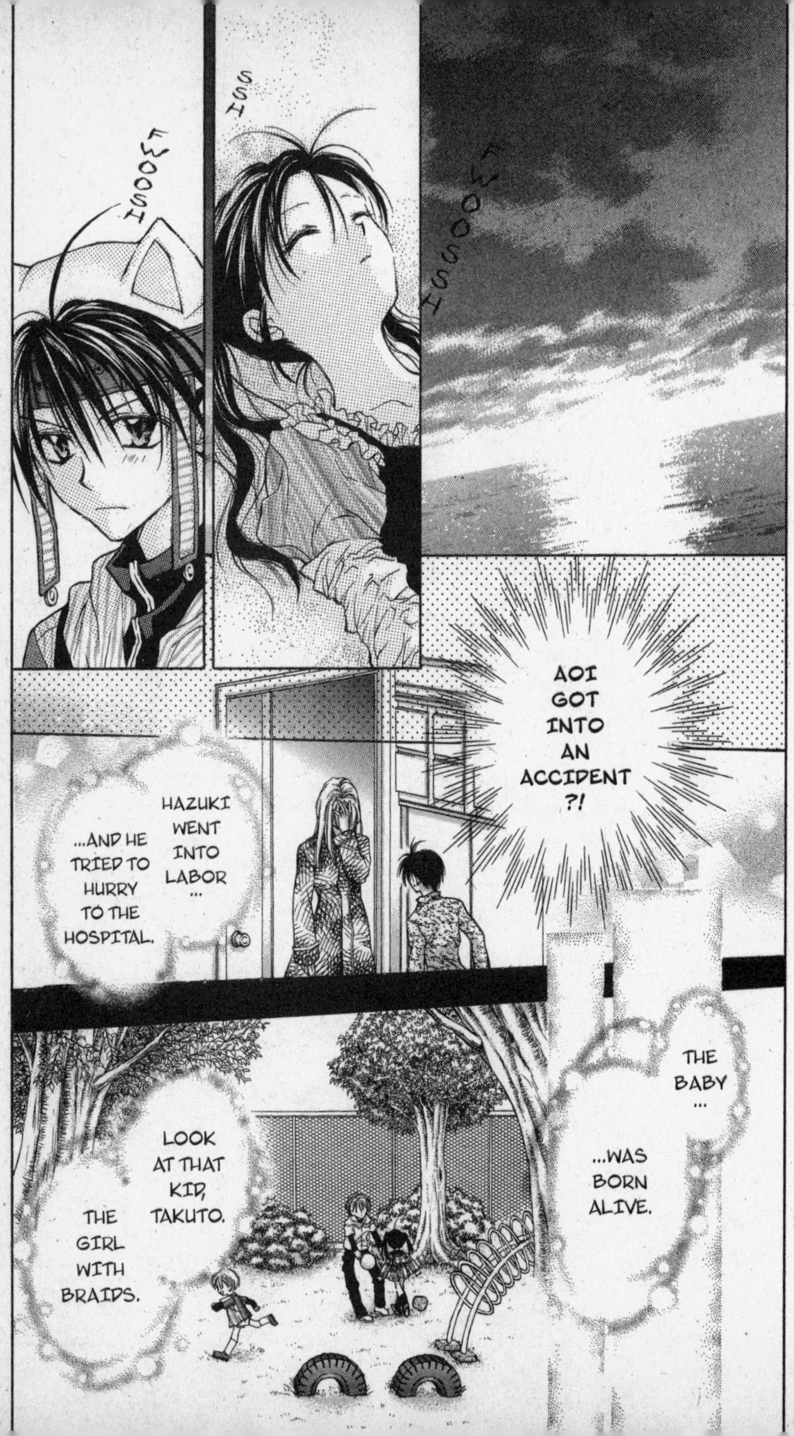
FWOOOSSH
SSH
FWOOSH
AOI GOT INTO AN ACCIDENT ?!
HAZUKI WENT INTO LABOR ...
...AND HE TRIED TO HURRY TO THE HOSPITAL.
THE BABY ...
...WAS BORN ALIVE.
LOOK AT THAT KID, TAKUTO.
THE GIRL WITH BRAIDS.

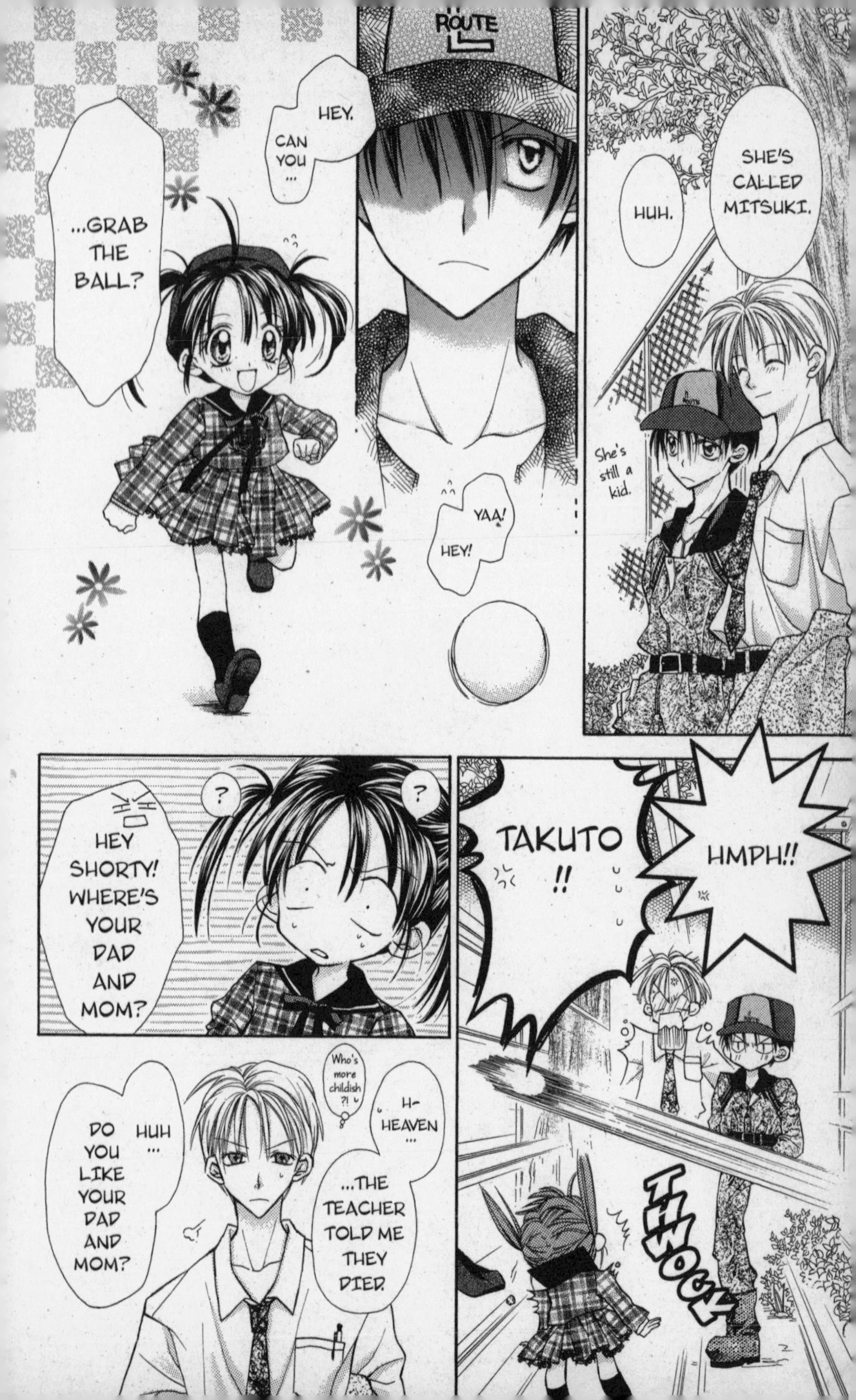
SHE'S CALLED MITSUKI.
HUH.
She's still a kid.
HEY.
CAN YOU ...
YAA!
HEY!
...GRAB THE BALL?
TAKUTO !!
HMPH!!
THWOCK
?
?
HEY SHORTY! WHERE'S YOUR DAD AND MOM?
H-HEAVEN ...
...THE TEACHER TOLD ME THEY DIED.
Who's more childish ?!
HUH ...
DO YOU LIKE YOUR DAD AND MOM?

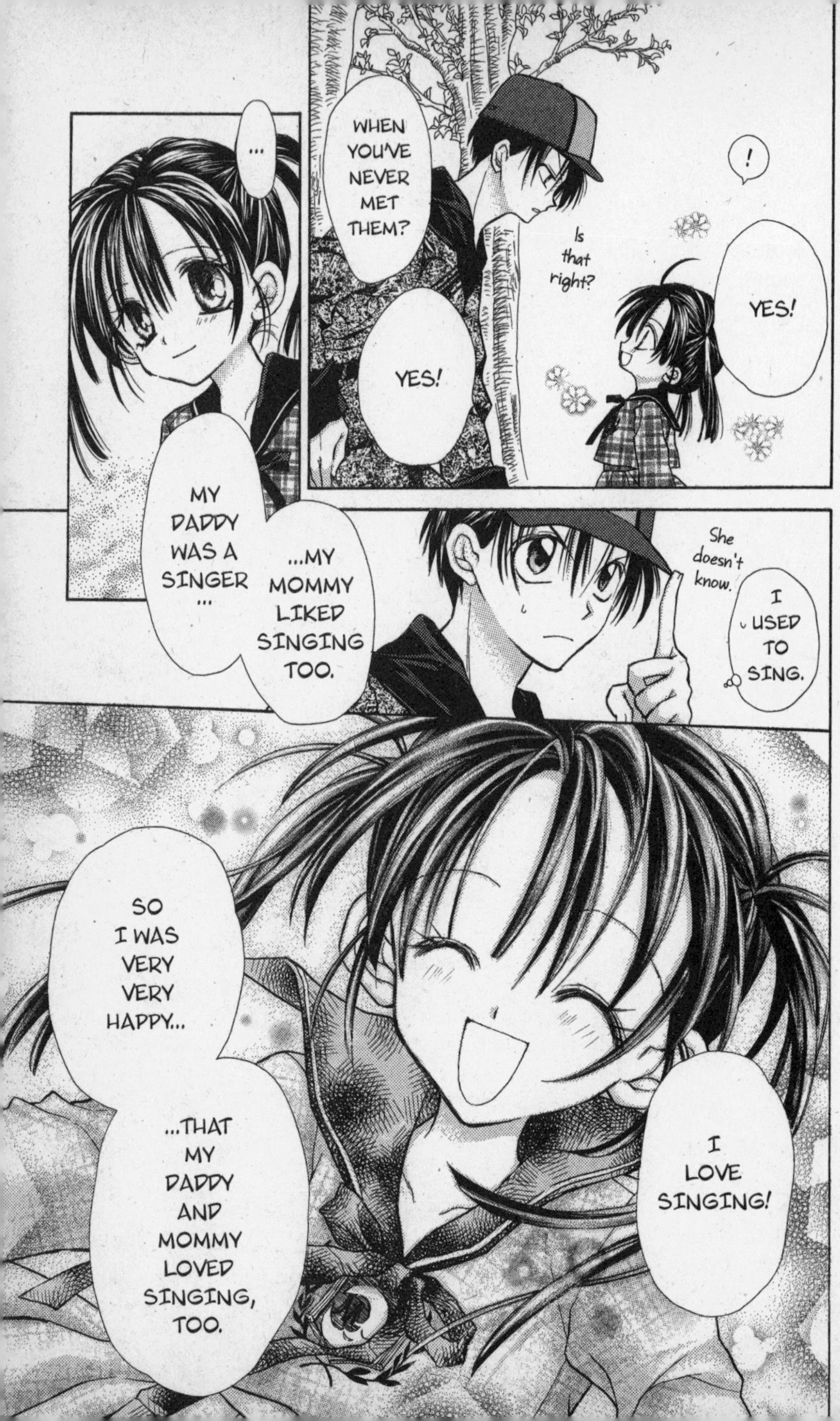
WHEN YOU'VE NEVER MET THEM?
YES!
Is that right?
YES!
!
...
MY DADDY WAS A SINGER...
...MY MOMMY LIKED SINGING TOO.
She doesn't know.
I USED TO SING.
I LOVE SINGING!
SO I WAS VERY VERY HAPPY...
...THAT MY DADDY AND MOMMY LOVED SINGING, TOO.

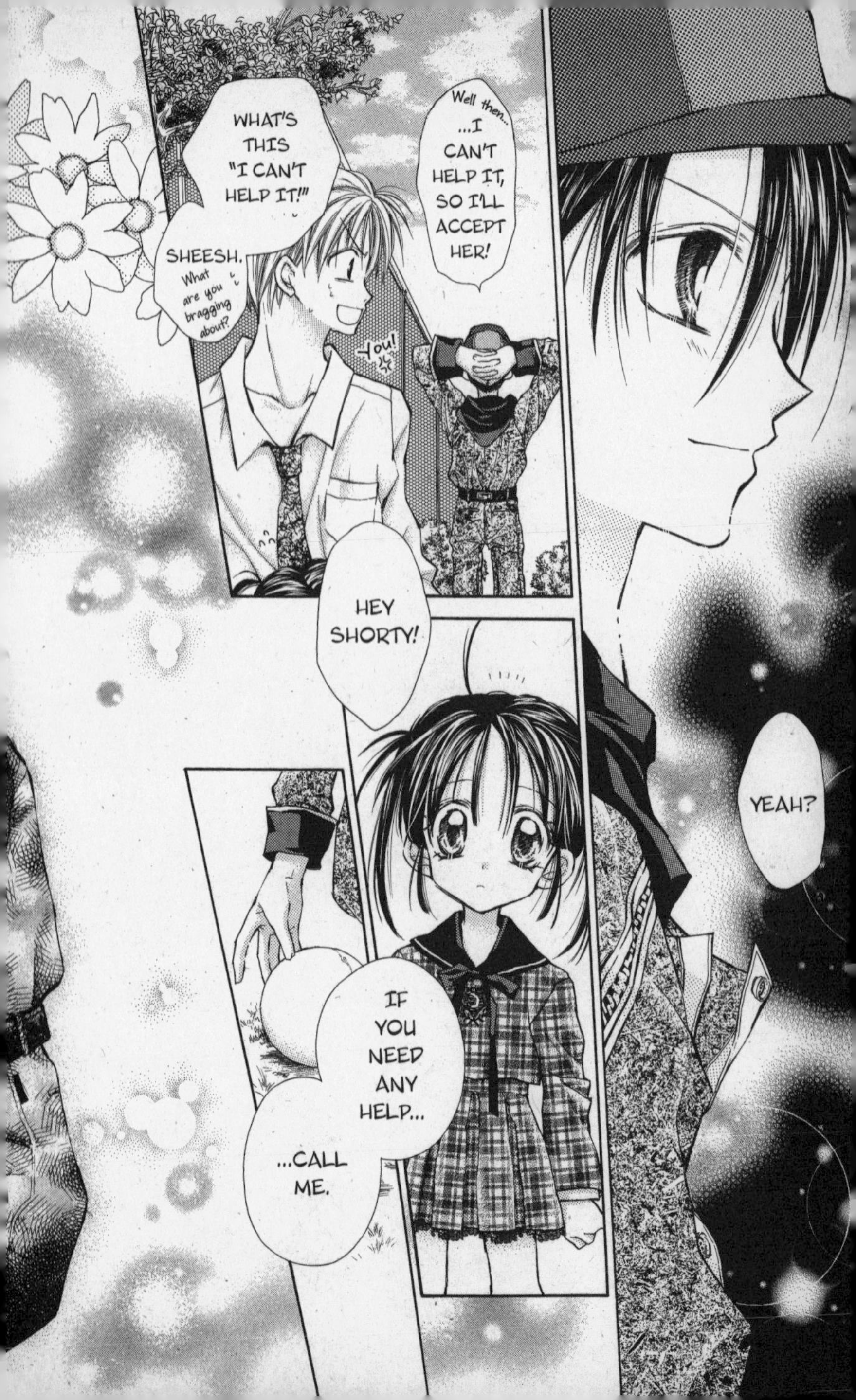
Well then... ...I CAN'T HELP IT, SO I'LL ACCEPT HER!
WHAT'S THIS "I CAN'T HELP IT!"
SHEESH.
What are you bragging about?
You!
HEY SHORTY!
YEAH?
IF YOU NEED ANY HELP...
...CALL ME.

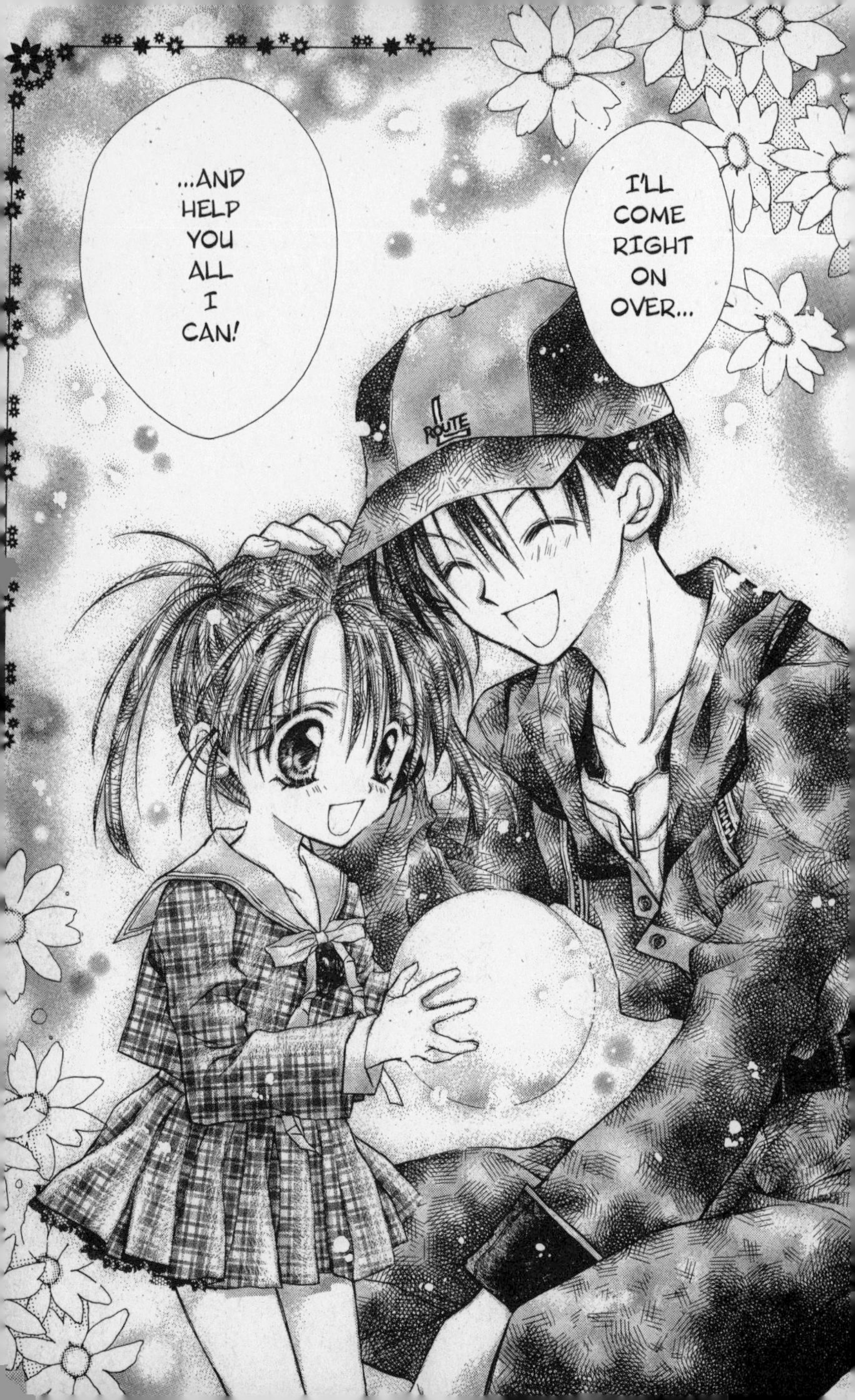
I'LL COME RIGHT ON OVER...
...AND HELP YOU ALL I CAN!

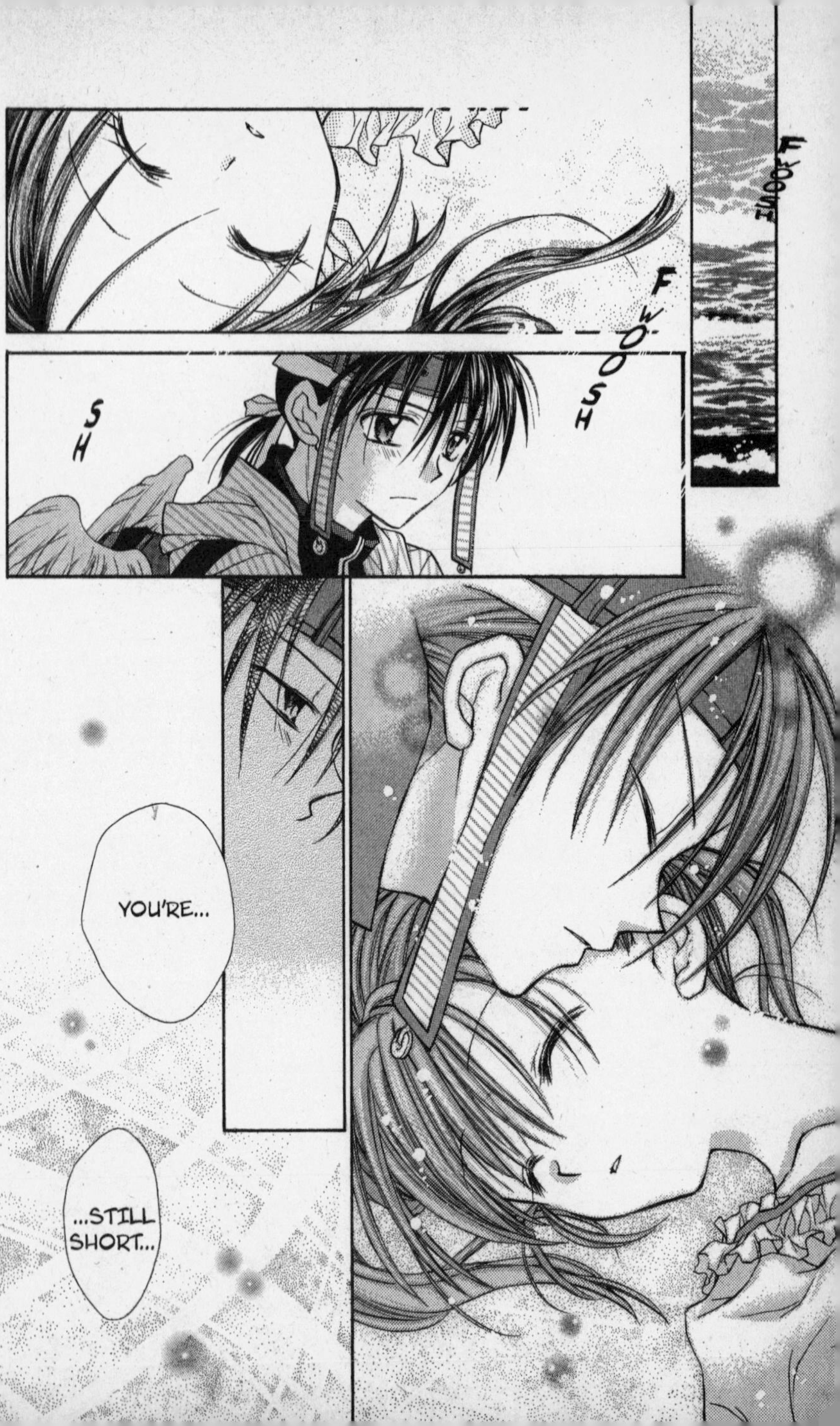
FWOOSH
FWOOSH
SH
YOU'RE...
...STILL SHORT...

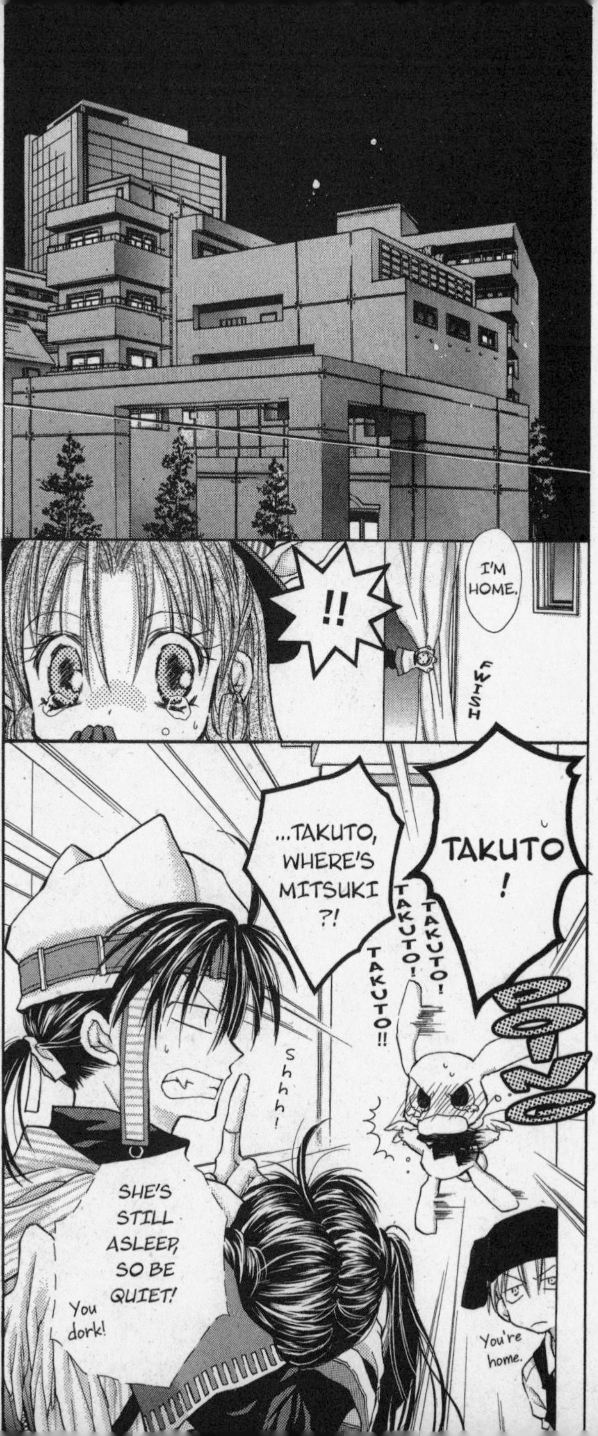
I'M HOME.
!!
FWISH
TAKUTO!
...TAKUTO, WHERE'S MITSUKI?!
TAKUTO! TAKUTO! TAKUTO!!
Shhh!
SHE'S STILL ASLEEP, SO BE QUIET!
You dork!
You're home.

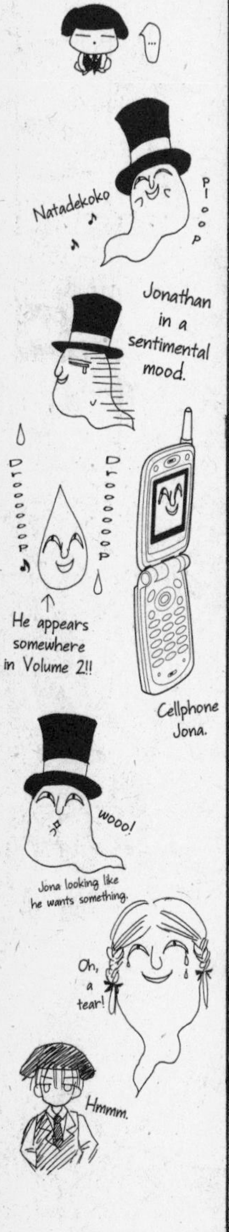
...
Natadekoko ♪ ♪
Ploop
Jonathan in a sentimental mood.
Droooooop ♪
Droooooop
He appears somewhere in Volume 2!!
Cellphone Jona.
wooo!
Jona looking like he wants something.
Oh, a tear!
Hmmm.

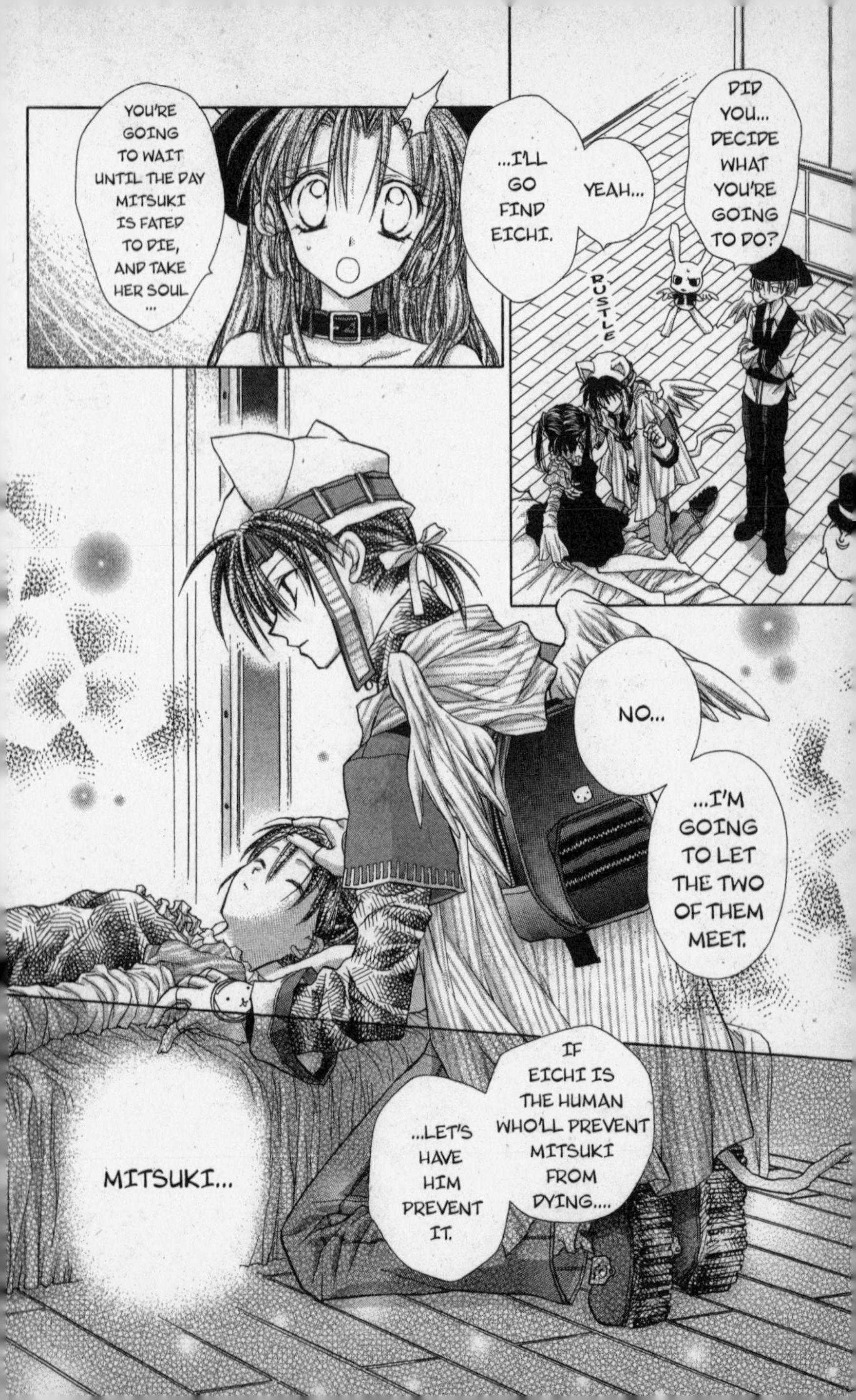
DID YOU... DECIDE WHAT YOU'RE GOING TO DO?
YEAH...
...I'LL GO FIND EICHI.
RUSTLE
YOU'RE GOING TO WAIT UNTIL THE DAY MITSUKI IS FATED TO DIE, AND TAKE HER SOUL...
NO...
...I'M GOING TO LET THE TWO OF THEM MEET.
IF EICHI IS THE HUMAN WHO'LL PREVENT MITSUKI FROM DYING....
...LET'S HAVE HIM PREVENT IT.
MITSUKI...

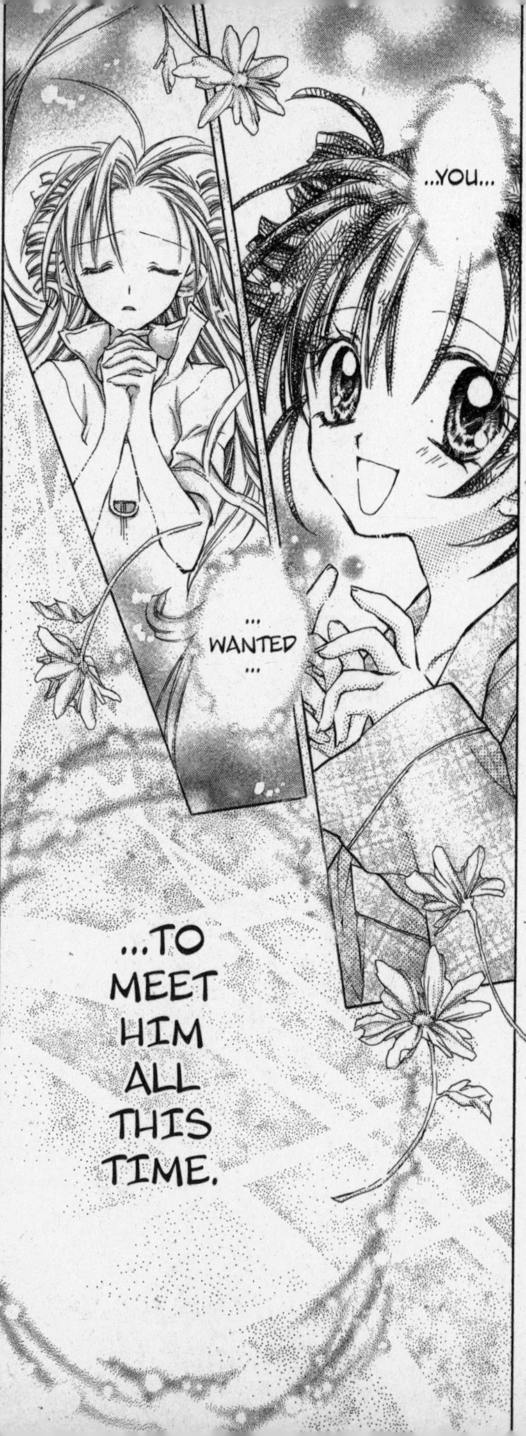
...YOU...
...WANTED...
...TO MEET HIM ALL THIS TIME.

5 Days Before

I do 8 to 10 pages of inking per day around this time...
Some pages take 30 minutes, some take three hours. The background team does inking of the background. The screentone team keeps applying screentones. Around this time, you only get to nap (everybody). I take 5 or 10 minutes for naps. I even go to the bathroom at super light speed.

Sigh... Ahaha...

4 Days Before

Today is the deadline for the first half of the chapter. After I've finished inking, I apply the finishing screentones after the screentone team has completed applying the basic screentones. I also give out detailed orders as necessary. The background team, when they've finished with their work, helps with the screentones, and everybody rushes to finish.

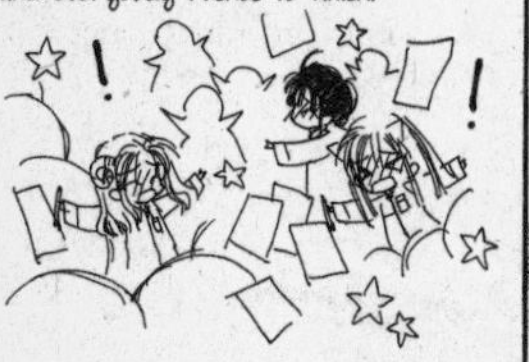

Lifeless shells.

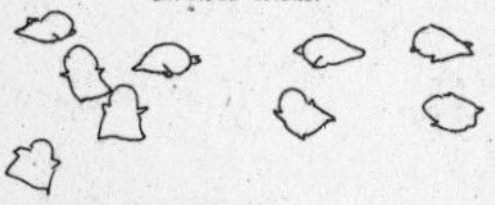

3 Days Before

I sleep for about six to seven hours, and do the penciling for the second half of the chapter. (Everybody else does things like cleaning the place.)
The staff gets to rest a little.
But the background team draws and draws when it's their turn.
The screentone team orders stuff, does laundry, and other stuff.
We joke, talk, and I finish the penciling no matter what by the end of the day. (This day, or...uh, until I get to take a nap?)

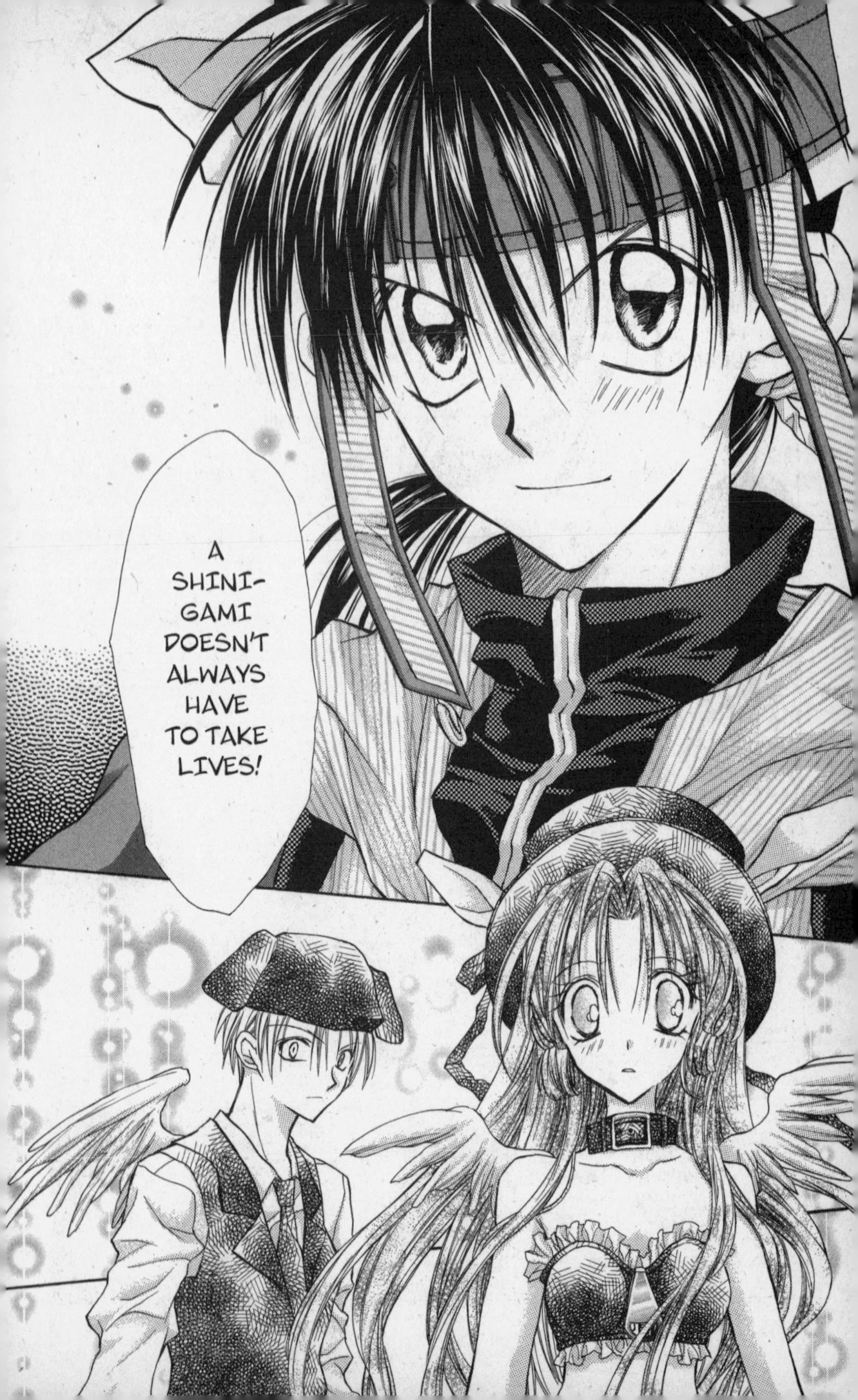
A SHINIGAMI DOESN'T ALWAYS HAVE TO TAKE LIVES!

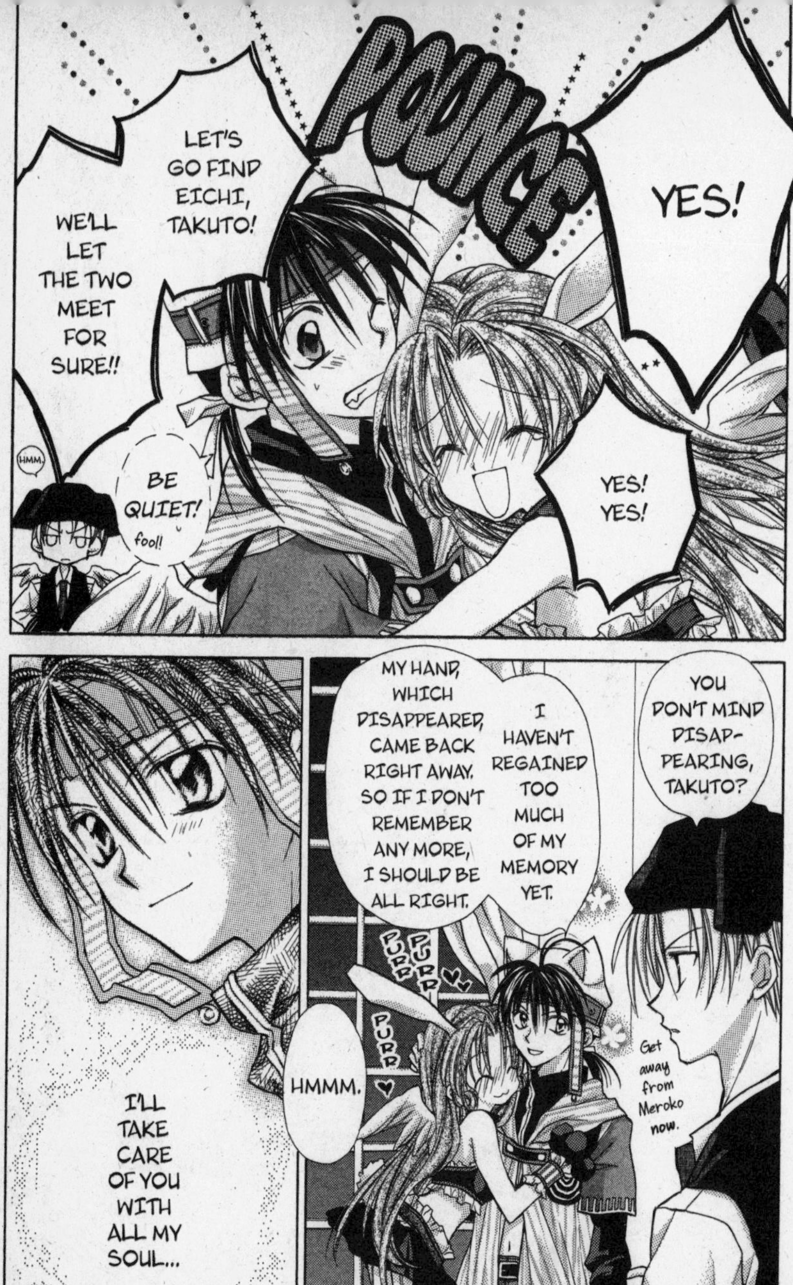
POUNCE
YES!
LET'S GO FIND EICHI, TAKUTO!
YES! YES!
WE'LL LET THE TWO MEET FOR SURE!!
BE QUIET! fool!
HMM.
YOU DON'T MIND DISAP-PEARING, TAKUTO?
I HAVEN'T REGAINED TOO MUCH OF MY MEMORY YET.
MY HAND, WHICH DISAPPEARED, CAME BACK RIGHT AWAY. SO IF I DON'T REMEMBER ANY MORE, I SHOULD BE ALL RIGHT.
PURR PURR
PURR
Get away from Meroko now.
HMMM.
I'LL TAKE CARE OF YOU WITH ALL MY SOUL...

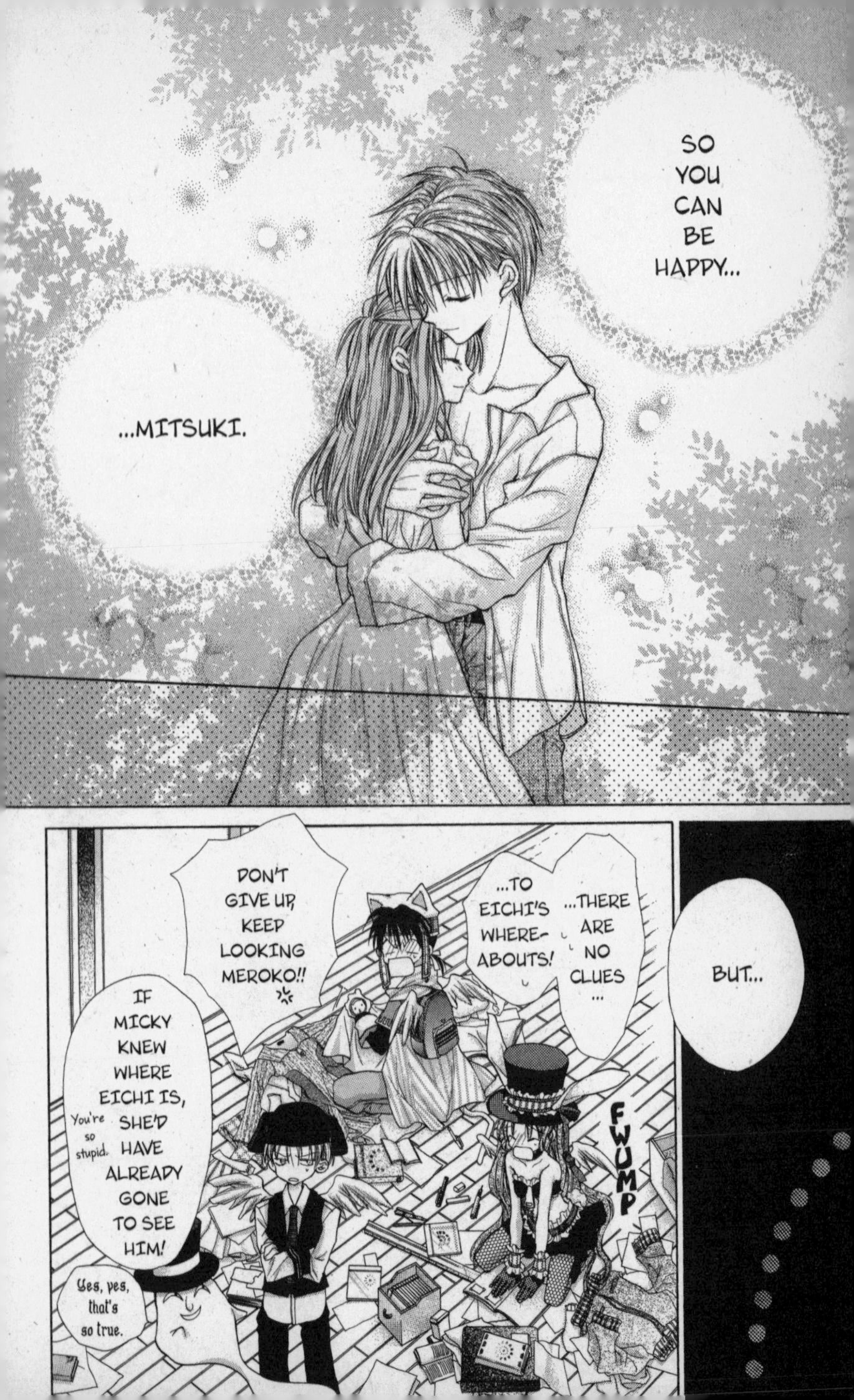
SO YOU CAN BE HAPPY...
...MITSUKI.
BUT...
...THERE ARE NO CLUES ...
...TO EICHI'S WHEREABOUTS!
DON'T GIVE UP, KEEP LOOKING MEROKO!!
FWUMP
IF MICKY KNEW WHERE EICHI IS, SHE'D HAVE ALREADY GONE TO SEE HIM!
You're so stupid.
Yes, yes, that's so true.

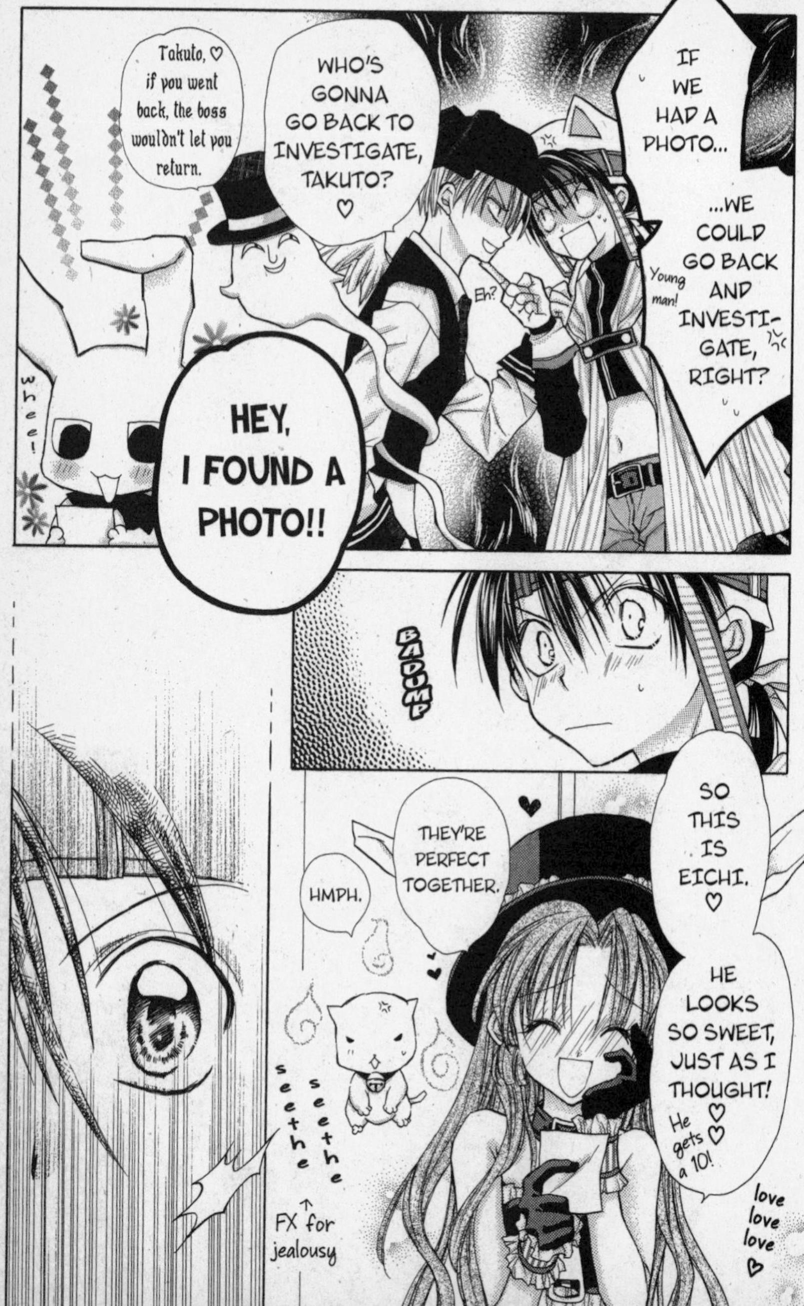
IF WE HAD A PHOTO...
...WE COULD GO BACK AND INVESTIGATE, RIGHT?
Young man!
Eh?
WHO'S GONNA GO BACK TO INVESTIGATE, TAKUTO? ♡
Takuto, ♡ if you went back, the boss wouldn't let you return.
HEY, I FOUND A PHOTO!!
whee!
BADUMP
SO THIS IS EICHI. ♡
HE LOOKS SO SWEET, JUST AS I THOUGHT! ♡
He gets a 10! ♡
love love love ♡
THEY'RE PERFECT TOGETHER.
HMPH.
seethe seethe
FX for jealousy

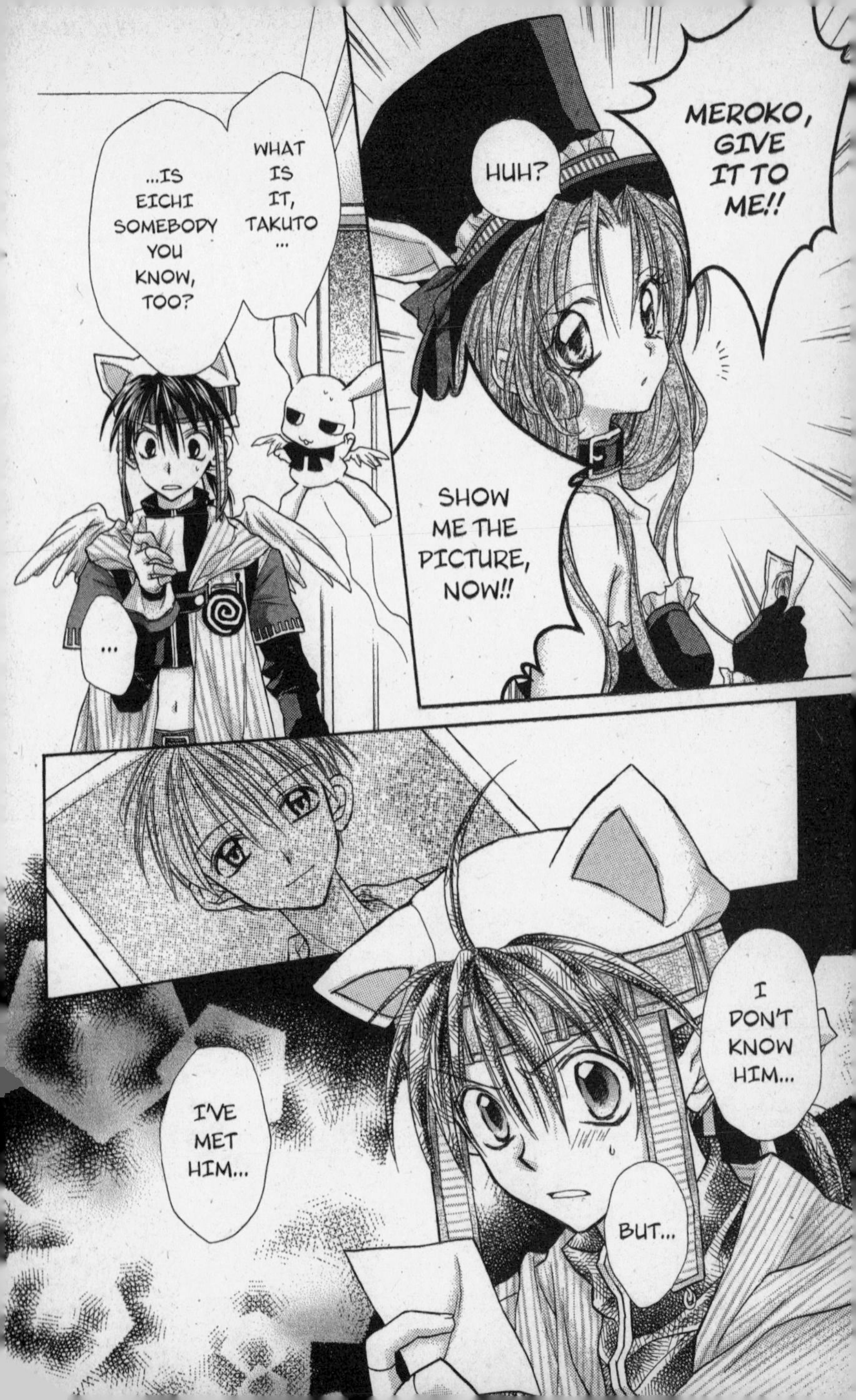
MEROKO, GIVE IT TO ME!!
HUH?
SHOW ME THE PICTURE, NOW!!
WHAT IS IT, TAKUTO ...
...IS EICHI SOMEBODY YOU KNOW, TOO?
...
I DON'T KNOW HIM...
BUT...
I'VE MET HIM...

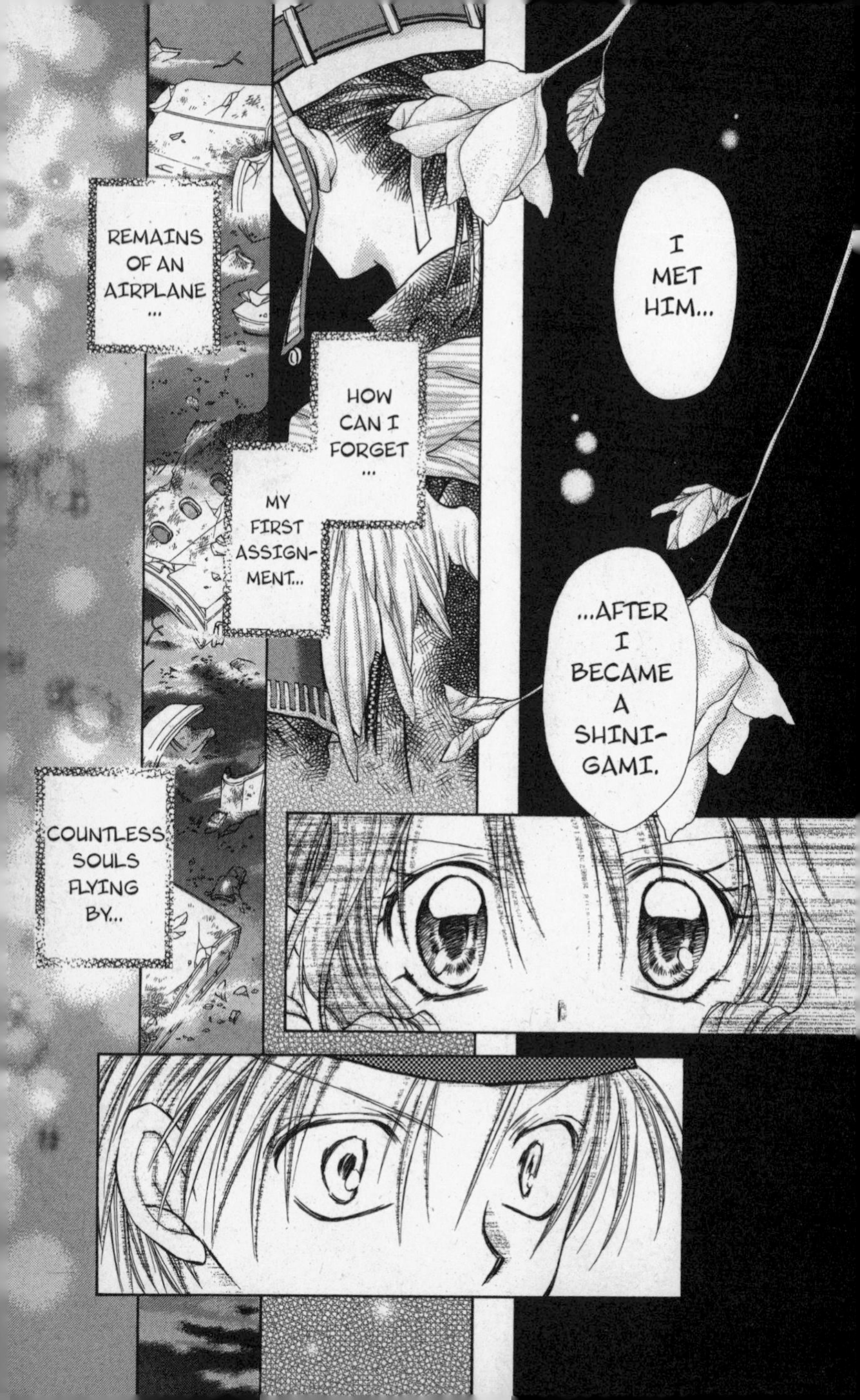
I MET HIM...
...AFTER I BECAME A SHINIGAMI.
HOW CAN I FORGET...
MY FIRST ASSIGNMENT...
REMAINS OF AN AIRPLANE...
COUNTLESS SOULS FLYING BY...

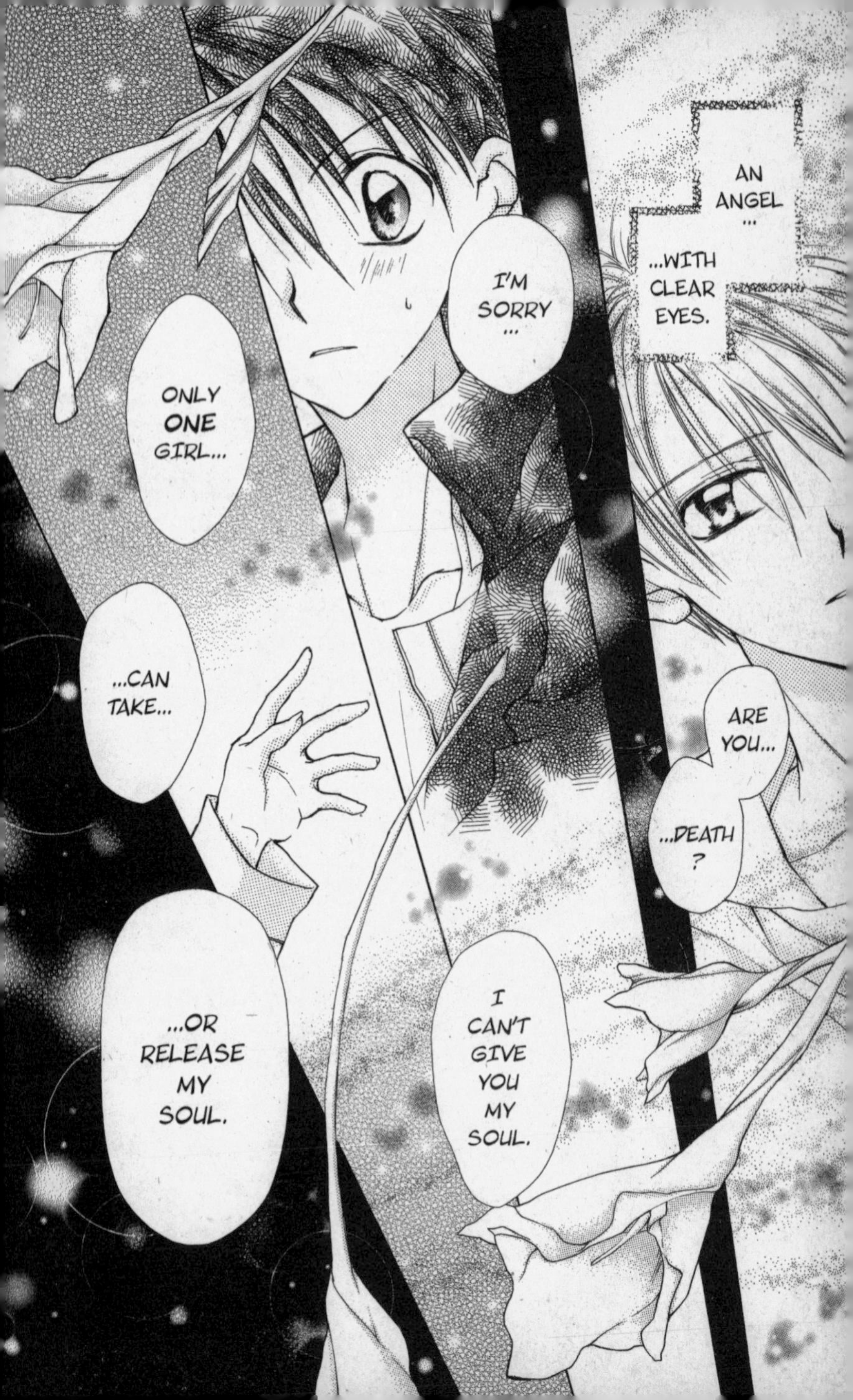
AN ANGEL...
...WITH CLEAR EYES.
ARE YOU...
...DEATH?
I'M SORRY...
I CAN'T GIVE YOU MY SOUL.
ONLY ONE GIRL...
...CAN TAKE...
...OR RELEASE MY SOUL.

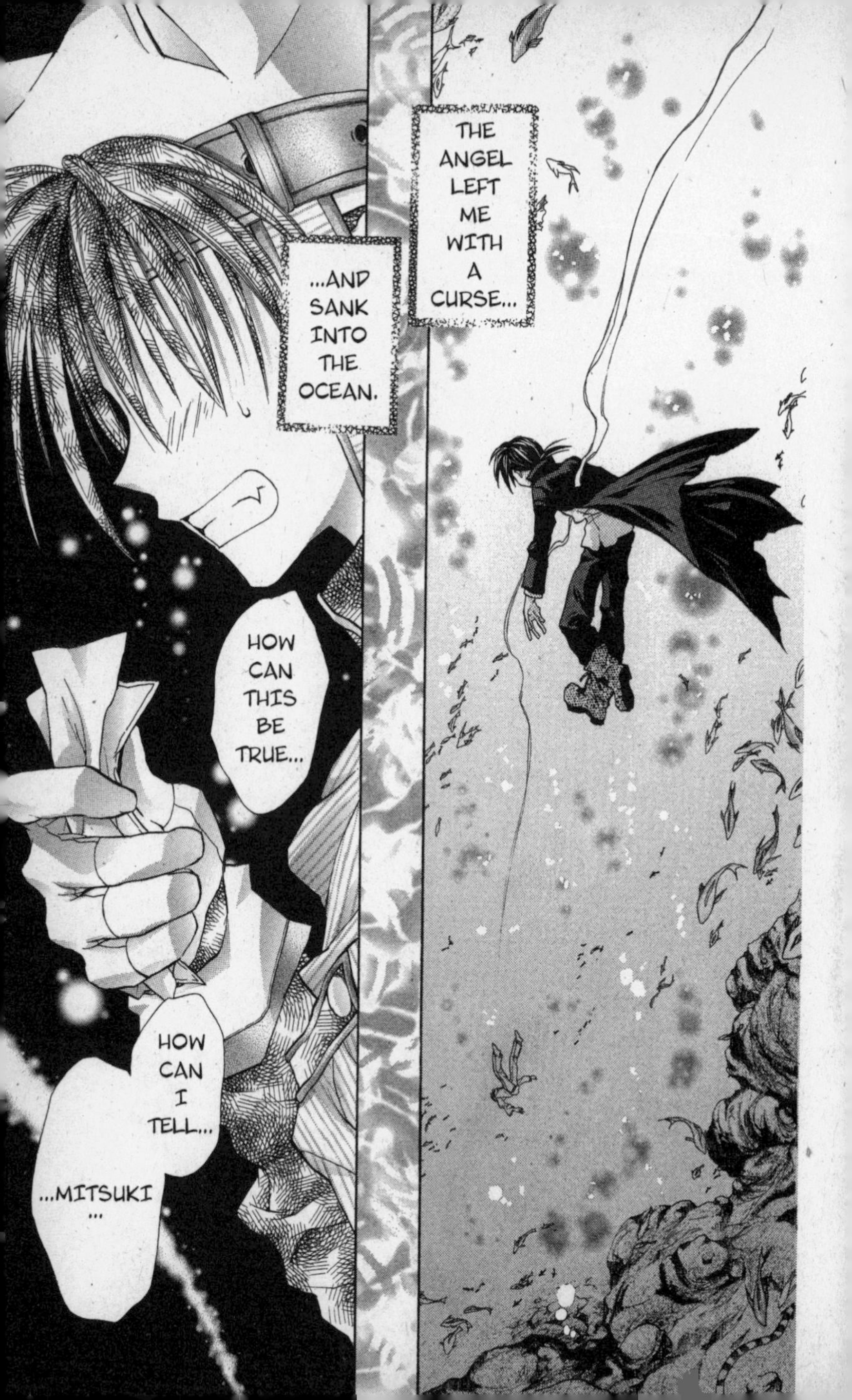
THE ANGEL LEFT ME WITH A CURSE...
...AND SANK INTO THE OCEAN.
HOW CAN THIS BE TRUE...
HOW CAN I TELL...
...MITSUKI...

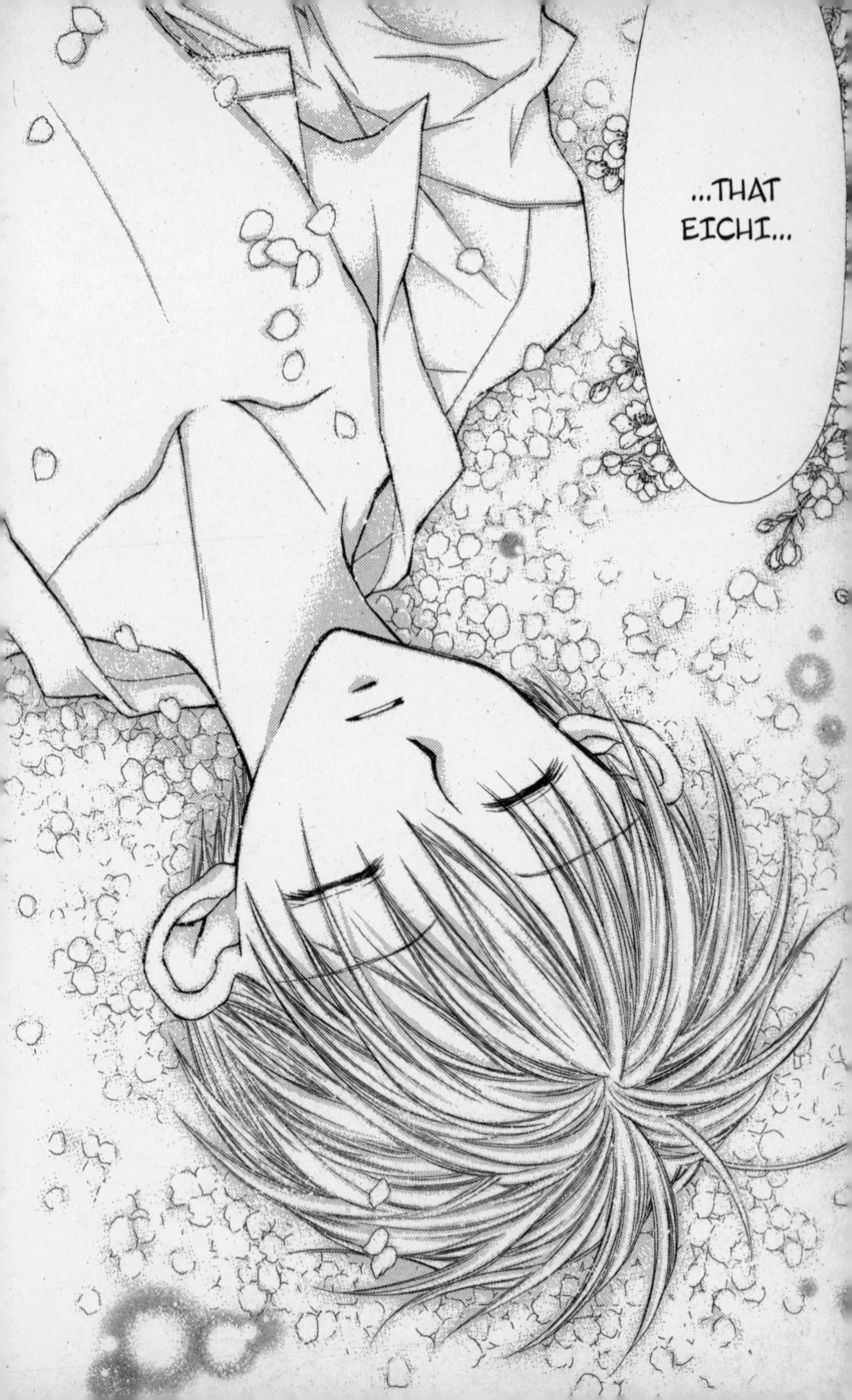
...THAT EICHI...

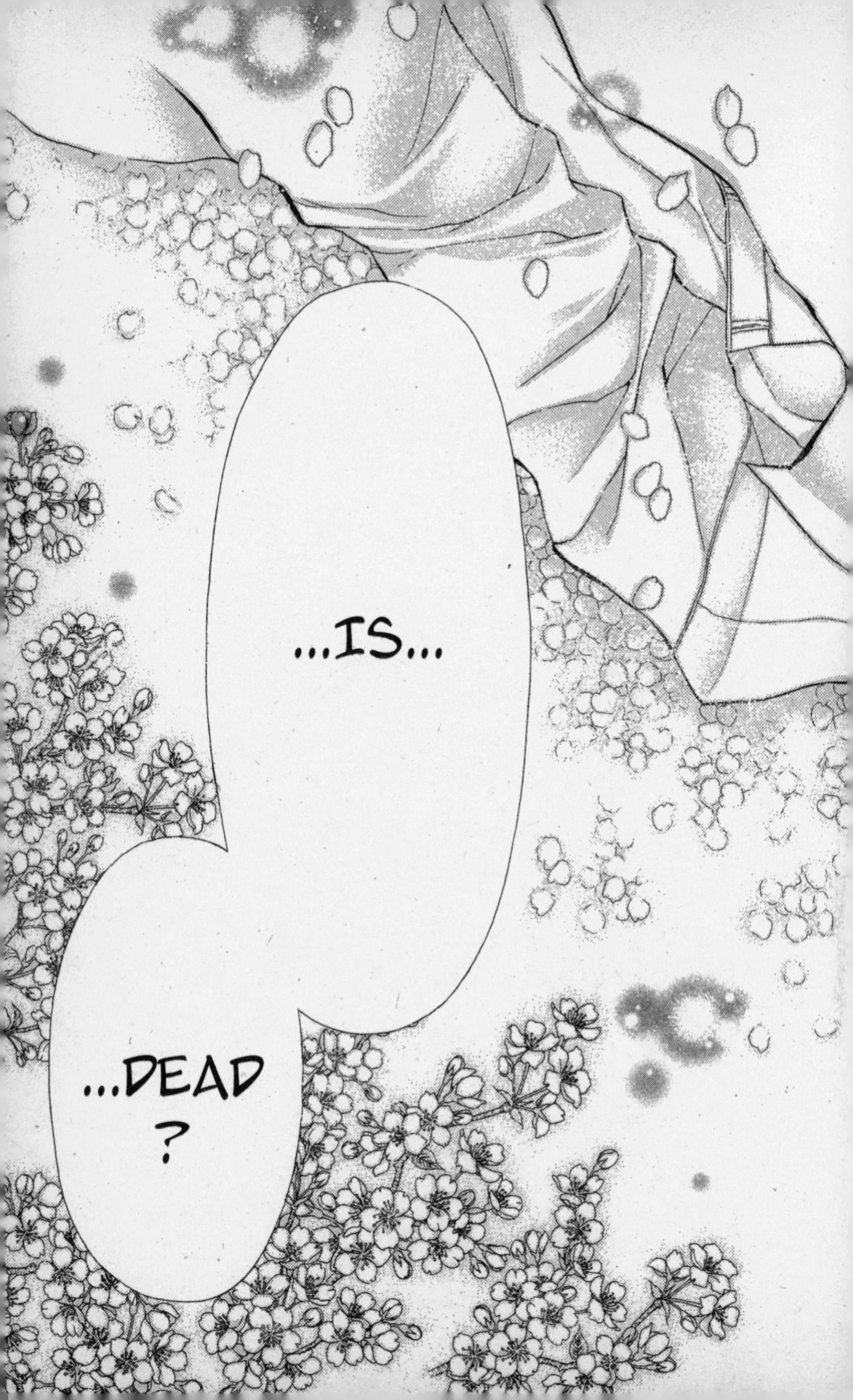
...IS...
...DEAD?

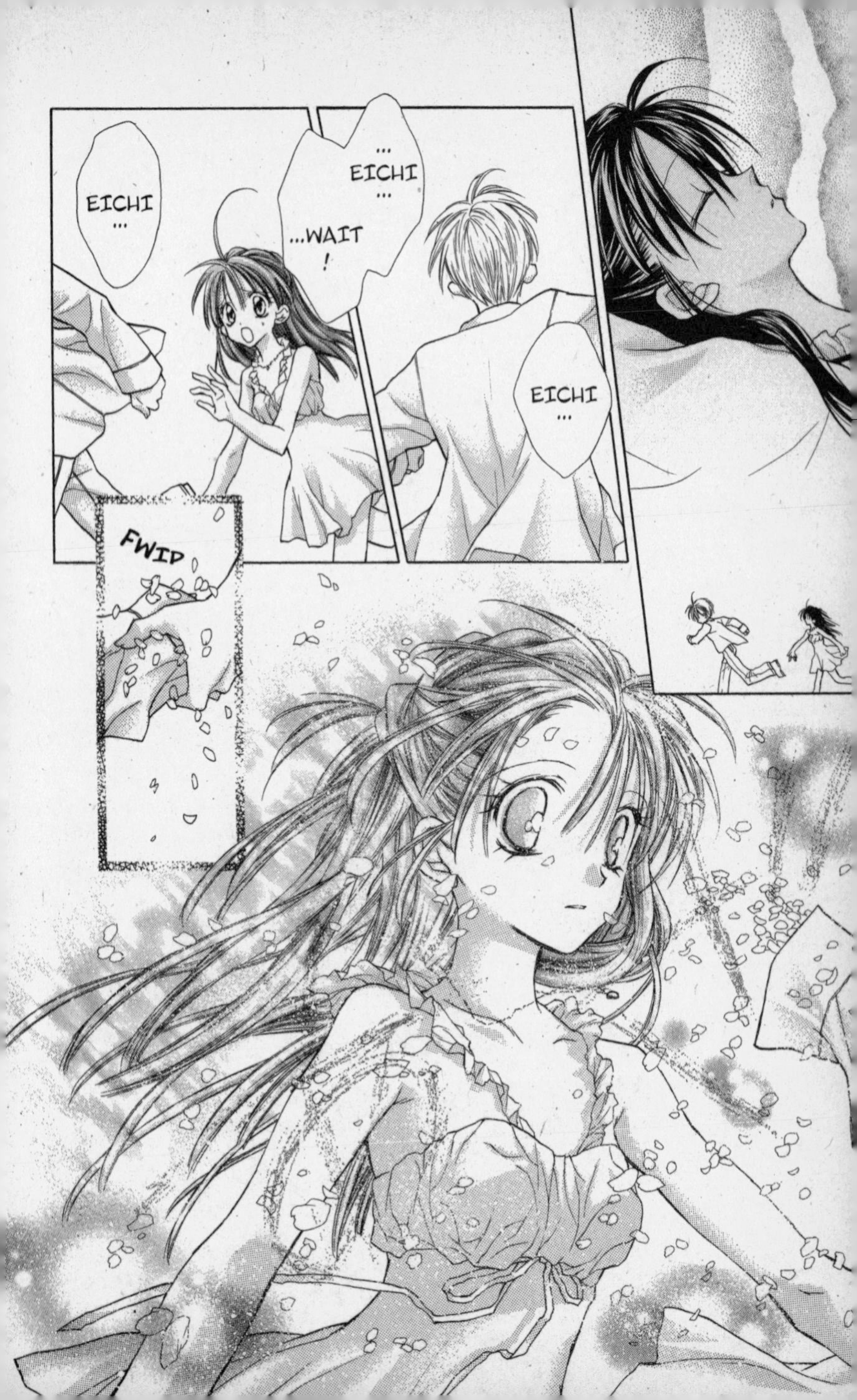
...EICHI...
EICHI...
...WAIT!
EICHI...
FWIP

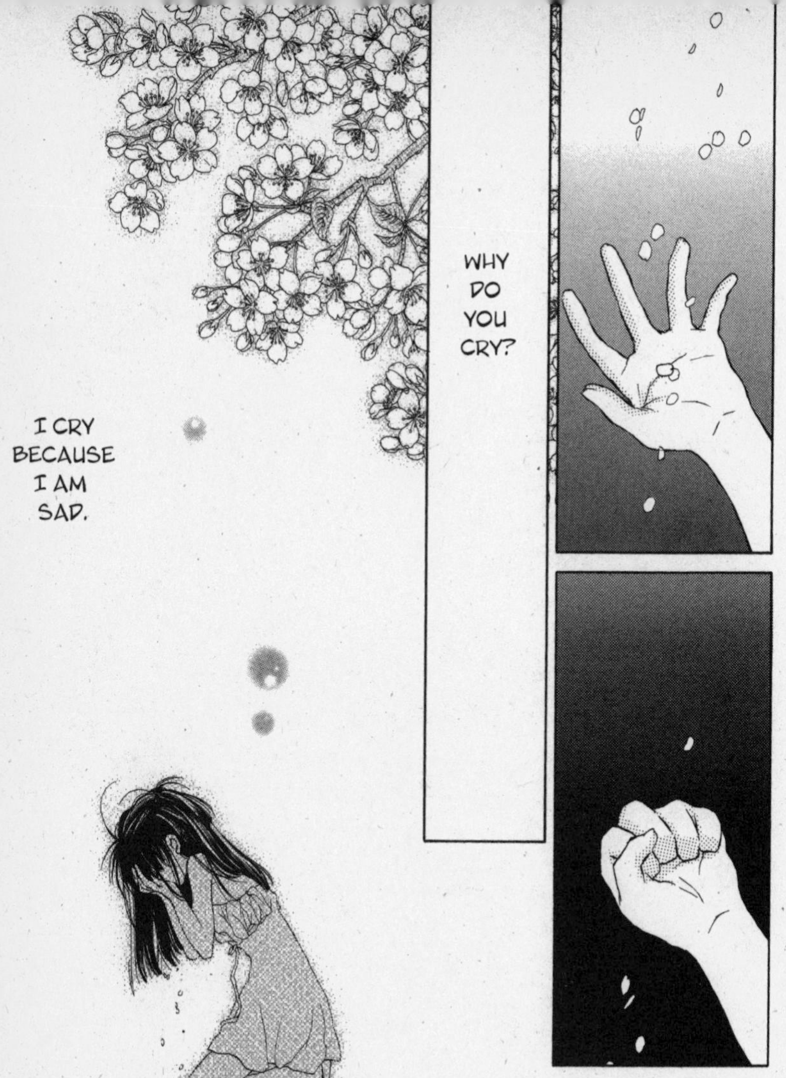
WHY DO YOU CRY?
I CRY BECAUSE I AM SAD.

—END CHAPTER 12—

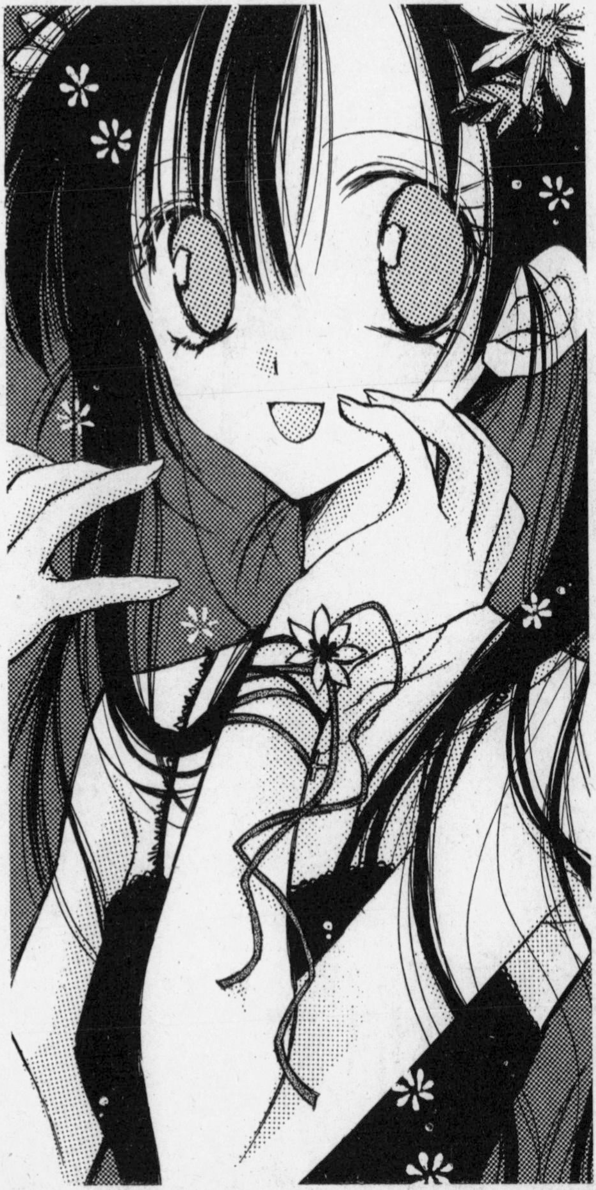

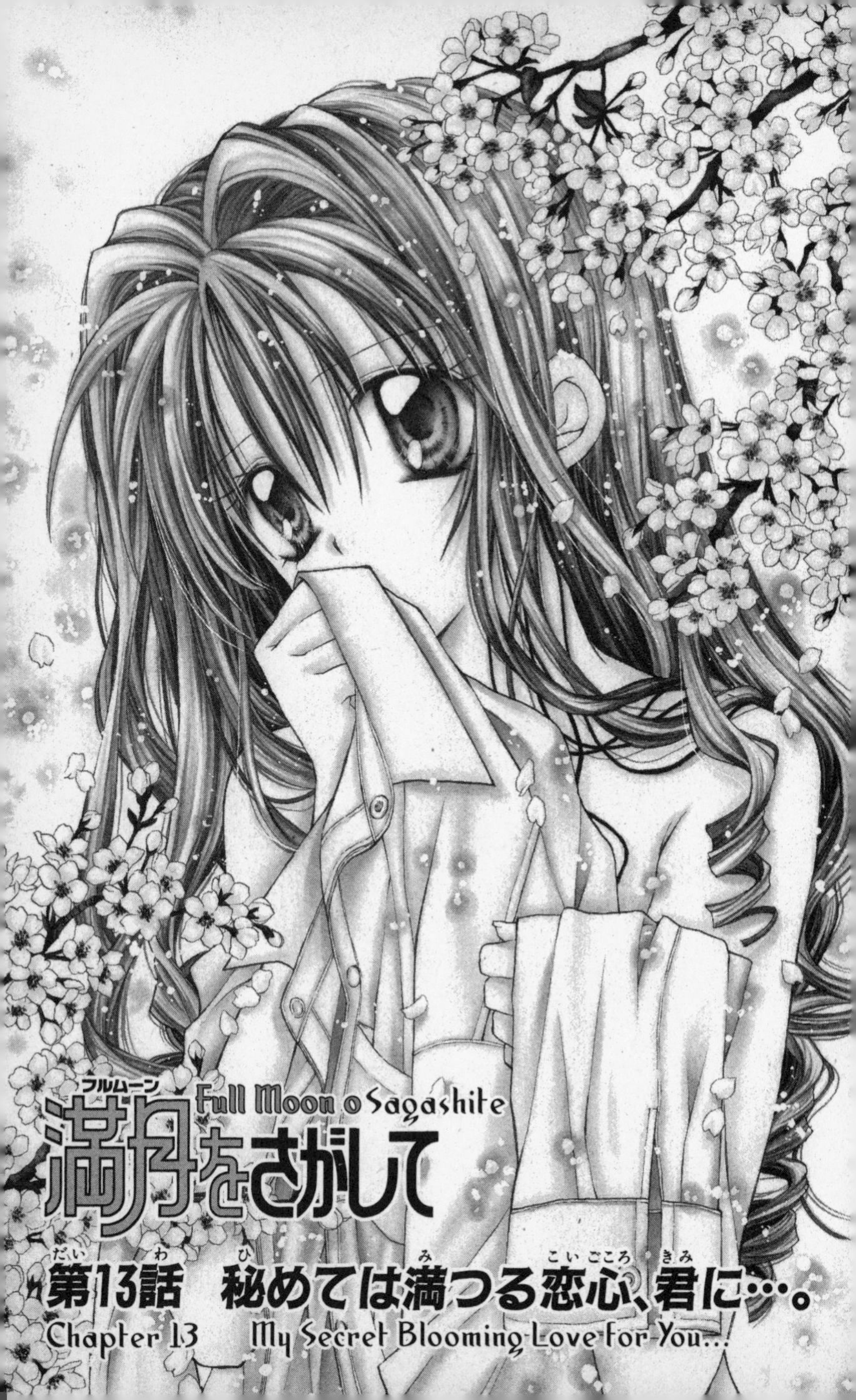
フルムーン
Full Moon o Sagashite
満月をさがして
第13話 秘めては満つる恋心、君に…。
Chapter 13 My Secret Blooming Love for You...

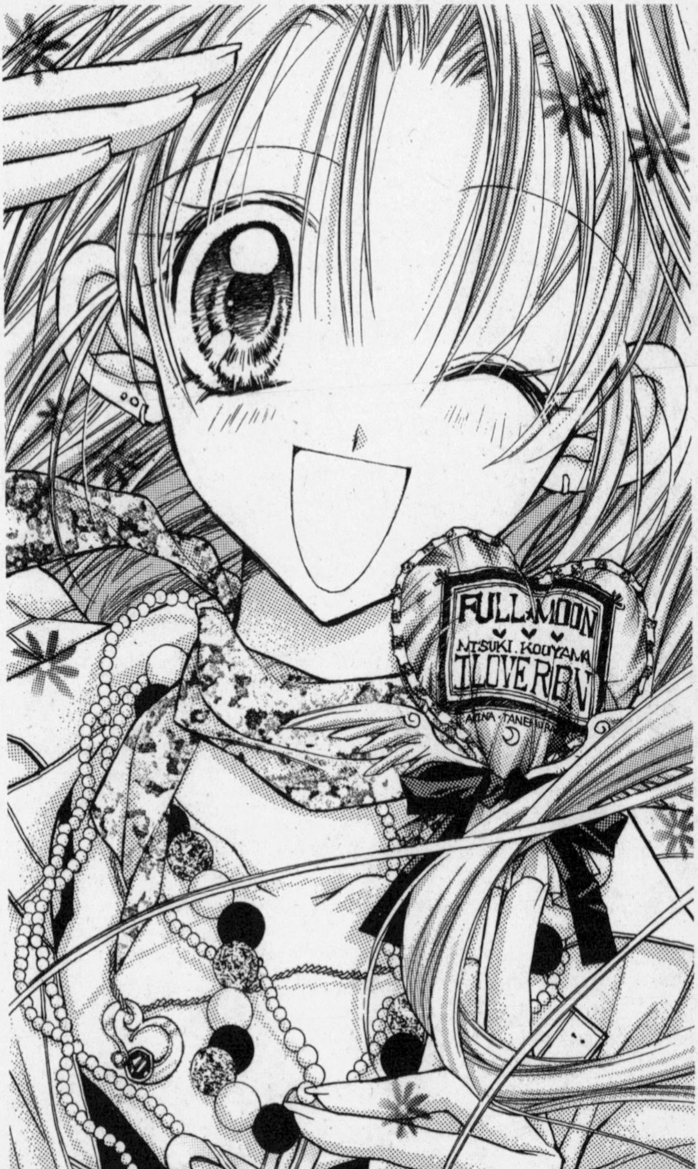
FULL MOON
MTSUKI. KOUYAMA
I LOVE RBN

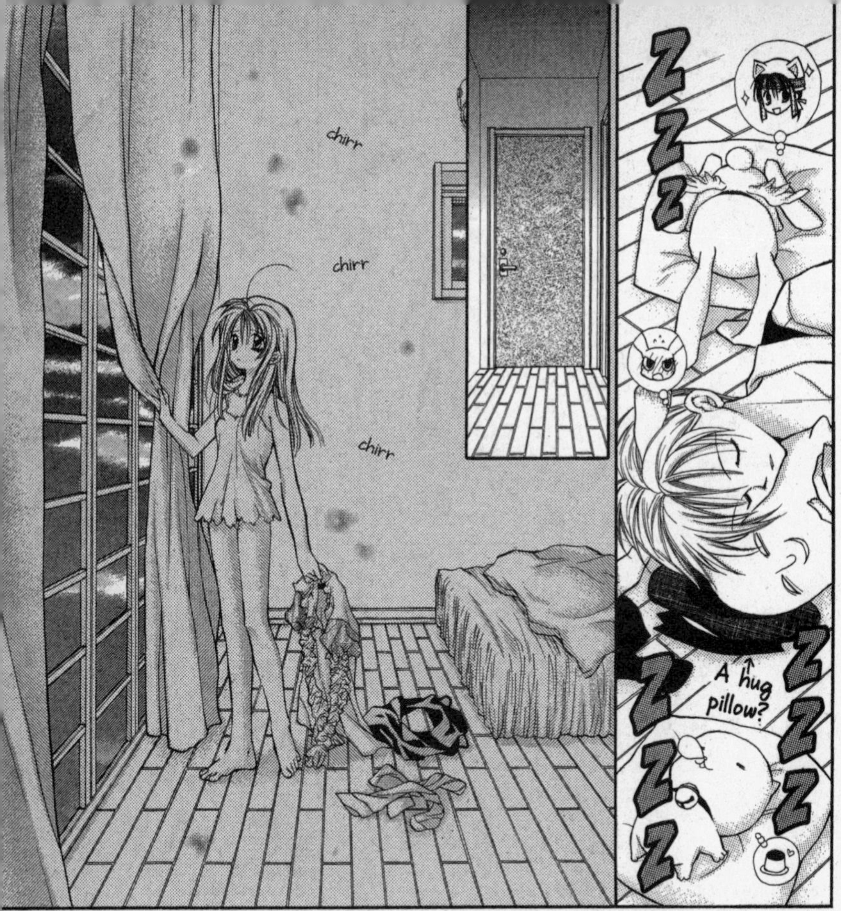
ZZZ
A hug pillow?
ZZZ
ZZZ
chirr
chirr
chirr

Chapter 13 My Secret Blooming Love for You... (spoilers follow)

Cover Copy **Eichi...your scent still holds me tight**

I wrote the cover copy myself. I had strong feelings for this chapter...
The cover illustration is how I perceive Mitsuki. She won't look us in the eye. She can't let go of Eichi's shirt. She can't get away from the cherry blossoms, and she can't look at them.

From the beginning of this series, I had already planned the flow of the story from the ending of the previous chapter up to the ending of this chapter. It was good that I could draw it.

There's nothing more that I can say.
I would like to keep watching Mitsuki-chan's heart by becoming the moon.

I wonder what's going to happen from now on...

Of course I know, but still...

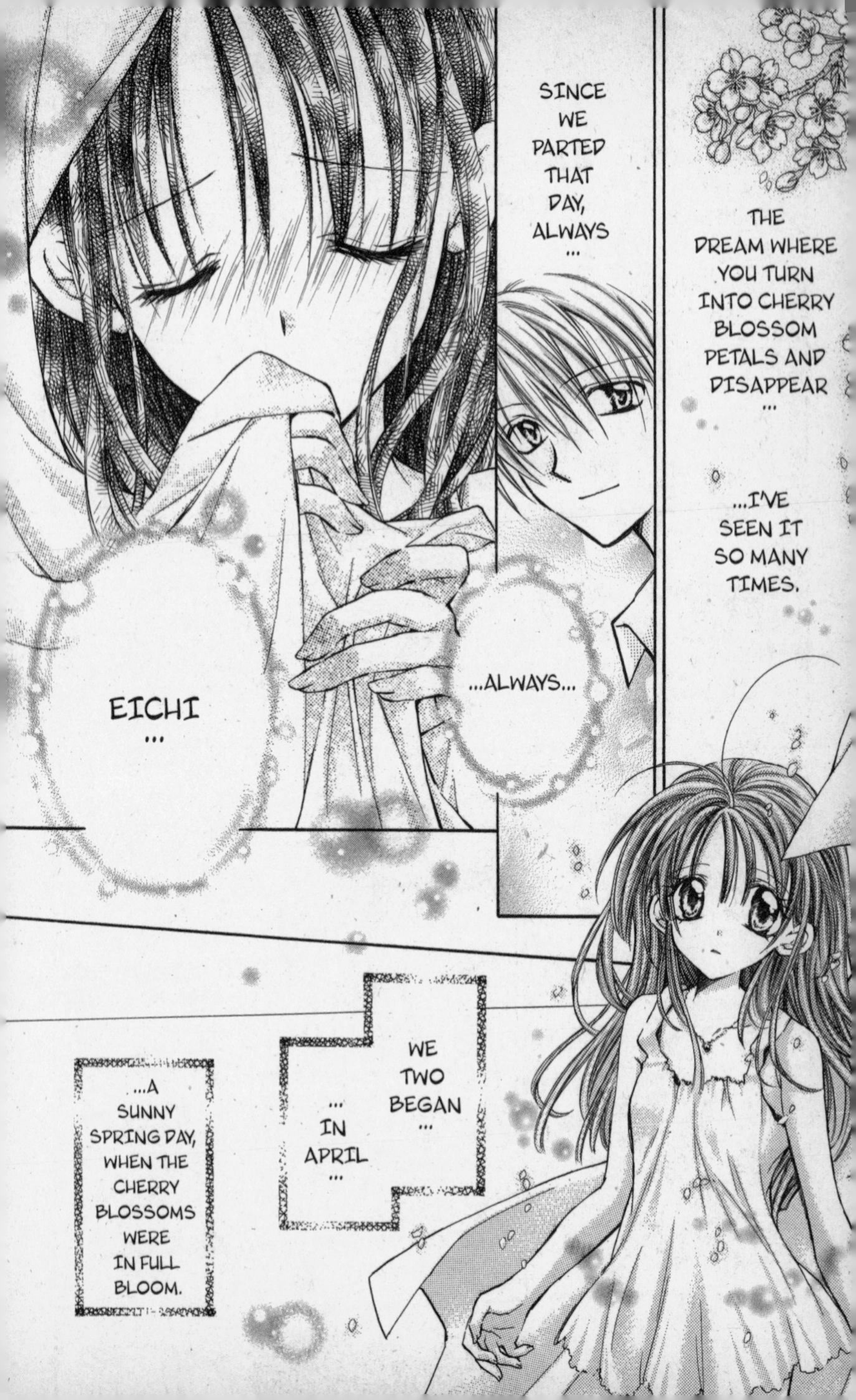
THE DREAM WHERE YOU TURN INTO CHERRY BLOSSOM PETALS AND DISAPPEAR ...
...I'VE SEEN IT SO MANY TIMES.
SINCE WE PARTED THAT DAY, ALWAYS ...
...ALWAYS...
EICHI ...
WE TWO BEGAN ...
... IN APRIL ...
...A SUNNY SPRING DAY, WHEN THE CHERRY BLOSSOMS WERE IN FULL BLOOM.

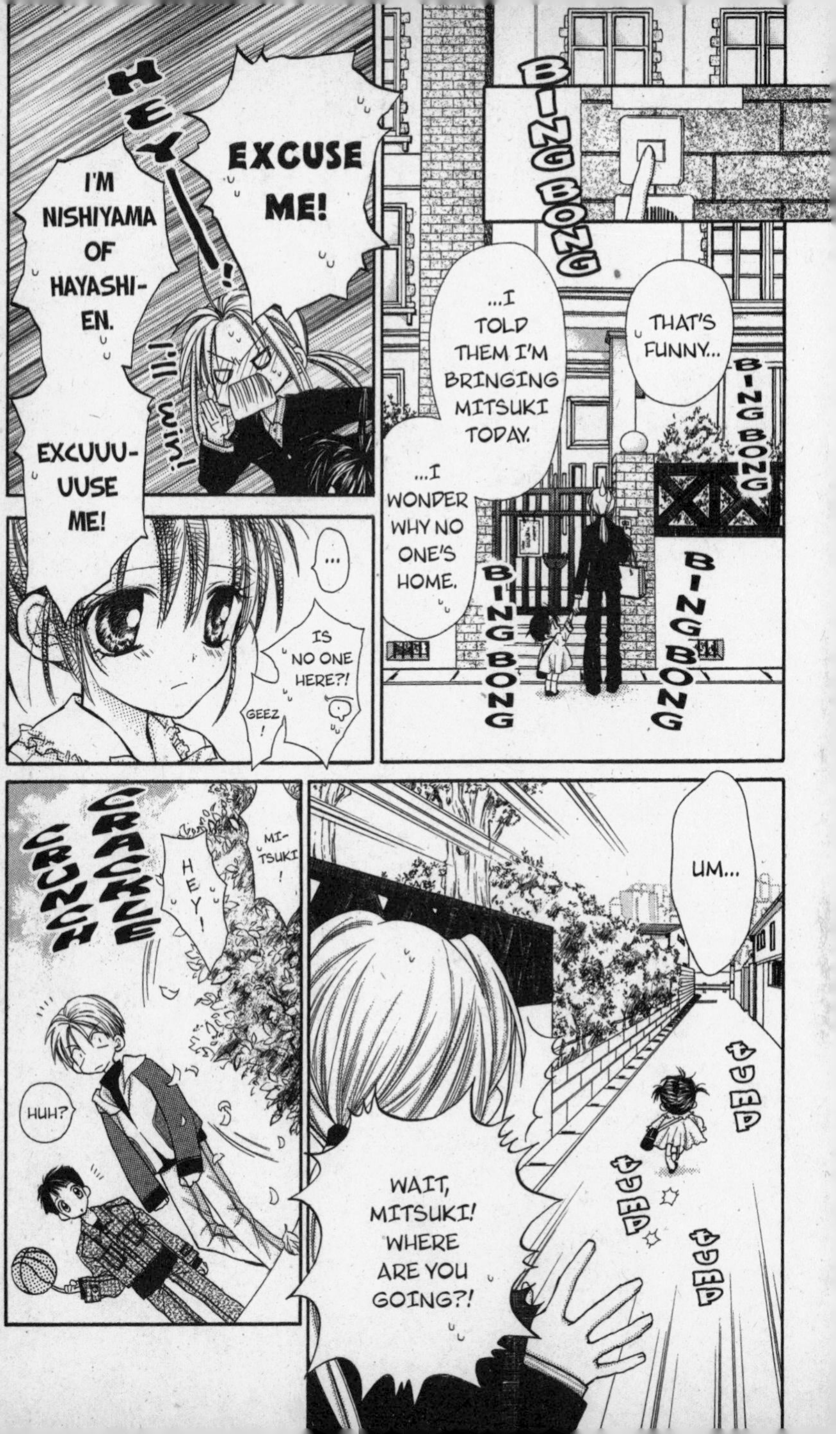
BING BONG
THAT'S FUNNY...
BING BONG
...I TOLD THEM I'M BRINGING MITSUKI TODAY.
...I WONDER WHY NO ONE'S HOME.
BING BONG
BING BONG
EXCUSE ME!
HEY—!
I'M NISHIYAMA OF HAYASHI-EN.
EXCUUU-UUSE ME!
...
IS NO ONE HERE?!
GEEZ!
UM...
TUMP
TUMP
TUMP
WAIT, MITSUKI! WHERE ARE YOU GOING?!
CRACKLE
CRUNCH
MI-TSUKI!
HEY!
HUH?

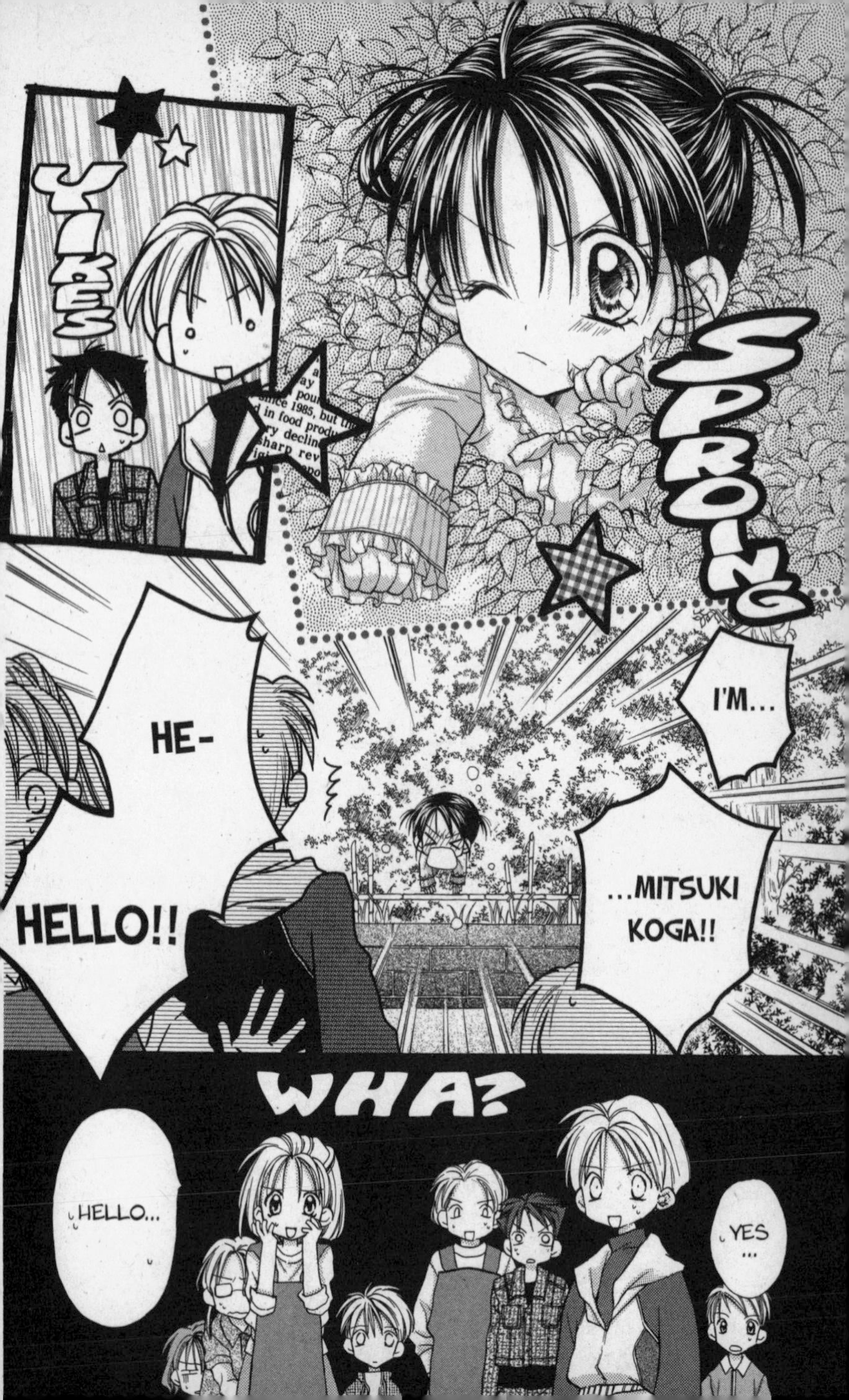
SPRONG
YIKES
I'M...
...MITSUKI KOGA!!
HE-
HELLO!!
WHA?
YES ...
HELLO...

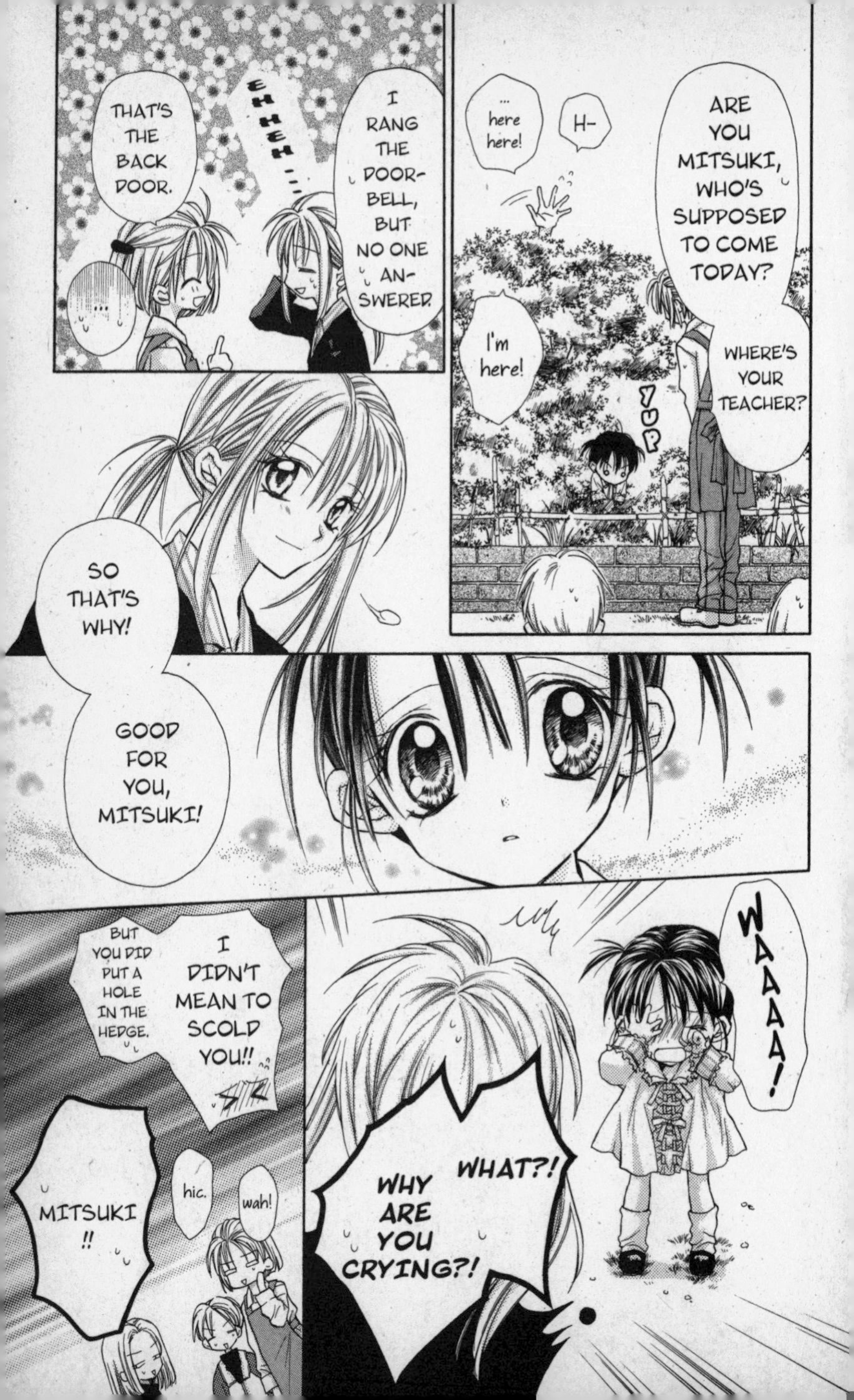
ARE YOU MITSUKI, WHO'S SUPPOSED TO COME TODAY?
H-
... here here!
WHERE'S YOUR TEACHER?
YUP
I'm here!
I RANG THE DOOR-BELL, BUT NO ONE AN-SWERED.
EH HEH...
THAT'S THE BACK DOOR.
...
SO THAT'S WHY!
GOOD FOR YOU, MITSUKI!
WAAAA!
WHAT?!
WHY ARE YOU CRYING?!
I DIDN'T MEAN TO SCOLD YOU!!
BUT YOU DID PUT A HOLE IN THE HEDGE.
wah!
hic.
MITSUKI!!

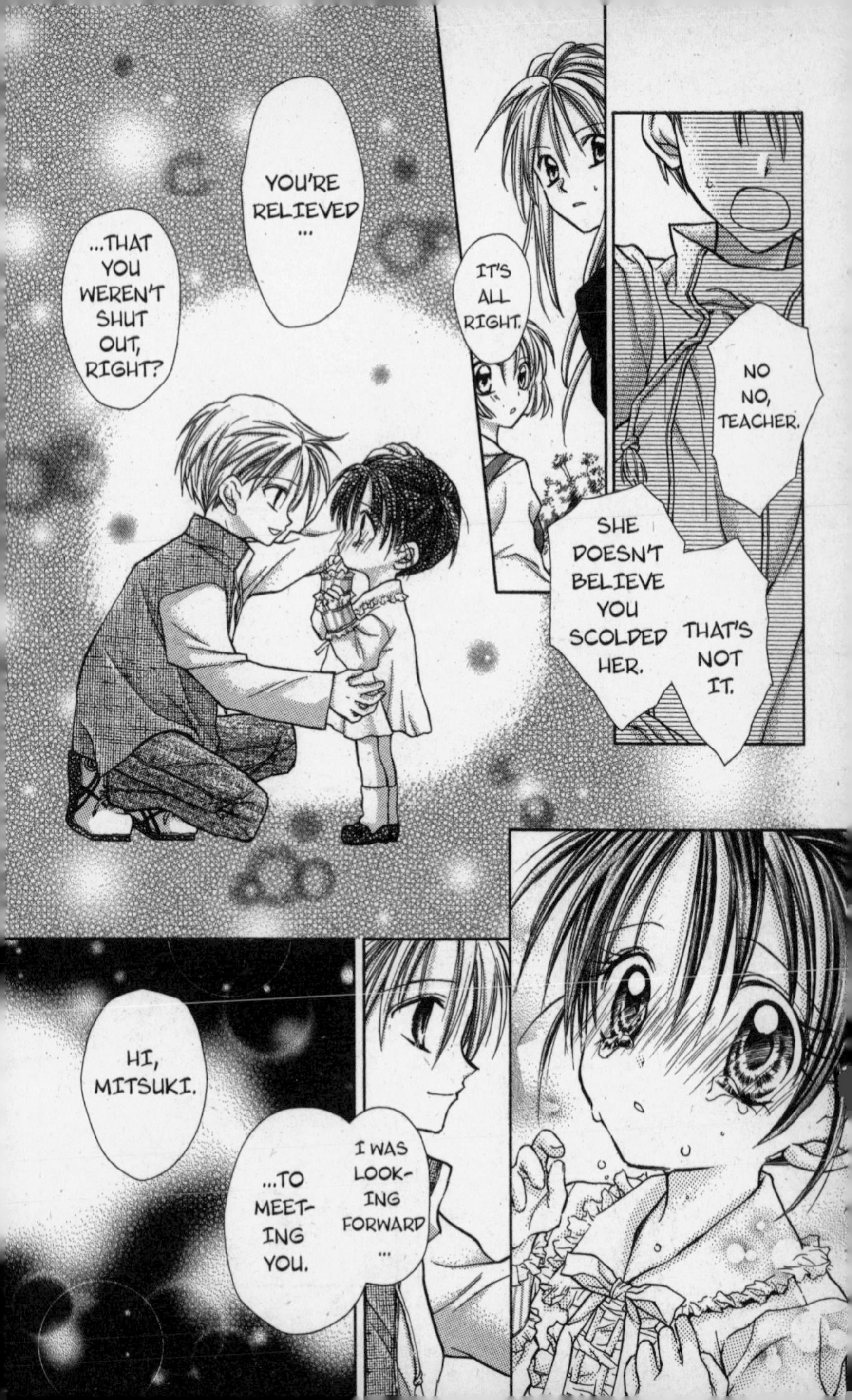
IT'S ALL RIGHT.
SHE DOESN'T BELIEVE YOU SCOLDED HER.
NO NO, TEACHER.
THAT'S NOT IT.
YOU'RE RELIEVED...
...THAT YOU WEREN'T SHUT OUT, RIGHT?
I WAS LOOKING-ING FORWARD...
...TO MEET-ING YOU.
HI, MITSUKI.

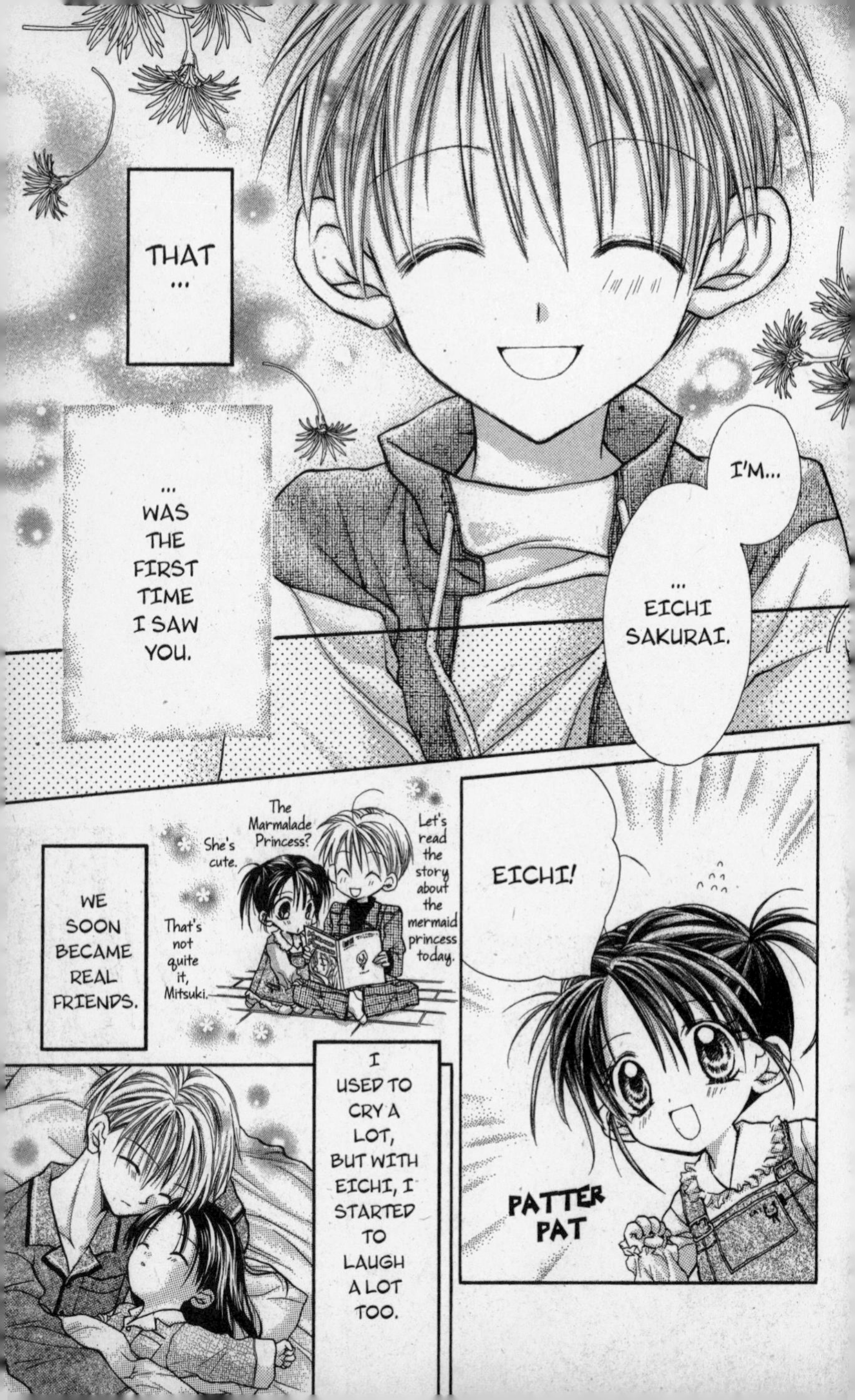
I'M...
... EICHI SAKURAI.
THAT ...
... WAS THE FIRST TIME I SAW YOU.
EICHI!
PATTER PAT
Let's read the story about the mermaid princess today.
The Marmalade Princess?
She's cute.
That's not quite it, Mitsuki.
WE SOON BECAME REAL FRIENDS.
I USED TO CRY A LOT, BUT WITH EICHI, I STARTED TO LAUGH A LOT TOO.

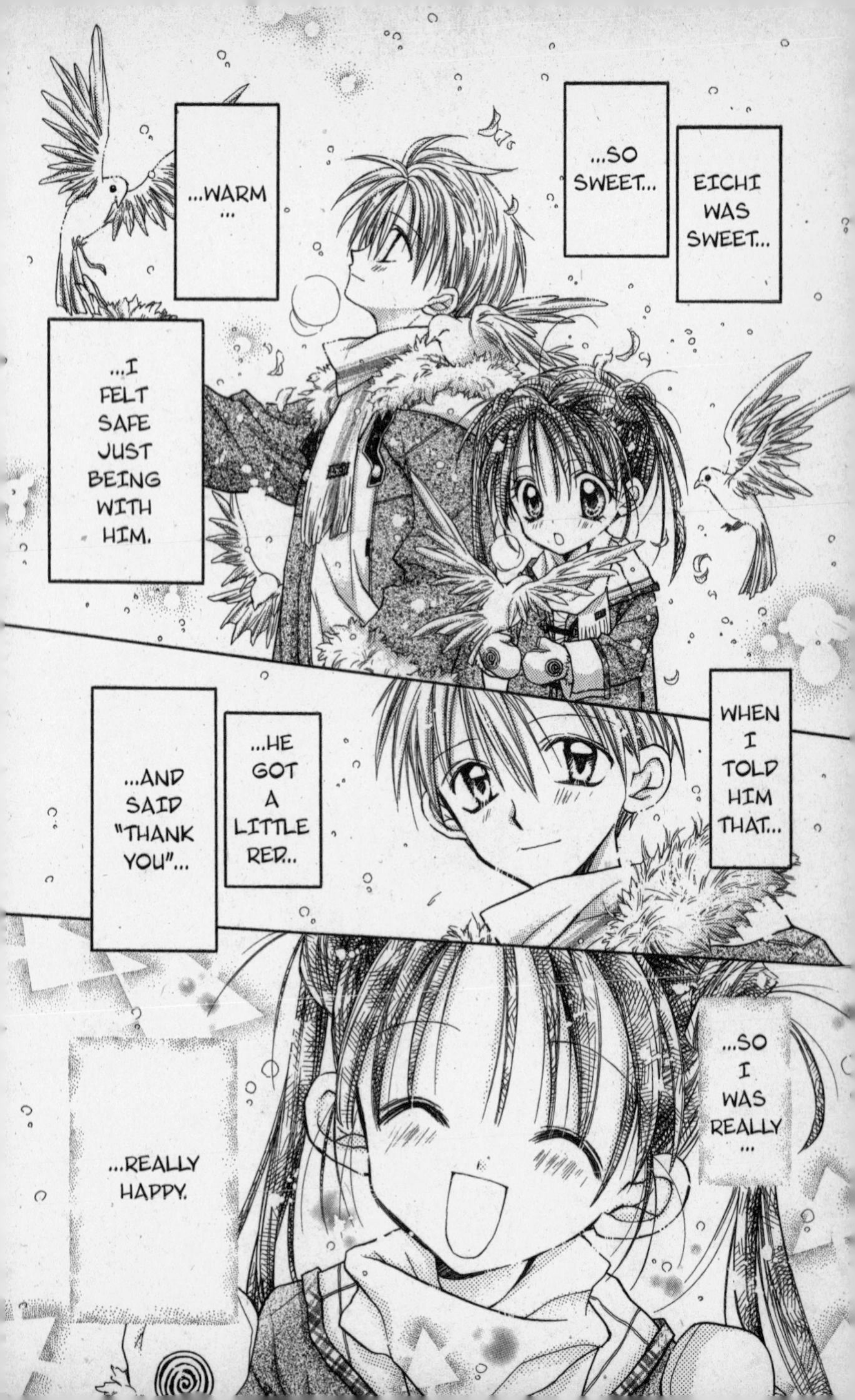
EICHI WAS SWEET...
...SO SWEET...
...WARM ...
...I FELT SAFE JUST BEING WITH HIM.
WHEN I TOLD HIM THAT...
...HE GOT A LITTLE RED...
...AND SAID "THANK YOU"...
...SO I WAS REALLY ...
...REALLY HAPPY.

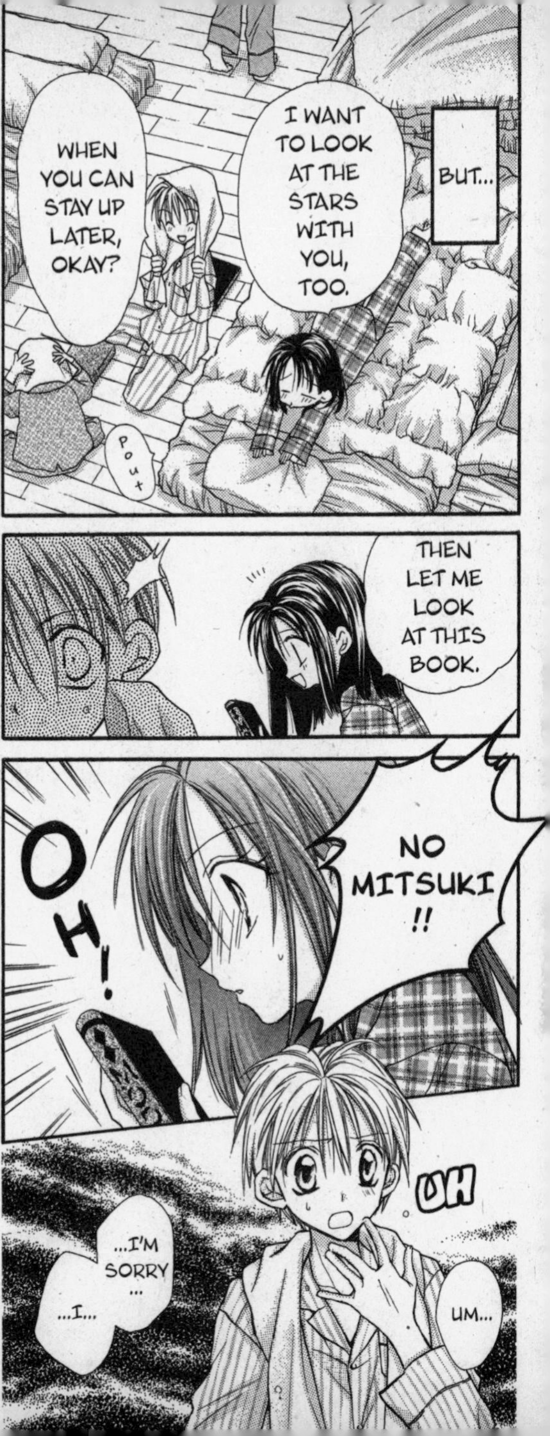
BUT...
I WANT TO LOOK AT THE STARS WITH YOU, TOO.
WHEN YOU CAN STAY UP LATER, OKAY?
Pout
THEN LET ME LOOK AT THIS BOOK.
NO MITSUKI !!
OH!
UH
UM...
...I'M SORRY...
...I...

2 Days Before

I shift into Supersonic-Arina and move at double speed. Inking is a maximum of one hour per page. But I don't want the quality to suffer. Gotta have your way! Arina!!

I return from the bathroom at Mach 5.

Because of fatigue, everybody sleeps like they're dead.

Nikisama sleeping, pointing. I found this impressive.

hee hee hee

She finally managed to play the Divine Move.

1 Day Before

Inking sometimes takes a little more time, if the hair is all black, or depending on the panel layout (and my condition), so I catch up here. ~...

But usually I don't have any problems keeping healthy. The only thing I can't win against is "that thing"...oops So there's no worry. I'd rather not sleep than drink Mocha.

Heh

A bad-tasting caffeine drink.

Deadline

Um.......................
....
....
.... hell?

Second Impact?

The danger zone approaches. Everybody gets out of control.

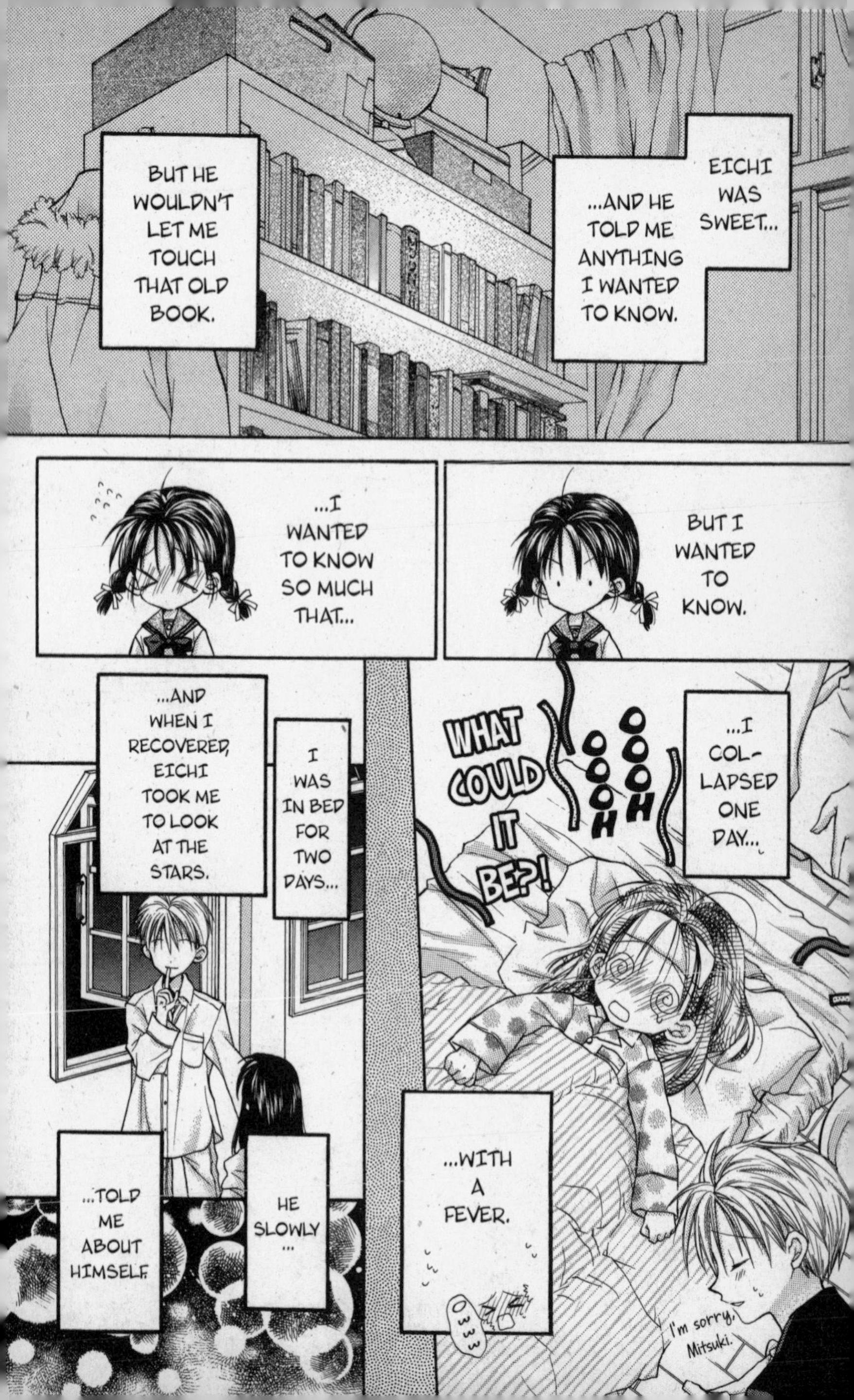
EICHI WAS SWEET...
...AND HE TOLD ME ANYTHING I WANTED TO KNOW.
BUT HE WOULDN'T LET ME TOUCH THAT OLD BOOK.
BUT I WANTED TO KNOW.
...I WANTED TO KNOW SO MUCH THAT...
...I COL-LAPSED ONE DAY...
OOOOH OOOH
WHAT COULD IT BE?!
...WITH A FEVER.
I'm sorry, Mitsuki.
I WAS IN BED FOR TWO DAYS...
...AND WHEN I RECOVERED, EICHI TOOK ME TO LOOK AT THE STARS.
HE SLOWLY...
...TOLD ME ABOUT HIMSELF.

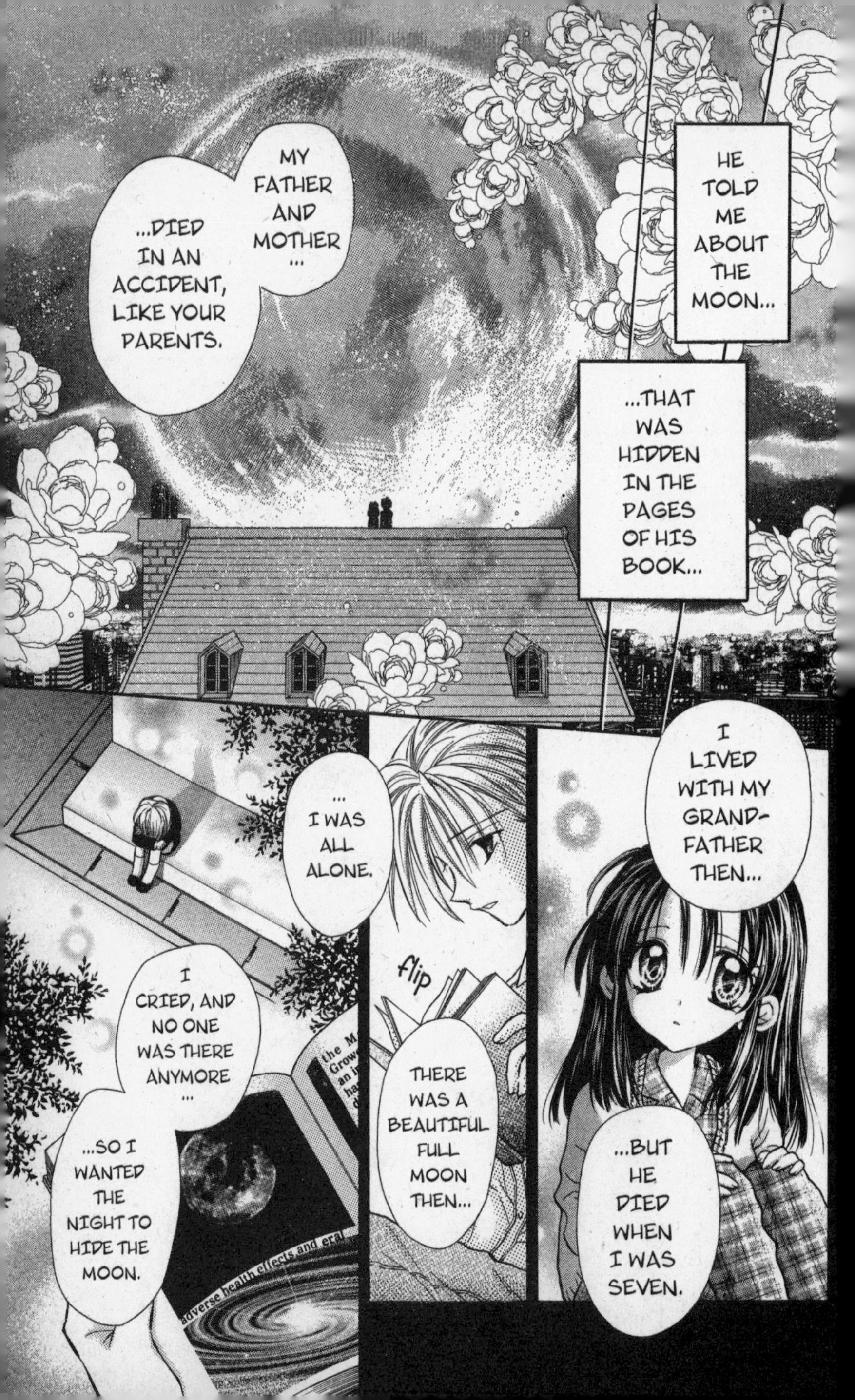
HE TOLD ME ABOUT THE MOON...
...THAT WAS HIDDEN IN THE PAGES OF HIS BOOK...
MY FATHER AND MOTHER...
...DIED IN AN ACCIDENT, LIKE YOUR PARENTS.
I LIVED WITH MY GRANDFATHER THEN...
...BUT HE DIED WHEN I WAS SEVEN.
... I WAS ALL ALONE.
flip
THERE WAS A BEAUTIFUL FULL MOON THEN...
I CRIED, AND NO ONE WAS THERE ANYMORE...
...SO I WANTED THE NIGHT TO HIDE THE MOON.

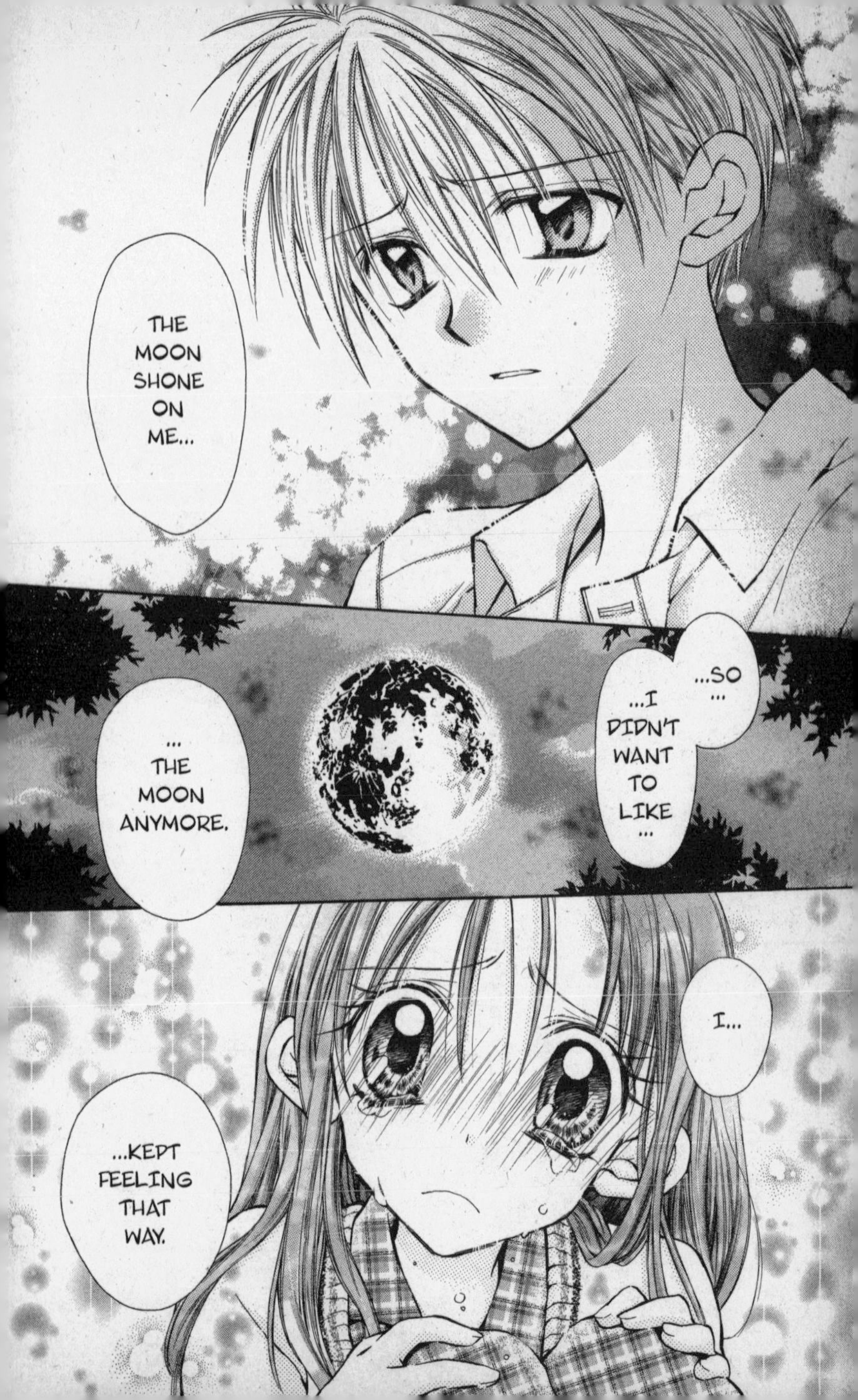
THE MOON SHONE ON ME...
...SO ...
...I DIDN'T WANT TO LIKE ...
... THE MOON ANYMORE.
I...
...KEPT FEELING THAT WAY.

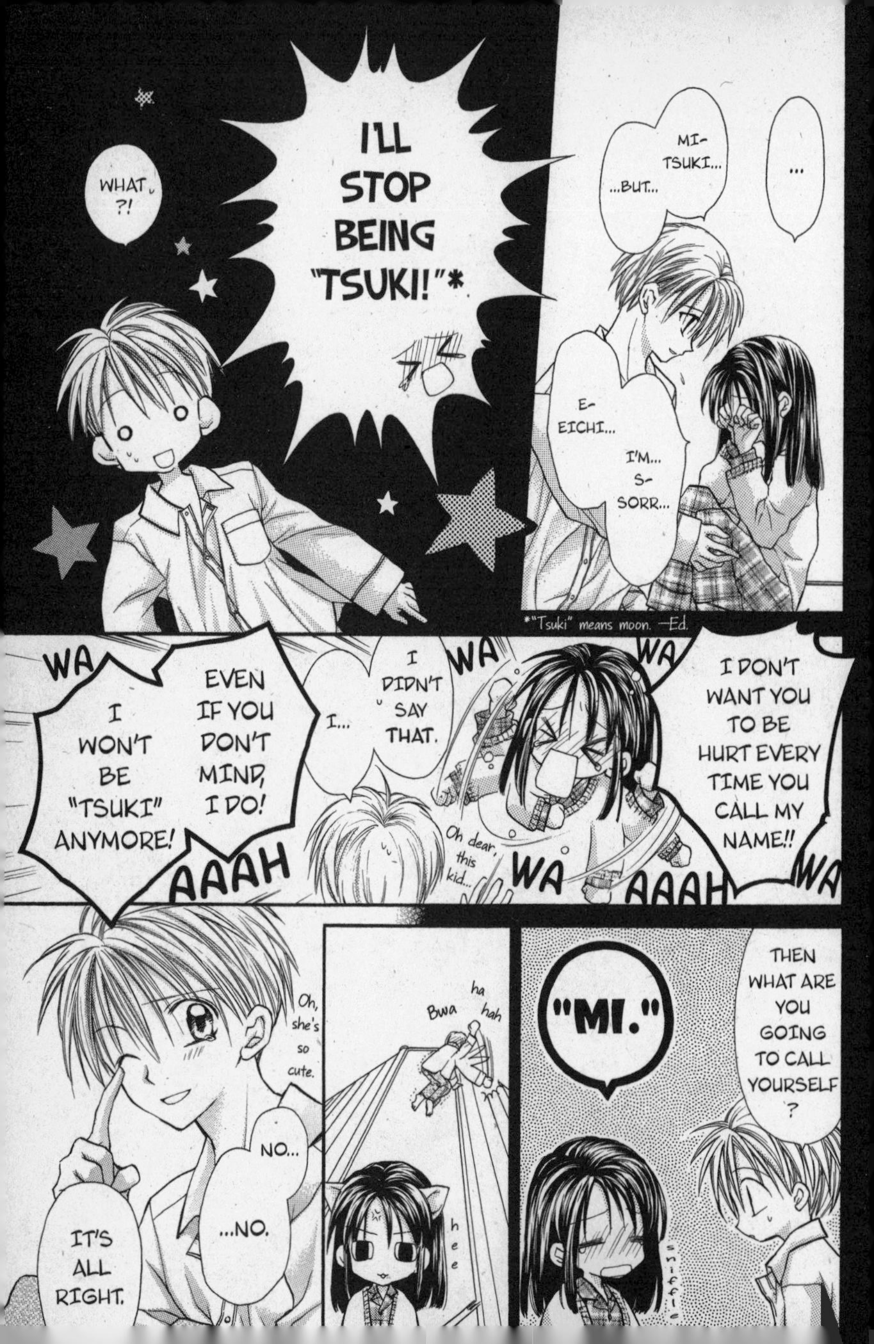
...
MI-TSUKI...
...BUT...
E-EICHI...
I'M... S-SORR...
I'LL STOP BEING "TSUKI!"*
WHAT?!
*"Tsuki" means moon. —Ed.
I DON'T WANT YOU TO BE HURT EVERY TIME YOU CALL MY NAME!!
WA
WA
WA
AAAH
WA
I DIDN'T SAY THAT.
I...
Oh dear, this kid...
EVEN IF YOU DON'T MIND, I DO!
I WON'T BE "TSUKI" ANYMORE!
WA
AAAH
THEN WHAT ARE YOU GOING TO CALL YOURSELF?
"MI."
sniffle
Bwa ha hah
hee
Oh, she's so cute.
NO...
...NO.
IT'S ALL RIGHT.

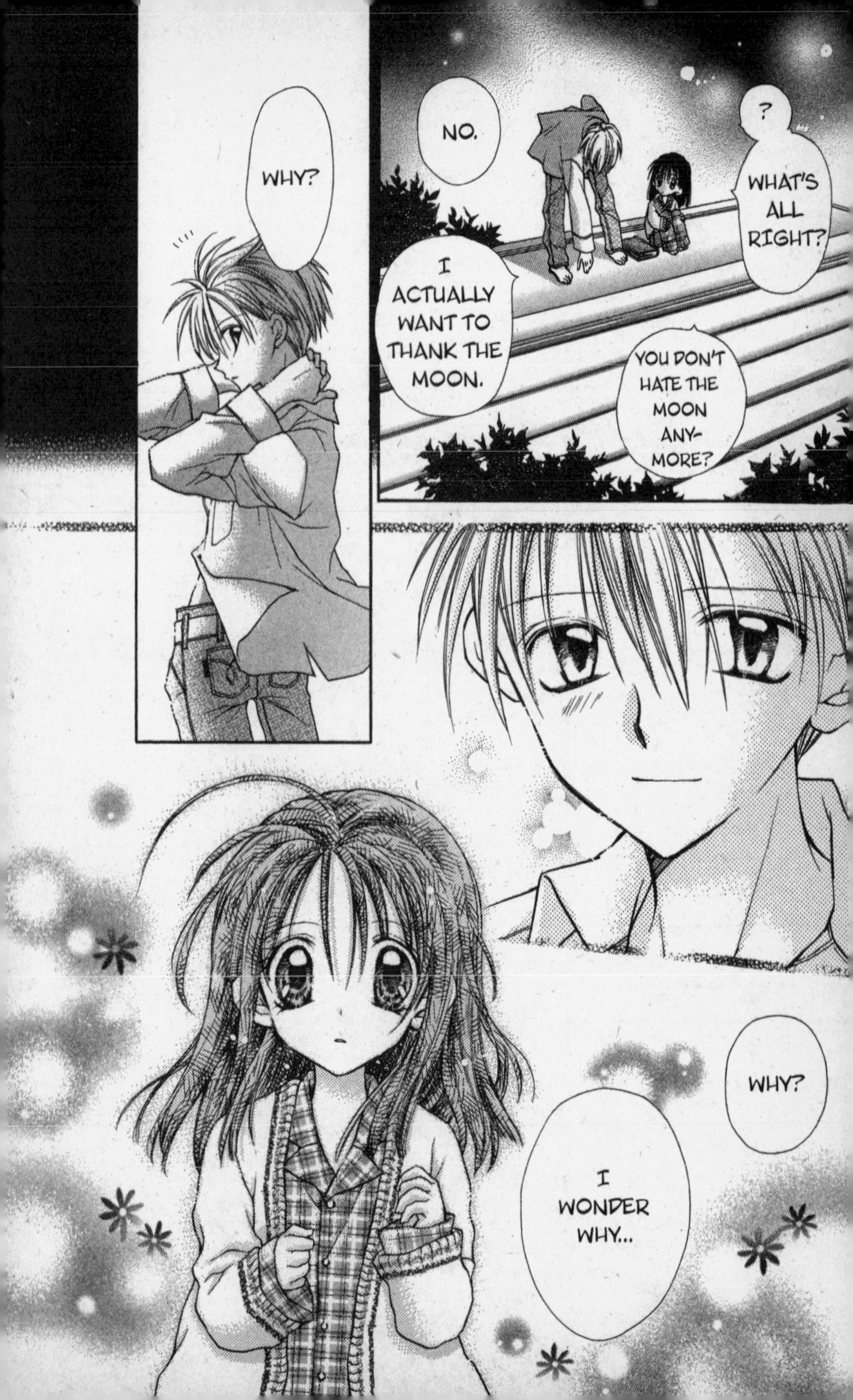
?
WHAT'S ALL RIGHT?
YOU DON'T HATE THE MOON ANY-MORE?
NO.
I ACTUALLY WANT TO THANK THE MOON.
WHY?
WHY?
I WONDER WHY...

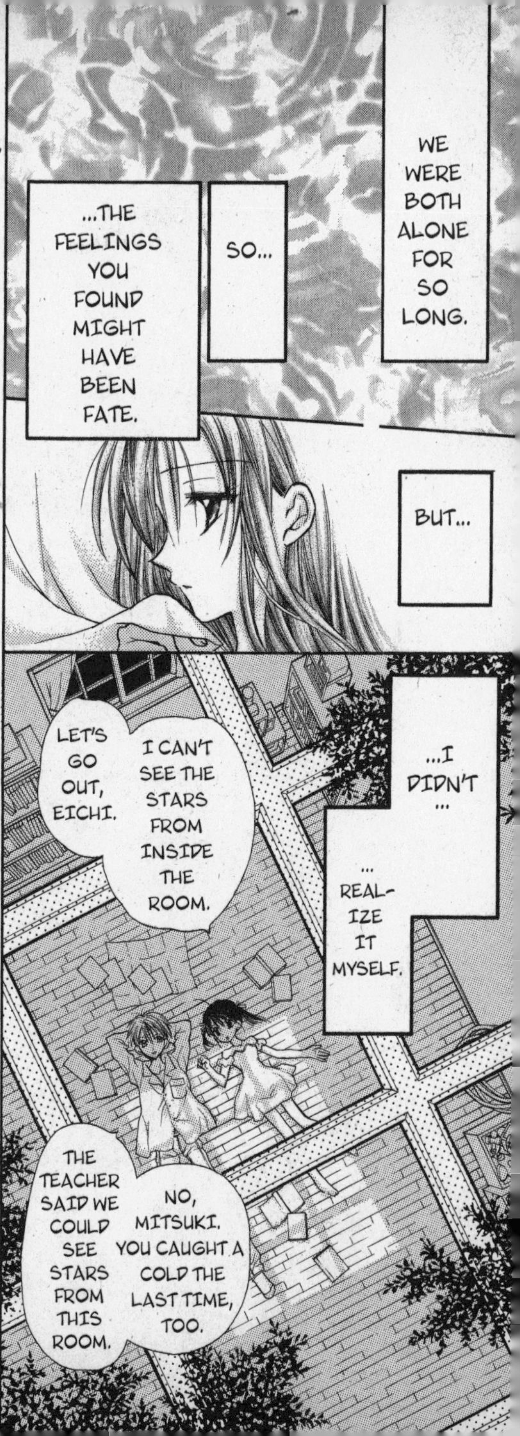
WE WERE BOTH ALONE FOR SO LONG.
SO...
...THE FEELINGS YOU FOUND MIGHT HAVE BEEN FATE.
BUT...
...I DIDN'T ...
... REAL-IZE IT MYSELF.
I CAN'T SEE THE STARS FROM INSIDE THE ROOM.
LET'S GO OUT, EICHI.
NO, MITSUKI. YOU CAUGHT A COLD THE LAST TIME, TOO.
THE TEACHER SAID WE COULD SEE STARS FROM THIS ROOM.

Well, was the "carnage" diary interesting? I really hate "carnage." Okay, see you. ♪

No, that's not true. I actually like working under that pressure.

I'm in danger now, too.
There's lots of work to do.
It's tough...
But fun...
I'm a masochist.

Special Thanks ☆

- Kanan Kiseki — Black joke happening. ♡
- Niki Seisou — Mysterious sleeping beauty.
- Kaya Asano — Yucchin Jyu R Yen, Time is Money!!
- Kyakya Asano — A coquettish Santa Claus. ♪
- Airi Teito — Toro melty chocolate. ♡
- Ai Minase — A joking idol.
- Rina Asuka — Anemic eating girl.
- Miwa Sawakami — Pote-miichan.
- Ruka Kaduki — Oh, "that."
- Konako — To where?
- Akoko Asakura — Well then, Karin.

Ribon Dept. and Koike-san!

Thank you so much! I love you all!

Chu!

Ammonite Limited

See you in Volume 4!!

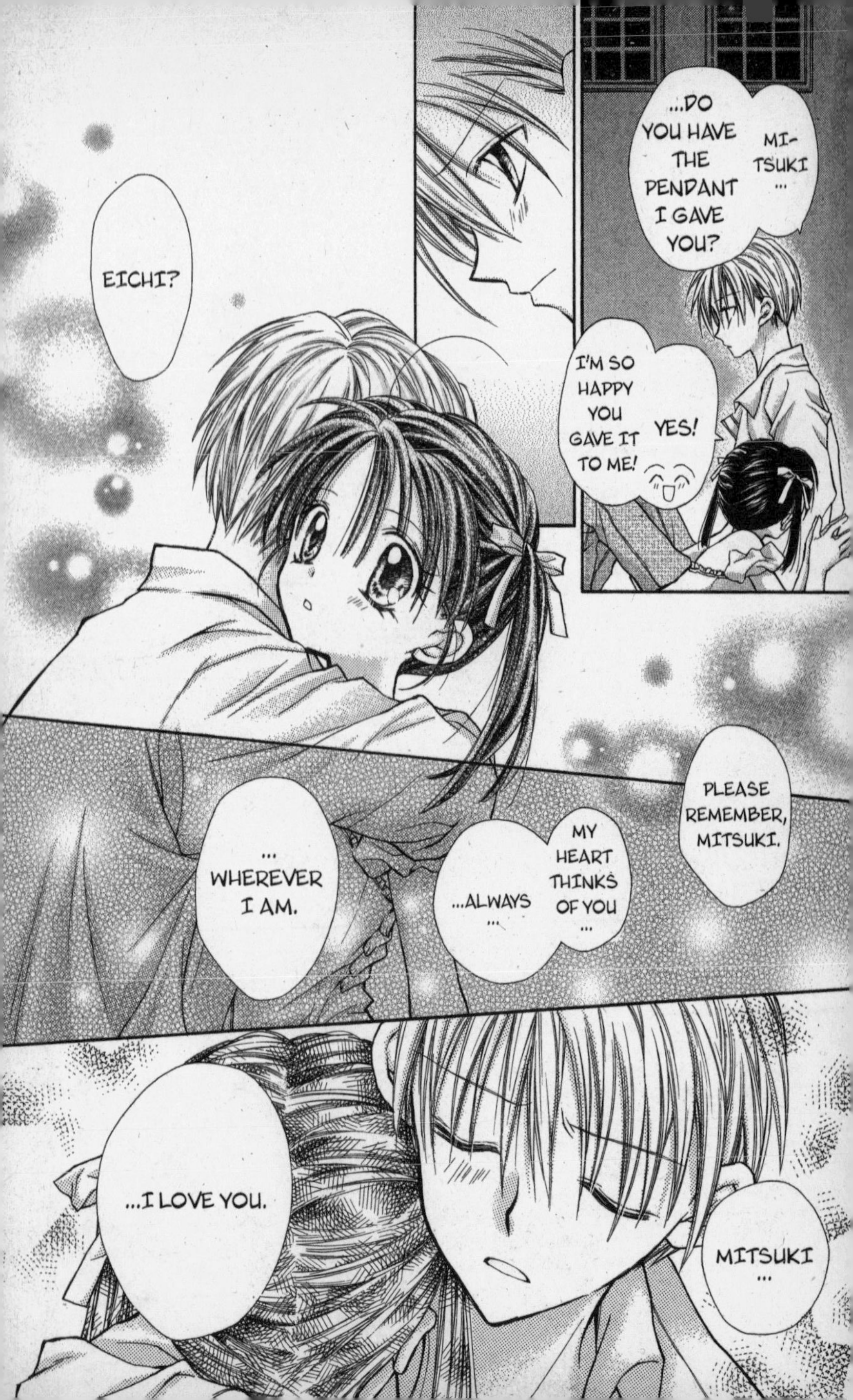
MI-TSUKI ...
...DO YOU HAVE THE PENDANT I GAVE YOU?
YES!
I'M SO HAPPY YOU GAVE IT TO ME!
EICHI?
PLEASE REMEMBER, MITSUKI.
MY HEART THINKS OF YOU ...
...ALWAYS ...
... WHEREVER I AM.
MITSUKI ...
...I LOVE YOU.

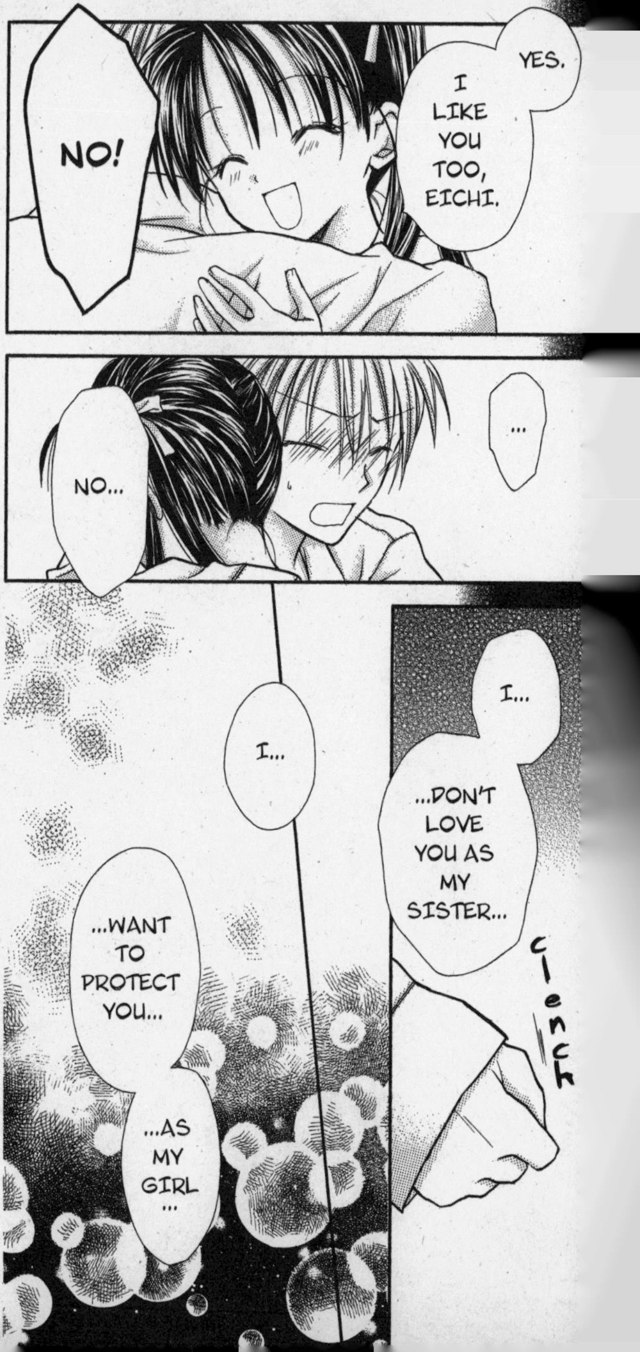
YES.
I LIKE YOU TOO, EICHI.
NO!
...
NO...
I...
...DON'T LOVE YOU AS MY SISTER...
clench
I...
...WANT TO PROTECT YOU...
...AS MY GIRL ...

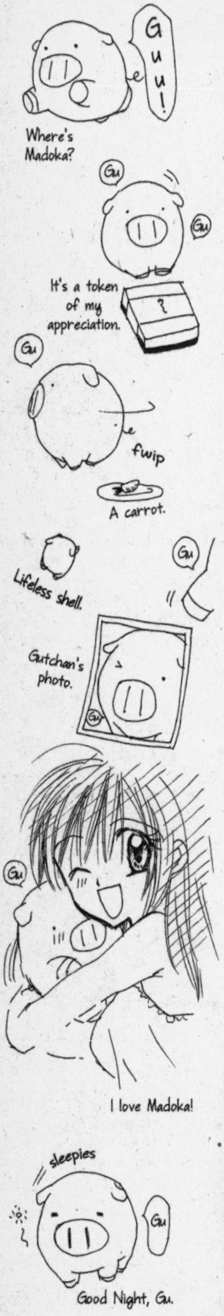
Guuu!
Where's Madoka?
Gu
Gu
It's a token of my appreciation.
?
Gu
fwip
A carrot.
Gu
Lifeless shell.
Gutchan's photo.
Gu
Gu
I love Madoka!
sleepies
Gu
Good Night, Gu.

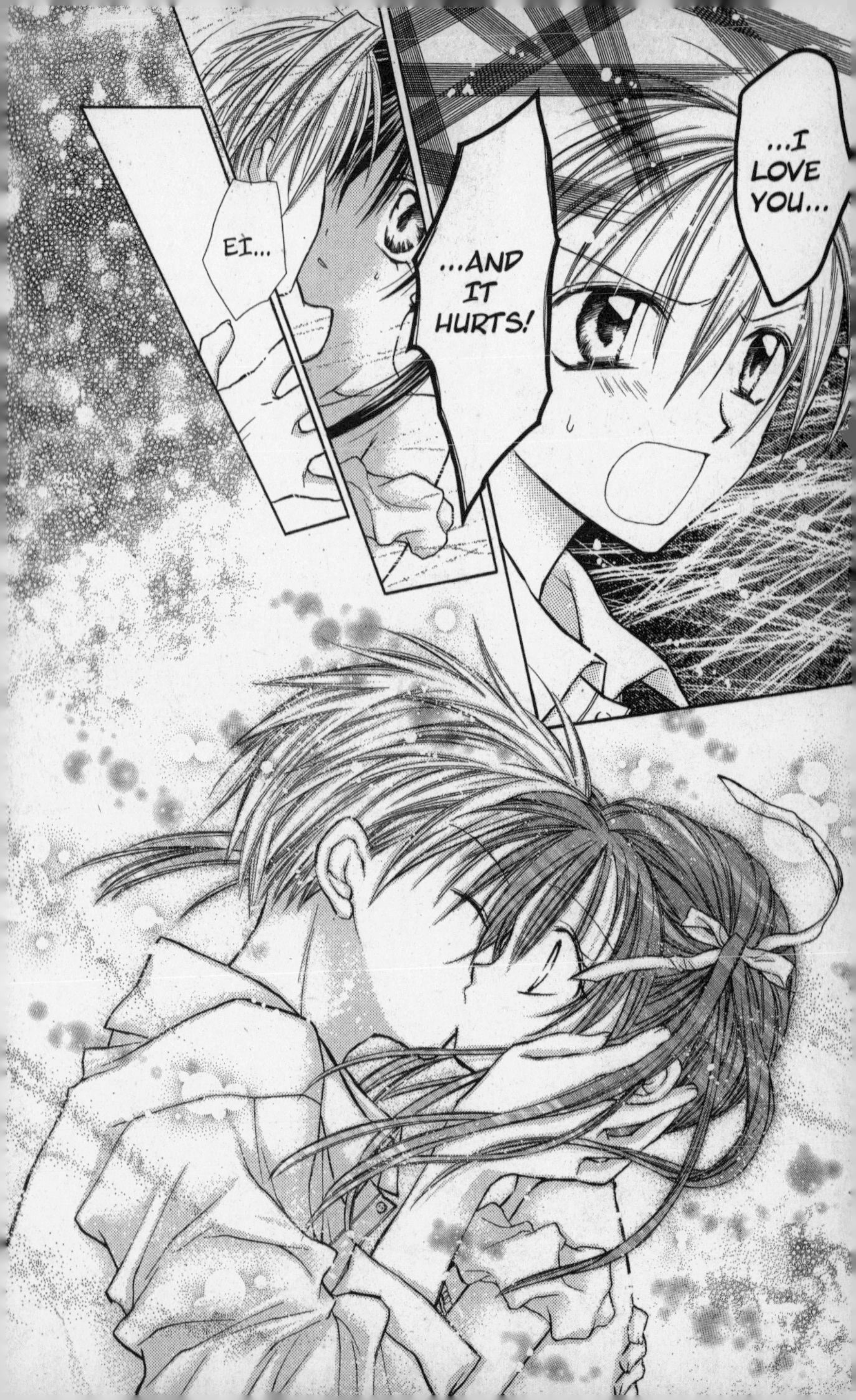
...I LOVE YOU...
...AND IT HURTS!
EI...

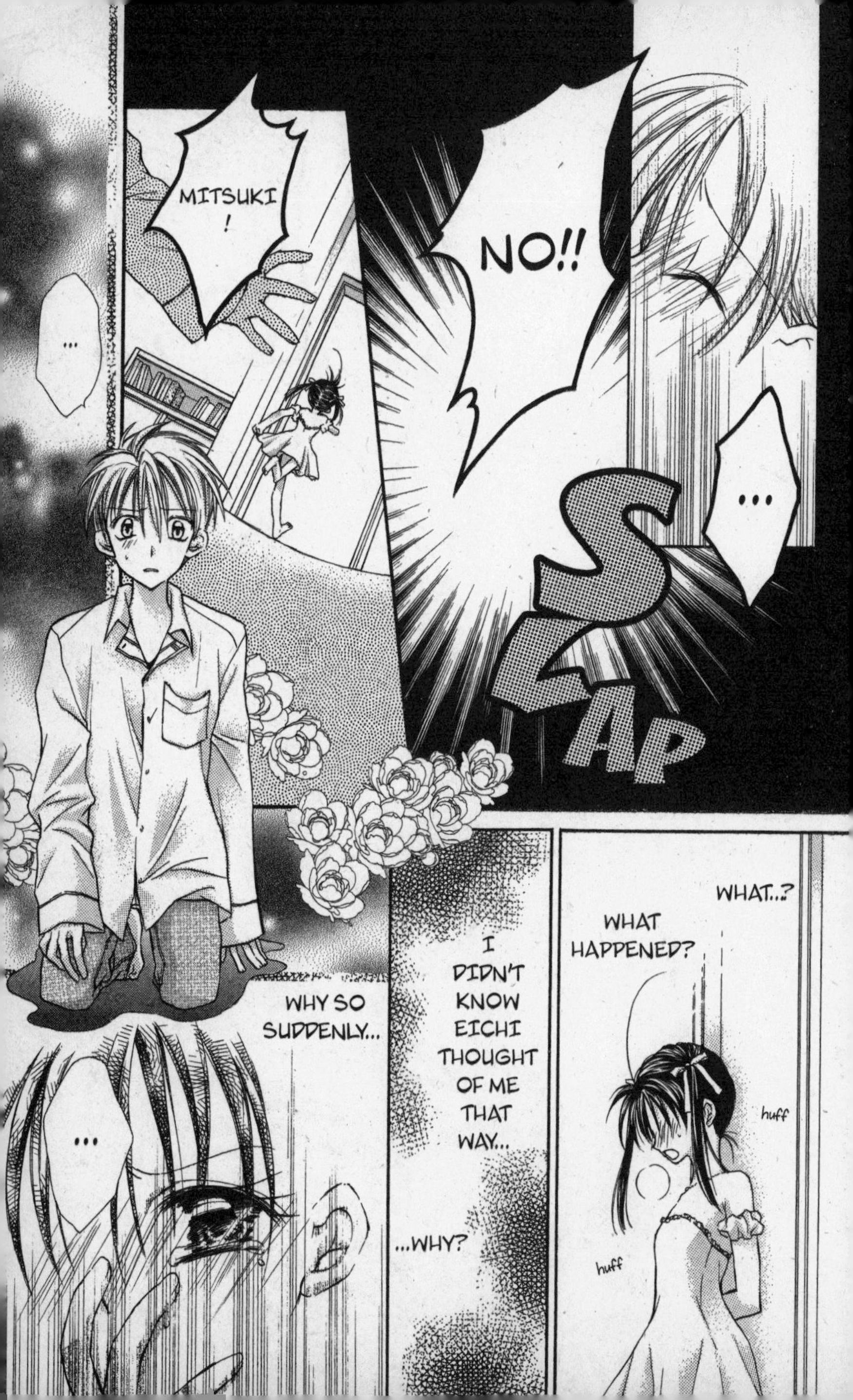
NO!!
...
SLAP
MITSUKI!
...
WHAT..?
WHAT HAPPENED?
huff
huff
I DIDN'T KNOW EICHI THOUGHT OF ME THAT WAY...
...WHY?
WHY SO SUDDENLY...
...

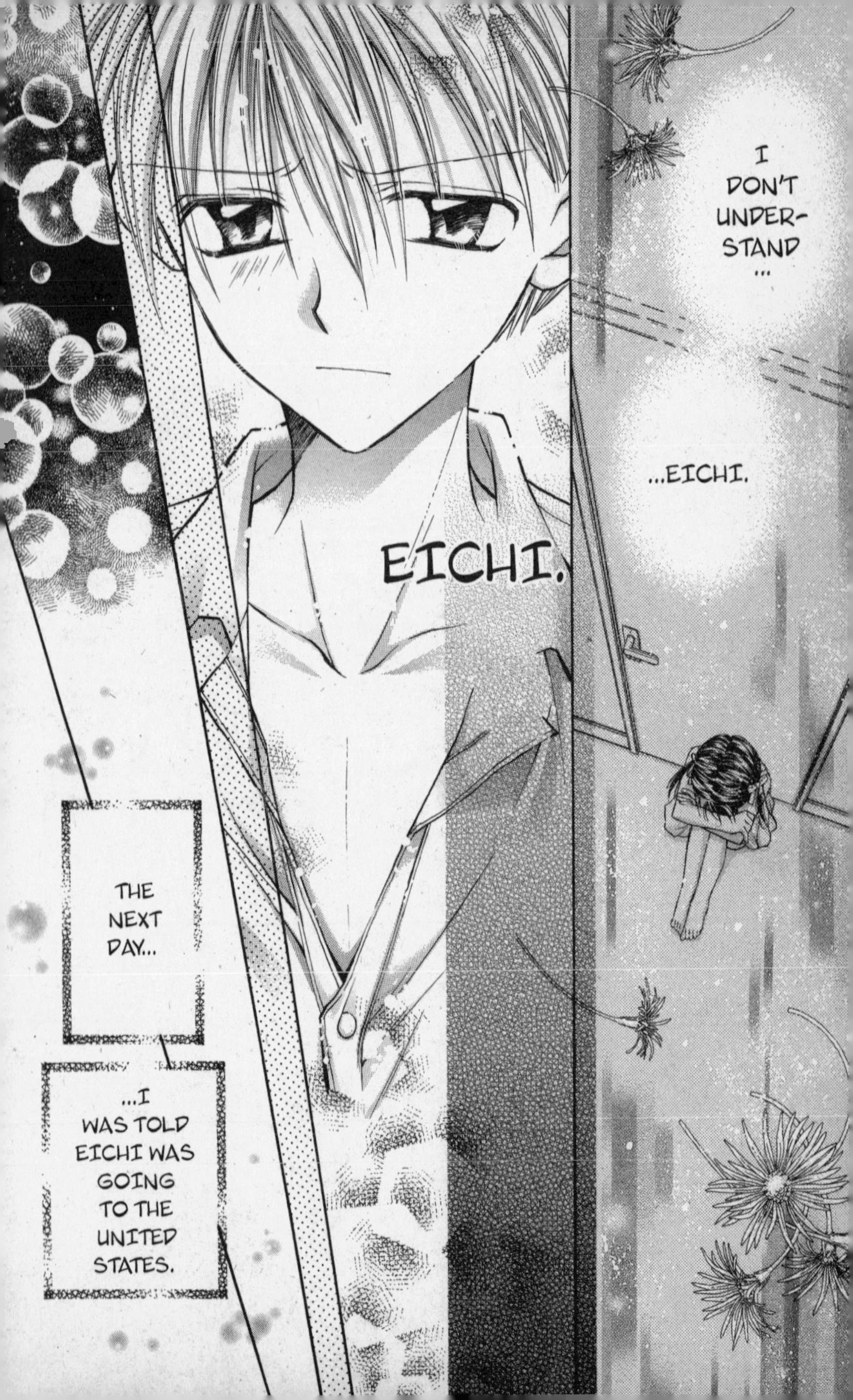
I DON'T UNDERSTAND ...
...EICHI.
EICHI.
THE NEXT DAY...
...I WAS TOLD EICHI WAS GOING TO THE UNITED STATES.

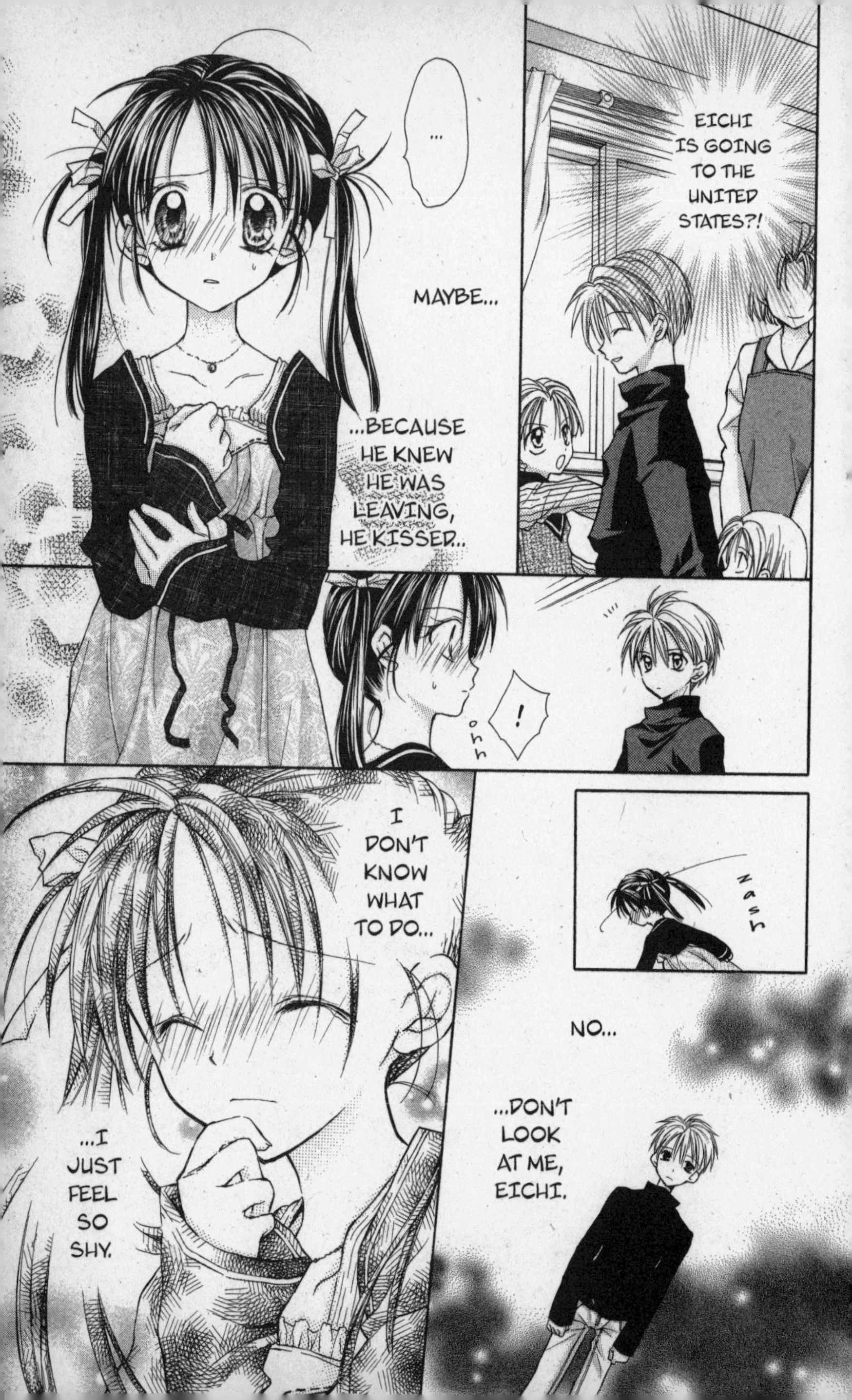

EICHI IS GOING TO THE UNITED STATES?!
!
ohh
...
MAYBE...
...BECAUSE HE KNEW HE WAS LEAVING, HE KISSED...
Zash
NO...
...DON'T LOOK AT ME, EICHI.
I DON'T KNOW WHAT TO DO...
...I JUST FEEL SO SHY.

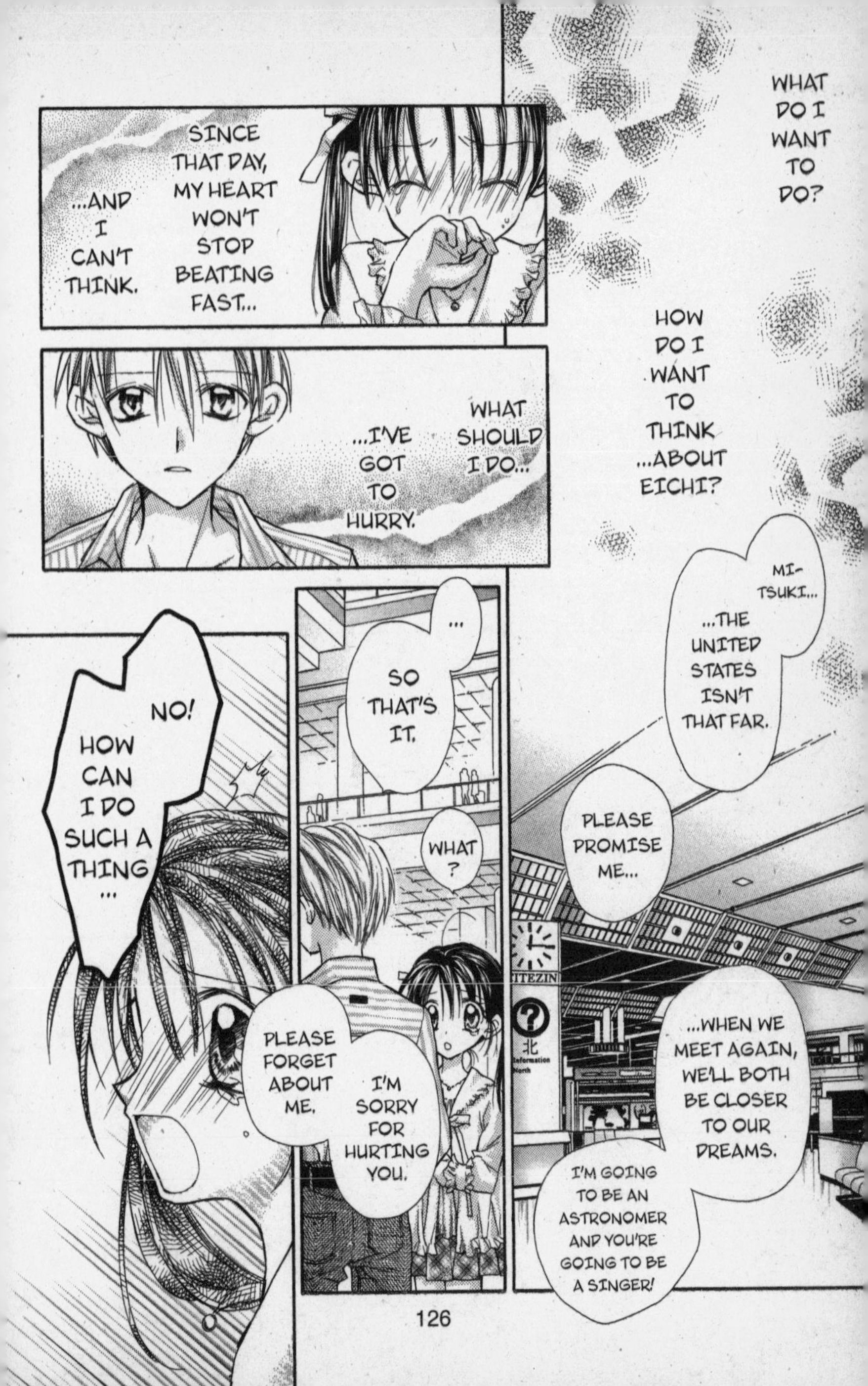
WHAT DO I WANT TO DO?
HOW DO I WANT TO THINK ...ABOUT EICHI?
SINCE THAT DAY, MY HEART WON'T STOP BEATING FAST...
...AND I CAN'T THINK.
WHAT SHOULD I DO...
...I'VE GOT TO HURRY.
MI-TSUKI...
...THE UNITED STATES ISN'T THAT FAR.
PLEASE PROMISE ME...
...WHEN WE MEET AGAIN, WE'LL BOTH BE CLOSER TO OUR DREAMS.
I'M GOING TO BE AN ASTRONOMER AND YOU'RE GOING TO BE A SINGER!
...
SO THAT'S IT.
WHAT?
I'M SORRY FOR HURTING YOU.
PLEASE FORGET ABOUT ME.
NO! HOW CAN I DO SUCH A THING...

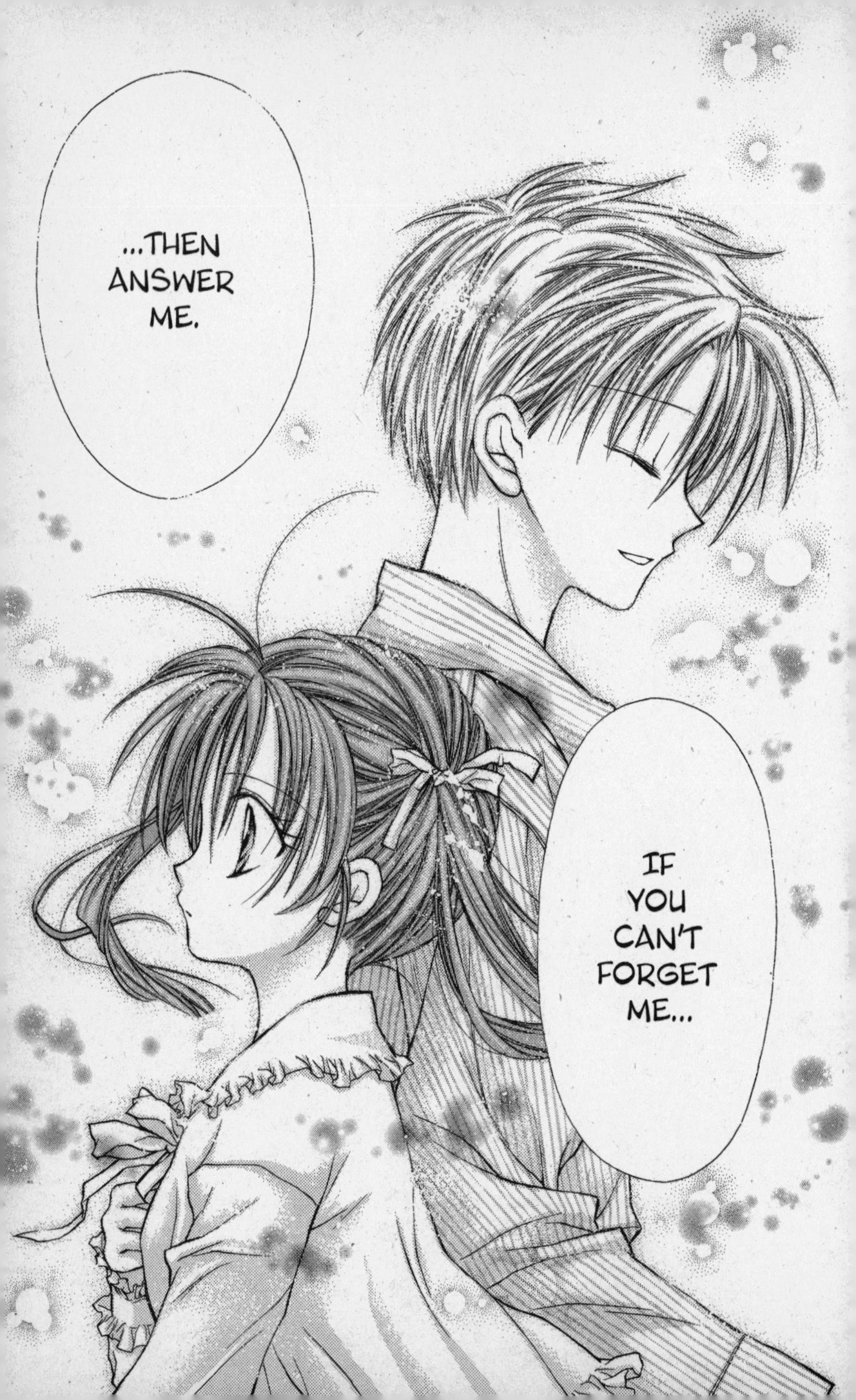
IF YOU CAN'T FORGET ME...
...THEN ANSWER ME.

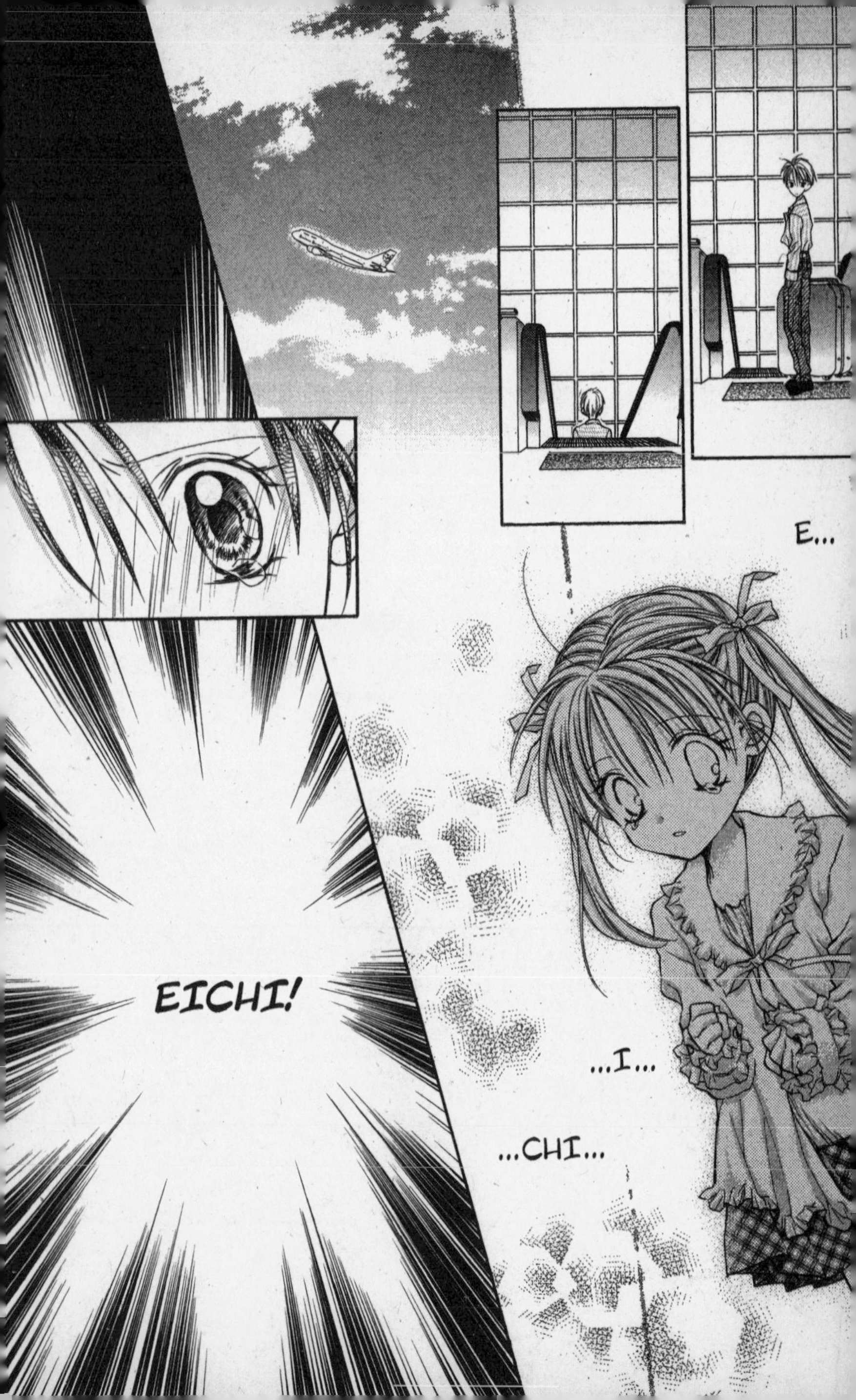
E...
...I...
...CHI...
EICHI!

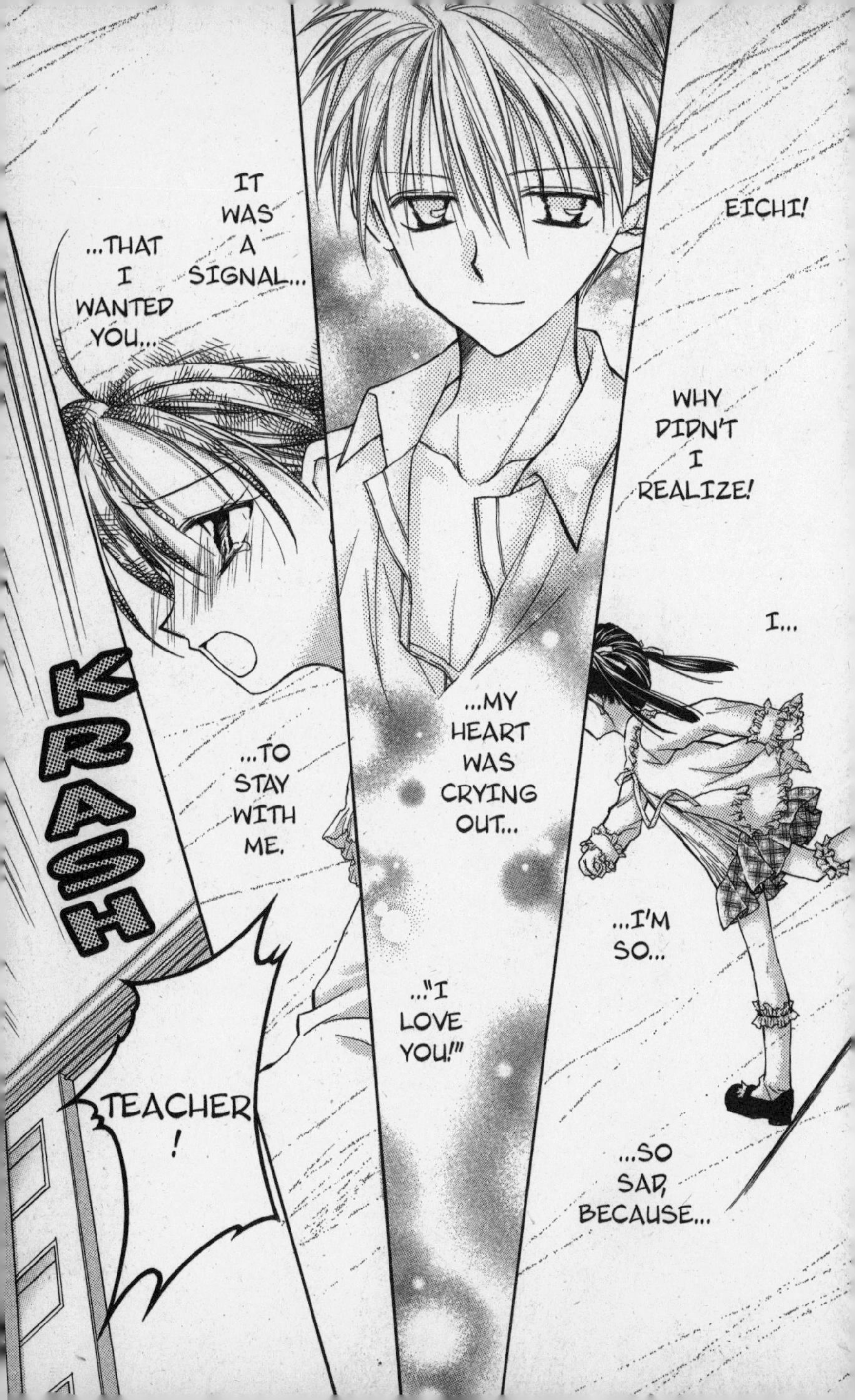
EICHI!
WHY DIDN'T I REALIZE!
I...
...I'M SO...
...SO SAD, BECAUSE...
...MY HEART WAS CRYING OUT...
..."I LOVE YOU!"
IT WAS A SIGNAL...
...THAT I WANTED YOU...
...TO STAY WITH ME.
KRASH
TEACHER!

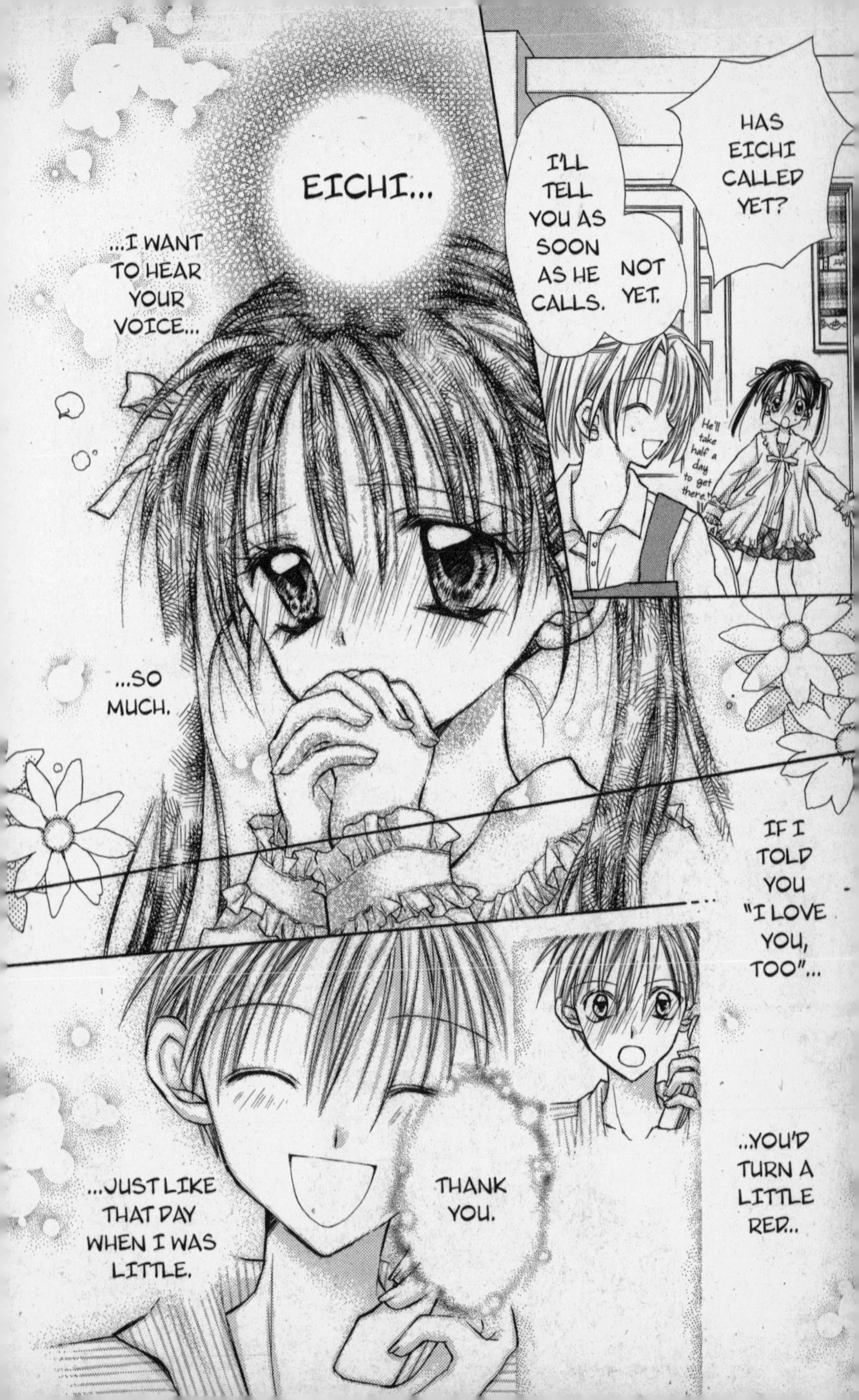
HAS EICHI CALLED YET?
NOT YET.
I'LL TELL YOU AS SOON AS HE CALLS.
He'll take half a day to get there.
EICHI...
...I WANT TO HEAR YOUR VOICE...
...SO MUCH.
IF I TOLD YOU "I LOVE YOU, TOO"...
...YOU'D TURN A LITTLE RED..
THANK YOU.
...JUST LIKE THAT DAY WHEN I WAS LITTLE.

THE PASSENGER LIST HAS JUST BEEN RELEASED

FLIGHT AR-112, WHICH LEFT NARITA FOR LOS ANGELES AT ONE O'CLOCK IN THE AFTERNOON...

THIS IS AN UPDATE ON THE ACCIDENT.

...CRASHED INTO THE PACIFIC OCEAN RIGHT AFTER TAKEOFF.

CAN YOU GET IT ON-SCREEN?

IT'S ON-SCREEN NOW!

MORIKAWA RIE	(25)	YAMADA AKIHIKO	(26)
SAKURAI KENSUKE	(39)	HORI KIMIYO	(66)
SAKURAI MIWA	(38)	HORI MARIKO	(52)
SAKURAI EICHI	(14)	NAKAMURA HIROMI	(15)
YAMADA TOMOMI	(20)	NAKAMURA ARATA	(21)
ASANO CHIHIRO	(22)	ASANO DAISUKE	(24)
KAYOKO	(31)	ASANO SADAHIDE	(30)
KAZUYO	(24)	ASANO MASAHIKO	(31)

UH, I REPEAT.

...EXPLODED AND BURST INTO FLAMES ABOVE THE PACIFIC OCEAN...

...THERE ARE NO CHANCES OF ANY SURVIVORS.

EICHI

FLIGHT AR-112, WHICH LEFT NARITA FOR LOS ANGELES AT ONE O'CLOCK IN THE AFTERNOON...

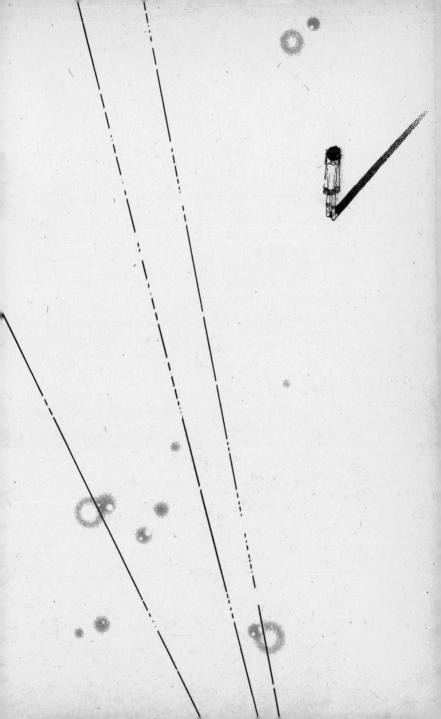

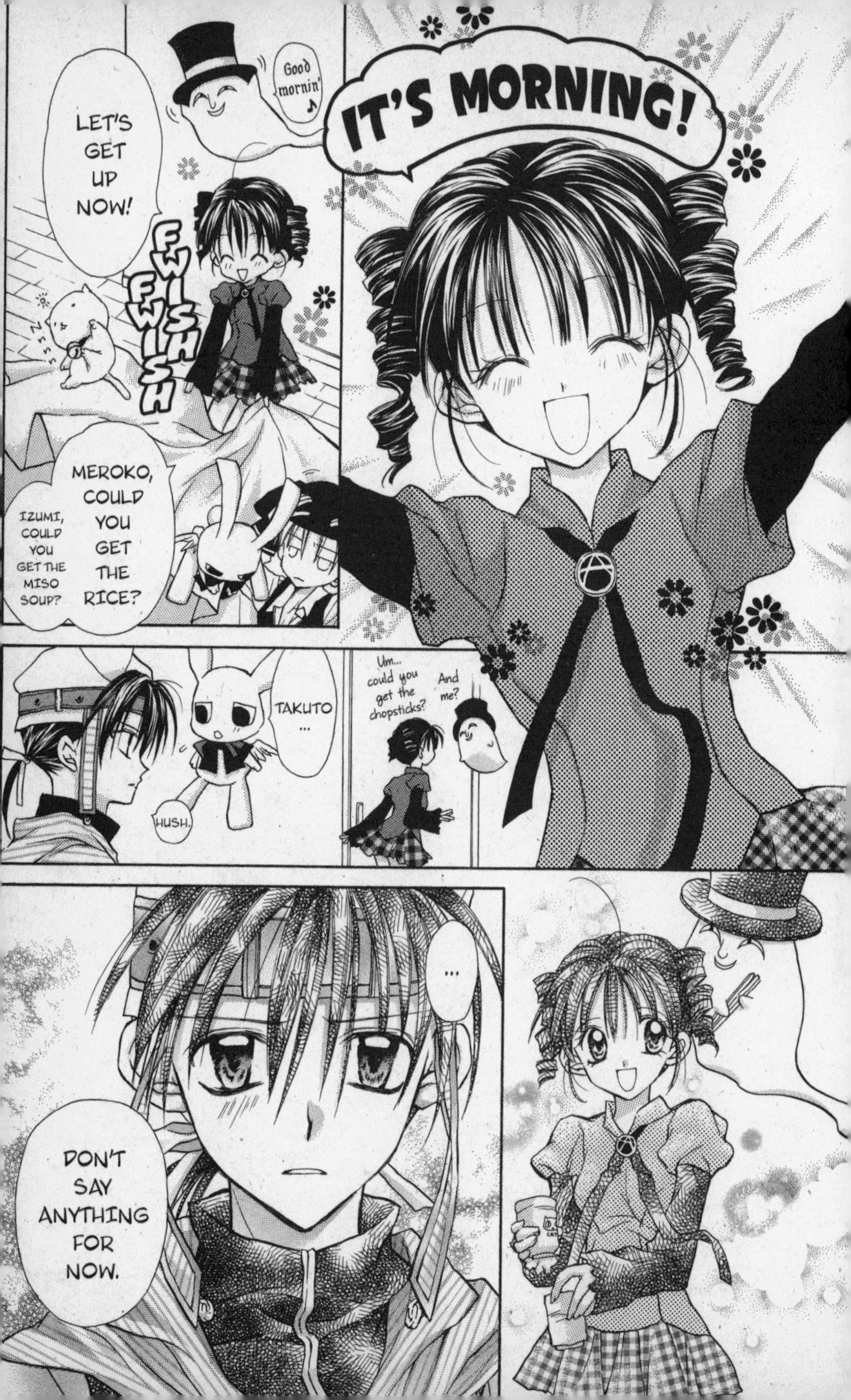
IT'S MORNING!
Good mornin' ♪
LET'S GET UP NOW!
FWISH FWISH
MEROKO, COULD YOU GET THE RICE?
IZUMI, COULD YOU GET THE MISO SOUP?
Um... could you get the chopsticks?
And me?
TAKUTO ...
HUSH.
...
DON'T SAY ANYTHING FOR NOW.

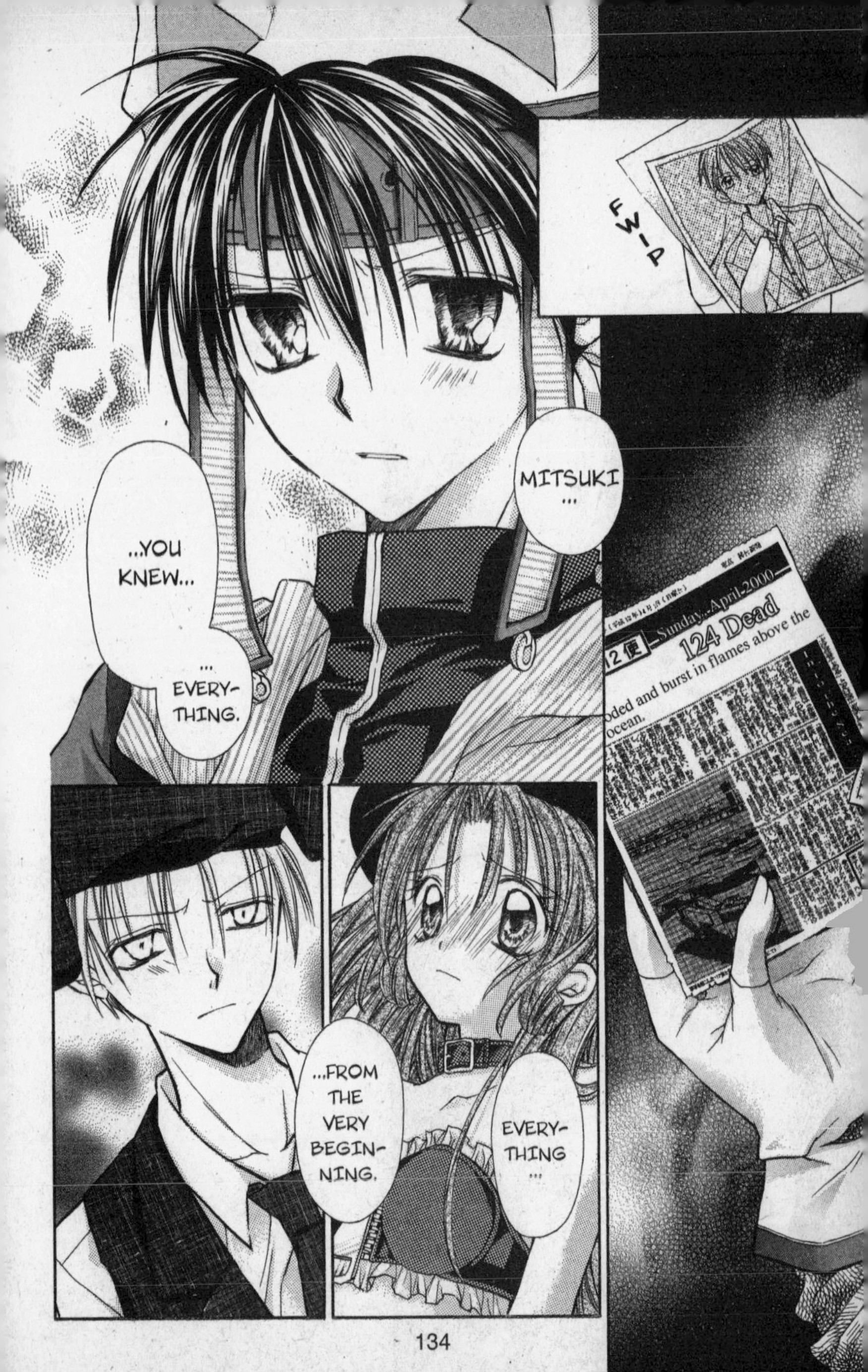
FWIP
—Sunday...April 2000—
124 Dead
oded and burst in flames above the
ocean.
MITSUKI ...
...YOU KNEW...
... EVERY-THING.
EVERY-THING ...
...FROM THE VERY BEGIN-NING.

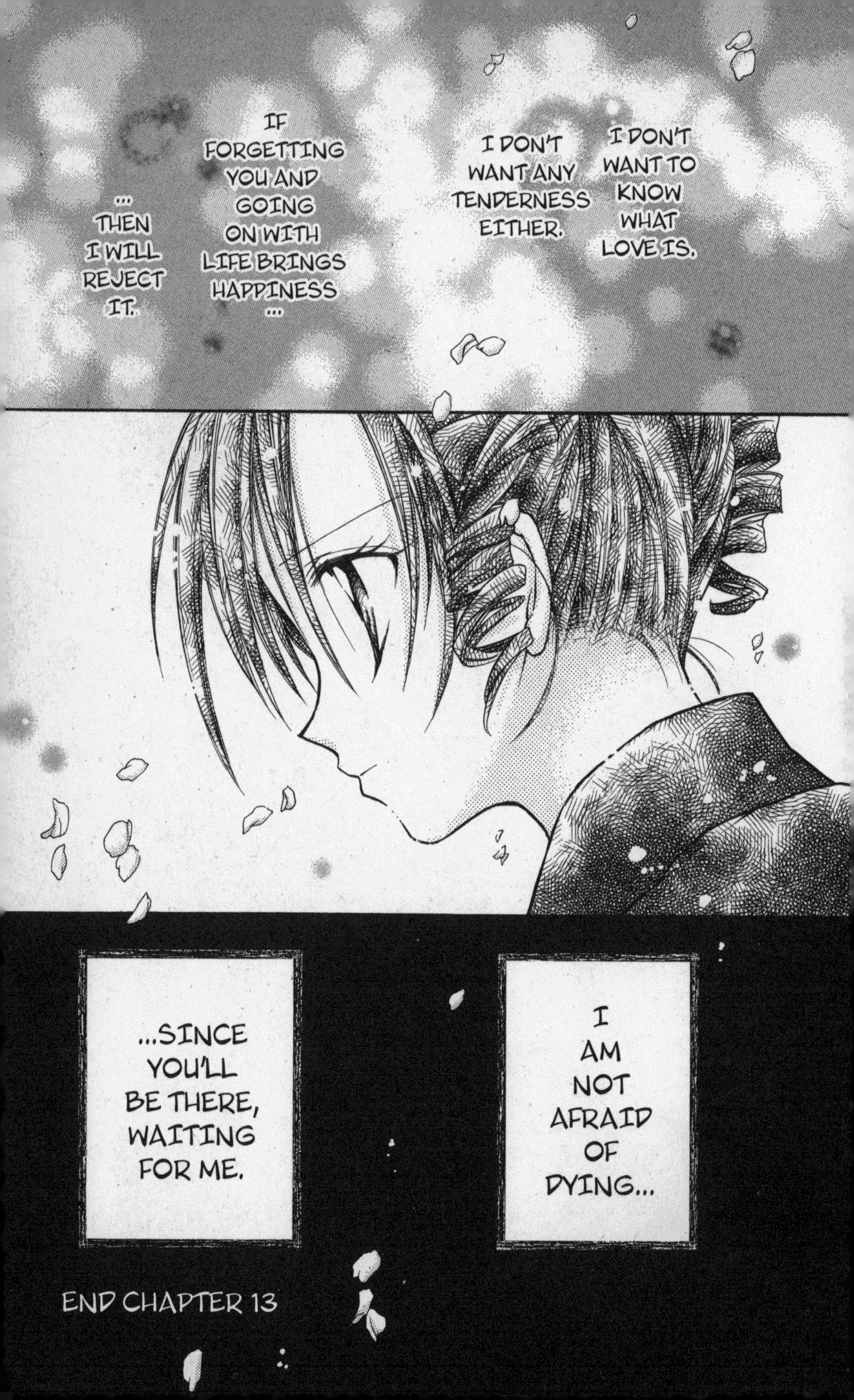
I DON'T WANT TO KNOW WHAT LOVE IS.
I DON'T WANT ANY TENDERNESS EITHER.
IF FORGETTING YOU AND GOING ON WITH LIFE BRINGS HAPPINESS...
...THEN I WILL REJECT IT.
I AM NOT AFRAID OF DYING...
...SINCE YOU'LL BE THERE, WAITING FOR ME.
END CHAPTER 13

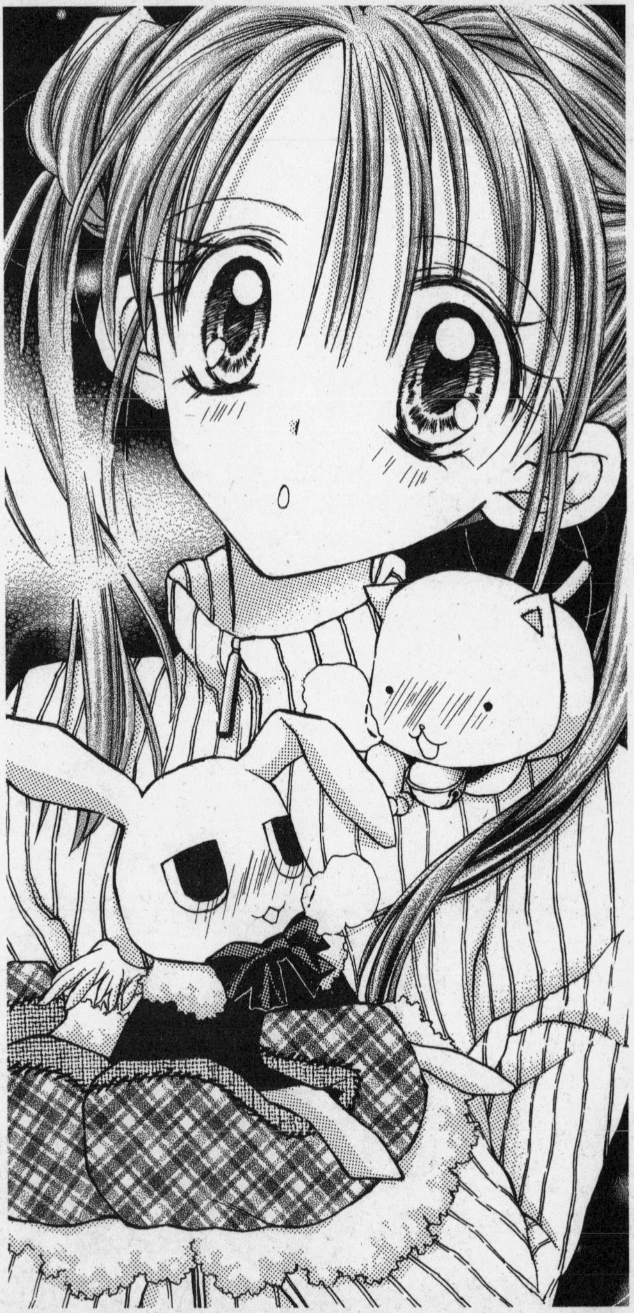

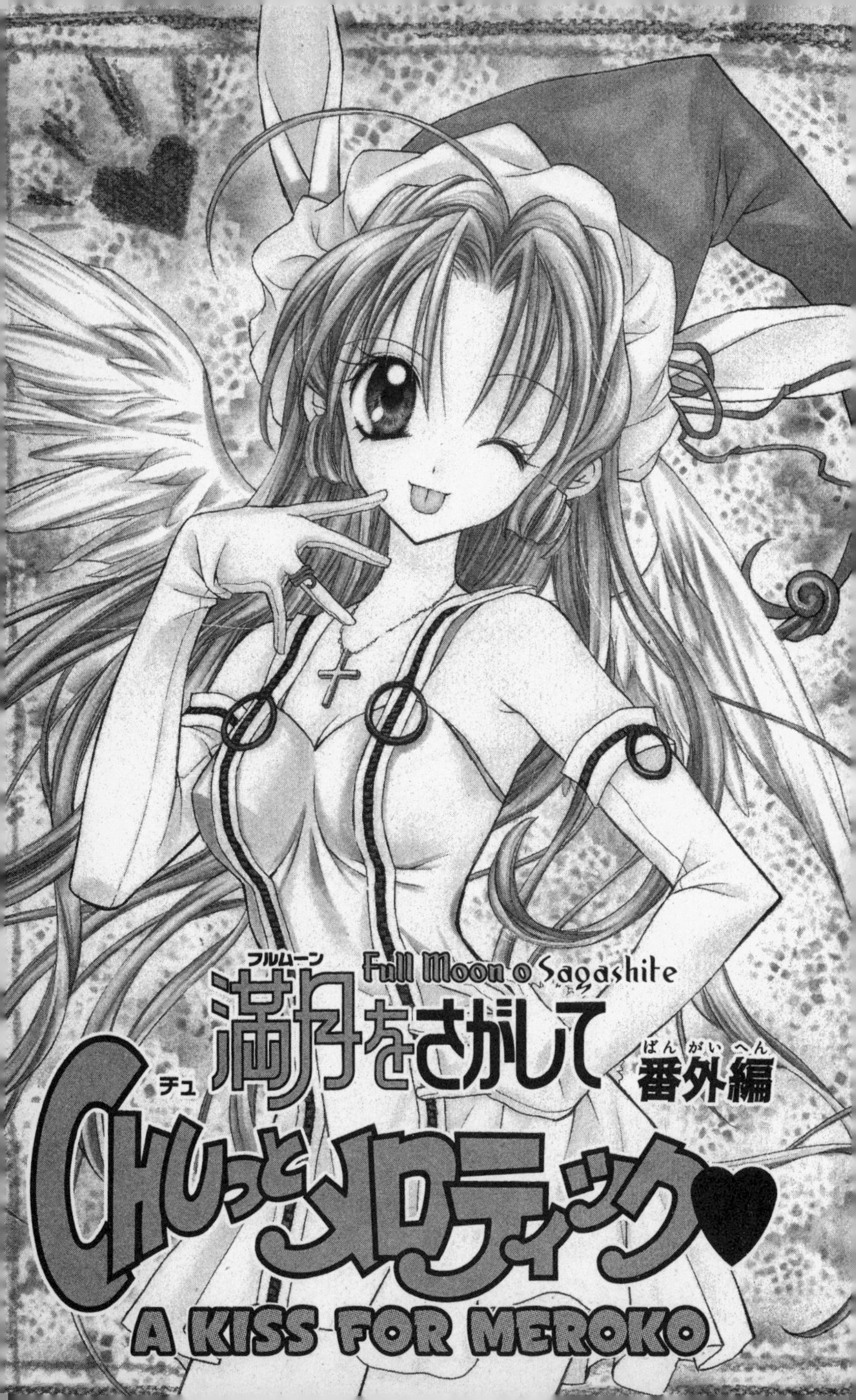

フルムーン
Full Moon o Sagashite
満月をさがして
ばんがいへん
番外編
チュ
CHUっとメロティック♥
A KISS FOR MEROKO

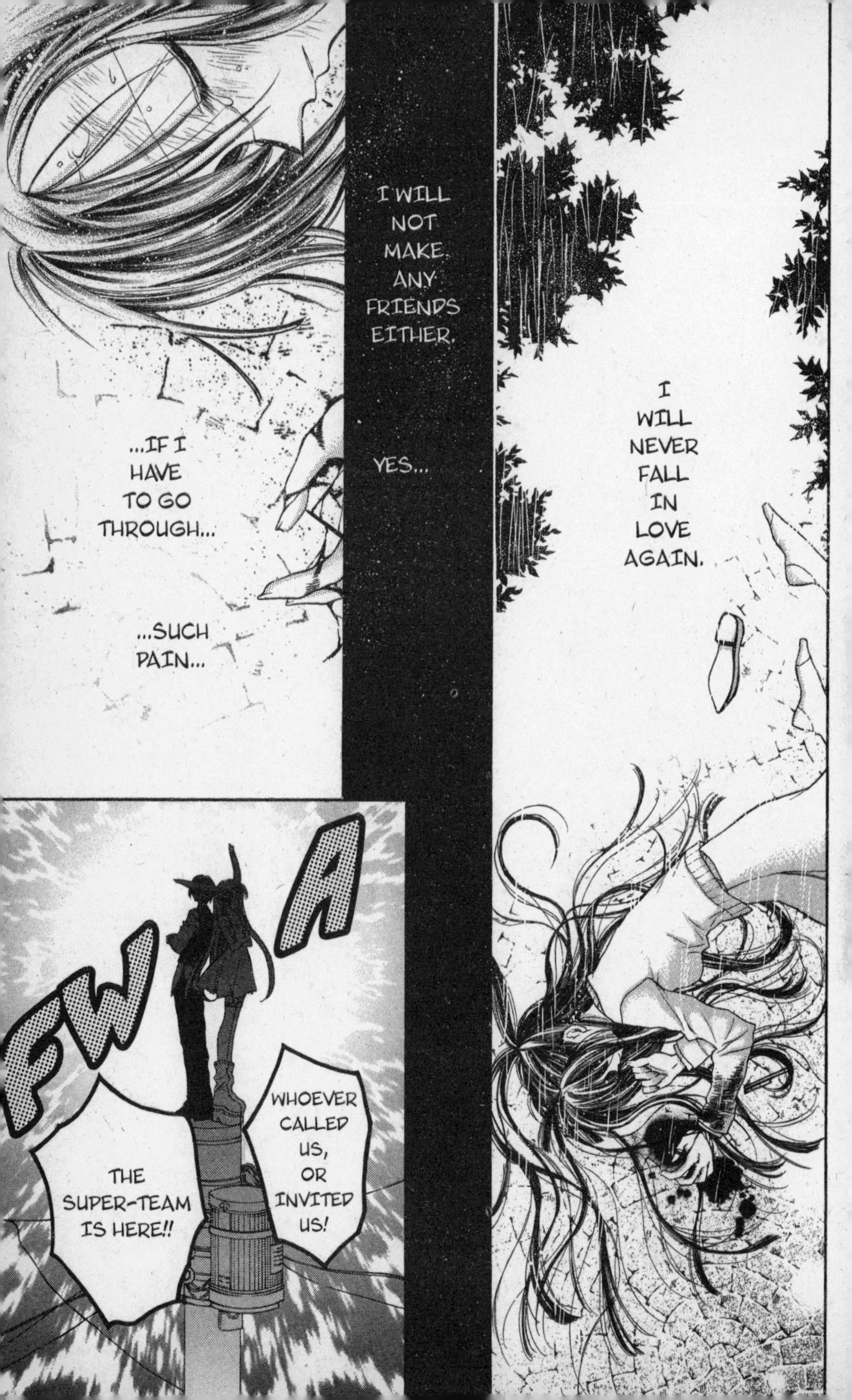

I WILL NEVER FALL IN LOVE AGAIN.
I WILL NOT MAKE ANY FRIENDS EITHER.
YES...
...IF I HAVE TO GO THROUGH...
...SUCH PAIN...
FWA
WHOEVER CALLED US, OR INVITED US!
THE SUPER-TEAM IS HERE!!

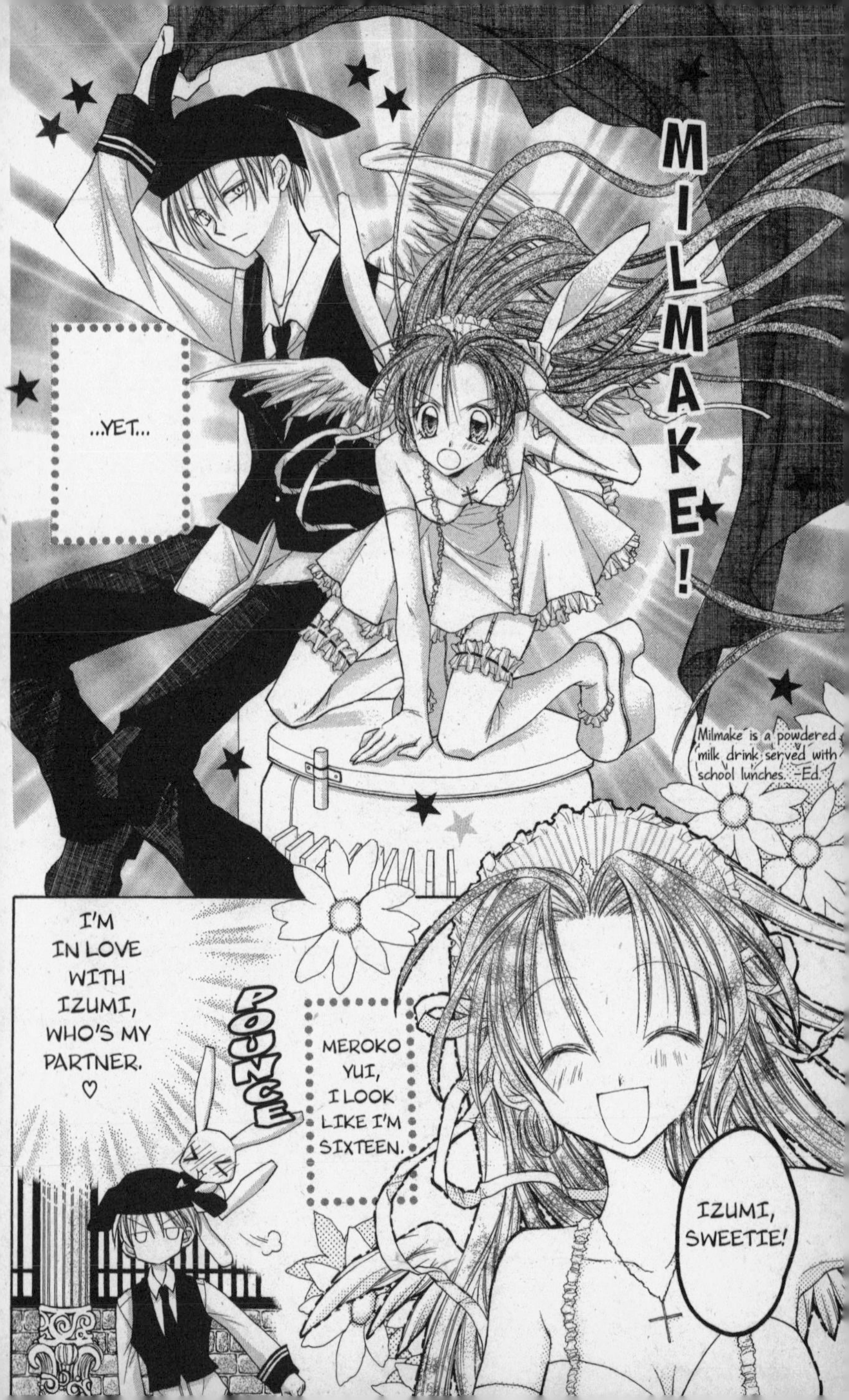
MILMAKE!
Milmake is a powdered milk drink served with school lunches. –Ed.
...YET...
IZUMI, SWEETIE!
MEROKO YUI, I LOOK LIKE I'M SIXTEEN.
POUNCE
I'M IN LOVE WITH IZUMI, WHO'S MY PARTNER. ♡

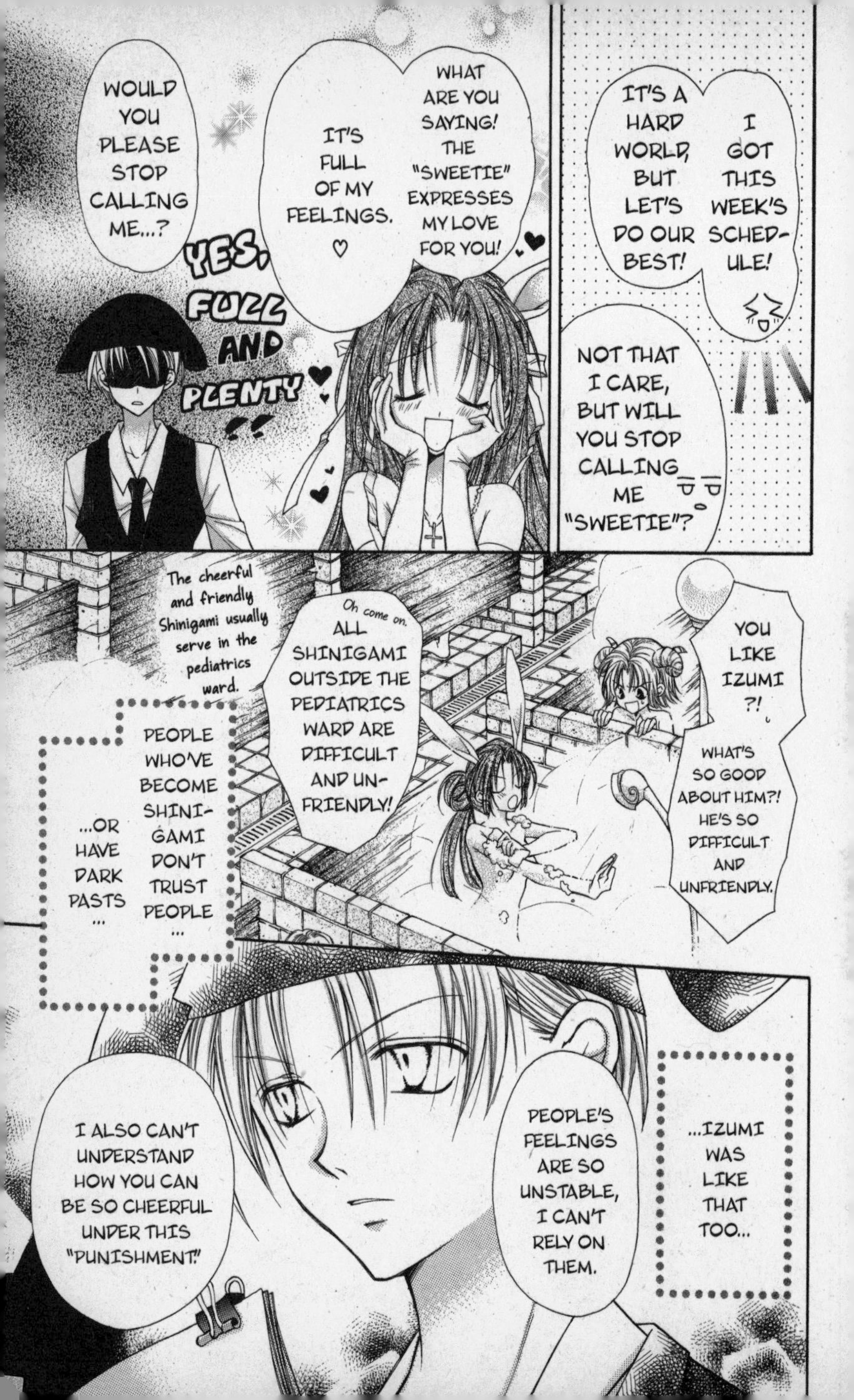
I GOT THIS WEEK'S SCHED-ULE!
IT'S A HARD WORLD, BUT LET'S DO OUR BEST!
NOT THAT I CARE, BUT WILL YOU STOP CALLING ME "SWEETIE"?
WHAT ARE YOU SAYING! THE "SWEETIE" EXPRESSES MY LOVE FOR YOU!
IT'S FULL OF MY FEELINGS. ♡
WOULD YOU PLEASE STOP CALLING ME...?
YES, FULL AND PLENTY
YOU LIKE IZUMI?!
WHAT'S SO GOOD ABOUT HIM?! HE'S SO DIFFICULT AND UNFRIENDLY.
Oh come on.
ALL SHINIGAMI OUTSIDE THE PEDIATRICS WARD ARE DIFFICULT AND UNFRIENDLY!
The cheerful and friendly Shinigami usually serve in the pediatrics ward.
PEOPLE WHO'VE BECOME SHINIGAMI DON'T TRUST PEOPLE...
...OR HAVE DARK PASTS...
...IZUMI WAS LIKE THAT TOO...
PEOPLE'S FEELINGS ARE SO UNSTABLE, I CAN'T RELY ON THEM.
I ALSO CAN'T UNDERSTAND HOW YOU CAN BE SO CHEERFUL UNDER THIS "PUNISHMENT."

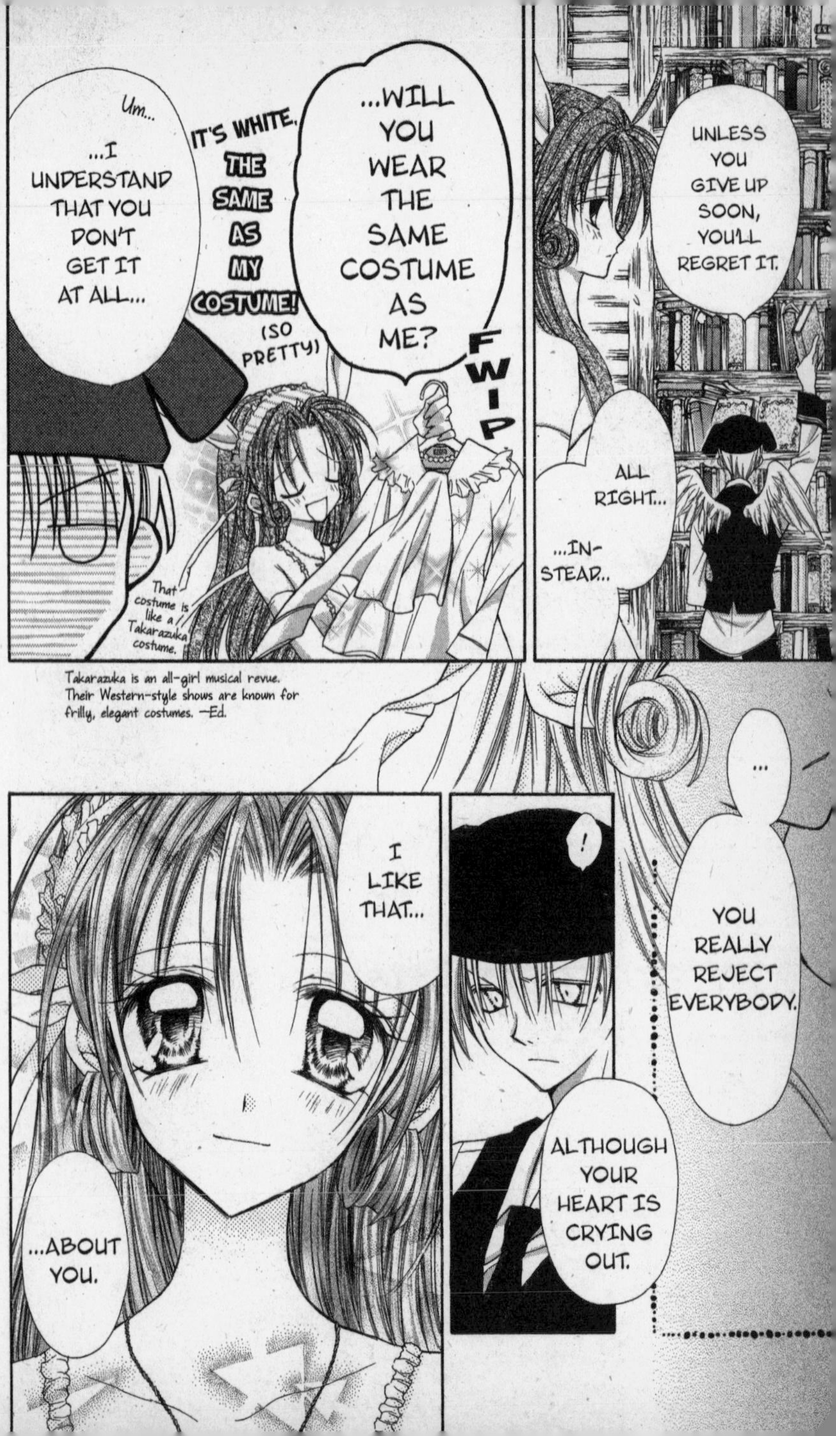
UNLESS YOU GIVE UP SOON, YOU'LL REGRET IT.
ALL RIGHT...
...INSTEAD...
...WILL YOU WEAR THE SAME COSTUME AS ME?
FWIP
IT'S WHITE. THE SAME AS MY COSTUME!
(SO PRETTY)
Um...
...I UNDERSTAND THAT YOU DON'T GET IT AT ALL...
That costume is like a Takarazuka costume.
...
YOU REALLY REJECT EVERYBODY.
!
ALTHOUGH YOUR HEART IS CRYING OUT.
I LIKE THAT...
...ABOUT YOU.

Takarazuka is an all-girl musical revue. Their Western-style shows are known for frilly, elegant costumes. —Ed.

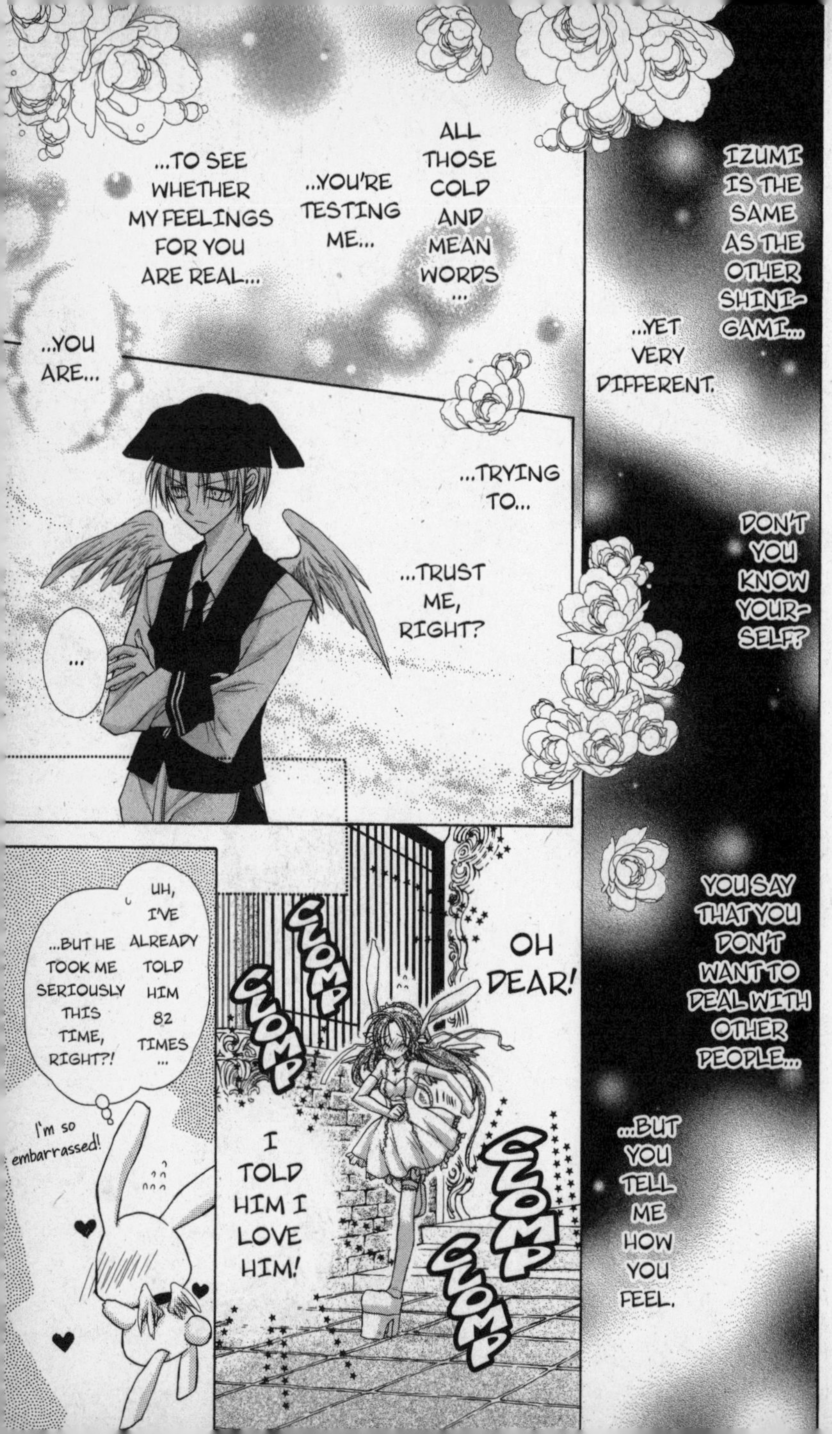
IZUMI IS THE SAME AS THE OTHER SHINIGAMI...
...YET VERY DIFFERENT.
ALL THOSE COLD AND MEAN WORDS...
...YOU'RE TESTING ME...
...TO SEE WHETHER MY FEELINGS FOR YOU ARE REAL...
...YOU ARE...
...TRYING TO...
...TRUST ME, RIGHT?
...
DON'T YOU KNOW YOURSELF?
YOU SAY THAT YOU DON'T WANT TO DEAL WITH OTHER PEOPLE...
...BUT YOU TELL ME HOW YOU FEEL.
OH DEAR!
CLOMP CLOMP
CLOMP CLOMP
I TOLD HIM I LOVE HIM!
UH, I'VE ALREADY TOLD HIM 82 TIMES...
...BUT HE TOOK ME SERIOUSLY THIS TIME, RIGHT?!
I'm so embarrassed!

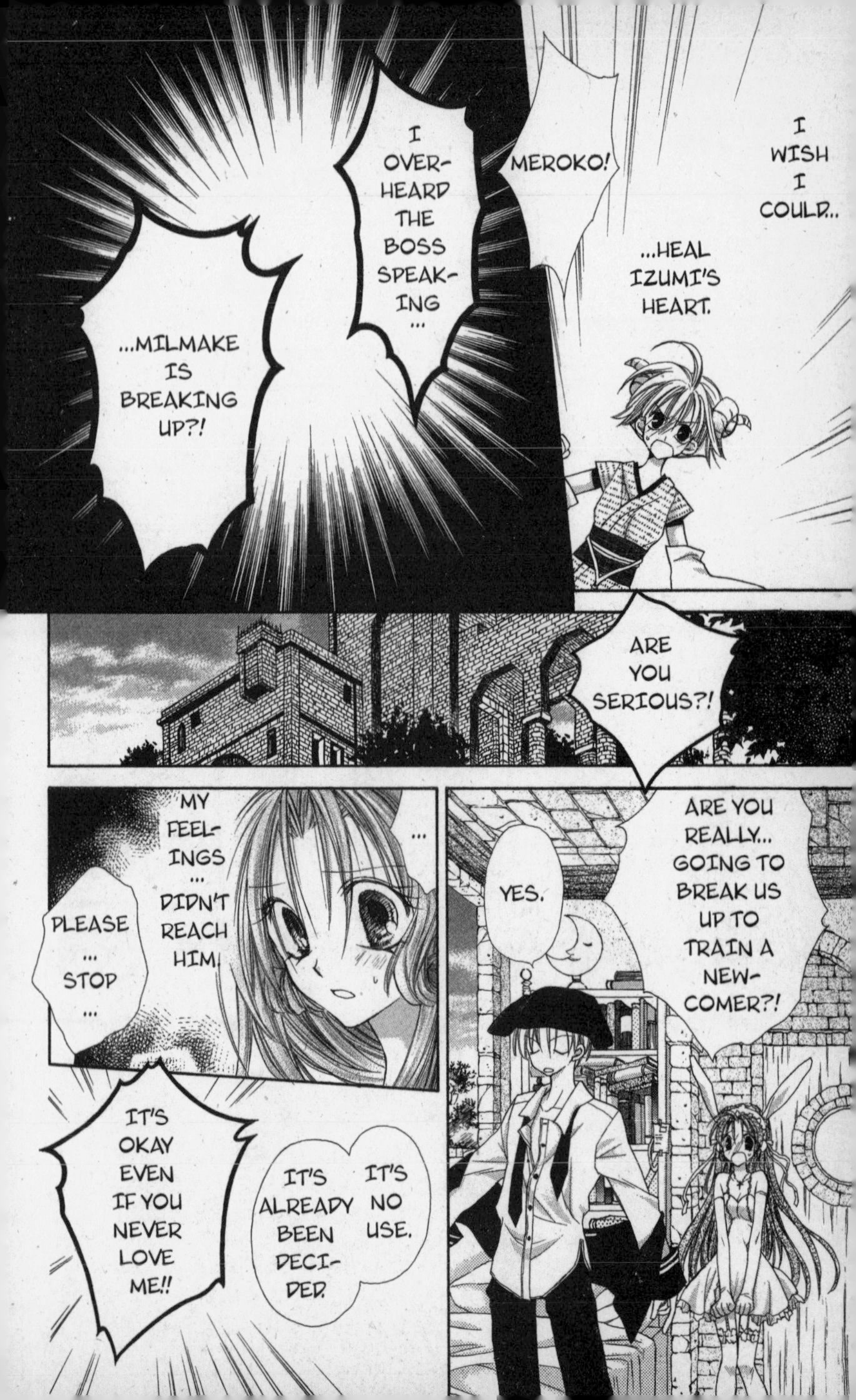
I WISH I COULD...
...HEAL IZUMI'S HEART.
MEROKO!
I OVERHEARD THE BOSS SPEAKING...
...MILMAKE IS BREAKING UP?!
ARE YOU SERIOUS?!
ARE YOU REALLY... GOING TO BREAK US UP TO TRAIN A NEWCOMER?!
YES.
...
MY FEELINGS... DIDN'T REACH HIM.
PLEASE... STOP...
IT'S NO USE.
IT'S ALREADY BEEN DECIDED.
IT'S OKAY EVEN IF YOU NEVER LOVE ME!!

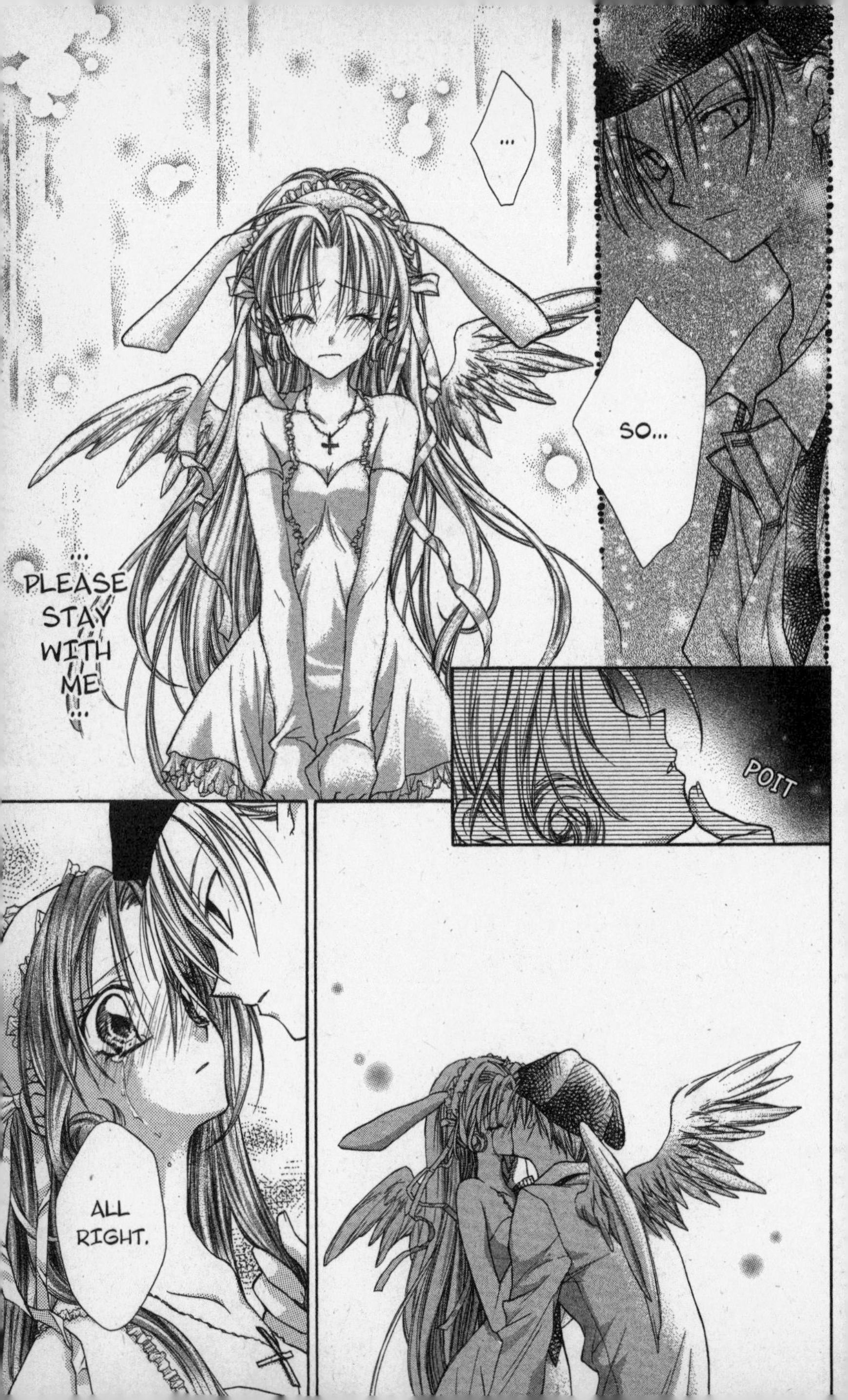
SO...
POIT
...
...PLEASE STAY WITH ME...
ALL RIGHT.

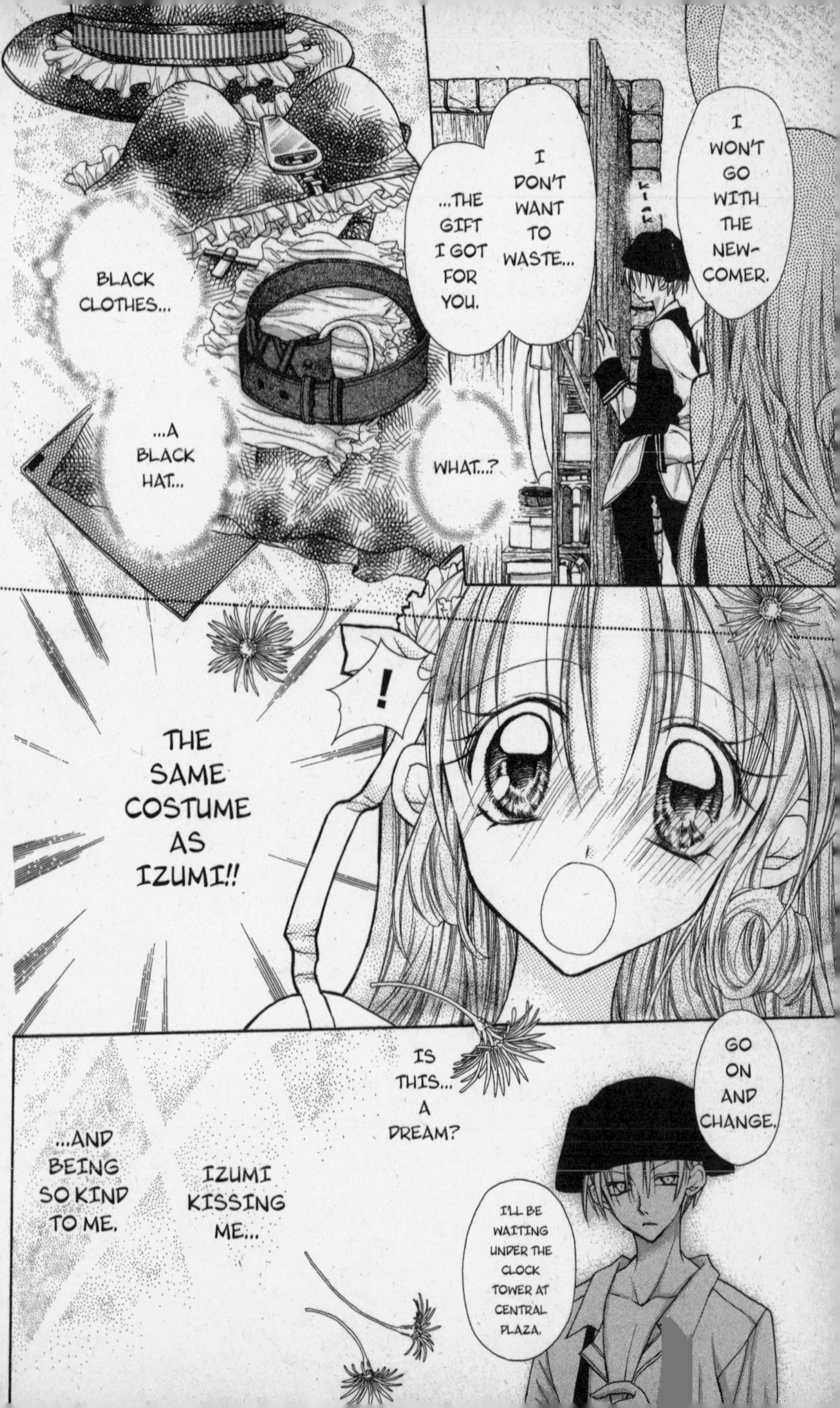
I WON'T GO WITH THE NEW-COMER.
I DON'T WANT TO WASTE...
...THE GIFT I GOT FOR YOU.
kick
WHAT...?
BLACK CLOTHES...
...A BLACK HAT...
!
THE SAME COSTUME AS IZUMI!!
GO ON AND CHANGE.
I'LL BE WAITING UNDER THE CLOCK TOWER AT CENTRAL PLAZA.
IS THIS... A DREAM?
IZUMI KISSING ME...
...AND BEING SO KIND TO ME.

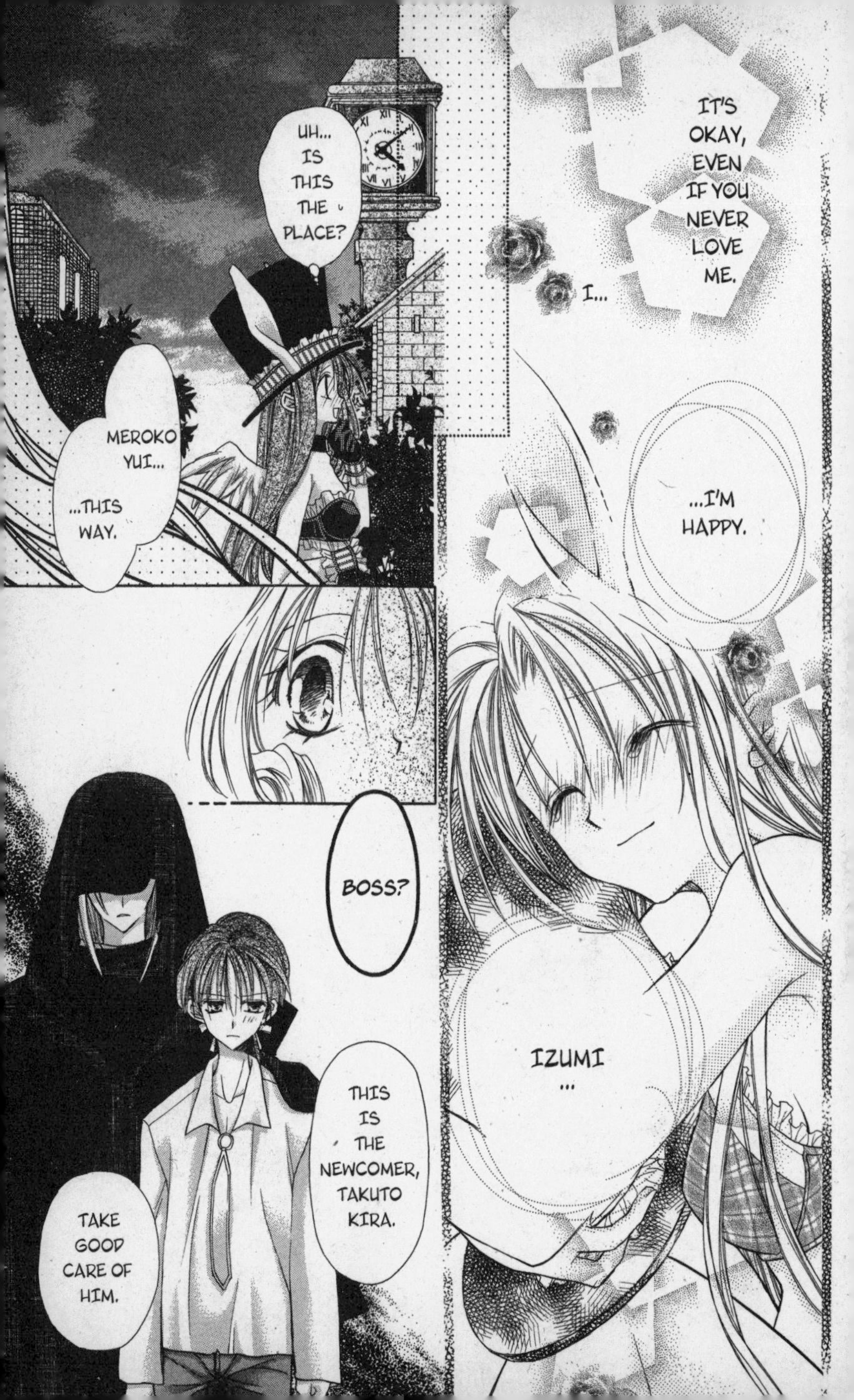
IT'S OKAY, EVEN IF YOU NEVER LOVE ME.
I...
...I'M HAPPY.
IZUMI ...
UH... IS THIS THE PLACE?
MEROKO YUI... ...THIS WAY.
BOSS?
THIS IS THE NEWCOMER, TAKUTO KIRA.
TAKE GOOD CARE OF HIM.

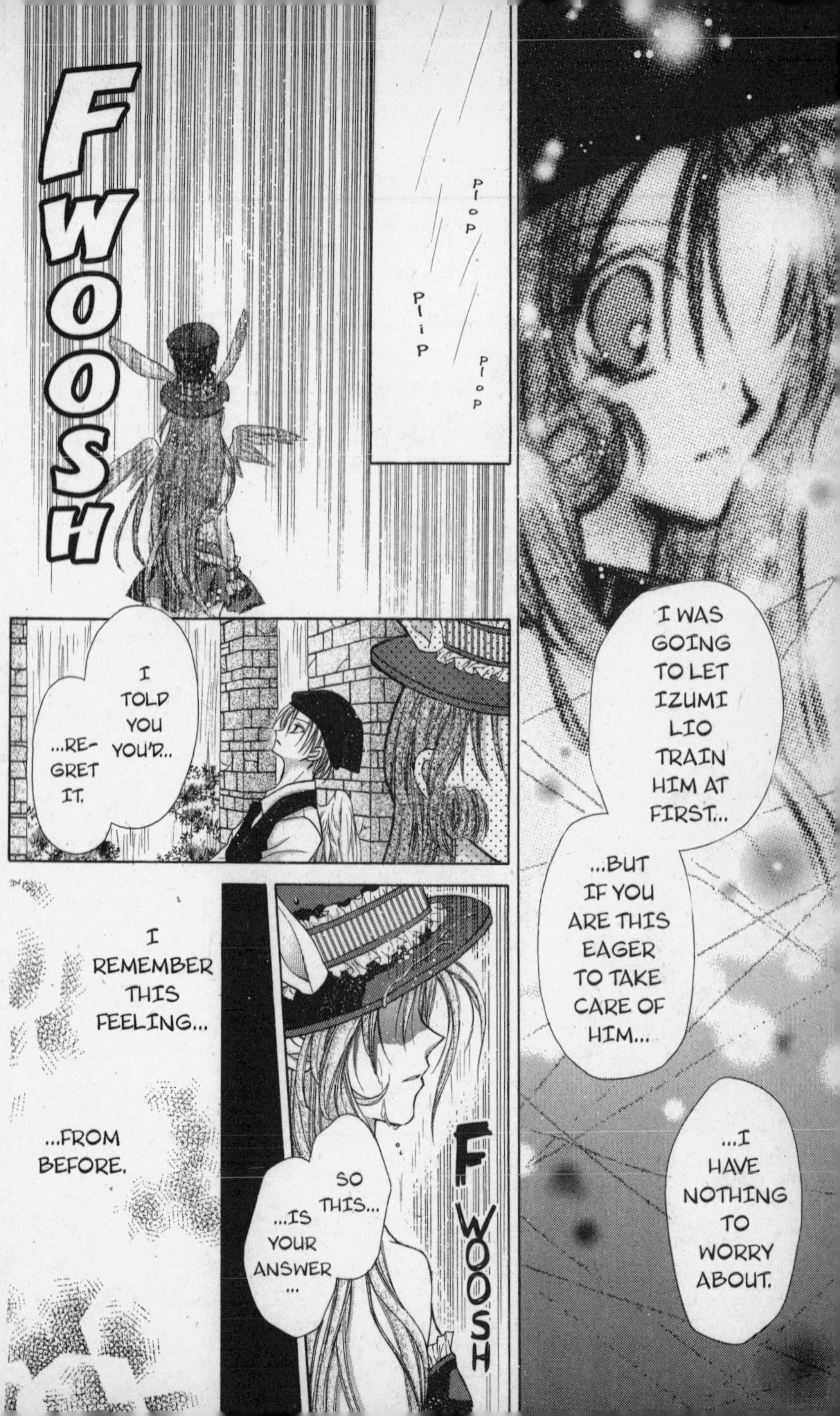
I WAS GOING TO LET IZUMI LIO TRAIN HIM AT FIRST...
...BUT IF YOU ARE THIS EAGER TO TAKE CARE OF HIM...
...I HAVE NOTHING TO WORRY ABOUT.
PLOP
PLIP
PLOP
FWOOSH
I TOLD YOU YOU'D...
...RE-GRET IT.
FWOOSH
SO THIS...
...IS YOUR ANSWER...
I REMEMBER THIS FEELING...
...FROM BEFORE.

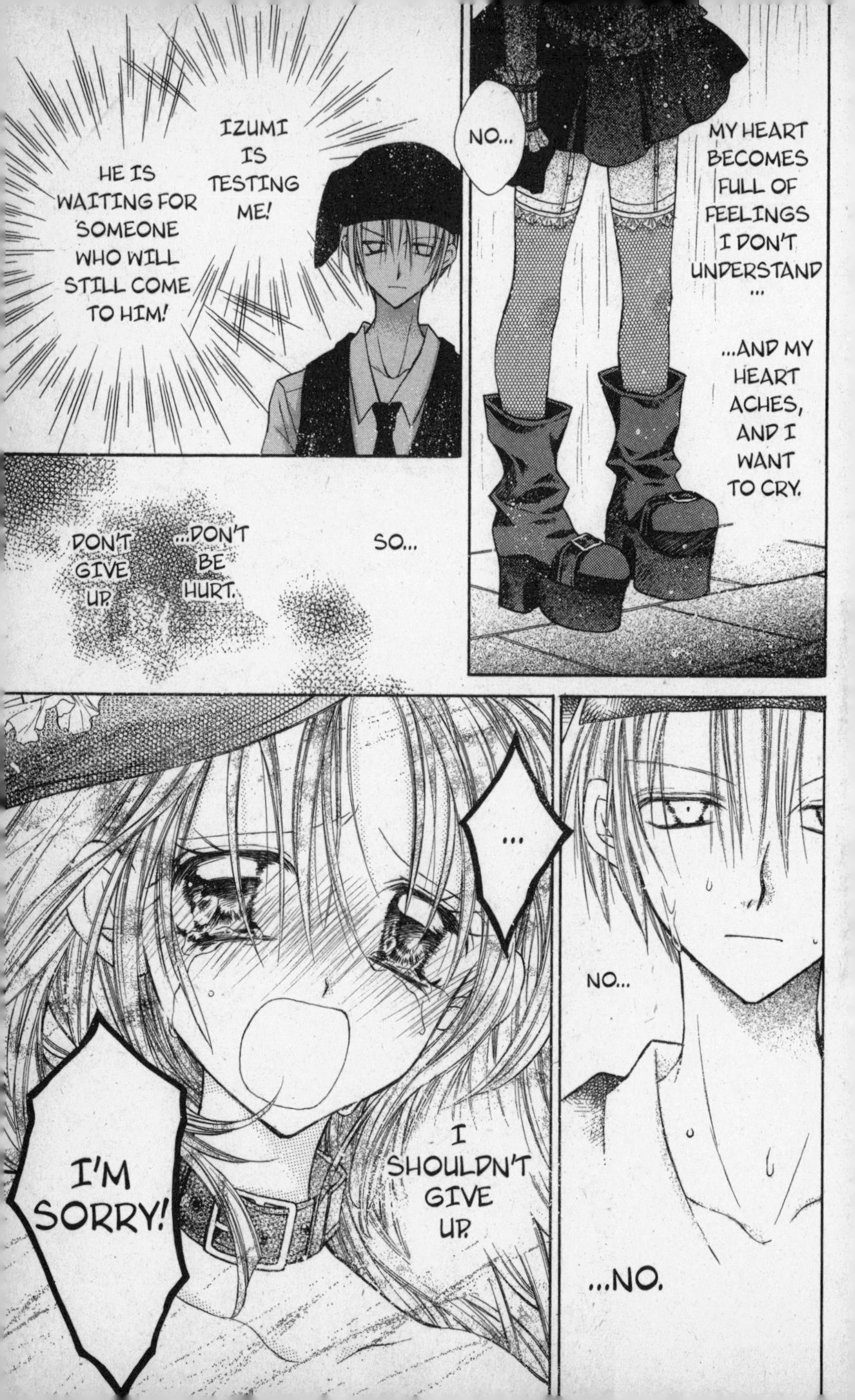
NO...
MY HEART BECOMES FULL OF FEELINGS I DON'T UNDERSTAND...
...AND MY HEART ACHES, AND I WANT TO CRY.
IZUMI IS TESTING ME!
HE IS WAITING FOR SOMEONE WHO WILL STILL COME TO HIM!
SO...
...DON'T BE HURT.
DON'T GIVE UP.
NO...
...NO.
...
I SHOULDN'T GIVE UP.
I'M SORRY!

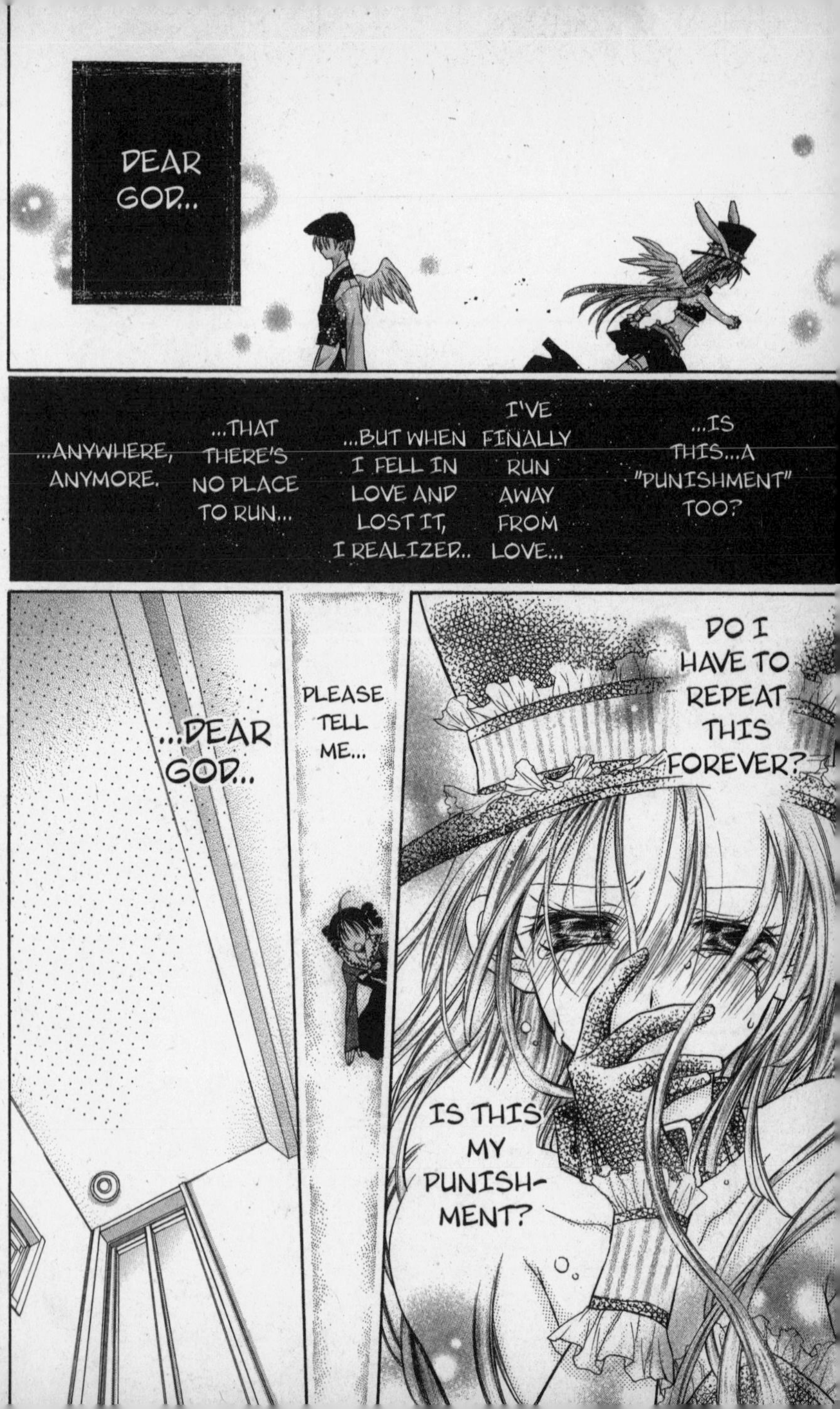
DEAR GOD...
...IS THIS...A "PUNISHMENT" TOO?
I'VE FINALLY RUN AWAY FROM LOVE...
...BUT WHEN I FELL IN LOVE AND LOST IT, I REALIZED...
...THAT THERE'S NO PLACE TO RUN...
...ANYWHERE, ANYMORE.
DO I HAVE TO REPEAT THIS FOREVER?
IS THIS MY PUNISHMENT?
PLEASE TELL ME...
...DEAR GOD...

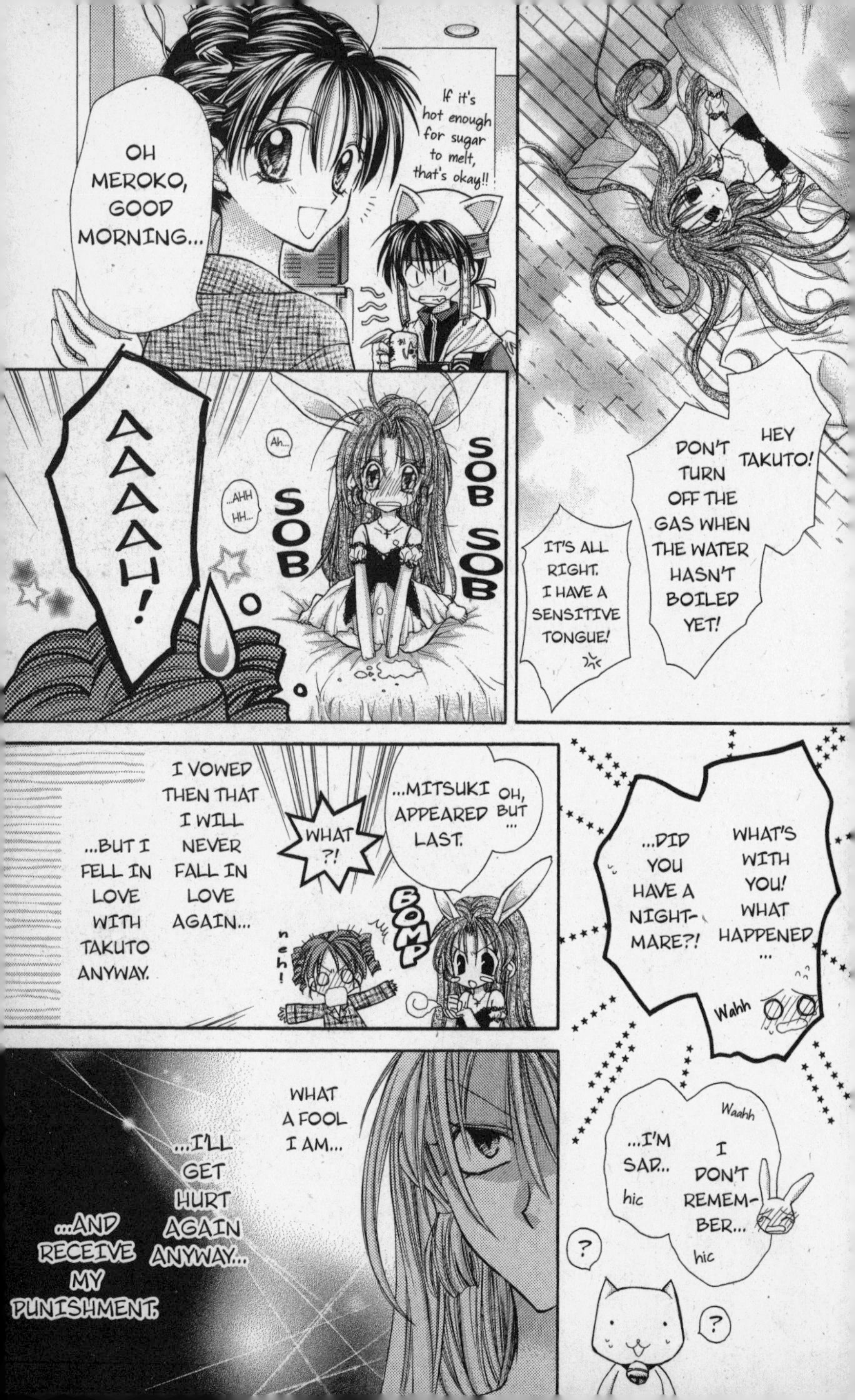
HEY TAKUTO! DON'T TURN OFF THE GAS WHEN THE WATER HASN'T BOILED YET!
IT'S ALL RIGHT. I HAVE A SENSITIVE TONGUE!
OH MEROKO, GOOD MORNING...
If it's hot enough for sugar to melt, that's okay!!
AAAAH!
Ah...
...AHH HH...
SOB SOB
SOB SOB
WHAT'S WITH YOU! WHAT HAPPENED...
...DID YOU HAVE A NIGHT-MARE?!
Wahh
OH, BUT...
...MITSUKI APPEARED LAST.
WHAT ?!
BOMP
neh!
I VOWED THEN THAT I WILL NEVER FALL IN LOVE AGAIN...
...BUT I FELL IN LOVE WITH TAKUTO ANYWAY.
Waahh
I DON'T REMEM-BER...
hic
...I'M SAD...
hic
?
?
WHAT A FOOL I AM...
...I'LL GET HURT AGAIN ANYWAY...
...AND RECEIVE MY PUNISHMENT.

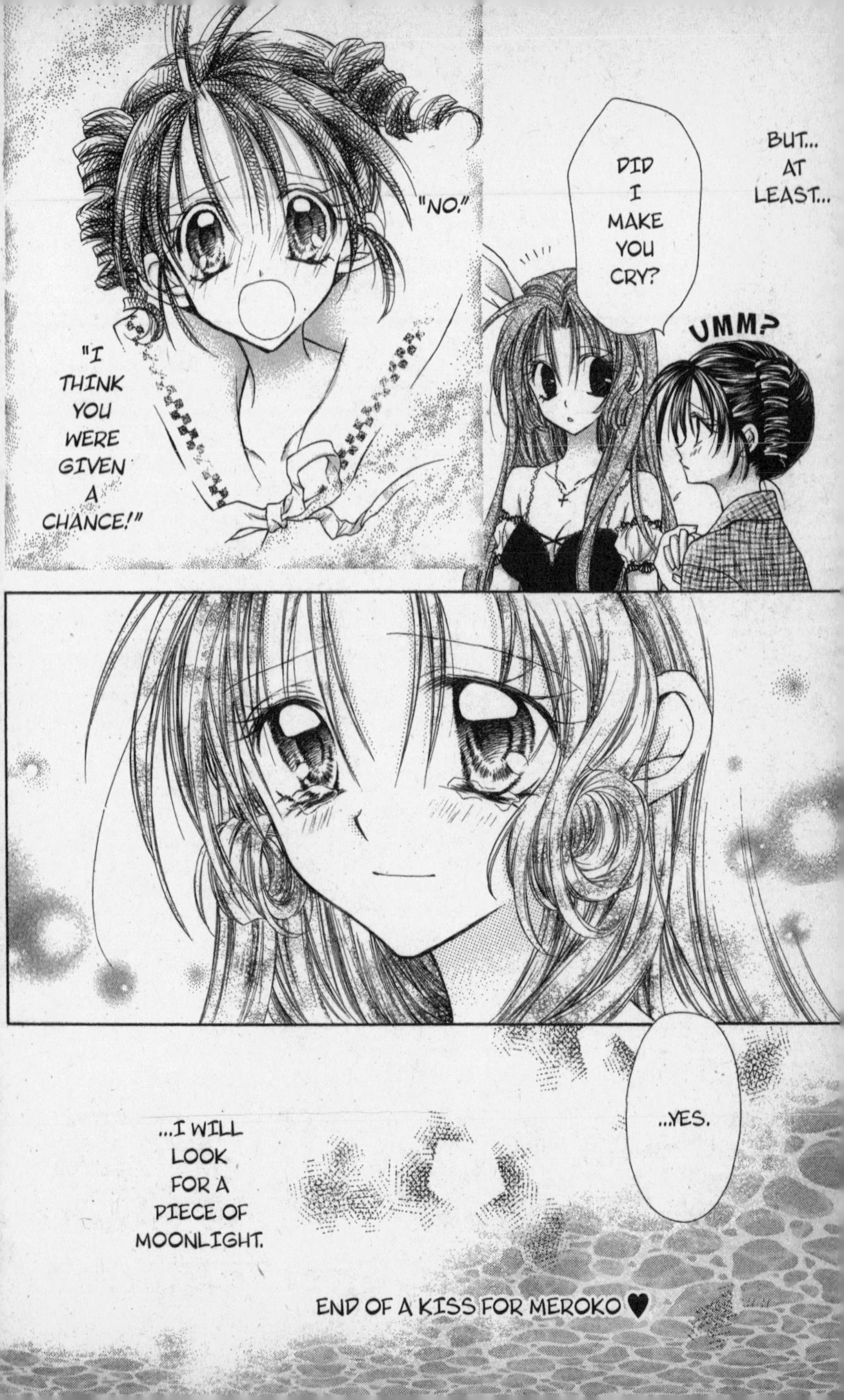
BUT... AT LEAST...
DID I MAKE YOU CRY?
UMM?
"NO."
"I THINK YOU WERE GIVEN A CHANCE!"
...YES.
...I WILL LOOK FOR A PIECE OF MOONLIGHT.
END OF A KISS FOR MEROKO ♥

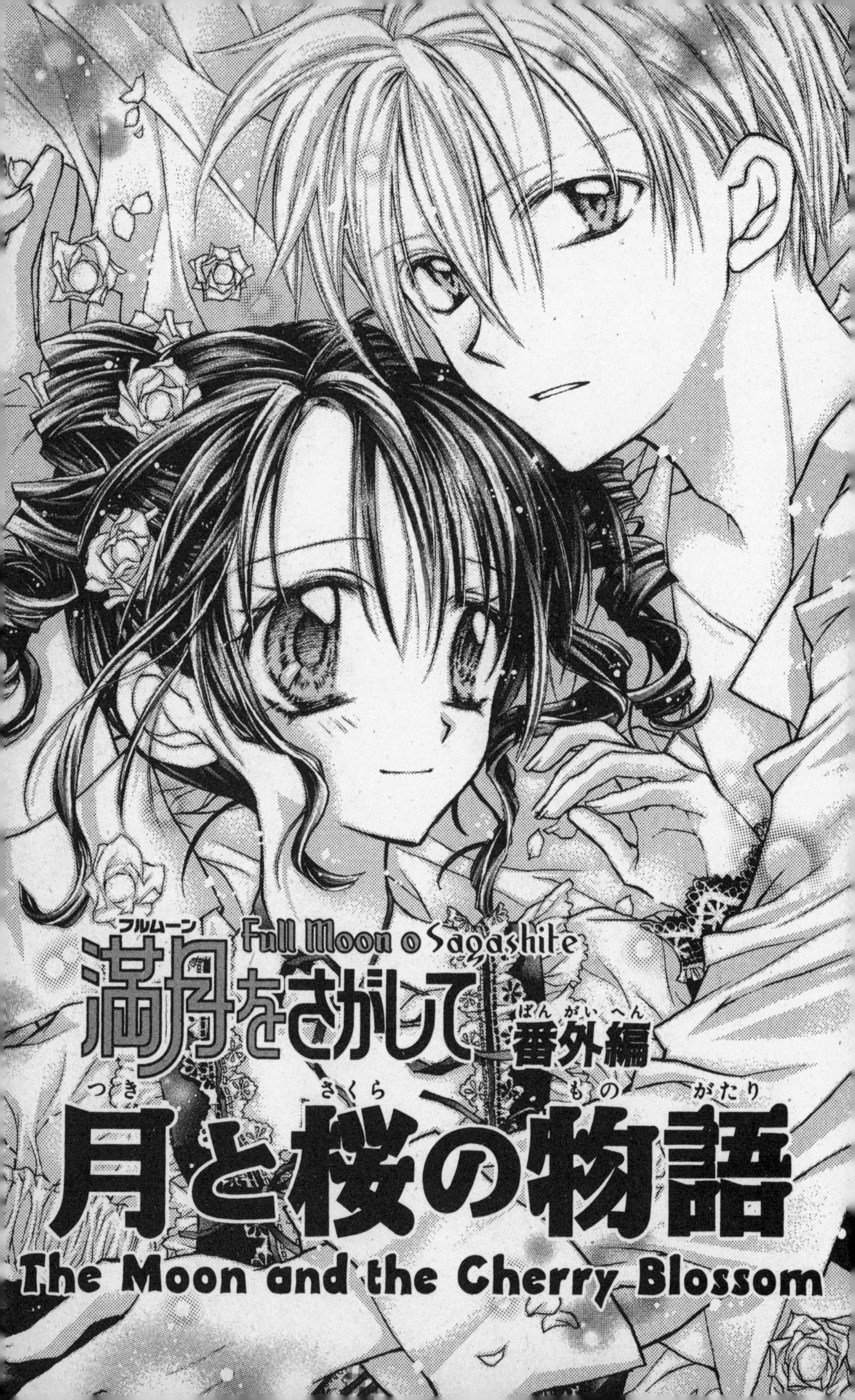

Full Moon o Sagashite
満月をさがして
番外編
月と桜の物語
The Moon and the Cherry Blossom

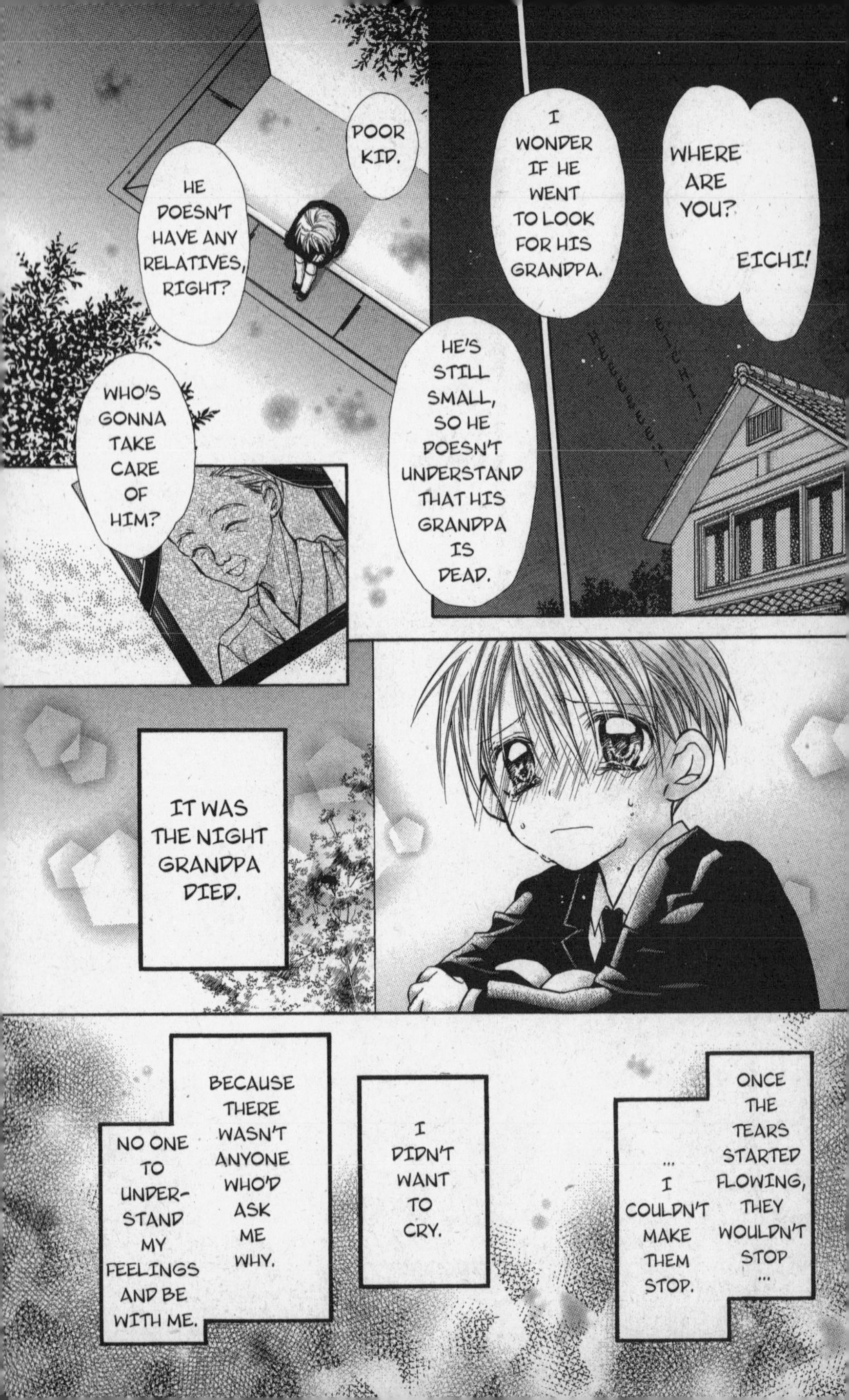
WHERE ARE YOU? EICHI!
I WONDER IF HE WENT TO LOOK FOR HIS GRANDPA.
HE'S STILL SMALL, SO HE DOESN'T UNDERSTAND THAT HIS GRANDPA IS DEAD.
POOR KID.
HE DOESN'T HAVE ANY RELATIVES, RIGHT?
WHO'S GONNA TAKE CARE OF HIM?
IT WAS THE NIGHT GRANDPA DIED.
ONCE THE TEARS STARTED FLOWING, THEY WOULDN'T STOP...
...I COULDN'T MAKE THEM STOP.
I DIDN'T WANT TO CRY.
BECAUSE THERE WASN'T ANYONE WHO'D ASK ME WHY.
NO ONE TO UNDER-STAND MY FEELINGS AND BE WITH ME.

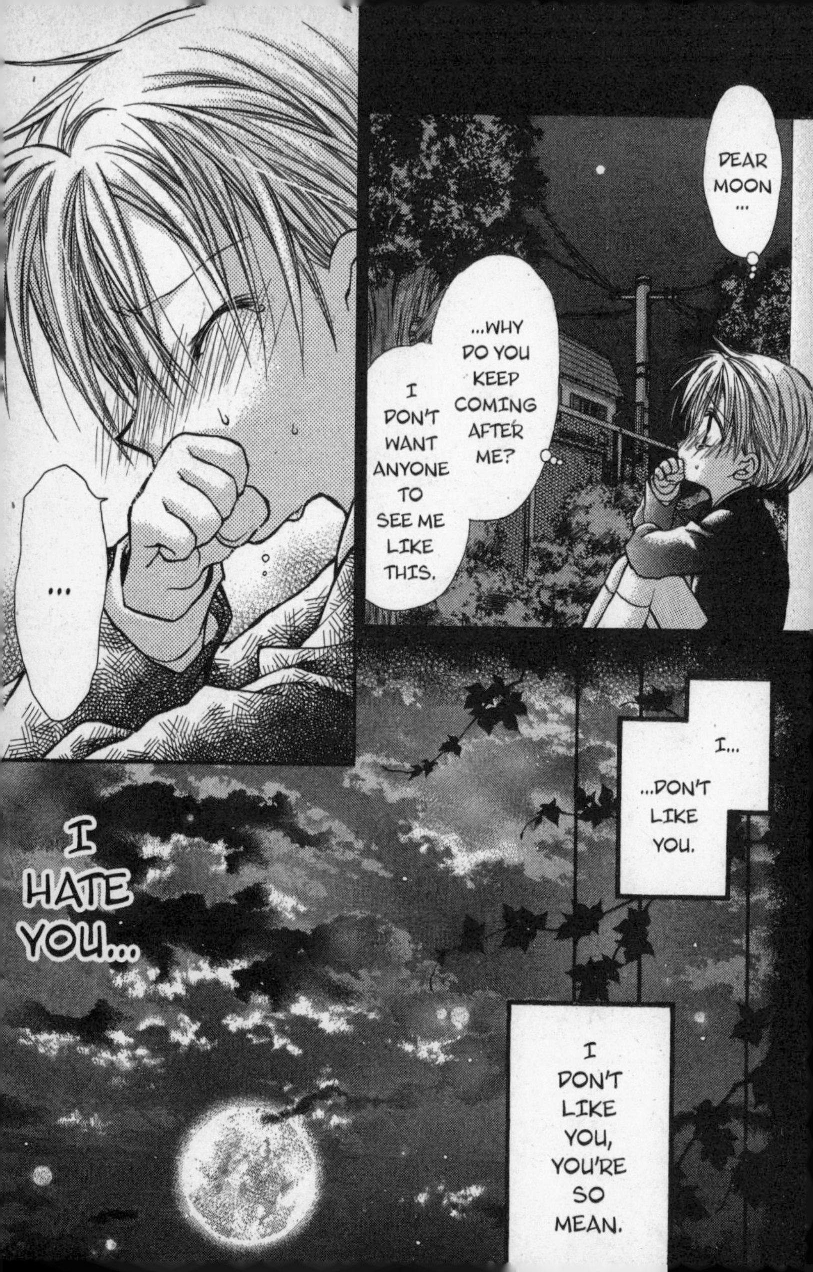
DEAR MOON ...
...WHY DO YOU KEEP COMING AFTER ME?
I DON'T WANT ANYONE TO SEE ME LIKE THIS.
...
I...
...DON'T LIKE YOU.
I DON'T LIKE YOU, YOU'RE SO MEAN.
I HATE YOU...

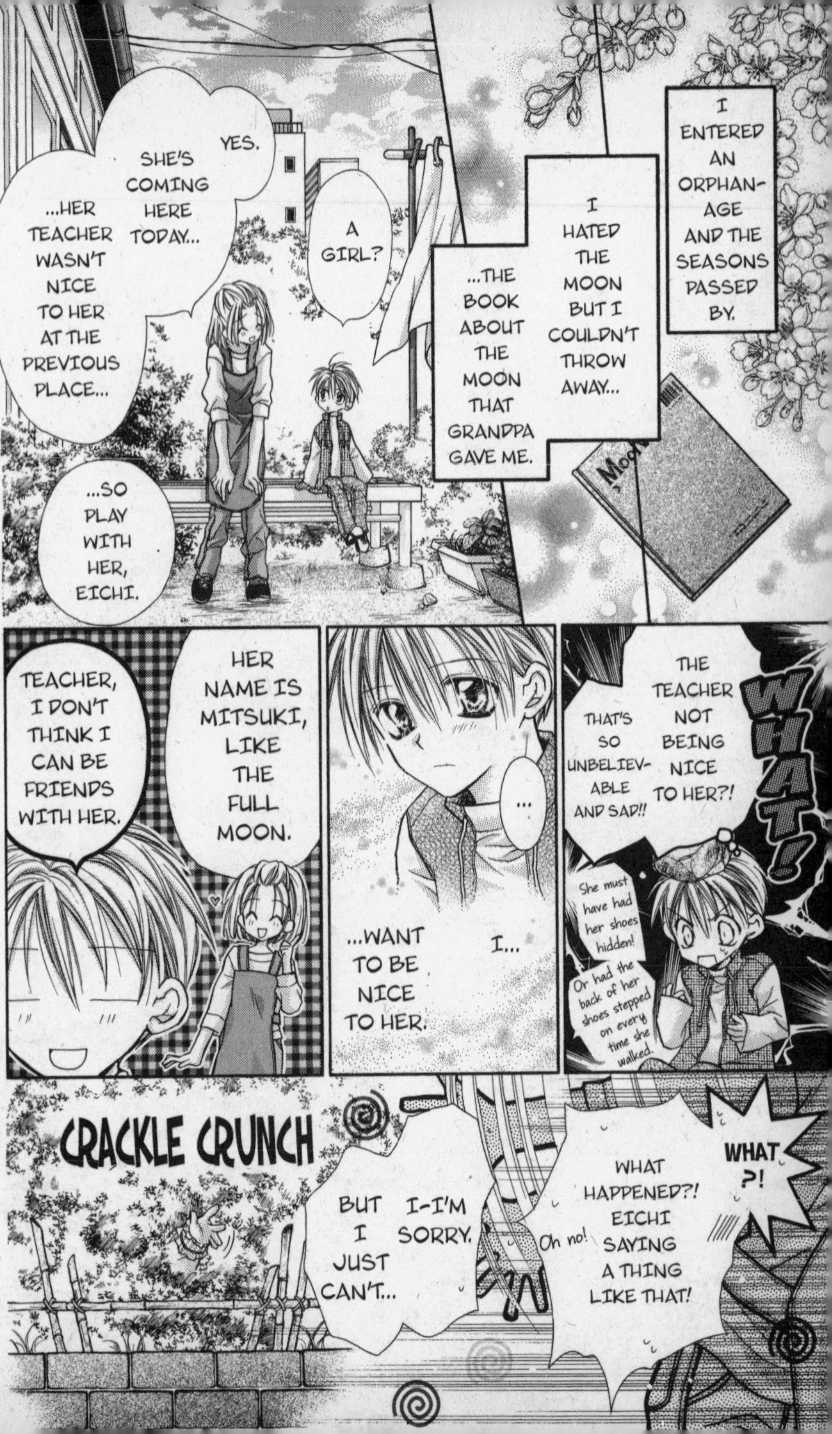
I ENTERED AN ORPHANAGE AND THE SEASONS PASSED BY.
I HATED THE MOON BUT I COULDN'T THROW AWAY...
...THE BOOK ABOUT THE MOON THAT GRANDPA GAVE ME.
A GIRL?
YES. SHE'S COMING HERE TODAY... ...HER TEACHER WASN'T NICE TO HER AT THE PREVIOUS PLACE...
...SO PLAY WITH HER, EICHI.
WHAT!
THE TEACHER NOT BEING NICE TO HER?!
THAT'S SO UNBELIEVABLE AND SAD!!
She must have had her shoes hidden!
Or had the back of her shoes stepped on every time she walked.
...
I...
...WANT TO BE NICE TO HER.
HER NAME IS MITSUKI, LIKE THE FULL MOON.
TEACHER, I DON'T THINK I CAN BE FRIENDS WITH HER.
WHAT?!
WHAT HAPPENED?! EICHI SAYING A THING LIKE THAT!
Oh no!
I-I'M SORRY.
BUT I JUST CAN'T...
CRACKLE CRUNCH

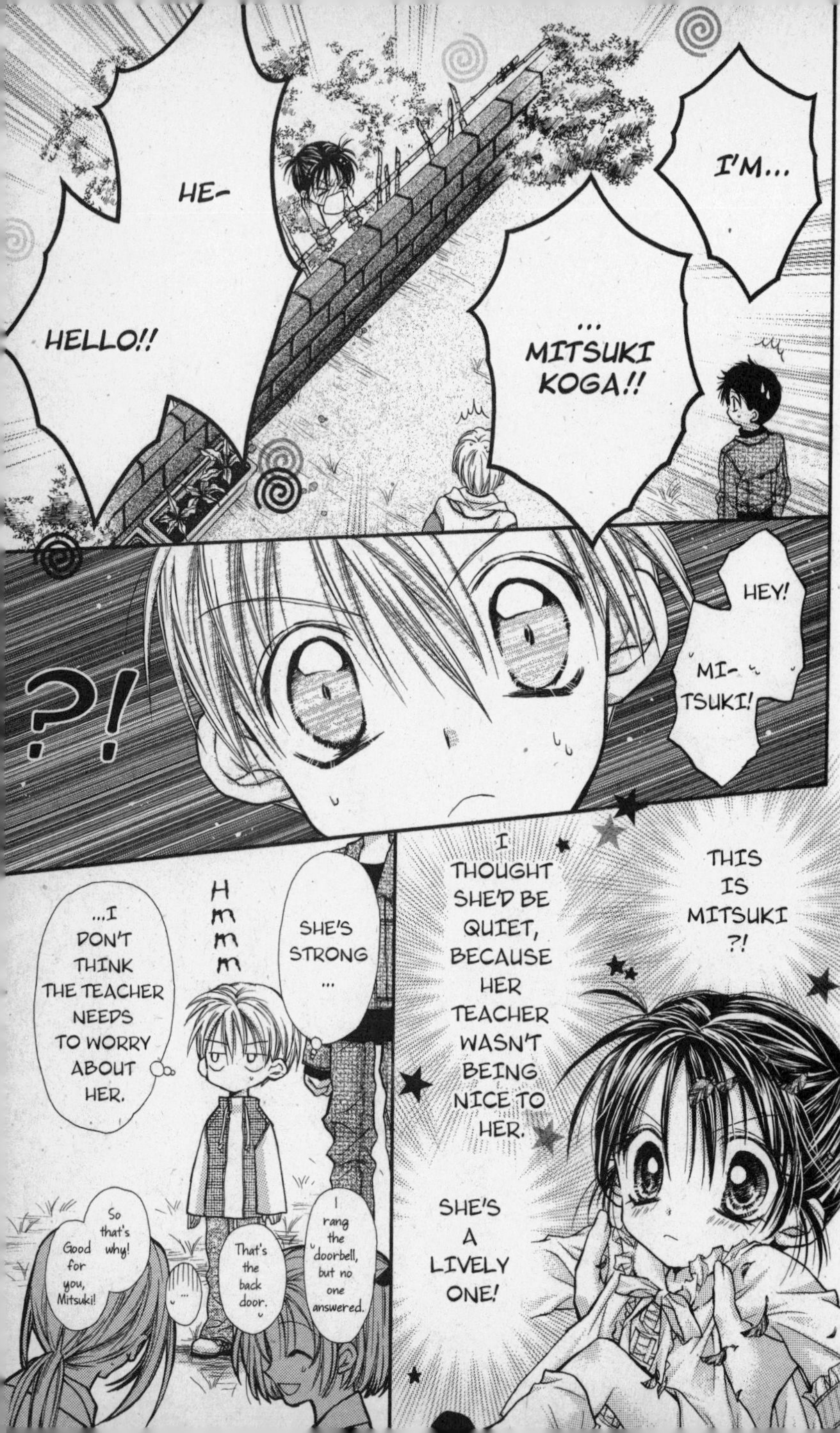
I'M...
...MITSUKI KOGA!!
HE-
HELLO!!
HEY!
MI-TSUKI!
?!
THIS IS MITSUKI ?!
I THOUGHT SHE'D BE QUIET, BECAUSE HER TEACHER WASN'T BEING NICE TO HER.
SHE'S A LIVELY ONE!
SHE'S STRONG ...
Hmmm
...I DON'T THINK THE TEACHER NEEDS TO WORRY ABOUT HER.
I rang the doorbell, but no one answered.
That's the back door.
...
So that's why! Good for you, Mitsuki!

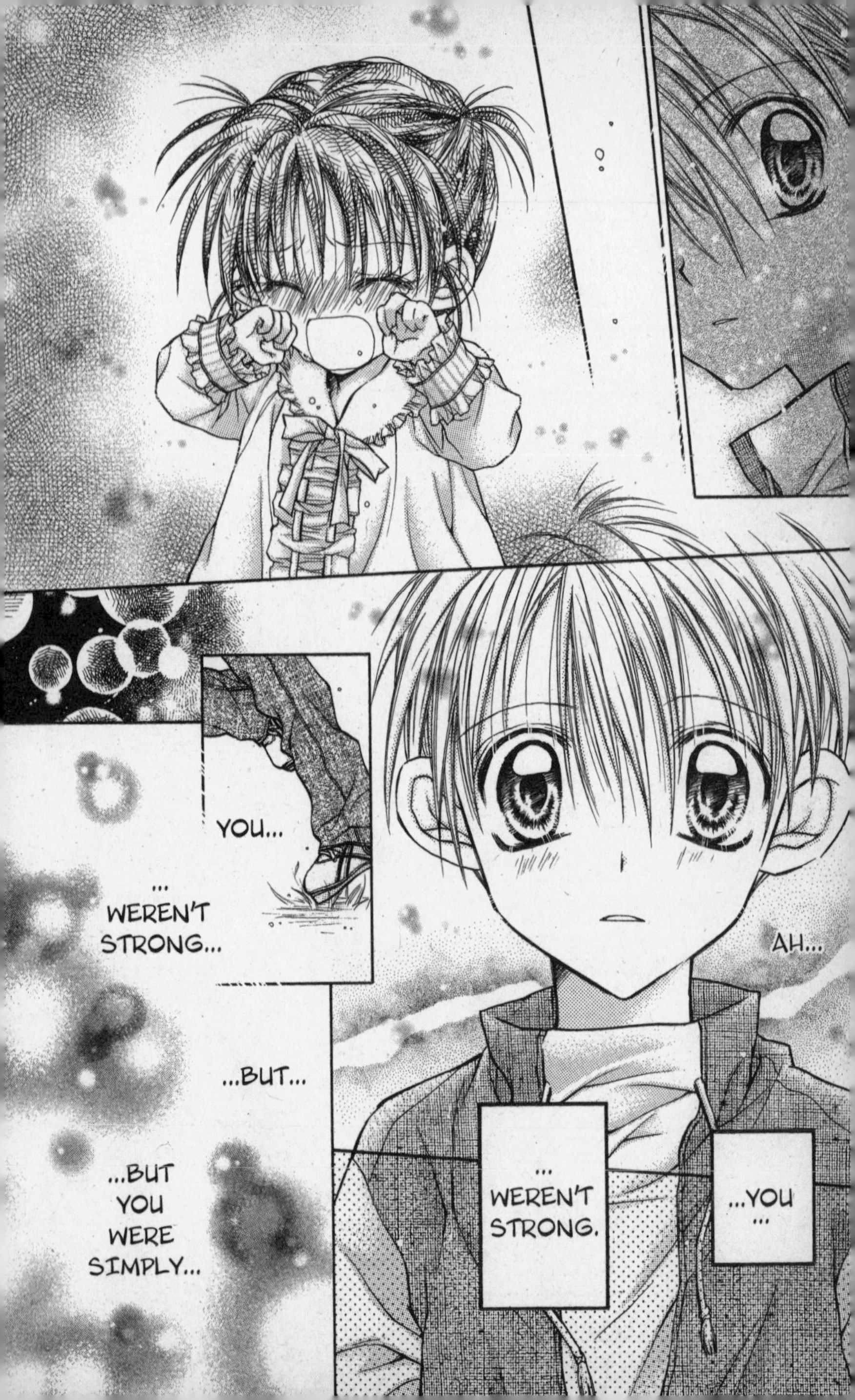
AH...
...YOU ...
... WEREN'T STRONG.
YOU...
... WEREN'T STRONG...
...BUT...
...BUT YOU WERE SIMPLY...

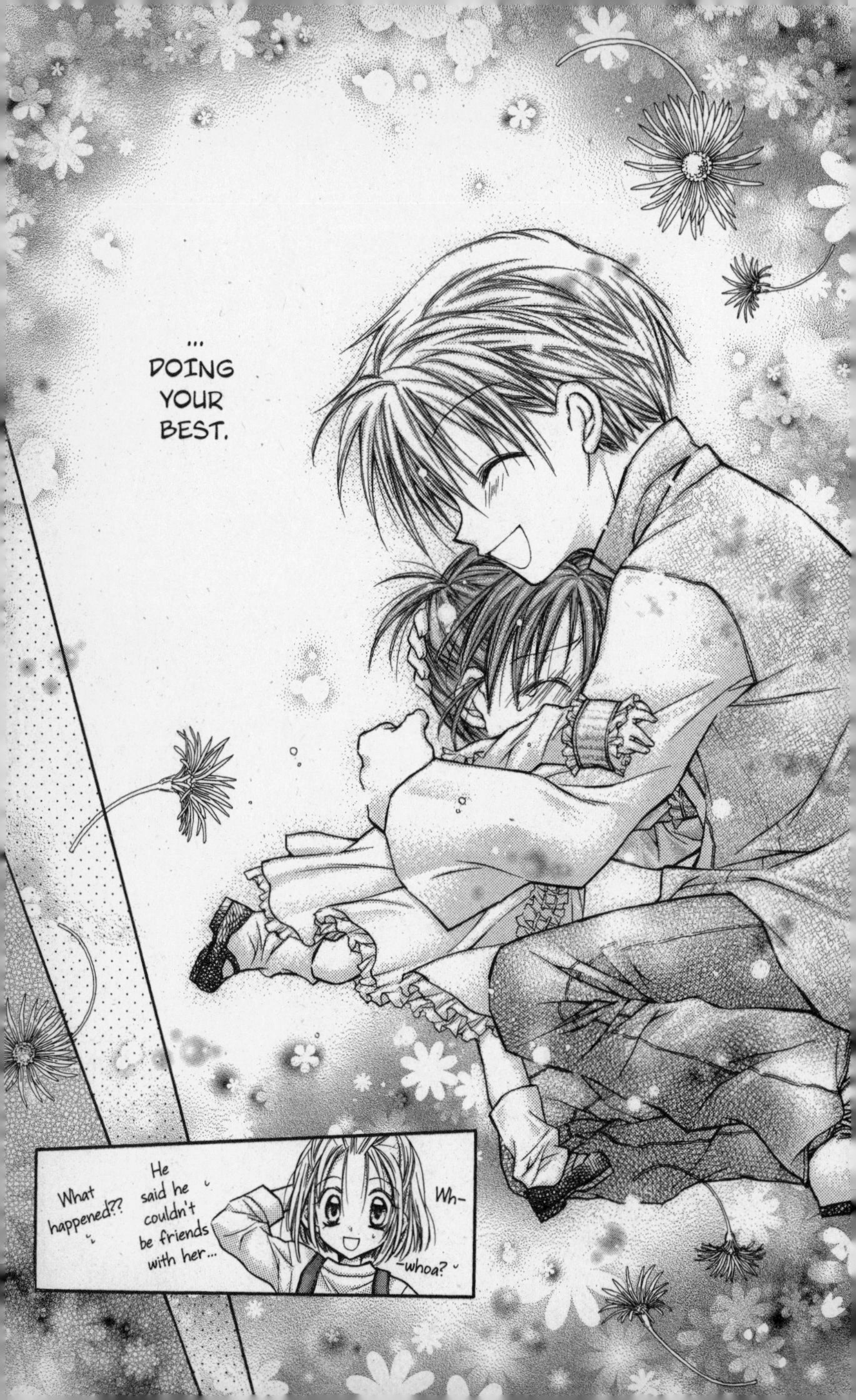
... DOING YOUR BEST.
Wh- -whoa?
He said he couldn't be friends with her...
What happened??

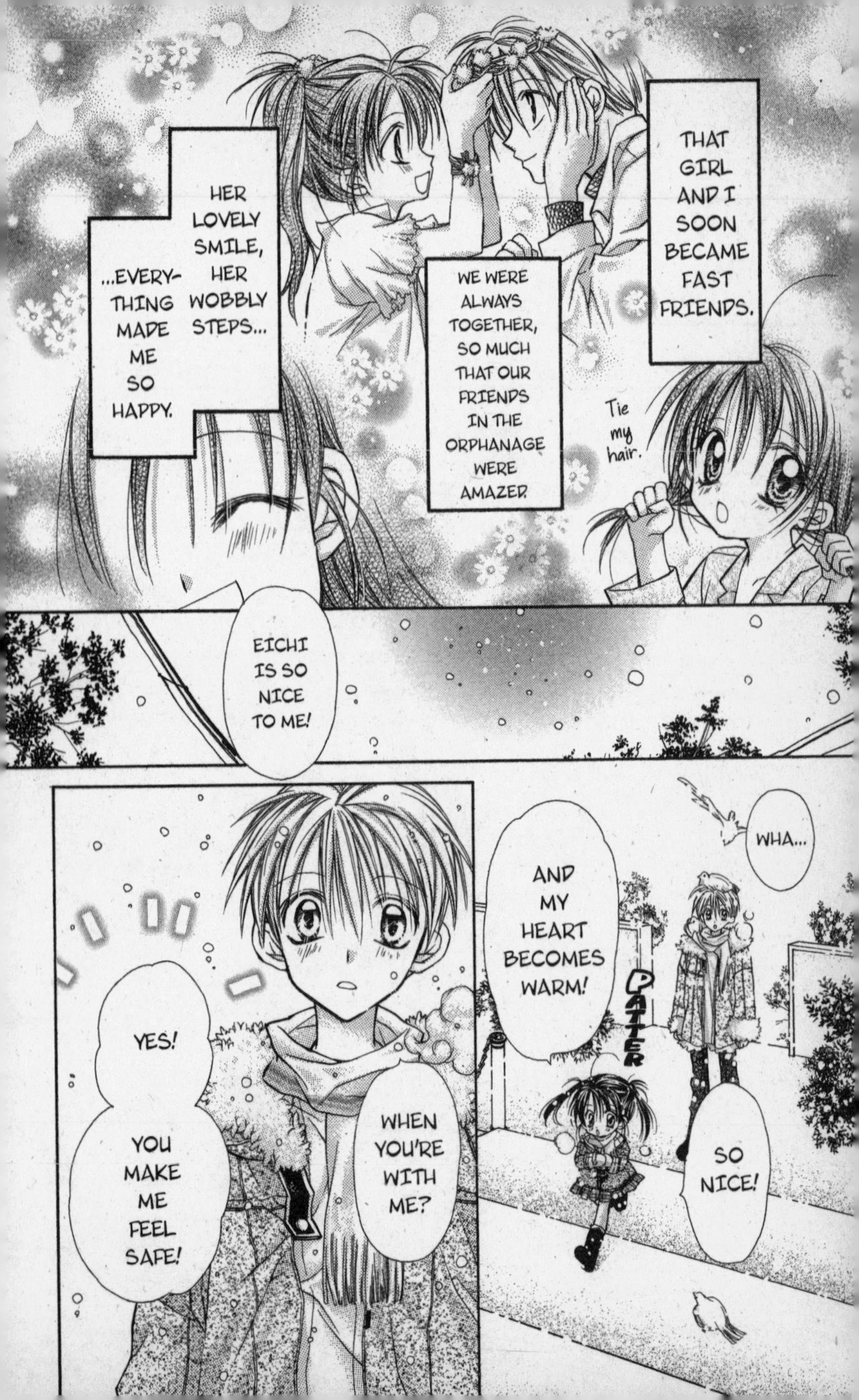
THAT GIRL AND I SOON BECAME FAST FRIENDS.
WE WERE ALWAYS TOGETHER, SO MUCH THAT OUR FRIENDS IN THE ORPHANAGE WERE AMAZED.
Tie my hair.
HER LOVELY SMILE, HER WOBBLY STEPS...
...EVERY-THING MADE ME SO HAPPY.
EICHI IS SO NICE TO ME!
WHA...
AND MY HEART BECOMES WARM!
PATTER
SO NICE!
WHEN YOU'RE WITH ME?
YES!
YOU MAKE ME FEEL SAFE!

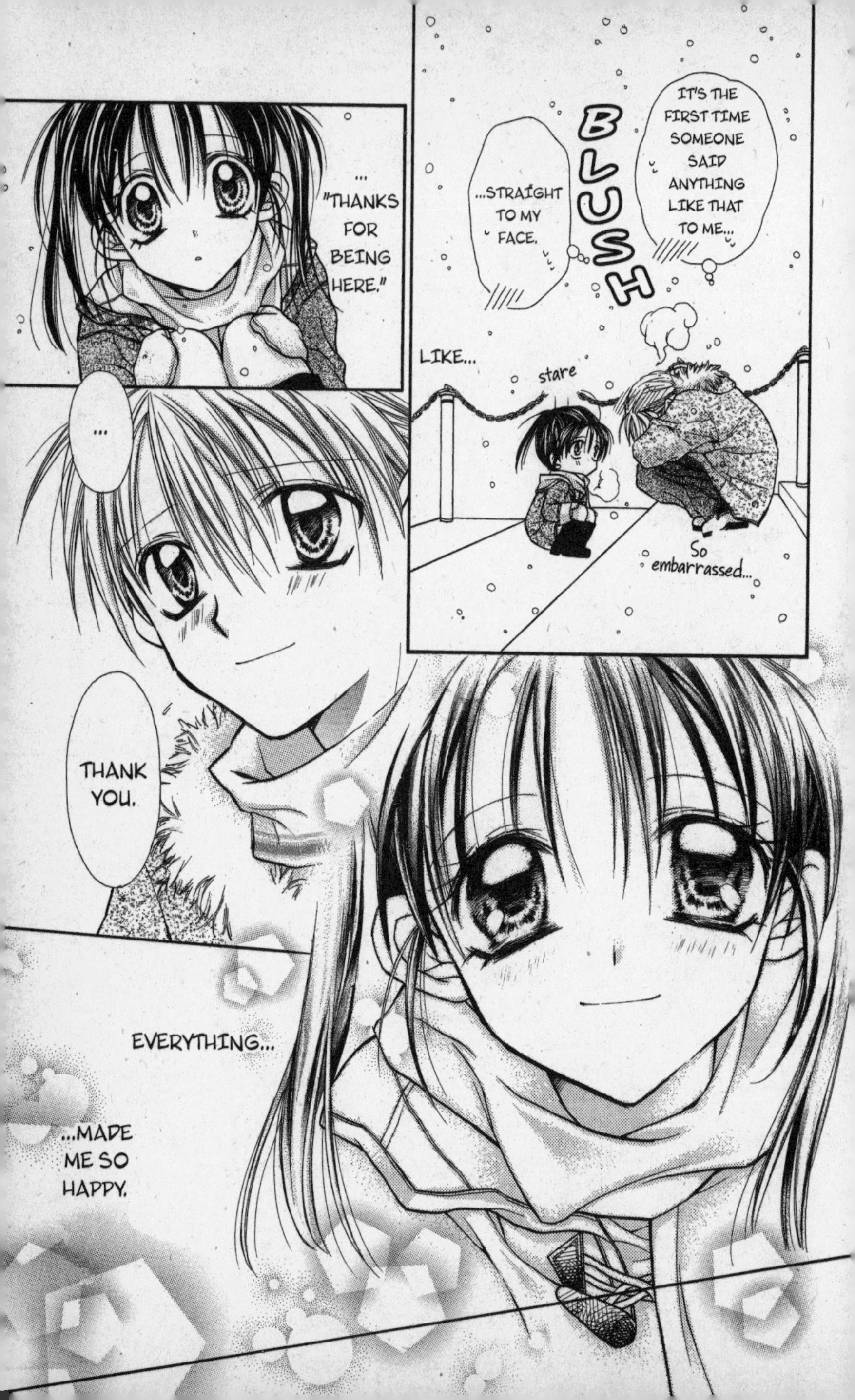
IT'S THE FIRST TIME SOMEONE SAID ANYTHING LIKE THAT TO ME...
BLUSH
...STRAIGHT TO MY FACE.
LIKE...
stare
So embarrassed...
... "THANKS FOR BEING HERE."
...
THANK YOU.
EVERYTHING...
...MADE ME SO HAPPY.

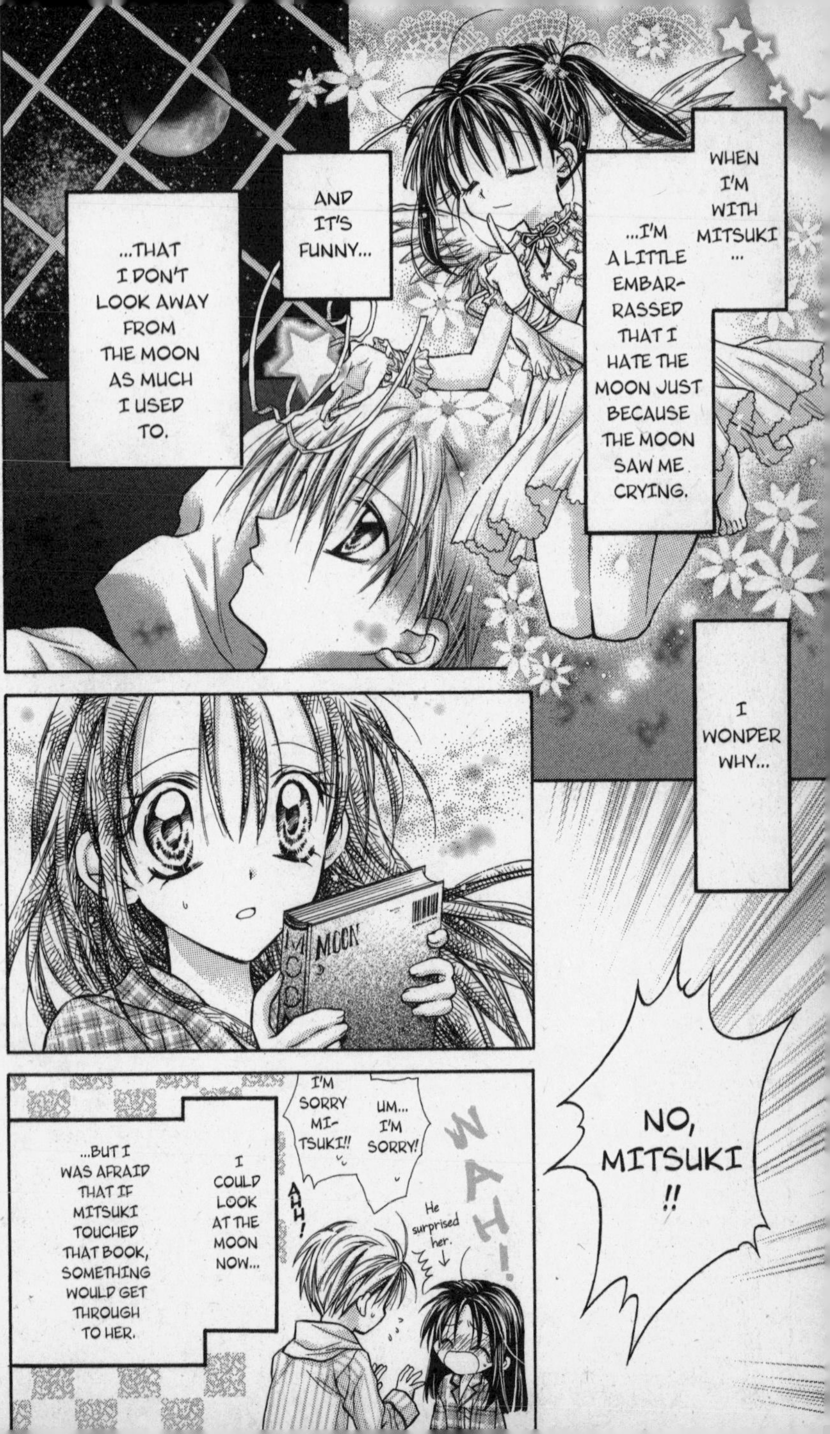

WHEN I'M WITH MITSUKI...
...I'M A LITTLE EMBARRASSED THAT I HATE THE MOON JUST BECAUSE THE MOON SAW ME CRYING.
AND IT'S FUNNY...
...THAT I DON'T LOOK AWAY FROM THE MOON AS MUCH I USED TO.
I WONDER WHY...
MOON
NO, MITSUKI!!
UM... I'M SORRY!
I'M SORRY MITSUKI!!
WAH!
He surprised her.
AHH!
I COULD LOOK AT THE MOON NOW...
...BUT I WAS AFRAID THAT IF MITSUKI TOUCHED THAT BOOK, SOMETHING WOULD GET THROUGH TO HER.

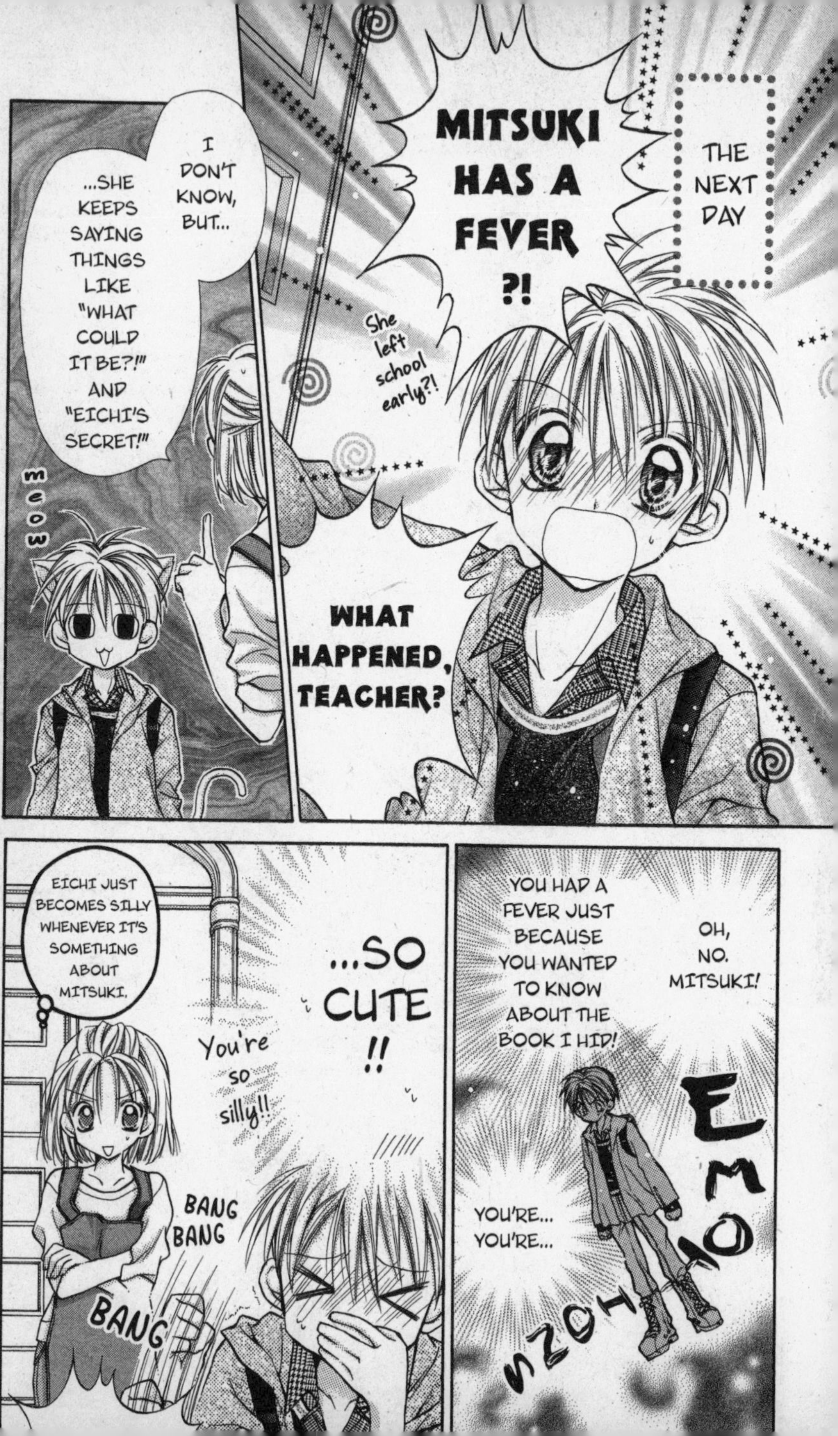
THE NEXT DAY
MITSUKI HAS A FEVER ?!
She left school early?!
WHAT HAPPENED, TEACHER?
I DON'T KNOW, BUT...
...SHE KEEPS SAYING THINGS LIKE "WHAT COULD IT BE?!" AND "EICHI'S SECRET!"
meow
OH, NO. MITSUKI!
YOU HAD A FEVER JUST BECAUSE YOU WANTED TO KNOW ABOUT THE BOOK I HID!
YOU'RE... YOU'RE...
EMO
EICHI JUST BECOMES SILLY WHENEVER IT'S SOMETHING ABOUT MITSUKI.
...SO CUTE !!
You're so silly!!
BANG BANG
BANG

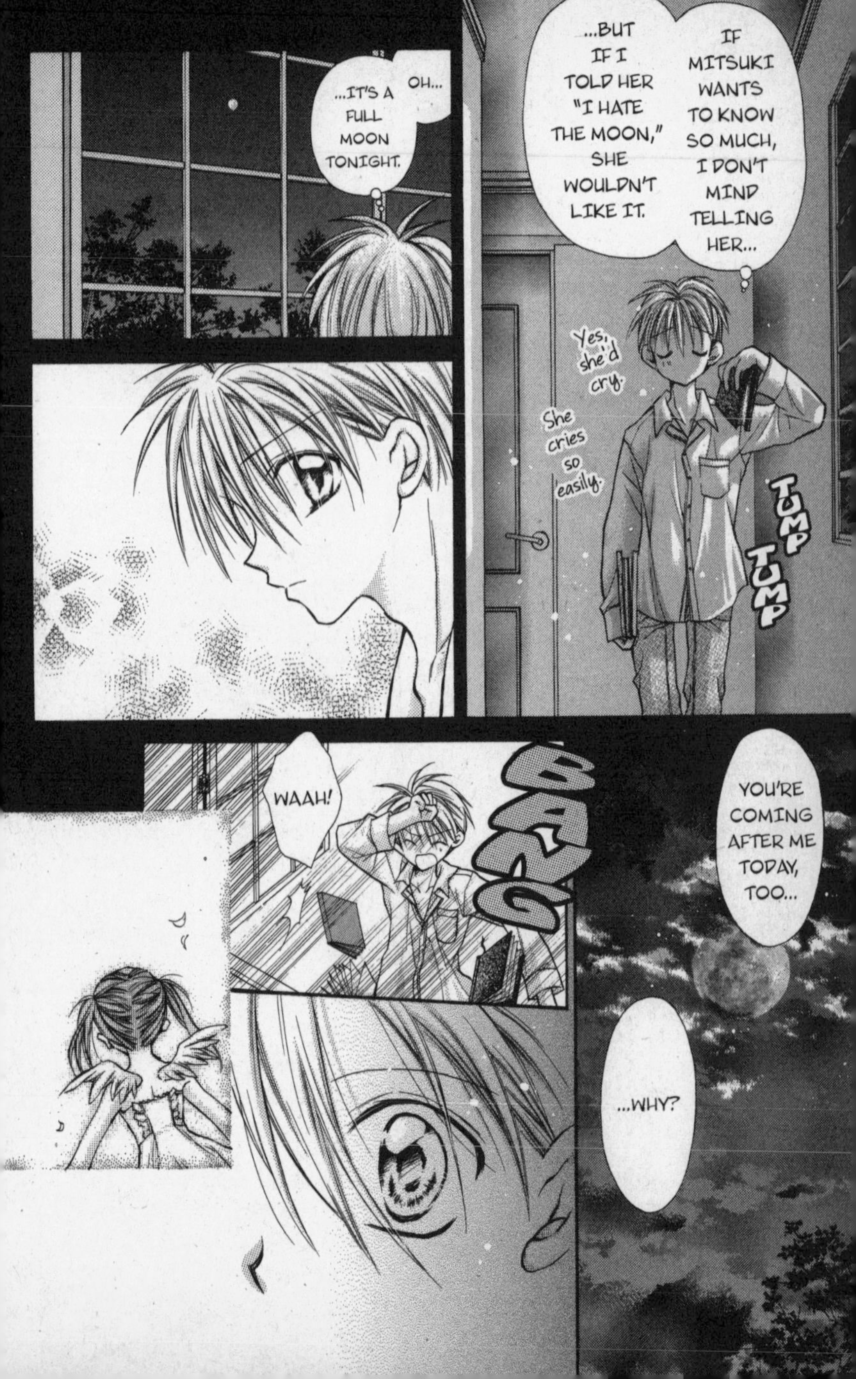
IF MITSUKI WANTS TO KNOW SO MUCH, I DON'T MIND TELLING HER...
...BUT IF I TOLD HER "I HATE THE MOON," SHE WOULDN'T LIKE IT.
Yes, she'd cry.
She cries so easily.
TUMP TUMP
OH...
...IT'S A FULL MOON TONIGHT.
YOU'RE COMING AFTER ME TODAY, TOO...
...WHY?
BANG
WAAH!

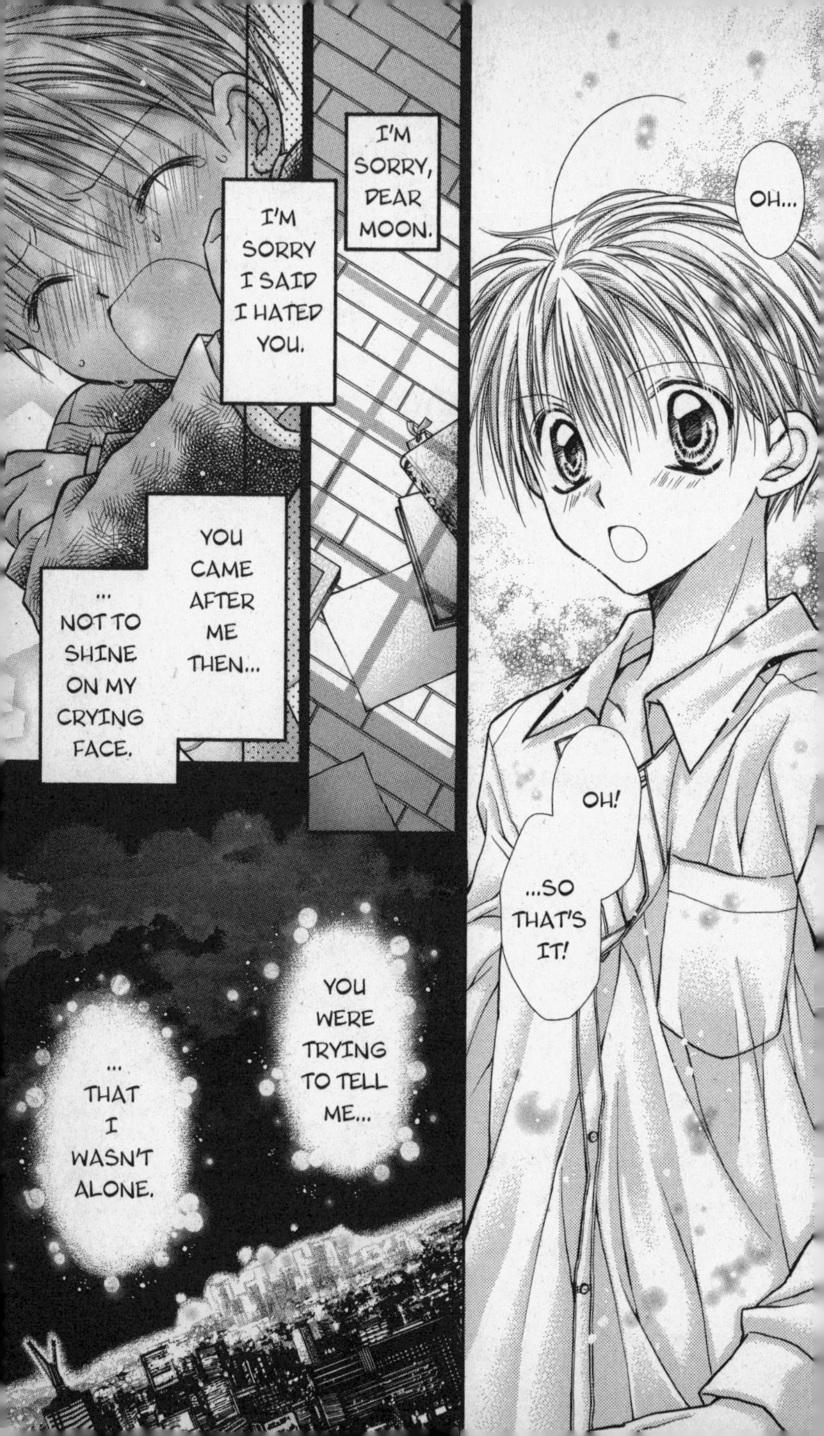
OH...
OH!
...SO THAT'S IT!
I'M SORRY, DEAR MOON.
I'M SORRY I SAID I HATED YOU.
YOU CAME AFTER ME THEN...
...NOT TO SHINE ON MY CRYING FACE.
YOU WERE TRYING TO TELL ME...
...THAT I WASN'T ALONE.

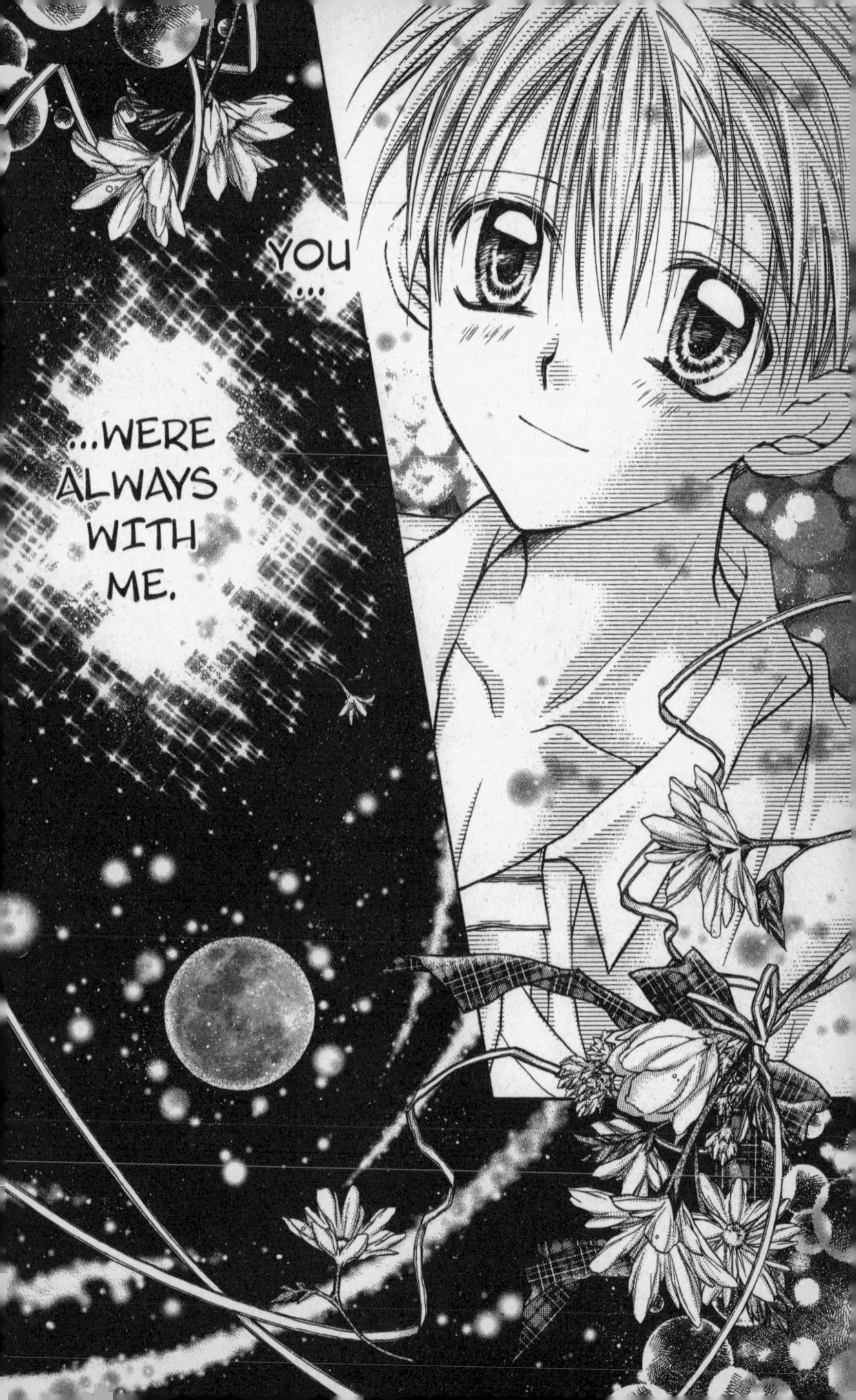
YOU ...
...WERE ALWAYS WITH ME.

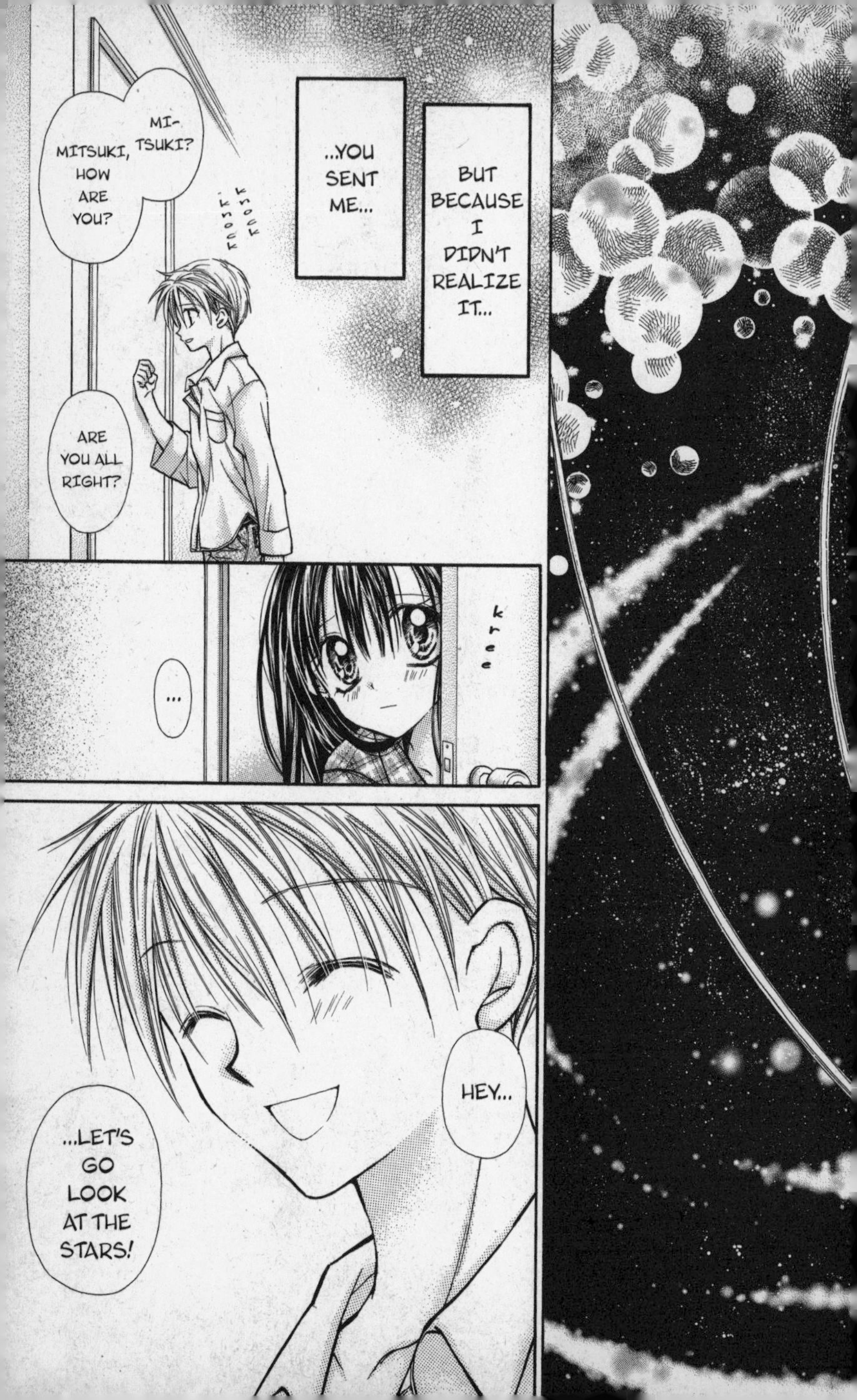
BUT BECAUSE I DIDN'T REALIZE IT...
...YOU SENT ME...
MI-TSUKI?
MITSUKI, HOW ARE YOU?
knock knock
ARE YOU ALL RIGHT?
kree
...
HEY...
...LET'S GO LOOK AT THE STARS!

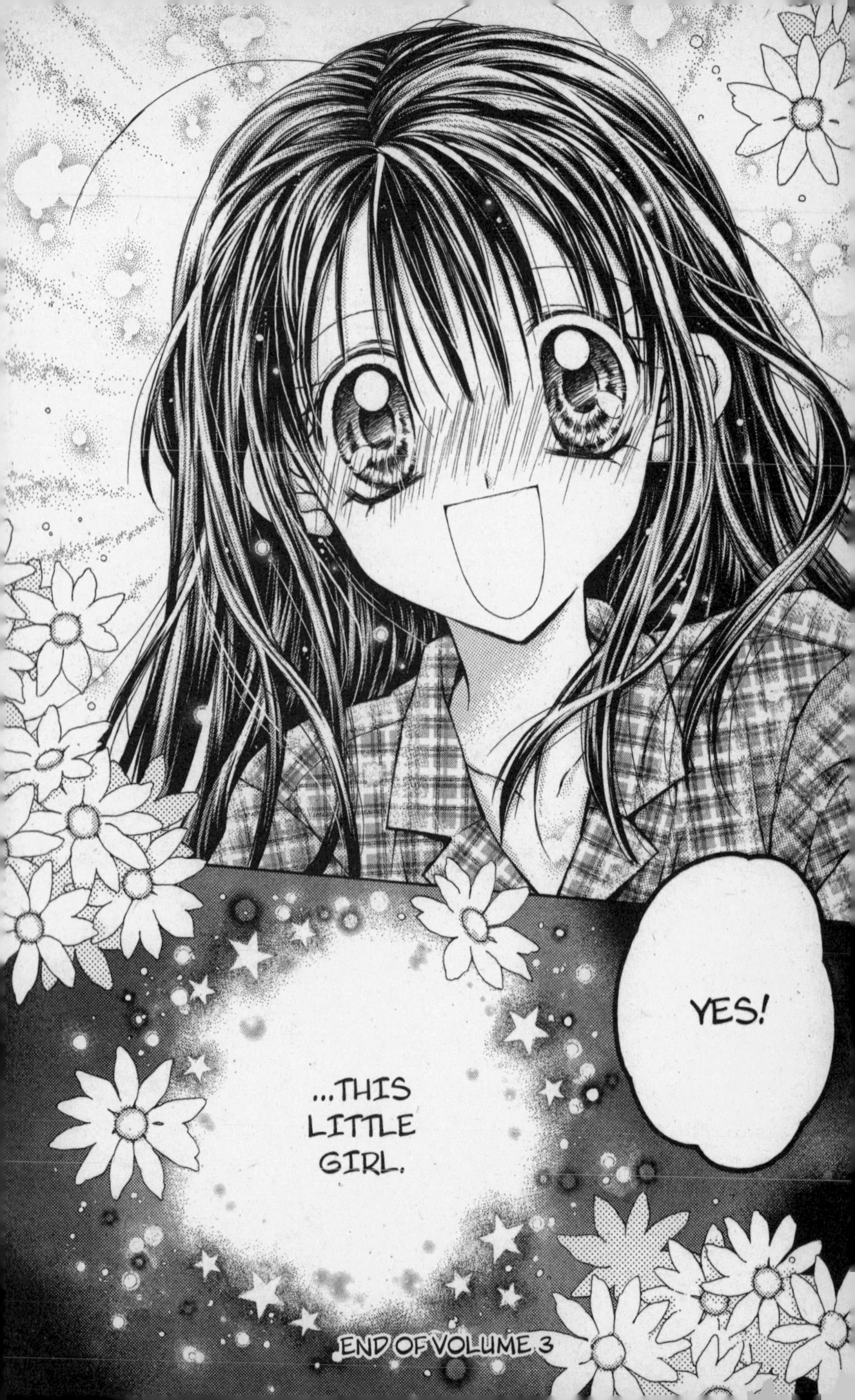
YES!
...THIS LITTLE GIRL.
END OF VOLUME 3

Author Bio

Arina Tanemura was born in Aichi, Japan.
She got her start in 1996, publishing
*Nibanme no Koi no Katachi (The Style of
Second Love)* in *Ribon Original* magazine.
Her early work includes a collection of short
stories called *Kanshaku Dama no Yuutsu
(Short-Tempered Melancholic)*. Two of her
titles, *Kamikaze Kaito Jeanne* and *Full
Moon,* were made into popular TV series.
Tanemura enjoys Karaoke and is a huge *Lord
of the Rings* fan.

Author's Note

Maaaaaaany things happened in
Volume 3. I guess everyone was
kept in suspense. The smiling
couple on the cover of this volume
is so sad, isn't it? Although I'd
decided on this from the first
chapter, as I was doing the
storyboards I kept asking myself
why I made the story this way. But
I can't turn back now, so I will keep
watch over everyone's feelings.

Full Moon o Sagashite

Vol. 3
The Shojo Beat Manga Edition

STORY & ART BY
ARINA TANEMURA

English Translation & Adaptation/Tomo Kimura
Touch-Up & Lettering/Elena Diaz
Graphics & Cover Design/Izumi Evers
Editors/Pancha Diaz & Nancy Thistlethwaite

Managing Editor/Megan Bates
Production Manager/Noboru Watanabe
Vice President of Publishing/Alvin Lu
Sr. Director of Acquisitions/Rika Inouye
VP of Sales & Marketing/Liza Coppola
Vice President & Editor in Chief/Yumi Hoashi
Publisher/ Hyoe Narita

Printed in the U.S.A.

Published by VIZ Media, LLC
P.O. Box 77064
San Francisco, CA 94107

Shojo Beat Manga Edition
10 9 8 7 6 5 4 3 2 1
First printing, September 2005

store.viz.com

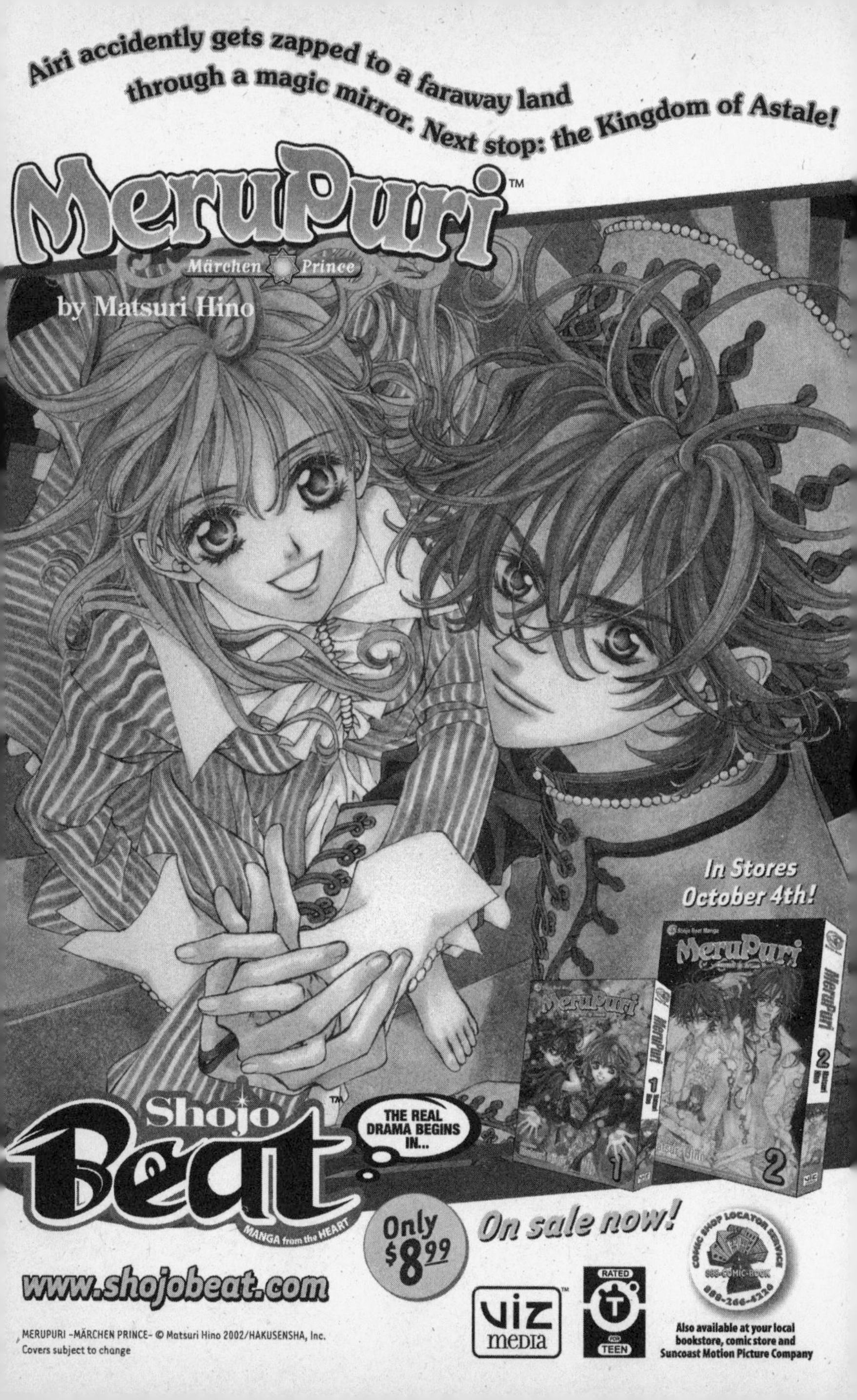

Airi accidently gets zapped to a faraway land
through a magic mirror. Next stop: the Kingdom of Astale!
MeruPuri™
Märchen Prince
by Matsuri Hino
In Stores
October 4th!
Shojo Beat™
MANGA from the HEART
THE REAL DRAMA BEGINS IN...
Only $8.99
On sale now!
www.shojobeat.com
viz media
RATED T FOR TEEN
COMIC SHOP LOCATOR SERVICE
888-COMIC-BOOK
888-266-4226
Also available at your local bookstore, comic store and Suncoast Motion Picture Company
MERUPURI -MÄRCHEN PRINCE- © Matsuri Hino 2002/HAKUSENSHA, Inc.
Covers subject to change

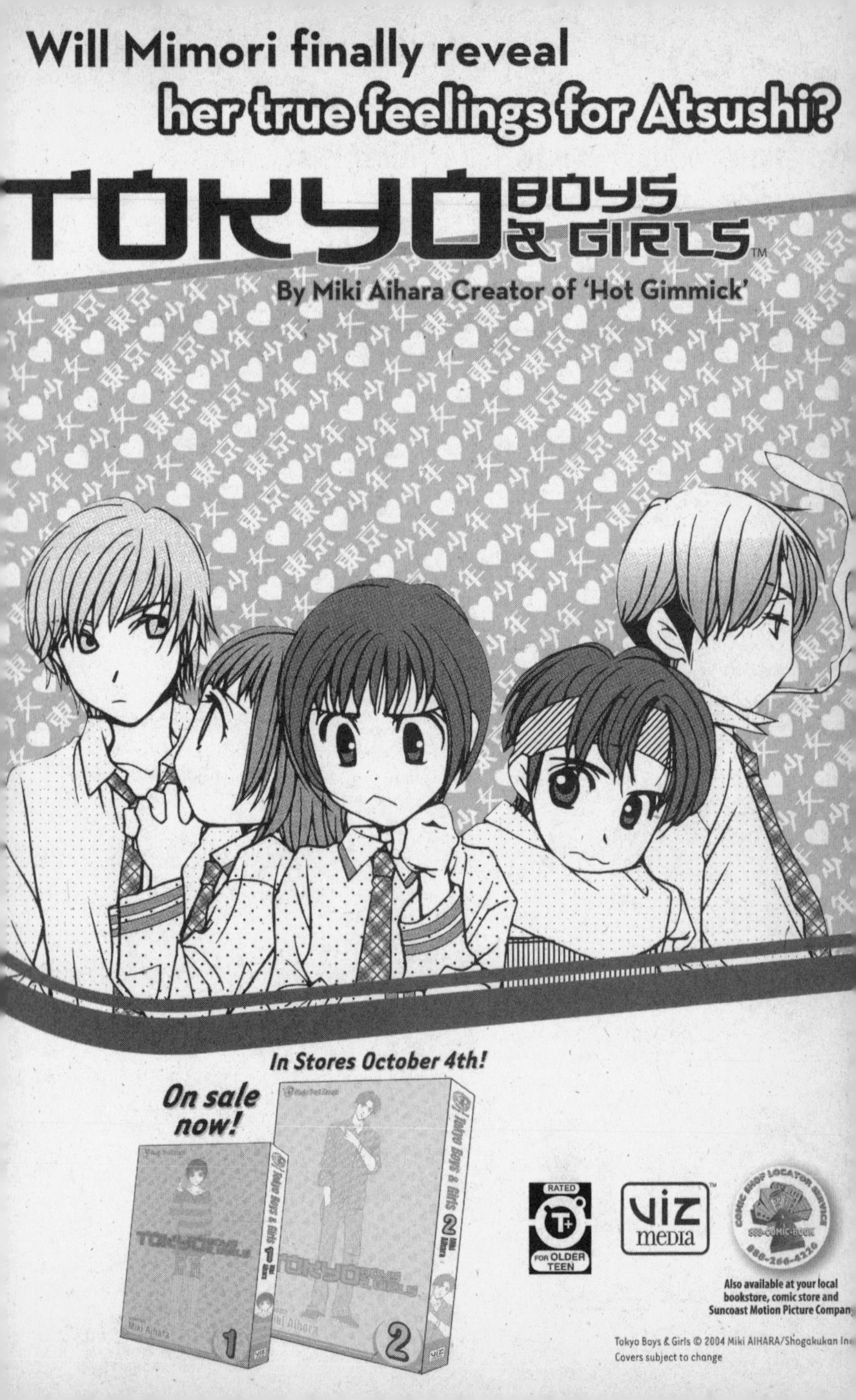
Will Mimori finally reveal
her true feelings for Atsushi?
TOKYO BOYS & GIRLS™
By Miki Aihara Creator of 'Hot Gimmick'
In Stores October 4th!
On sale now!
Tokyo Boys & Girls 1
Miki Aihara
Tokyo Boys & Girls 2
Miki Aihara
RATED T+ FOR OLDER TEEN
VIZ media
COMIC SHOP LOCATOR SERVICE
888-COMIC-BOOK
888-266-4226
Also available at your local bookstore, comic store and Suncoast Motion Picture Company
Tokyo Boys & Girls © 2004 Miki AIHARA/Shogakukan Inc.
Covers subject to change

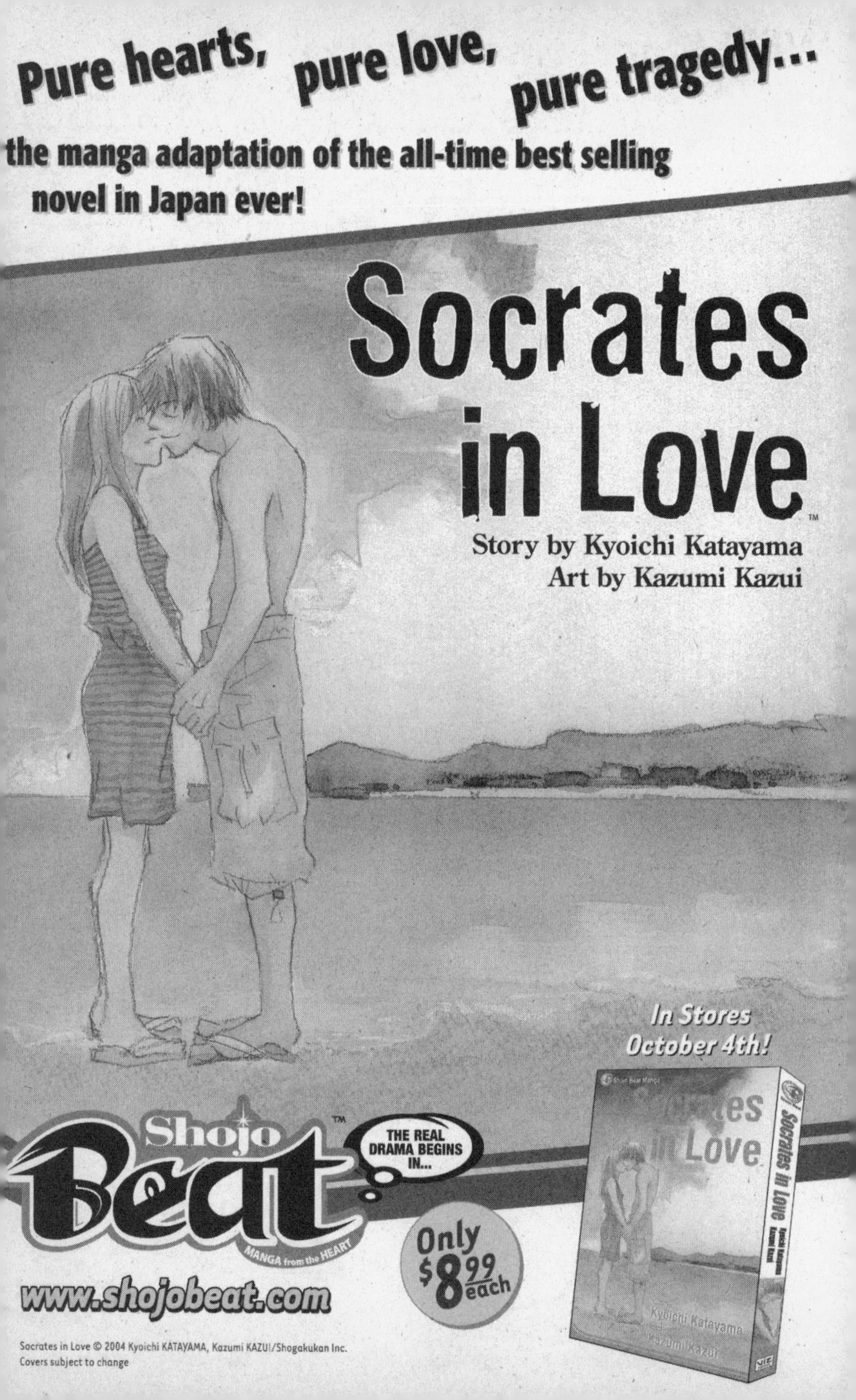
Pure hearts, pure love, pure tragedy...
the manga adaptation of the all-time best selling novel in Japan ever!
Socrates in Love™
Story by Kyoichi Katayama
Art by Kazumi Kazui
In Stores October 4th!
Shojo Beat™
MANGA from the HEART
THE REAL DRAMA BEGINS IN...
Only $8.99 each
www.shojobeat.com
Shojo Beat Manga
Socrates in Love
Kyoichi Katayama
Kazumi Kazui
Socrates in Love © 2004 Kyoichi KATAYAMA, Kazumi KAZUI/Shogakukan Inc.
Covers subject to change

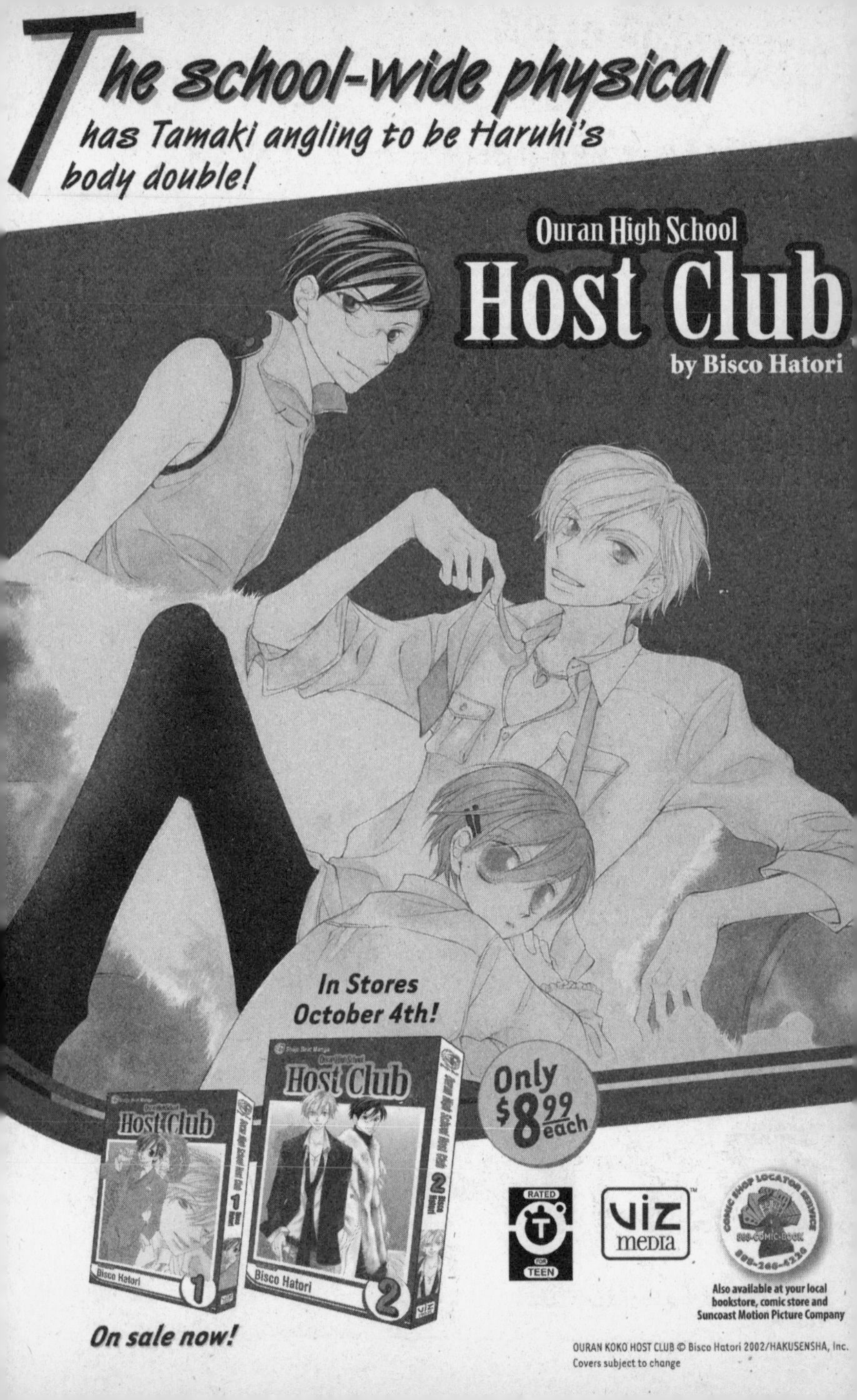
The school-wide physical
has Tamaki angling to be Haruhi's
body double!
Ouran High School
Host Club
by Bisco Hatori
In Stores
October 4th!
Host Club
Bisco Hatori
2
Only
$8.99
each
Host Club
Bisco Hatori
1
On sale now!
RATED
T
FOR
TEEN
viz
media
COMIC SHOP LOCATOR SERVICE
888-COMIC-BOOK
888-266-4226
Also available at your local
bookstore, comic store and
Suncoast Motion Picture Company
OURAN KOKO HOST CLUB © Bisco Hatori 2002/HAKUSENSHA, Inc.
Covers subject to change

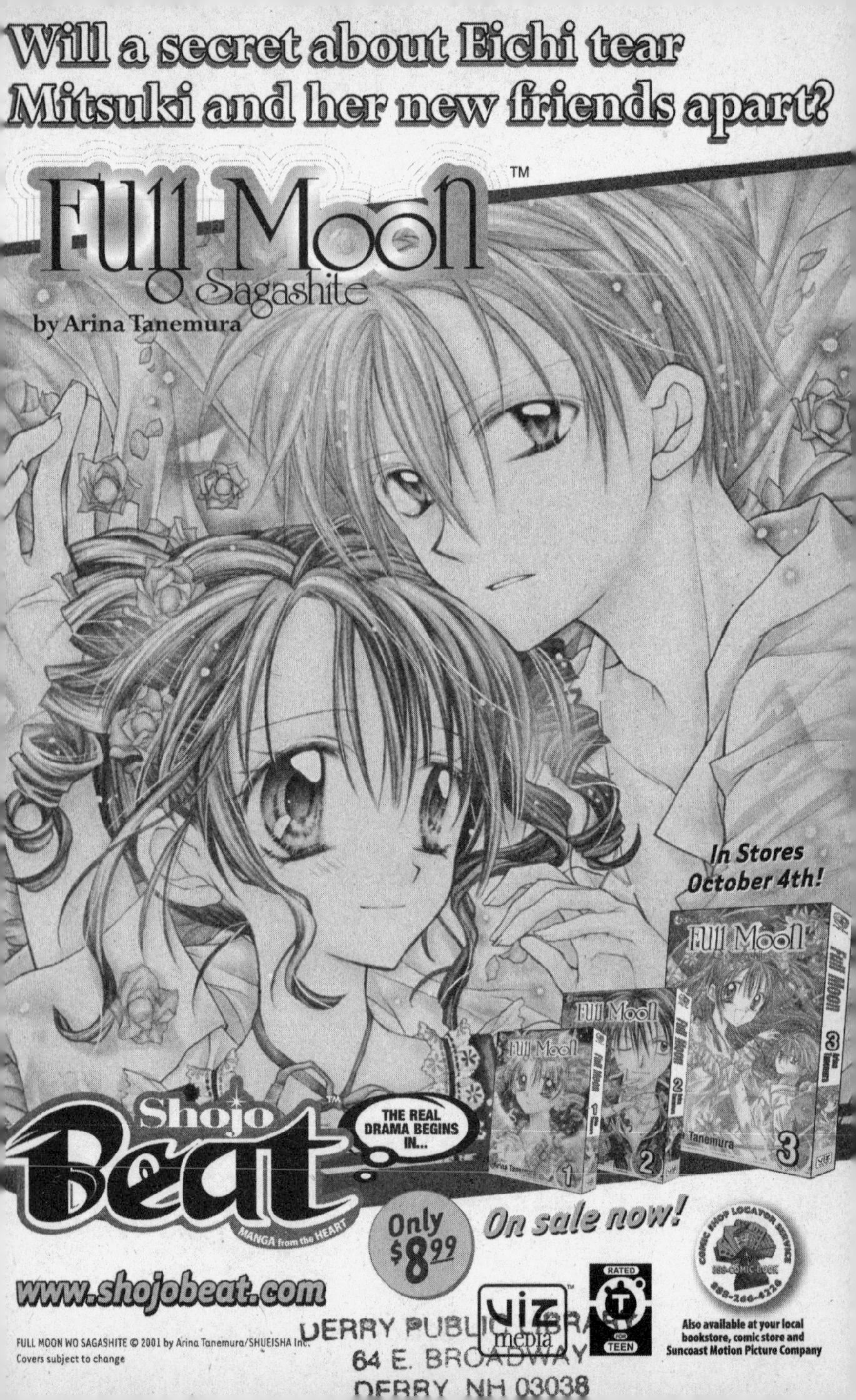
Will a secret about Eichi tear Mitsuki and her new friends apart?
Full Moon™
O Sagashite
by Arina Tanemura
In Stores October 4th!
Full Moon
Tanemura
3
2
1
Shojo Beat™
MANGA from the HEART
THE REAL DRAMA BEGINS IN...
Only $8.99
On sale now!
www.shojobeat.com
viz media™
RATED T FOR TEEN
COMIC SHOP LOCATOR SERVICE
888-COMIC-BOOK
888-266-4226
Also available at your local bookstore, comic store and Suncoast Motion Picture Company
FULL MOON WO SAGASHITE © 2001 by Arina Tanemura/SHUEISHA Inc.
Covers subject to change

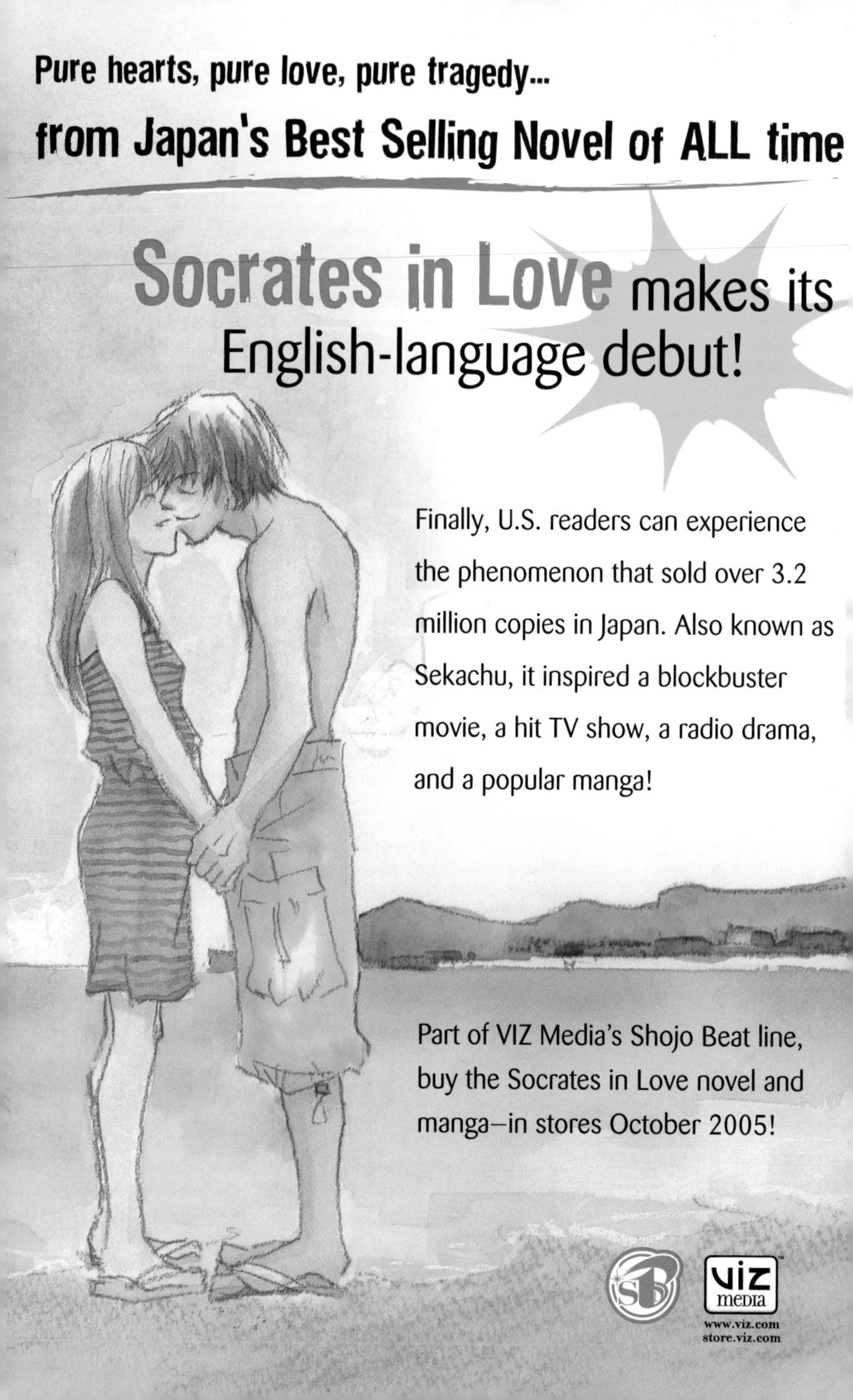
Pure hearts, pure love, pure tragedy...
from Japan's Best Selling Novel of ALL time
Socrates in Love makes its English-language debut!
Finally, U.S. readers can experience the phenomenon that sold over 3.2 million copies in Japan. Also known as Sekachu, it inspired a blockbuster movie, a hit TV show, a radio drama, and a popular manga!
Part of VIZ Media's Shojo Beat line, buy the Socrates in Love novel and manga—in stores October 2005!
VIZ MEDIA
www.viz.com
store.viz.com

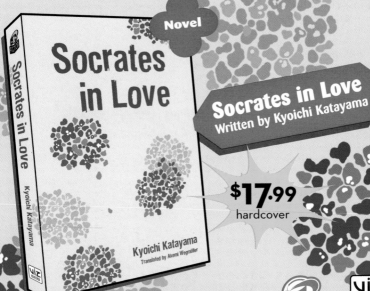

Find the Beat online!
Check us out at

www.shojobeat.com!